Mic
pb

BY THE SAME AUTHOR

Crowned in a Far Country

The Serpent and the Moon

Cupid and the King

FIVE ROYAL PARAMOURS

Her Royal Highness

PRINCESS MICHAEL OF KENT

A TOUCHSTONE BOOK
PUBLISHED BY SIMON & SCHUSTER
NEW YORK   LONDON   TORONTO   SYDNEY

TOUCHSTONE
Rockefeller Center
1230 Avenue of the Americas
New York, NY 10020

Originally published in Great Britain in 1991 by HarperCollins Publishers

First Touchstone Edition 2005

TOUCHSTONE and colophon are registered trademarks of Simon & Schuster, Inc.

For information regarding special discounts for bulk purchases, please contact
Simon & Schuster Special Sales at 1-800-456-6798 or
business@simonandschuster.com.

Designed by Jan Pisciotta

Manufactured in the United States of America

1   3   5   7   9   10   8   6   4   2

Library of Congress Cataloging-in-Publication Data
Michael, of Kent, Princess.
Cupid and the king : five royal paramours / Princess Michael of Kent.—
1st Touchstone ed.
    p.   cm.
"A Touchstone book."
1. Europe—Kings and rulers—Mistresses—Biography.
2. Courtesans—Europe—Biography.   I. Title.
D107.7.M52   2005
940.2092'2—dc22   [B]   2005054087

ISBN-13: 978-0-7432-7086-1
ISBN-10: 0-7432-7086-X

Acknowledgments

As this book has been a long project, there are a number of people I would like to thank.

In France: Danielle Gallet at the Archives nationales for her help and corrections to Madame de Pompadour; at the Louvre: Catherine Belanger, Marie-Catherine Sahut, Amaury Lefebure; Geneviève Monnier for her help at the Elysée Palace and Jean-Gabriel Mitterrand for making the inspection possible; Mme Marthe Bernous at the Grand Palais; Bernard Chevallier and Alain Pougetoux at Malmaison; Marie Walewska's descendant le Comte Hubert d'Ornano for his help, corrections and original material; Daniel Meyer at Versailles; Mme A. Malle at the Musée National De Céramique de Sèvres; Jean-Marie Moulin at Compiègne; the Musée David Stewart; François Mathey at the Musée des Arts décoratifs; the Musée Comondo; Mlle Mongellas at Saumur; the Musée des Beaux-Arts de Chartres; the Musée de l'Isle de France à Sceaux; Daniel Marg; M. and Mme Menier at Chenonceau and their curator; Mme Samoyault-Verlet at Fontainebleau; the Baron Guy de Rothschild for allowing me access to his collection of Renaissance ceramics and enamels; Prince Michael of Greece for all his support and advice.

In Britain: Alison Bailey, Mrs. Charles Bronage and others at the British Library; Paul Dove at the British Museum; the ever helpful staff of the London Library; the many departments of the Victoria and Albert who lent assistance, especially in the Library, Philip de Bey and Robert Sayle; Helen Smails at the Scottish National Portrait Gallery; Anthony Camp at the Society of Genealogists; for reading the manuscript, encouraging and advising: the late Lady (Elizabeth) Longford, Andrew Sinclair, Tony Buzan, Alan Brooke, Arianna Huffington, Christine Sutherland, who also allowed me to use her original research material; Kate Macintyre for giving me a year's hard work as a research assistant; the British Film Institute library; the Duke of Buccleuch for advice and material; Helen Menzies and others at the Hulton Picture Library; Shruti Patel and others at the National Portrait Gallery; Camera Press; Anthony Pie-Jeary for his generous help on book design; the Earl of Derby; Geoffrey Bailey at Hatchards; Mrs. S.M. Willey at Nell Gwynn House; M. Pierre Hivermat, Cultural Attaché at the French Embassy; Earl Spencer; Sarah Goodbody, Frances Diamond and others at the Royal Collection; and all those at Sony who have helped me overcome my technical ineptitude and master my word processor.

I would particularly like to mention the exceptional work of Leo van de Pas for all his genealogical corrections to the text and other suggestions. I am also greatly indebted to the original team at HarperCollins, in particular Robert Lacey, my sharp, cruel, perceptive editor, and Eddie Bell for making the 1991 edition happen. Special acknowledgment for patience and hard work well beyond any call of duty must go to my personal assistant Emma Fellowes and my secretary Katie Garrod. I wish to thank my U.S. editor, Trish Todd at Touchstone Fireside, for having faith in me and for editing the new chapter on Lillie Langtry. Julia Harris-Voss and Jo Walton deserve special thanks for their patience and efficiency in the picture attributions.

And lastly, my gratitude must go to my agent Suzanne Gluck for all her sterling efforts on my behalf. Most of all I would like to thank my brother for his invaluable support, advice and help, my husband for his patience and encouragement, and the many friends who made this reissue possible.

Contents

Author's Note

Cupid and the King is a natural successor to *Crowned in a Far Country*, my biography of eight princesses who, through obedience and duty to their royal fathers, became pawns in the great political game of dynastic marriage in order to secure thrones, treaties, prosperity and peace. The book's theme was the way in which each of them adapted to her husband and to her new country, and her influence on its politics, lifestyle and arts. In *Cupid and the King* I focus on the women whom the mighty ruler, the richest and most powerful man in the kingdom, *chose* to love. Faced with the prospect of a loveless political marriage, to whom did such a ruler turn to share his heart, his thoughts and his concerns, to open his soul and comfort his body?

I have chosen five such women, each of them the great love of a king, as the subjects of this book. Their names will be known to most of my readers, but their lives are often shrouded in so much fantasy and falsehood that the only attribute which is never denied them is the mystique attached to a woman who won, and held, the heart of a king. This is not a study in bedroom politics, nor a jolly romp through royal boudoirs, littered with legends surrounding *les grandes horizontales*. Nor is my sole concern the passion of women and the favor of kings. The royal courtesans in this book were not fleeting relationships or conquests of the night. These were not women possessed and discarded without care or consideration. They should not be seen merely as "the other woman"—there was much more at stake than just an *affaire* or a domestic upheaval. They all represented a great passion, the *grand amour* of the sovereign. In differing ways, each one altered the monarch's life—and sometimes the course of history. My aim here is to explore the alternatives chosen by five rulers committed to political or loveless marriages. What was the reasoning behind their choice? What was the outcome of their decision to pick one of the principals of this book? This is the story of five fascinating women whose lives span three centuries. Their backgrounds differed dramatically, yet each became the beloved paramour of a monarch. It is a study of female ambition and motivation, of greed and also self-lessness, of love and hate, passion and devotion as well as self-destruction. Throughout history human nature has demonstrated a deep and enduring need for gods and goddesses, heroes and heroines, just as men and women, kings and courtesans, have never ceased to yearn for romance.

United in their eternal theme of love, each of my chosen heroines was beautiful, intelligent, charming; and the kings whose hearts they won were men worth winning. I do not seek to glorify or excuse them, nor to make moral judgments on their behavior. People must be seen against the background of their time, their lives assessed within the framework of their own society. Just as the private life of a great man is public property, the same seems to apply to the women in his life. The public has a desire to share in their great moments, their sorrows and joys, often for no better reason than that these women have lived their lives alongside a great man.

The fashion for biography swelled in the nineteenth century but, particularly when the subjects lived in an earlier time, they were often judged by the intolerant standards of the moralists of the day. Fame or notoriety attracts biographers, and as the course of history was sometimes affected by these women, their lives have been chronicled by academics and historians. Indeed, most famous women have been written about by men, many of whom have not always been sensitive to the events in the lives of these women, or to the women themselves. Male historians are not necessarily the best-qualified judges of female behavior, and I would question whether many academics, with their restricted lives, would have much feel for such a woman's world or psyche.

Once I decided to tell the stories of my five chosen subjects, I travelled in their footsteps as much as possible, retracing the paths of their adventurous lives, visiting the houses in which they lived, the gardens they planned, the works of art they commissioned. I have gazed at their portraits and possessions throughout Europe, feeling their presence, smelling the perfume on their clothes. Occasionally I stumbled upon something as touching as the miniature of Marie Walewska, a little past her days of beauty, which was found in Napoleon's calèche when it was captured by the Prussians at Waterloo. Their passion was over but sentiment remained.

After researching the lives of these five women for several years, I feel as if I have lived with them and in their time. Madame de Pompadour was a perfectionist, and her need to excel was often misunderstood and attacked as ambition. Yet, can excellence and achievement not be desired for their own sake? How could the gentle Marie Walewska resist the overwhelming charisma and magnetism of Napoleon? How could she insist he keep the promises for Poland he made to her? Lola Montez was the victim of her fiery Irish temperament and total lack of discipline. Life for her never had a dull moment. "Pretty, witty Nell" Gwyn had such honesty and gusto that she well deserved the love of her king and country.

As their new friend, I have come to cherish their virtues while freely acknowledging their faults. In another life, another place, another time, perhaps the king might even have chosen the companion of his heart as his lawful wife. My readers must make their own judgments, but I choose to think of each of them as their king's beloved paramour.

I have no doubt that Lillie Langtry's practical ambition motivated her relationship with King Edward VII, but her personality and charm were strong enough to keep his loyalty and affection for the rest of his life.

When this book was first published in 1991, my first chapter was devoted to the sixteenth-century beauty Diane de Poitiers, mistress of Henri II of France. I have since written her biography, *The Serpent and the Moon,* and so she is no longer included in this book.

Introduction

"There are only two precious things on earth: the first is love; the second, a long way behind it, is intelligence."

GASTON BERGER

"A Prince should always be a perfect model of virtue, all the more since he lives in a glass house. If, however, we yield in spite of ourselves, we must observe two precautions . . . First, that the time allotted to a *liaison* should never prejudice our affairs. . . . Secondly—and more difficult to practise—that in giving our heart we must remain absolute master of our mind. . . ."

LOUIS XIV, Testament Politique

"I saw pale kings, and princes too,
Pale warriors, death-pale were they all;
Who cry'd—'La belle Dame sans merci
Hath thee in thrall!'"

KEATS, "La Belle Dame sans Merci"

"I can do no more than to implore virtuous ladies . . . to rouse themselves and to show the world that, even if our sex were not born to command, we ought not to be despised as companions (whether in public or in private) of those who are born to rule: to rule and to be obeyed."

The courtesan Louise Labé in a letter
to a Sapphic friend, September 1548

*P*ower is the greatest aphrodisiac," said Henry Kissinger, para-phrasing Napoleon. A king who married, for the sake of his country's peace and prosperity, an unappealing princess—or simply a woman he could not love—found no shortage of candidates waiting to fill the space in his heart and his bed. But the situation of a king's mistress was fraught with anxiety. Established as the highest lady in the land after the queen, and often more powerful, hers was a precar-ious position filled with permanent, gnawing uncertainty about her future. At a moment's notice she could find herself dismissed in favor of a younger, or more beautiful, or more cunning rival. Mistresses were even passed on to friends, as in the case of Alexander the Great's lovely Greek Campsaspe,* or Emma, the future Lady Hamil-ton, who came "into the possession" of the British consul in Naples as part payment of a bad debt of his nephew's.

THE NAMES OF famous royal courtesans sprinkle the pages of his-tory. Often they exercised more influence on the monarch, for good

---

* Commissioned by his friend the king to paint his mistress naked, the painter Apelles fell in love with Campsaspe while working on his masterpiece. Alexander was said to have been so touched by the strength of Apelles' love for his mistress, and by the beauty of her portrait, that he gave Campsaspe to the artist as a gift. Plutarch in his *Lives* recounts that in her old age Flora the courtesan told the story of how in her youth she had so loved the young Pompey that she could not succumb to his friend Germinius, despite his entreaties. Germinius himself then ap-proached Pompey, who happily gave him Flora. She is said to have been "sick for a long time with grief and longing," but neither her feelings, nor Campsaspe's, were considered of the least importance by their lovers.

or ill, than ministers or the queen. Who were they? What was their background, their training? How did they achieve their position? What did they gain? And—the most intriguing question—how did they retain their hold over the ruler?

Beauty was the invariable key to the door of a monarch's chamber and even to his heart, yet those who remained by his side succeeded, often tenuously, by keeping cool heads. Until recent times, beauty had a short life, and although a splendid marriage was the ultimate goal of most courtesans, few were successful in catching, and keeping, a king.

The primary qualification for a courtesan was to be attractive to men, at least to the man on whom she focused her ambition; if she succeeded in winning his favor, she had to be clever, cunning and lucky if she was to hold on to her position and its perquisites. It was not easy to keep the most prestigious and best-paid post in the land without the sanction of the Church or the law. No woman had more rivals than a king's mistress, and her dismissal or banishment could come at a whim and without warning.

How did they survive, these great courtesans of history, when time had ravaged their beauty and delicious young rivals were dangled continually before their royal masters by unscrupulous manipulators? How did they use their positions as uncrowned queens? How did they spread their very considerable resources, power and influence? What was in their hearts? Did the promise and possession of glory lead them to sacrifice their emotions to the struggle for supremacy in the court, where survival of the fittest was as much the rule as in the rainforests of Brazil or the African veld?

The concept of the complete liberation of women is a recent one, and it is easy to forget the immense power and influence exercised by women in the past as the partners of rich and powerful men. A clever woman understood the loneliness and isolation of absolute monarchy. She knew how a king, faced with an endless choice of ambitious bedfellows, laid much value on normality, tradition, and the comfort of habit. Should he find a wise, dignified and charming companion, who created for him an illusion of security and dependability in a world dominated by the quest for power, he was indeed fortunate. As she knew that her beauty would fade and aspirants would gather at her master's door, many a king's mistress recognized that her tenure of office might be brief. From the first day, most began securing their future by acquiring as much wealth as they could and, if possible, titles for themselves and great marriages for their children. The image of the royal courtesan became, unfairly, that of a calculating, grasping woman, an odalisque with the character of a Salomé.

Throughout history, courtesans have been a feature of royal courts. Beautiful women armed with intelligence, independence and social graces have flocked to try their luck in the entourage of a ruler. Often they succeeded in making their mark and rose to prominent positions as the mistress of a powerful man. Some even rose to share the life of the ruler as his consort in all but name, like Aspasia, who was said to possess divine wisdom, and who became the beloved mistress of Pericles.

According to Demosthenes, Athenian men "had courtesans for the sake of pleasure, concubines for the daily health of our bodies, and wives to bear us lawful offspring and be the faithful guardians of our homes." The Greeks recognized the very clear dichotomy between the mother and the courtesan, just as it was understood by the Ancien Régime and the Victorians. To keep house, and to perpetuate the race with legitimate offspring, the lawful wife was essential; whereas the courtesan fulfilled not only erotic but also social needs, by acting as a hostess able to associate freely with men.

The ancient Greeks and Romans idolized beauty, bestowing moral virtues on those who possessed it. Ugliness was synonymous with shame, and artists often used the loveliest of the hetaerae* as models for images of their deities.

In the East, the secrecy surrounding the harem made it difficult to study the rise of a particular "favorite"—the Sublime Porte took care to conceal the Sultan's private pleasures. Some names, though few likenesses, drifted westward: the beautiful Caucasian Roxelana, thought to be a Russian or Polish slave, ruled the harem of Suleyman the Magnificent. Another who rose to share the Ottoman throne was Aimée de Rivary, a Creole like her alleged kinswoman Josephine de Beauharnais. While sailing between France and her home in Mar-

---

* Literally "female courtiers," from the Greek *hetairos*—a friend or companion.

tinique as a young woman, she was captured by pirates and sold as a slave. Her blond beauty distinguished her in the Topkapi harem, and her influence over the Sultan led to the Porte's pro-French policy. Aimée de Rivary was known as the French Sultana when she became co-regent with her son.

Wu Chao, a concubine in the time of the T'ang Emperor T'ai Tsung, should have retired into a convent on her master's death. Instead, she succeeded in returning to court, displacing the chief concubine and taking the place of the empress. Once on the throne, she eliminated all opposition, killing even her own son, and effectively ruled for the next fifty years. Her grandson inherited a united, prosperous China at the peak of the T'ang culture.

The Byzantine empress Theodora was the daughter of a bear-keeper in Constantinople's Hippodrome. A woman of powerful and controversial character, she rose through a series of liaisons until she finally married the Emperor Justinian, with whom she was jointly crowned in A.D. 523. With spirit and courage, she helped him to rule wisely and well.

But these exceptions were rare. In most cases, concubines remained cloistered and anonymous.

In medieval times, marriage among the privileged was usually a business contract, in which love played little part. Once noble rank became established as hereditary throughout Europe, purity of descent became highly prized, and added to the dignity of women of the nobility. They found themselves placed on pedestals, their role exalted, their femininity admired, their "weaker sex" defended. Gallantry was born, and rules were set for the art of love. But the valiant knight, inspired by the wandering troubadour, spent most of his chivalric life away from home—with the ultimate focus of his chivalry, love and homage almost invariably not his lawful wife.

Through the influence of prominent ladies such as Marie de Champagne,* a phenomenon arose throughout Provence and Burgundy in the late twelfth century known as the Courts of Love. A "Prince of Love" would be appointed to initiate debates which took the form of hypothetical amorous lawsuits. The ladies would reward

---

* Marie de France, daughter of Louis VII, married Henri I of Champagne in 1164.

the winners in a manner of their choosing. By her controversial avowal that real love was impossible between man and wife, as "true lovers give freely without being compelled by external circumstances such as prevail in the married state," Marie de Champagne set the tone for an era, and the cult of adulterous passion for the elite was sanctioned thereafter. Although pure, aesthetic love did not exclude sexual enjoyment, unfulfilled or "impossible" love, *"amor de lonh"*— love from afar, for a woman perhaps as yet unseen—appealed to many romantics, and produced such enduring legends as that of Tristan and Isolde. During the Hundred Years War chivalric courtesy gradually evolved until it reached such a peak that a knight was more readily spurred into action to fight for the love of his lady than of his God.

It was not until the advent of the Courts of Love that the station of the courtesan inspired respect, though at times she had earned admiration. During this era the roles of the concubine and the courtesan fused to appear, and be accepted, as a high social position: the "titular mistress" had arrived. Secure at last in her self-image, she still chose to present herself as a goddess to be adored. Through vanity, and in homage to the classical past, she allowed artists to portray her radiantly naked.

In fifteenth-century France, artists took advantage of classical precedents to flatter important patrons into posing for them as gods and goddesses in mythological settings. In a strange reversal, great ladies of the French court, as well as courtesans, posed naked in imitation of famous courtesans from the Roman Empire, who had themselves been portrayed as the heroines of ancient Greece. To justify their exposure in such paintings, these beautiful women were given the names of famous classical heroines, whose stories, it was suggested, related in some way to their own. Such was the case of the wondrous School of Fontainebleau portrait entitled *Sabina Poppaea,* after Nero's concubine whom he later married. With the revival of courtly love as practiced in Provence, so much emphasis was placed on the intellectual and platonic overtones of ideal love that the courtesan became a fascinating means of conveying the artist's double entendre—a combination of allegory and provocation. The courtesan appeared simultaneously as divine and venal, and she became the rich, aristocratic patron's carnal ideal.

In the Italian courts of the fifteenth century, the term *cortigiana,* the feminine of *cortigiano,* a courtier, distinguished a sophisticated, ambitious beauty with an entrée (her own or her lover's) to the court, from a mere prostitute. Although each offered herself for some kind of profit, the prostitute could not afford the luxury of choice. As Renaissance Italy worshipped beauty and sensuality, such women were able to make a profession out of love and giving pleasure. Although the courtesan, sometimes referred to as *"la grande putana,"* was driven by ambition, deliberately setting out to enchant and capture the prize of her choice, she was not a common whore.

This rebirth of the spirit of Greece and Rome shifted the cultural epicenter of the world from the austerity of the cold Gothic north back to the relaxed sensuality of the Mediterranean. Art rejoiced once again in the human form, and particularly in that of the courtesan.

During the first quarter of the sixteenth century, until the sack of the Holy City in 1527, the patronage of the papal court attracted the greatest artistic talents and most powerful personages of the Italian peninsula. This was the courtesan's Golden Age. Amid the increasing decadence and corruption of Rome, the courtesan was seen as beautiful, intellectual and cultured, society's victim as well as its parasite. As in classical times, the Renaissance outlook on woman was blatantly pagan: what intelligence she had she would use, like her body, in the service of man. The great humanists, revered for their freedom of thought and rational philosophy, can in fact be held responsible for the revival of the hetaerae. These enlightened followers of Petrarch were male elitists and misogynists as extreme as their classical counterparts, holding that a woman's intellect had value only in increasing her sensual awareness. Lorenzo Valla's *De Voluptate,* which advocates female promiscuity and proclaims prostitutes more useful than nuns, almost became the humanist bible.

A number of courtesans, however, did have a marked impact on the cultural life of the times. The most refined and cultured of the Renaissance hetaerae were deemed perfectly suitable companions for Rome's many secular princes of the Church and for important ambassadors and merchants. The best became known in the sixteenth century as *cortesane honeste,* creating a new role-image for their kind. Many won acclaim and respect for their intelligence, culture and femininity: the Pope's banker, Agostino Chigi of Siena, had the famous courtesan Imperia de Cugnati as his mistress. Fluent in Latin and Greek, she was painted by Raphael as Sappho and lived like a princess, her palace superbly appointed. Fiammetta, courtesan and mistress of Cesare Borgia, left considerable property when she died. Beatrice de Ferrara, mistress of Lorenzo de' Medici (grandson of the Magnificent), posed for Raphael's *Fornarina* and Giulio Romano's *Lovers with Procuress*. The tall, cultured Tullia d'Aragona was the daughter of a courtesan and, it was said, a cardinal. Though not beautiful, Tullia won countless admirers with her poems and philosophical dialogues about love, and her "two devilish eyes that as they skipped about, inflamed men's hearts."

BEFORE THE RENAISSANCE, the courtesan was often like a concubine, clandestinely kept by an official who had to maintain an appearance of celibacy, or exclusively the mistress of a rich or powerful man. As the private delight of a magnate, she enjoyed a shadowy if luxurious existence, but the stigma of the "kept woman" remained. There were, of course, outstanding and dignified exceptions. The former courtesan Laura Dianti shared the life of Alfonso d'Este, widower of Lucrezia Borgia, so openly that both Aretino and Vasari wrote about her as his wife and his duchess. As her son succeeded his father, he must have secretly married her.

THE ROLE PLAYED by religion is highly relevant to the development of the courtesan. In Greco-Roman times, the joys of sexuality were a vital ingredient of life, with neither thoughts nor deeds confined by dogma. The advent of Christianity brought a theology of love and forgiveness, though the sin of Eve was not so easily forgiven. God had to send his only son to earth to save mankind, banished from the Garden of Eden by the weakness of woman. The ultimate repudiation of evil could only be achieved through the rejection of woman, and religious orders were formed pledged to chastity and celibacy. There was only one path to "holiness"—abstinence from sex outside matrimony, and not too much of it or too much joy from it even within marriage.

Most ancient civilizations had worshipped a mother/earth goddess, and the early Christians turned from the rising tide of misogyny by establishing the Virgin Mary as a woman worthy of adoration. Obsession with Eve's sin had become so fanatical in some societies that family life and growth was endangered. Mother of Christ and handmaiden of the Lord, Mary was perceived as the antithesis of Eve the Sinner. In Mary, immortal and raised up bodily to be Queen of Heaven, man had found an ideal woman he could unashamedly worship.

Despite Eve's sin, the medieval Church had protected and supported women's access to education and the professions, particularly when the need arose during the Crusades. Aristocratic ladies had usually sided with the Pope on major issues and advocated peaceful solutions in time of international strife. Until the dawn of the Renaissance, unless a woman was born into the upper classes, where there were a few shining examples of literate great ladies and learned *religieuses,* the only choices available to her were marriage, servitude, the nunnery, prostitution or witchcraft.

As the winter of the Middle Ages thawed into the spring of the Renaissance, humanism returned, and with it an end to the repression of mind and body, releasing man at last from the doctrine of Original Sin. Education was encouraged, business acumen and management ability admired. Shame was lifted from the naked human form, which emerged triumphant in art, no longer concealed by shapeless masses of drapery. Women wore cosmetics and beautiful clothes once again, and in Venice even the breasts were uncovered, with nipples lightly rouged (as they would be again during the classical revival following the French Revolution). Freed from the moral constraints of medieval Christianity, many women abandoned Mary and reverted to Eve as their spiritual heroine. With the return of sexually liberated women and the cult of the body beautiful, the courtesan reemerged to appear as she had in ancient times—intelligent, charming and financially independent.

The Reformation reversed women's position in ecclesiastical thinking, just as the Renaissance and humanist philosophy had altered their secular lives a century earlier. The Roman Church had offered women a life of contemplation, study and charitable work in religious orders and convents as an alternative to domestic drudgery. Martin Luther's teachings closed convents and sent women back to the hearth and home and childbearing. "Take women from their house-wifery, and they are good for nothing," he wrote. "If women tire and die of bearing, there is no harm in that; let them die as long as they bear; they are made for that." Luther's preaching taught Protestants to regard woman once again as Eve, not in the voluptuous Renaissance sense but as the cause of man's damnation. Among the European civilizations of the sixteenth century there was as great a need for the Reformation as there had been for the Renaissance in the fifteenth, but with the reformers encouraging superstition and emphasizing the evil in women, it is not surprising that the great witch-hunts began, their flames fanned by a combination of ecclesiastical fear and the terror of the superstitious public.

IN THE PAST, politics, power and dynastic unions were the basis of royal marriages. The blood relationships which created the alliances of peace or defense, war or expansion, only ceased to be relevant in this century. The king truly ruled, and no man needed comfort and relaxation from the cares of state more than he did.

Of all the royal courtesans, the French titular mistresses were the most powerful and prominent. This book originally began with one of the greatest in Diane de Poitiers,* but I must mention the most dazzling of her predecessors, Agnès Sorel. She was the first of the great French royal mistresses (or "left-handed queens," as the French called them) with the attributes of a great courtesan. Ravishingly beautiful, this gentle blond lady-in-waiting to Isabelle de Lorraine caught the eye of King Charles VII of France, who became so smitten "that he dreamed of her while awake and did not believe that sleep could bring more lovely dreams."† He made her *maîtresse de beauté*

---

* See her biography, *The Serpent and the Moon,* by this author.
† Olivier de la Marche.

by giving her the castle of that name on the River Marne as well as many others, and he covered her in diamonds. Painted by the greatest artists of the time, her wondrous image has come down through the centuries. Young and extravagant, and delighting in outrageous costumes, Agnès Sorel nonetheless appears to have "done much good for the kingdom of France." According to the contemporary chronicler Olivier de la Marche, she played a significant and positive role in politics, and as she was a shrewd judge of character, she ably assisted the king in the choice of his excellent ministers. "Burning with desire for her to the extent he could not bear for her to be away from him for an instant: at meals, in bed, at the council, she always had to be at his side." It was for Agnès Sorel that the title *maîtresse en titre* was created for the official mistress of the King of France. Charles VII rewarded and honored her in every way possible, even at the expense of his queen. Agnès Sorel gave the king four daughters* before dying in childbirth, repentant and devout, at the age of forty-one.†

Before the close of the sixteenth century, the King of France, Henri IV, who was said to have had as many mistresses as there were days in the year, fell under the spell of an extraordinary young woman, Gabrielle d'Estrées. Despite Voltaire's later eulogy to her as the pure young maiden of his *Henriade,* Gabrielle d'Estrées came from a family of courtesans—her seven aunts were known as "the seven deadly sins," and her mother ran off with her lover. Henri IV fell so deeply in love with the "marvelous blonde of Picardy" that he resolved to have his marriage to his queen annulled and to marry his mistress. For some time France had been torn apart by civil war between Protestants and Catholics; it was largely thanks to the benign influence of Gabrielle d'Estrées that the king promulgated the Edict of Nantes granting freedom of religion throughout France. She was the only woman to whom the king "could communicate his secrets

---

* The eldest was Charlotte, Bâtarde de France, the mother of Louis de Brézé, husband of Diane de Poitiers.

† Once they were established by the side of the ruler and secure in their power, almost all the subjects of this book began a quest for God and respectability, and all became devout in later life. At times, when I found the sincerity of their repentance difficult to accept, I wondered whether, as they approached the end of their lives, their ambition for position and gain in an earthly royal court was simply transferred into a desire for a prominent place in the Court of Heaven.

and troubles and receive . . . a familiar and gentle consolation," and for this he paid her many royal honors. Shortly before the papal bull annulling the king's marriage arrived from Rome, Gabrielle d'Estrées, her wedding dress prepared, died from convulsions brought on by a premature labor—some said poison.

In the seventeenth century, France's Sun King Louis XIV also had his considerable share of mistresses, most notably Madame de Montespan, described by Saint-Simon as "beautiful as the day." This intelligent and witty blonde with large blue eyes, who came from one of France's oldest families, was avid for money and power, and succeeded in obtaining all she desired. The Marquise de Montespan held the king's fascination during a thirteen-year reign of sensuality, her body massaged for two or three hours a day with pomades, "thus spicing her real beauty with all the artifices in use with the courtesans."

LOUIS XIV WAS still in his prime and enthralled by the glorious Montespan when his cousin King Charles II was restored to the English throne in 1660. The "merriest" of England's monarchs, he had already sired several bastards and enjoyed the favors of a number of mistresses. The most notable to date were Lucy Walters, mother of the future Duke of Monmouth, and Barbara Villiers, later made Duchess of Cleveland. The English sovereign may have thought that love was a game in which his emotions played the smallest part, but by nature he was astoundingly generous.

Unlike the grand mistresses of the King of France, Charles II's, Nell Gwyn (1650–1687) was born in squalor, most probably in Hereford, on the border of Wales. As a child she had helped fill tankards in a brothel, sold oranges at the new theater in London's Drury Lane, and progressed step by step up a ladder of conquests to become a popular actress in Restoration comedy. Once "pretty, witty Nellie at The King's House" caught the eye of Charles II, this bawdy, high-spirited redhead loved only the king. She refused to leave the stage and her audience for some years, and although she had to share the king with a number of rivals, she remained faithful to Charles II all his

life. None of King Charles' many mistresses had any real political influence over him, and all were loathed by his subjects, except for Nell,
the "Protestant whore" (as she described herself), who was beloved
by the English people until her death.

BROADLY SPEAKING, ONE could say that the fifteenth century was
dominated by the Renaissance spreading from Italy, the sixteenth by
the Reformation swelling from Germany, and the seventeenth and
eighteenth by France developing and then imposing its cultural superiority and influence over the entire Continent and into the New
World. This Golden Age of French civilization could not have been
created were it not for the nature of the French, so unlike any other
European people, and the subtle, refining qualities of their extraordinarily feminine women.

While the majority of upper-class ladies in eighteenth-century England could not even read or write, the overall cultural level in France,
and the talents of the country's inhabitants, were higher by far than
among any other nation in Europe. This phenomenon began with the
birth of the literary salons of France's aristocratic ladies, who mixed
together for the first time the most brilliant and cultured members of
all classes. Conversation became an art. Patronage was encouraged,
and ideas exchanged to raise the standard and quality of life. Dazzled,
Europe's courts religiously copied the protocol, etiquette, manners
and fashions of the court at Versailles and the salons of Paris.

Almost one hundred years after an illiterate actress had won the
heart of King Charles II of England and been accepted by the court
and the people, Madame de Pompadour (1721–1764), a beautiful,
rich, cultivated Parisian bourgeoise, was considered insufficiently
grand for King Louis XV of France. The classes may have mixed in
the salons, but the *maîtresse en titre* had always been an aristocrat.
Created Marquise and then Duchesse de Pompadour, she became acknowledged as the most accomplished and civilized woman of her
time, an enchantress with exquisite taste; her creative mind made its
influence felt on everything she touched, until her whole era was described as being *à la Pompadour.* Although she was not a passionate

woman (the relationship between her and the king was once described as a *"scandale de convenance"*), her devotion to Louis was single-minded and obsessive, and through her intelligence, her personality and her incomparable zest for life, she succeeded in holding on to this hot-blooded, libertine King of France until her death.

THE FRENCH REVOLUTION brought a temporary halt to the reign of royal courtesans, though not to liaisons. The enchanting Josephine de Beauharnais was the mistress of the young Napoleon Bonaparte and, although he made her his wife and his empress, this graceful Creole remained in essence a courtesan. When his love for her was soured by her constant infidelities, Napoleon considered divorce, but he did not act until he met Marie Walewska (1786–1817). This beautiful blond Polish noblewoman had been married at seventeen to a man fifty years her senior for the sake of her debt-ridden family. A devout Catholic and patriot, she had resigned herself to dedicating her life to her husband, her son and Poland. Marie Walewska did not seek Napoleon's love, and initially resisted his advances. Persuaded that her virtue was a small price to pay for her country's freedom, she succumbed—and fell in love with him. By bearing the Emperor of France a son she proved to him that his dynastic ambitions could be achieved, and thereby lost the man she loved.

THE NINETEENTH CENTURY saw a dramatic swing back to religion, piety and morality throughout Europe. If the seventeenth and eighteenth centuries had been dominated by France, the nineteenth belonged to the Industrial Revolution and the British Empire. Following the defeat of Napoleon, a new self-awareness possessed the British as they saw the red of the empire cover most of the globe. There was always an upper-class Byronic element in society, which worshipped beauty and nonchalantly espoused sin as being frankly more fun, but in public the British aristocracy appeared as virtuous, domesticated and fecund as their exemplary monarchs, Victoria and

Albert. Royal mistresses, made unfashionable by Victoria's licentious uncles, seemed obsolete.

Exploding onto the Victorian scene like a meteor, Lola Montez (1818–1861) was to have a spectacular life. Born in Ireland, she spent her childhood in the India of the British Raj. A hasty marriage at the age of fifteen ended in divorce—social death at the time. As her only alternatives appeared to be the stage or the streets, Lola travelled to Spain to study dancing. A few months later she returned to conquer London, masquerading as an Andalusian dancer of noble birth. For some years she led an eventful life in the theaters and among the high society of Europe, courting influential patrons and disasters with equal aplomb, until she arrived in the Bavaria of King Ludwig I. Her wild Irish beauty totally captivated the elderly monarch, and he fell hopelessly in love. Almost overnight Ludwig described Lola as his "best friend," and within weeks she effectively ruled Bavaria. Her every wish was granted, and her caprices became legendary. Royal honors, privileges and German gold rained down on her, until her meddling in government and her uncontrollable temper cost Ludwig I his throne. To be fair to Lola—and few biographers of the nineteenth century were—the 1840s heralded an era of revolution when thrones toppled almost indiscriminately, for one reason or another.

If the people demanded middle-class morality of their sovereigns, the latter demanded middle-class comforts in return. What was considered gemütlich in the Germanic world and cozy in the Anglo-Saxon was exactly what the Pompadour had brought to the Petits Appartements of Louis XV—a feeling of bourgeois well-being. Except for state occasions, royalty abandoned grand palaces in favor of relaxed shooting boxes, hunting lodges, chalets in the Alps and villas on the Riviera. It was now the kings and the princes who stole away into their mistresses' domain, and no longer the mistress who was raised up to circulate within the sphere of her royal lover.

Edwardian society tolerated almost any liaison, as long as everyone played their discreet part in the masquerade. The courtesan was back in fashion with a vengeance, and remained at the pinnacle of society until the Belle Epoque ended in 1910 with the death of England's King Edward VII.

WHETHER IN SOCIETY, romanticized art or fiction, the popular image of a courtesan in today's idiom has not strayed far from the "grand voluptuary" or *poule de luxe* of the nineteenth century. The last century too saw its share of royal mistresses, but as access to the upper classes has been widespread since the First World War, the courtesan/mistress has ceased to be a status symbol of international society's gentlemen.

As few monarchs remained on their thrones after the last war, there was even less demand for the *maîtresse en titre*. Fluidity of movement within the classes, and an open society in many countries, have enabled the demi-mondaine to be thoroughly integrated into today's society. Indeed, the courtesan's twentieth- and twenty-first-century incarnation could be seen as the cinema or television actress/pop star/cover girl, energetically filling the vacuum left by her predecessor. Glamorously exposed through the "artists" of the popular media, recognition, rather than beauty or talent, is her fortune.

Today, in a sense, there are many more kings once again, but they sit on different thrones: their kingdoms are industry, music, the media, entertainment, large corporations. The fortunes of these self-made monarchs often exceed the gross national product of small nations, and they of course have their mistresses. This book does not concern them, and as today's royalty no longer has the same need or duty to contract political marriages as in previous times, today's princes are free to marry their hearts' desire.

LILLIE LANGTRY (1853–1929) was born on the Channel Island of Jersey, the daughter of the minister. Brought up with five rough-and-tumble brothers, she shared their life of freedom and wild escapades. When her only escape to London and liberty was marriage, the ravishing Jersey Lillie married Edward Langtry, a dull gentleman who was not as rich as Lillie supposed. At a London reception, she was noticed by a group of influential artists, and soon her likeness appeared on postcards as one of society's "professional beauties." Oscar Wilde promoted her, and inevitably Lillie caught the roving eye of Edward, Prince of Wales, and became his first official mistress. Bankruptcy and divorce from the wretched Edward Langtry left Lillie no choice but to go on the stage, automatically placing herself "beyond the pale" of English society. Lillie sought and gained her fortune abroad, mainly in America, but Edward VII's patronage and friendship never wavered until her death.

```
                                              CHRISTIAN I
                                              King of Denmark
                                              1426–1481

         MARGARET OF
          DENMARK
          1456–1486

           JAMES IV
          King of Scots
           1473–1513

  LADY KATHERINE            JAMES V
     STEWART               King of Scots
                            1512–1542

  LADY MARGARET               MARY
    DOUGLAS               Queen of Scots
                            1542–1587

   LADY ANNE                JAMES I                        ANNE OF DENMARK
    HAMILTON            King of Great Britain                 1574–1619
                            1566–1625

  GEORGE GORDON          ELIZABETH OF
  1st Marquess of Huntly    ENGLAND
     1563–1626             1596–1662

  GEORGE GORDON         SOPHIA OF THE          HENRIETTA ANNE
  2nd Marquess of Huntly  PALATINATE              1644–1670
     ?–1649               1630–1714

  LADY CATHERINE          GEORGE I            ANNE OF ORLÉANS
    GORDON               King of England         1669–1728
    1635–1691             1660–1727

  COUNTESS ISABELLA       GEORGE II          MARIE ADELAIDE
    MORSZTYN             King of England        OF SAVOY
    1671–1758             1683–1760            1685–1712

 PRINCESS CONSTANZA     FREDERICK LOUIS         LOUIS XV
   CZARTORYSKA          Prince of Wales      King of France
    1700–1759            1707–1751            1710–1774

     CASIMIR             GEORGE III
 Prince Poniatowski     King of England
    1721–1800            1738–1820

   STANISLAUS              EDWARD           MARIE      NAPOLEON I
 Prince Poniatowski      Duke of Kent      WALEWSKA   Emperor of France
    1754–1833          and Strathearn                  1769–1821
                         1767–1820

    ISABELLA             VICTORIA
  PONIATOWSKI         Queen of Great Britain
     1805               and Ireland
                        1819–1901

   MARIA ANNA  LILLIE   EDWARD VII
    DI RICCI  LANGTRY  King of Great Britain    COUNT ALEXANDER
    1823–1912           and Ireland                WALEWSKI
                        1841–1910                  1810–1868
```

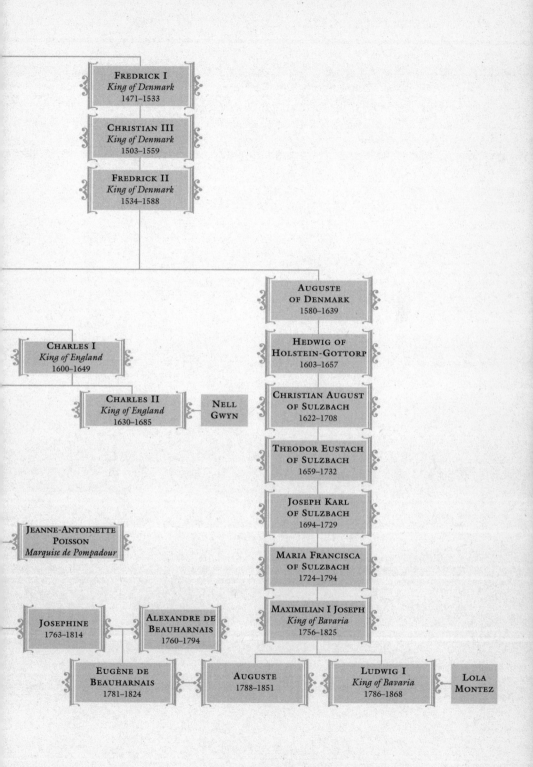

FREDRICK I
King of Denmark
1471–1533

CHRISTIAN III
King of Denmark
1503–1559

FREDRICK II
King of Denmark
1534–1588

AUGUSTE
OF DENMARK
1580–1639

CHARLES I
King of England
1600–1649

HEDWIG OF
HOLSTEIN-GOTTORP
1603–1657

CHARLES II
King of England
1630–1685

NELL
GWYN

CHRISTIAN AUGUST
OF SULZBACH
1622–1708

THEODOR EUSTACH
OF SULZBACH
1659–1732

JOSEPH KARL
OF SULZBACH
1694–1729

JEANNE-ANTOINETTE
POISSON
Marquise de Pompadour

MARIA FRANCISCA
OF SULZBACH
1724–1794

JOSEPHINE
1763–1814

ALEXANDRE DE
BEAUHARNAIS
1760–1794

MAXIMILIAN I JOSEPH
King of Bavaria
1756–1825

EUGÈNE DE
BEAUHARNAIS
1781–1824

AUGUSTE
1788–1851

LUDWIG I
King of Bavaria
1786–1868

LOLA
MONTEZ

Cupid and the King

1

Nell Gwyn

1650–1687

MISTRESS OF CHARLES II OF ENGLAND

"The amours of a good king are always deemed a pardonable weakness, providing they are not attended with injustice or violence."

Anti-Machiavelli

"Permit me, Sir, to help you to a whore:
Kiss her but once, you'll ne'er want Cleveland more.
She's Buckhurst's whore at present, but you know—
When sovereign wants a whore, the subject must forgo."

ETHEREGE (Dedicated to Charles II, about Nell Gwyn)

"He [Charles II] thought no man sincere, nor woman honest, out of principle; but that whenever they proved so, humour or vanity was at the bottom of it. No one, he fancied, served him out of love, and therefore he endeavoured to be quits with the world by loving others as little as he thought they loved him."

GILBERT BURNET, Bishop of Salisbury, 1643–1715

*N*o one can be sure exactly where Nell Gwyn* was born, but most of her biographers agree that her birth occurred in miserable circumstances in Hereford, on February 2, 1650. Her father may have come from a respectable Welsh family, and was rumored to have been a captain, most probably a Royalist.

Like so many others caught up in the army in those troubled times, Thomas Gwyn was broken by the Civil War. When he married Eleanor Smith of London's St. Martin-in-the-Fields at Oxford, the union was considered beneath him, and he could scarcely have married lower. Mrs. Gwyn, who had come to Royalist Oxford at the start of the Civil War, was an alcoholic who shared out her favors most liberally. After the war, Thomas Gwyn returned to his father's birthplace of Hereford and kept a tavern—and most probably a brothel as well. It is likely that both Nell and her older sister Rose were born here. After lying low for a few years, Gwyn returned to Oxford, where he was promptly put in prison for his Royalist sympathies. Mrs. Gwyn and her daughters fled to St. Martin-in-the-Fields, where they lived in a cellar in the squalid Coal Alley Yard, Drury Lane. Thomas Gwyn died in Oxford in prison before the Restoration, without ever seeing his family again.

While their mother worked ostensibly selling ale at Mrs. Ross' "house of ill repute," the barefooted Nell and Rose hawked fish and oysters in the filthy streets around their home. Both girls quickly learned to live on their wits and entice customers with their cheeky repartee. By the time pert little Nellie was nine, she had joined her mother and sister at Mrs. Ross's. But although Nell later maintained that her duties involved no more than filling the customers' cups with "strong waters," John Wilmot, Earl of Rochester, had his doubts when he wrote that she was

> *By Madame Ross exposed to town,*
> *I mean to those who will give half-a-crown*

---

* Nell spelt her name variously Gwyn, Gwine, Gwin, Gwynne and Gwinne.

—the going rate for her whores. But then Nell Gwyn's name was often coupled with that of Rochester, and she may even have been his mistress before she met the king.

Two districts of London were the main centers of activity at this time: the City and the Whitehall Palace area. Here the money was made and business was done, and inevitably the need for relaxation and entertainment, as well as blessed relief from Cromwell's Puritan restrictions, led to the rapid spread of taverns and brothels.

✵

NELL GWYN WAS ten years old in the summer of 1660 when Charles Stuart returned to England to be restored as the rightful king. No one in London on that bright May day, least of all an impressionable young girl, could forget the sight of the darkly handsome young monarch, riding at the head of a procession of twenty thousand cavalry and soldiers, smiling and waving to his cheering subjects. The sun shone, the streets were garlanded and the children ran in front of his prancing charger throwing petals in its path.

After years of austerity and the horror of civil war, England rejoiced and relaxed. Among the main factors in favor of the Restoration of Charles II had been the fear in the minds of thinking people that the country would be dominated by the army. Charles had endured exile and the knowledge that his father had lost his crown, and his head, as a result of his intolerance, inflexibility and apparent lack of charm. His son determined that he would lack none of the qualities needed "to regain his throne, retain his throne, and maintain the legitimate succession to that throne" (Imbert-Terry), and swore he would never go on his travels again.

Hypocrisy had characterized the Puritan domination of England during the Commonwealth years; with the Restoration, the people's reaction to the end of the enforced restriction of their pleasures was an orgy of immorality. For Charles, tolerance became the keyword of his reign, and the easygoing attitude of the monarch permeated all aspects of society.

In questions of behavior, tone or fashion, the people looked to the king and his court, an entourage dominated by wits and beauties.

This was a court of youth—Charles was twenty-nine, his brother James, Duke of York, was twenty-seven. Of the king's closest companions, the Duke of Buckingham was thirty-two, the earls of Sunderland, Dorset and Arran were in their twenties, and the cleverest, wittiest and most debauched of them all, the Earl of Rochester, was still in his teens.* Inevitably, these young men, exiled for years and deprived of their homeland by joining their king abroad, made merry with their monarch on his triumphant return. They had all suffered hardship and danger, and the strain of an uncertain future. The restored Charles could now reward their constancy and loyalty by granting his friends titles and positions which would guarantee great prestige and yield them enormous incomes.

AT THE TIME of the Restoration, London's inns hung out their old signs again: The King's Head, The Duke's Head and The Crown. Their patrons spilled into the streets, overfed and usually drunk. Strict observance of the Sabbath was no longer enforced, and morals were extremely lax. The streets were filthy—muddy in wet weather and dust-filled when dry, unsafe to walk because of the likelihood of attack by footpads and rogues, and incredibly noisy, the cries of the hawkers, porters and watermen mixing with the myriad signs creaking over almost every doorway, and the crash and clatter of horses, carriages and carts over the uneven cobbles. Much traffic centered on the river, as it was the only swift, safe avenue of conveyance (except when shooting the rapids under London Bridge) through the capital. The old city was concentrated along the banks of the Thames.

Maypoles were re-erected on their former sites and traditional dances performed around them once more. The common folk and the gentry dressed in bright colors again, the fashionable covered in a profusion of ribbons, ruffles and lace, broad-brimmed feathered hats, short cloaks and square-toed high-heeled shoes. Ladies favored green silk stockings with diamond-buckled black velvet garters below the

---

* Etherege wrote of Rochester: "I know he is a Devil, but he has something of the Angel yet undefac'd in him."

knee, though the French ambassador, le Comte de Comminges, reported to his sovereign that the English ladies often preferred to show "their white satin skins by wearing none." Gentlemen wore powdered periwigs and fringed, scented gloves, and carried special combs for their wigs and quizzing glasses with which to examine those of their neighbors. Pocket watches were worn, snuff was used, and both men and women carried muffs. Ladies dyed their hair in exotic colors, sported loose curls on their foreheads and stuck black beauty patches on their white-powdered faces.

The king was famous for his courtesy and courtly manners (just as he was for his amours), but the bad language adopted by his young courtiers while in exile was enthusiastically copied by all classes of society. The courtiers' table manners were appalling, and swearing was energetic and commonplace. When the Grand Duke Cosimo III of Tuscany visited London, his secretary noted:

> there are no forks, nor vessels to supply water for the hands, which
> are washed in a basin full of water that serves for all the company;
> or perhaps at the end of dinner, they dip the end of the napkin into
> the beaker of water set before each guest, and with this they clean
> their teeth, and wash their hands.

The gossip and scandals of the court and society were recorded with relish by the diarists of the day, such as Samuel Pepys (who, at the age of twenty-six, had come from Holland on the same ship as the king), John Evelyn, Aubrey and le Comte de Grammont, and dozens of lesser known and anonymous writers. The middle classes lived lives as dissolute as those of the courtiers they emulated.

One of the first decisions taken by King Charles was to restore the theatrical life of London, which had been banned for twenty-three years. Starved of entertainment during the lackluster years of the Commonwealth, the people looked to the revival of the theaters as the preminent source of amusement and social life. Two theaters were immediately commissioned: the King's House in Drury Lane, known simply as "The Theatre," and the Duke's House (known as "The Opera"), named in honor of the Duke of York.

The dashing young men of the court were matched by the talented, and equally young, writers of the day—Dryden, Etherege, Wycherley and Sedley—all in their twenties. The young king at the center of this high-spirited, brilliant society was himself charming, witty and generous. He encouraged a series of glittering entertainments to be staged so that he could meet and be seen by his people. The highways of the kingdom were choked with coachloads of subjects making their colorful way to London—a huge caravanserai, all anxious to catch a glimpse of the sovereign.

The king was a fine and worthy sight to see. Tall and slender and immensely fit, due to his constant pursuit of sport of all kinds, Charles Stuart always rose early and rode or walked briskly in St. James's Park before breakfast, exhausting his slower entourage. He played tennis or pall-mall (a kind of croquet) almost daily. He was dark, and his face was long and marked by deep lines of suffering, which made him look older than his years. He did not follow the current fashion and wear a wig, but allowed his fine black hair to fall to his shoulders in ringlets. His best feature was his eyes, alert, intelligent and as black as his hair. His mouth, sensual and sardonic, was quick to smile and reply to any witticism with one of his own, in a melodic, deep voice. His subjects, men and women, all agreed: their sovereign was most attractive to his people.

A carnival atmosphere permeated all classes of society throughout that glorious summer of 1660. When the queen mother and her daughter, Charles's adored sister Henrietta Anne (Minette), arrived from France in the autumn, the festivities began all over again. No sooner had the country finished celebrating the return of their king than it was time to celebrate his coronation. Charles II was crowned with all the pageantry of monarchy, and to the rejoicing of his people.

By 1662, with England's king firmly established on his throne, it was thought time for the succession to be assured. Charles already had five illegitimate children, four boys and a girl. Some thought he might be willing to legitimize the eldest, James Scott, Duke of Monmouth, when his mother, the much-maligned Lucy Walters, was dead, but under English law this would not allow Monmouth to become his father's heir. The queen mother also objected strongly; in 1659, Charles had forced his brother James to marry the commoner he had made pregnant. (Anne Hyde, Duchess of York, was to be the mother of the next two queens, Mary and Anne.) There has always been speculation that Charles had actually married Lucy Walters, but in his later years the king himself denied this.

The consort chosen for Charles was Catherine de Braganza, daughter of King John IV of Portugal. She was rich, though sadly deformed, plain, dull and in bad health. To make matters worse, according to the Spanish ambassador, it was common knowledge in both Spain and Portugal that she could not have children. However, as the king took exception to the ambassador's overbearing manner, he chose to ignore this piece of information. The union would certainly please France's Louis XIV, who had sided with Portugal in its long-drawn-out struggle against Spain for independence. Although France was at peace with Spain, this did not prevent Louis from coveting the Spanish Netherlands. The marriage would bring England firmly into the French network of European alliances. (Catherine's dowry included Tangiers and Calcutta, which marked the beginning of England's interference in India. She is probably best remembered for introducing tea to England. Drinking chocolate was also first imported at this time from Madrid, and *vin pétillant*, or champagne, from France became fashionable.)

Pious and good, the little queen devoted herself to her religious duties and to trying to please her husband, whom she was to adore all her life. Charles was always kind to her, but faithful he could not be. Although Catherine suffered terribly from jealousy at first, she reconciled herself to her husband's infidelities, and even came to quite like some of his mistresses. Her efforts to join in the gaieties of Charles' court endeared her to him, and gently eased her own pain.

DURING THE PREVIOUS year, 1661, the eleven-year-old Nell had witnessed the construction of the King's House theater in Drury Lane. Charles II had commissioned Tom Killigrew, dramatist and royal jester, the son of one of his most respected courtiers, to form a company of players. Killigrew had befriended Rose Gwyn and offered her and Nell jobs as "orange girls" in the new theater. A friend of Mrs. Gwyn known as "Orange Moll" had the license to sell oranges, lemons, fruits and sweetmeats to the thirsty theatergoers; "strong waters" were banned in case they should inflame the tempers of the patrons. Orange Moll supervised the girls, dressed them and trained them to sell her fruit for whatever they could get above her basic price. Competition was fierce to attract buyers in the audience, as "orange girls" were considered little better than prostitutes, and success depended as much on a girl's looks as on her line of patter.

London's theatrical life had lain dormant for so long that its revival brought a number of changes. Men had always played the female roles, but now, for the first time, at the express wish of the king, women were allowed to appear on the stage. All the scenery was new, and the queen, her ladies, and some of the richer courtiers gave their own clothes to be worn in productions. Formerly, sovereigns had only attended the court theaters attached to their palaces, and would never visit a public playhouse. Now that the king and his brother were each patrons of a company, they attended regularly, as did the queen, the Duchess of York, the courtiers and their ladies.

To make best use of the daylight streaming through the open roof, performances began at three in the afternoon. Ladies who joined the beaux in the pit audience wore vizards or masks to hide their identity or their blushes, and to spy unrecognized on their husbands. Prostitutes also wore black visors and plied their wares in the pit. The actresses were all given the courtesy title of "Mrs." or "Mistress" ("Miss" in those days had less respectful connotations—a "miss" was a whore!). Such courtesy did not extend to the orange girls, whose exchanges with the town beaux were ribald to the point of bawdiness and were considered part of the interval entertainment. Thomas Shadwell in *The Sullen Lovers* summed up the times: "Methinks it's as pretty an honest, drinking, whoring age as a man would wish to live in."

Pert little Nellie, with her red curls, cheeky turned-up nose and dimples, sold oranges in the pit for eighteen months. During that time "sweet Nell of old Drury" became, at twelve years old, the mistress of a Captain Duncan (who was said to be "Nell-sick" with love), and although kept by him at the Cock and Pie Inn next to the theater, she merrily "entertained" others.

Nell's sister Rose had become the mistress of "Lying" Harry, son of Thomas Killigrew. When he cast her off without the traditional gratuity on parting, she married a highwayman and indulged in a little whoring to make ends meet. Rose and her husband were caught burgling the house of one of her customers and thrown into Newgate Prison. Due to Nell's pleas, Thomas Killigrew used his influence to free his son's former mistress. This brought Nell to his attention, and eventually to the stage. Killigrew could not help being impressed and amused by Nell's ingenuous approach when she pointed out that " 'twas surely a pity and a waste to let a young whore scarred with neither the pox nor infected with the clap to languish in prison." Rose's pardon and release were duly arranged.

Like most of the young girls of London, Nellie thought of the king as her romantic ideal. His marriage, she said, had broken her heart, leaving her no reason (she added with a laugh) to hold on to her virginity.

> Next in the Playhouse she took her degree
> As men commence at University.
> No doctors, till they've masters been before:
> So she no player was till first a whore.*

Stagestruck and very pretty, Nell soon caught the eye of the playwright John Lacy and Shakespeare's great-nephew Charles Hart. Lacy taught her to dance while Hart trained her for the stage (and, it was said, "all else beside"). She was totally illiterate (she could only form a crude E.G. for her signature all her life), and had to learn all her roles by rote, but she had a good memory and learned quickly. Her first appearance on the stage, aged fifteen, was in a play by Dryden, *The Indian Emperor*, and she acquitted herself well. An intelligent girl, Nell had an instinct for invention and impromptu lines. Pepys was a regular in the audience, and he claimed that she saved many a poor play with her ready wit and humor, and said her voice was good and carried well over the noise of the rowdiest audience. A born comedienne, she never succeeded in tragic parts. Her debut was an immediate success, and she was invited to join the company of the King's House.

---

* Rochester's "Panegyric on Nellie."

Small and slim, with lovely legs and tiny feet, Nell was left remarkably unscarred by her years of running barefoot in London's filthy streets. She was justifiably proud of her thick hair—auburn with golden highlights—which hung in loose waves below her shoulders. Her eyes were a deep blue, framed by well-shaped brows and long, dark eyelashes, a striking contrast with her hair. Her skin was clear, with rosy cheeks, and her full, invariably laughing mouth (described by an admirer as "an out-mouth that makes mine water at it") showed perfect small teeth. The whole effect was of an enchanting, merry urchin. Besides her beauty, Nell's greatest assets were her sense of fun and her good humor. Laughter suffused her whole face, and she infected all around her with her vitality. Pepys thought her delightful, and described her at fifteen as "pretty, witty Nellie at The King's House."

Dryden was so taken with the young actress's fresh beauty and eagerness to learn that he offered to write for her as long as she was taught to act and given a wardrobe. The sponsorship of such an influential playwright was all-important, as actresses had to supply their own accessories—petticoats, collars, neckerchiefs, silk stockings, fans, garters and so on; the theater supplied only the basic costumes. As well as learning to act—which consisted of posturing, pouting and generally flinging her arms about—Nell had to be seen "on the town" in order to further her career and improve her station in life. Accompanying Charles Hart, Nellie was able to observe the courtiers, rakes and gallants on the rampage, whether drunk and disorderly at the Cock and Pie or dining with the members of King Charles' newly formed Royal Society. Fortunately for Nellie, Restoration manners were as uncouth as the language at Charles' court. Hundreds of broadsheets, bawdy songs and ballads were printed to entertain the masses, often ridiculing members of society. Nell had had few opportunities to hear fine English spoken, other than the occasional sermon at St. Martin-in-the-Fields, and although the struggle for survival in Coal Alley Yard and in Mrs. Ross' brothel may have sharpened her wits, it had done little to dilute her dreadful swearing. In every way,

Nell Gwyn could be said to have epitomized the true spirit of the people during the merry Restoration.

> *Fate now for her did its whole force engage,*
> *And from the pit she's mounted to the stage,*
> *There in full lustre did her glories shine,*
> *And, long eclipsed, spread forth their light divine.**

Still only fifteen, Nell moved from one stage success to the next and became officially, as a member of the theater's company, a King's Servant, with the attached privileges and social status, a salary of three pounds a week and her own dressing room. But the outbreak of the plague in 1665 forced the playhouses to close, and a frustrated and frightened Nell had to gather up her mother and her belongings and flee with the court to Oxford for more than a year. When the playhouses reopened, the Great Fire emptied London once again a year later.

However, it was not long before the theaters were rebuilt, and by the end of 1666 Nell's conquest of her public was assured—a public which included two of the most influential members of the king's inner circle: the brilliant young wit and writer the Earl of Rochester, and George Villiers, Duke of Buckingham, satirist and "lord of useless thousands." Pepys commented of the actresses in a new play at the King's House that they did "very well, but above all, little Nelly." The king, too, had seen Nell Gwyn in a number of performances, and had particularly admired her in roles for which she dressed as a boy. He even went so far as to pay for some of her costumes, especially some "Rhinegraves"—wide divided skirts which flew up, displaying a tantalising glimpse of lovely leg, when Nell twirled and danced on the stage. When Queen Catherine noticed her husband's penchant for shapely calves, she too adopted male attire to show off her own pretty legs, starting a fashion for trouser-suits for the ladies of the court.

---

* Rochester's "Panegyric."

A YEAR LATER the theaters had to close again, this time as a result of the constant wars with the Dutch. Nell found herself on the dole, albeit the royal dole. In need of a protector, she turned to her new friends Buckingham and Rochester for a solution. With their help, by the summer of 1667 she was able to transfer her favors from Charles Hart (who had to give up Nellie, as he was very poor and needed to find a "Lady Wealthy" to keep him) to Charles Sackville, Lord Buckhurst, a considerable move up the social ladder. Heir to the earldoms of Dorset and Middlesex, Buckhurst was known as one of the most cultured, witty and charming young rakes at court, as well as one of the wildest. Nell and Hart were both resourceful and practical, and came to an agreeable financial arrangement with the handsome, and very rich, Lord Buckhurst. The balladeers took full advantage:

> *"Take her, my lord," quoth Hart, "since you're so mean*
> *To take a player's leavings for your quean,*
> *For though I love her well, yet as she's poor,*
> *I'm well contented to prefer the whore."*

All that summer Nell dallied at Epsom with her new protector and his friend, the equally amusing poet and "rakehell" Sir Charles Sedley and his young daughter, riding on the Downs, laughing and drinking.* This is how Rochester described his two friends, Nell's summer companions:

> *For pointed satyrs I would Buckhurst choose,*
> *The best good man, with the worst natur'd muse,*
> *For songs and verses, mannerly obscene,*
> *That can stir nature up by spring unseen,*
> *And without forcing blushes please the queen.*
> *Sedley has that prevailing, gentle art,*
> *That can with a resistless charm impart*
> *The loosest wishes of the chastest heart,*
> *Raise such a conflict, kindle such a fire*

---

* Five years earlier, Buckhurst and Sedley, already partners in debaucheries, had indulged in a famous frolic at Oxford Kate's tavern in Covent Garden, appearing naked on the balcony and preaching to the crowd gathered below.

Betwixt declining virtue and desire,
Till the poor vanquish'd mind dissolves away
In dreams all night, in sighs and tears all day.

A newly fashionable spa, Epsom was patronized by the court and society for the cure of every kind of overindulgence. The three made merry throughout the summer until, inevitably, they fell out over one of their silly pranks which went too far. Nell and Buckhurst parted, and to the relief of her audience as well as her friends, she came back to London and the stage.

Finding herself temporarily without a sponsor, Nell befriended Mary (Moll) Davis, a rival actress from the Duke's House whom she had often wickedly mimicked, to the delight of her audience. Moll was a blacksmith's daughter who claimed an illegitimate descent from the first Earl of Berkshire, but despite this tenuous connection with nobility, she was as vulgar and coarse as Nell. Moll was an excellent dancer, though Nell was perhaps the better actress; both declared they would never make real money on the stage, so they teamed up to find a rich patron. The court had moved to Tunbridge Wells, where Queen Catherine was taking the waters in a last attempt to conceive, though the spa's reputation for helping conception might have had more to do with the ample opportunities it offered for amorous digressions than the beneficial qualities of the water. Nell and Moll, prompted by the queen's request for theater, packed their prettiest dresses and headed for the spa.

Fashionable Tunbridge Wells was a center for society, especially for those hoping to enter it through a useful liaison. One who had was the king's long-established mistress, Barbara Villiers, Lady Castlemaine. A harridan and a nymphomaniac (she happily consoled, and kept, Charles Hart after Nell's transfer to Buckhurst), she was visibly losing her hold on Charles. Barbara was one of those women whom men love despite themselves. She exerted a magnetic fascination over Charles, and this proud and intelligent man had been reduced by her to a condition approaching slavery. Her power had been such that there was nothing she could not extract from him—money, land, privileges and titles. Nor was her avarice confined to the king. Barbara Villiers exchanged her favors for money wherever it was offered, but was equally prepared to pay for anyone she desired and could not get for free. Though Rochester's kinswoman, she did not escape his "profane wit"* or acid pen. He recorded all her infidelities: Monmouth and Cavendish, Henningham and Scrope, "scabby Ned," "sturdy Frank" and many more.

> When she has jaded quite,
> Her almost boundless appetite . . .
> She'll still drudge on in tasteless vice,
> As if she sinn'd for exercise.

Once an unusually acrobatic rope dancer called Jacob Hall attracted her perverted fancy at a fair, and tales of their sexual diversions shocked even this licentious court.

Barbara Villiers' poor but handsome young cousin, John Churchill, the future warrior Duke of Marlborough, founded his fortune and position on what Barbara paid him for his services. One day when the king came to visit their children, he spied young Churchill hurriedly leaving Barbara's bedroom by the window, and called out to him, almost in sympathy: "I forgive you sir, for I know you do it only for the money." When Barbara felt her hold over the king slipping, she resorted to the age-old technique of procuring lovely young girls stupid enough for her to manage in order to entice her royal lover back to her own boudoir.

For some time King Charles had been engaged in a fruitless pursuit of one such protégée of Barbara's, "La Belle" Frances Stewart,† but his complete lack of success tempted him toward new conquests.

☙

IT WAS DURING Nell and Moll Davis' first sojourn at Tunbridge Wells that Rochester and Buckingham encouraged the two young actresses to aim for the most influential patron of all in order to oust Barbara Villiers as official mistress. For, despite her assurances to her

---

* John Evelyn's description.

† Until decimalization, her perfect profile featured as Britannia on the coins of the realm.

cousin and lover Buckingham, Barbara had not kept her promises to advance his interests with the king, and the ambitious duke wanted to replace her with a more malleable mistress.

It was Moll's provocative song-and-dance routine "My Lodging Is on the Cold Ground" which prompted the queen to leave the room and the king to take Moll to his bed. The contemporary wit John Downes remarked that the performance had been so effective it had "raised the fair songstress from the cold ground to the bed royal." Moll was soon pregnant and installed by the monarch in a fine house in Suffolk Street, London. But while she was castigated by Mrs. Pepys as being "the most impertinent slut in the world," publicly flaunting her condition as well as Charles' gift of a valuable ring, rumors were circulating that the king's interest had already moved on. There was also a story that Moll and Nell had fallen out after Nell had laced Moll's sweetmeats with julap, a strong purgative, when she was due to dine with the king. The result must have been dramatic, as Moll never forgave her rival. Rochester summed up the king's amorous predilections with an irreverent ditty:

> *Restless he rolls about from whore to whore,*
> *A merry monarch, scandalous and poor.*
> *Nor are his high desires above his strength;*
> *His sceptre and his —— are of a length.*

In any other reign Rochester would have been sent to the Tower for such treasonable libel, but Charles II was ever lenient with wit, even when directed against himself.

In April 1668, within a year of Moll's conquest of the king at Tunbridge, Nell, accompanied by a distant cousin of Buckingham's, attended the first night of Etherege's *She Would If She Could* at the Duke's House. In the next box sat the duke himself with his brother the king, who immediately struck up a conversation with Nell, inviting her and her companion to supper. Leaving his brother to distract her escort, Charles bantered with Nell, but when he was presented with the bill, as usual he had no money. Nor had James, and Nell was left to pay for the party. Delighting in the king's discomfort, she exclaimed: "Oddsfish!" mimicking his favorite expression, "This is the poorest company I ever was in!" From that moment, Nell Gwyn would enchant, delight and amuse her sovereign for the rest of his life. This was one of the last occasions on which the Duke of York would visit "his" theater, as he announced his conversion to Catholicism within the year and lost interest in his playhouse.

As spring came, Nell's success on the stage continued in a series of new plays and revivals. She was now famous, and the best-loved comedienne of her day. Her success with the monarch kept pace, and all the town knew that the king "had sent for Nellie."

When Barbara Villiers discovered that Charles had established a new mistress, the scenes at court were terrible. But the more Barbara raged and terrorized everyone within her orbit, the more Nell mimicked her tantrums, to the delight of the courtiers.

Charles II had tolerated Barbara Villiers' greed and infidelities for long enough and, although he continued to treat her generously, he had her put out of her rooms in Whitehall Palace, though somehow they remained on good terms. Moll Davis' impertinence had matched her avarice, and she and her daughter by Charles, Lady Mary Tudor,* had been pensioned off with a thousand pounds a year. The timing was right for Nell Gwyn's conquest of Charles II.

Word soon reached Nellie's adoring fans that she had become a regular visitor to the king's private apartments in Whitehall. If approval could have been measured by her success at the theater, it would appear that this time most Londoners agreed with their sovereign's choice. Nell seemed to fit the lines Dryden wrote for her:

> Sweet ladies! be not frighted, I'll be civil.
> I'm what I was, a harmless little devil.

When Charles made Barbara Villiers his mistress, he compensated her husband with an earldom. When he took on Nellie, he did not forget her previous attachment to Lord Buckhurst, and appointed him, most appropriately, a groom of the bedchamber, with a salary of a thousand pounds a year. This august position involved waiting on

---

* She married Francis Ratcliffe, second Earl of Derwentwater. Their two sons became prominent Jacobites and were executed after the rebellions of 1715 and 1745 respectively.

the king when he ate in private, and sleeping on a pallet-bed in the king's bedroom all night. The office was a great honor, given only to the highest nobility, including Buckingham, Rochester and others of the king's "merry gang."

Naturally, Charles wanted Nell to himself, but despite his pleading she would not leave the stage. At eighteen, Nell Gwyn was at the height of her beauty and popularity. London was at her feet, and this had enabled her to win the attention and affection of the highest in the land. Her situation at the theater had also changed with her social status; she was allocated a new dressing room, new costumes and new lodgings. She became known as "Mrs. Ellen Gwyn," and only her closest friends and her "public" could call her "Nellie." She called the king her "Charles III," as he followed Charles Hart and Charles Buckhurst in her affections. Inevitably, it all went a little to Nellie's head. She became more particular about the company she kept, insisted her costumes had to be remade, and generally lorded it over her rivals on the stage.

Often Charles would come to watch Nellie perform at his theater and then leave with her, but when affairs of state kept him away, a suitable escort would be found for her, usually the ubiquitous Buckingham. Strangely enough, Charles was rarely jealous and, although Nell was considered "a bold merry slut who lay laughing there upon people" (Pepys Diary, January 7, 1669), once she became his mistress she never took another lover. Despite rumor, and a poem attributed to Rochester (but not worthy of him), describing Nell's body in thoroughly indecent detail, her constancy to the king was genuine. Rochester did write about Nell:

> Much did she suffer, first on bulk and stage,
> From the blackguards and bullies of the age;
> Much more her growing virtue did sustain
> While dear Charles Hart and Buckhurst su'd in vain.
>
> In vain they su'd; curs'd be the envious tongue
> That in her undoubted chastity would wrong;
> For should we fame believe, we then might say
> That thousands lay with her as well as they.

Among the first gifts Nell received from Charles were stables at Epsom, as he complained that she rode badly. Not that her lack of skill deterred her from backing the horses. Nellie loved to gamble, and as Newmarket had eclipsed Epsom as the great center of English racing by this time, she often accompanied the king there, where his stables were said to be "all wainscotted and sculptured and the horses fed with new-laid eggs and Spanish wine." Charles greatly enjoyed these visits to the country, where he could relax in a simpler way of life, away from the intrigues of the court and the pressures of parliament. His visits to Newmarket became an annual routine, always accompanied by Nell. Sometimes he brought the court, and occasionally even the queen. Christopher Wren was commissioned to build Nell a house at Newmarket, and the king enlarged his own stables. Like all the Stuarts, Charles was a superb rider with a passion for horse racing, often taking part in races himself as well as hunting to hounds in the neighborhood.

In London, Nell was first installed in a small house in what is now Aldwych. Here her royal protector would visit her daily, delighting in a newfound domesticity. If ministers or ambassadors needed to see the king they would find him at Nell's house. Petitions and state matters were all discussed in the congenial atmosphere Nellie provided there, and Charles discovered the value of a discreet confidante and the advantage of doing business away from the spies in his palace. By the summer of 1669, Nell Gwyn was expecting the king's child, and she moved to a small house in Pall Mall.

Her quick wit and humor, which had saved many a play from disaster, also endeared Nell to Charles. Time and again the king forgave courtiers whom he could, and possibly should, have sent to the Tower, because of the quality and sharpness of their wit—in particular Rochester. Wit was the secret of Nell's success with Charles; she made the king laugh, and her company would guarantee his good humor. He adored her "buffooneries" and, for the first time in his life, Charles had fun with a woman. He could have had his pick of beautiful and aristocratic ladies for his mistresses, and he did, but this cheeky, common redhead with the infectious laugh had the natural confidence to talk to his ministers, entertain his friends and brazenly treat her rivals at court as her equals.

Nell's value as Charles Stuart's pretty mistress was greatly enhanced by her shrewdness as a judge of character, her total reliability concerning his business, and her loyalty. She was a good listener and a good friend, and her discretion as a political hostess compensated for her lack of education. With Nell, Charles found the freedom to relax with his friends and put off for a time the heavy burden of ruling and his ever-increasing financial worries. She alone of his mistresses never accepted any of the many bribes she was offered or traded in titles and privileges, and aptly described herself as "a sleeping partner in the ship of state." James, Duke of York, also had his mistresses, but when Charles considered them he would shake his head and declare them so ugly that they must have been chosen by James' confessor as a penance.

As THE WARS between France, the Netherlands and the Austrian Empire continued their steady destruction of the Continent, the question of the religion of Charles' successor troubled many at home—as well as King Louis XIV at Versailles, and the Pope in the Vatican.

For some time the French had tried to use Barbara Villiers (who was always amenable to bribery) to influence Charles in matters of religion as well as in affairs of state. Now that she was out of favor—though Charles would give her the lovely palace of Nonsuch* and create her Duchess of Cleveland in 1670 in recognition of her long "service," as well as awarding her a most handsome pension—a new opportunity arose for Louis XIV to influence the Protestant King of England to support the Vatican. Charles' brother was Catholic, as was his queen, and his dearly beloved sister Minette, wife of the homosexual Duc d'Orléans, Louis XIV's brother "Monsieur," was so miserable in her marriage that she had buried her unhappiness in devout Catholicism. In December 1668, Minette conceived a secret treaty between England and France which she hoped would help her brother out of his financial difficulties, cast him as France's ally against Holland, and make England Catholic once again.†

* Which she was to destroy in 1682.

† According to the memoirs of James, Duke of York, the idea for the Treaty of Dover originated at a secret conference between himself and several of Charles' senior ministers the following January, and represented a reconciliation between the royal brothers. But letters which passed between Charles and Minette one month earlier prove the treaty to have been their idea.

Unlike his father, Charles repeatedly succeeded in charming Parliament into acceding to his wishes, often in spite of its most ardent resolutions. Nevertheless, both people and Parliament criticized the amounts he spent, especially on his mistresses. The wars with the Dutch were depleting the treasury, and the army and navy badly needed to be re-equipped and refitted. The king did not relish his habitual role as petitioner before Parliament for funds both private and public.

It is not surprising that Charles was pleased by Louis' offer of 2 million livres a year, which would solve many of his more immediate problems and give him his independence. In return for this largesse, Charles II was to agree to be Louis XIV's "perpetual ally," supplying troops and ships in support of France; to become Catholic himself; to repeal all anti-Catholic legislation and, in the long term, to bring England and Scotland back into the Catholic fold. Charles' brother James was not alone in his concern regarding the validity of the Church of England. Even so, bearing in mind the king's relaxed attitude toward religious matters, it is hard to believe James' account in his memoirs of Charles tearfully announcing his belief in Catholicism at a secret meeting in January 1669. Sanguine and cynical as he was, it is far more probable that the king proposed *suggesting* to Louis XIV he *might* consider his own conversion and that of England if the King of France were to meet specific, primarily financial, conditions.

The king's ministers were fairly evenly divided in their sympathies between Catholics and Protestants, and Charles himself appears to have been ambivalent, disliking discrimination yet refusing to be drawn. The French terms were discussed and debated at length by Charles and his few trusted ministers in the greatest secrecy at Nell's house. By May 1670, more than a year later, all was agreed.

Charles II's "dear, dear sister" Minette, Duchesse d'Orléans, accompanied by a huge French suite, sailed to Dover where, under the pretext of a happy family reunion, Charles signed the secret Treaty of Dover, or *Traité de Madame*. Surrounded by the court, brother and sister exchanged fond embraces and presents: silver, paintings, jewelry and spaniels for Minette, and among her gifts for Charles, many charming little items for the lovely young actress who was about to give birth (on May 12) to his latest child. For the rest of his life, the King of England would be in the pay of the King of France.

During his long exile, however, Charles had learned the hard lessons of survival and perfected the art of dissimulation. Other than being France's political ally, fighting the Dutch and lessening the discrimination against Catholics, England's king did little to comply with the terms of the treaty. For his part, Louis XIV rarely paid on time or in full.

The secret agreement may appear to have favored French interests, but England ultimately gained more, for despite his outward nonchalance and genuine tolerance, Charles II was probably the most astute politician of his time. Both England and France wanted to reduce the power of the Dutch—France on land and England on the high seas. France failed on land, whereas England, helped by French financing of its fleet, succeeded in establishing its superiority on the water, which led to the extension of the British Empire.

Although the king willingly returned to London to be with Nell and his new son following Minette's departure, his attentiveness to one of his sister's maids of honor, the young and beautiful Louise-Renée de Penancoet de Kéroualle, had not gone unnoticed by the observant of the English and French courts. But despite her brother's interest, Minette insisted that as the girl had been entrusted to her by her parents she would have to return with her to France.

CHARLES STUART LOVED his children, not least as proofs of his virility, and granted Nellie's wish to name the boy after himself.* Following her son's birth, Nell was eager to return to the stage and bask once again in the adulation of her audience, but the king needed her. On June 30, 1670, just three weeks after Minette's return to France,

---

* Four of the king's sons were named Charles, two of them James. Barbara Villiers' third son was christened Henry but was known as Harry. The girls had mostly Stuart names—Anne or Mary—and his daughter by Elizabeth Killigrew was given the then uncommon name of Charlotte. Surnames used were blatantly royal—Fitzcharles, Fitzroy, even Tudor. Monmouth used his guardian's surname of Crofts while in exile before the Restoration, and took his wife's name of Scott after his marriage.

news had come of her sudden death. The suspicion that she had been poisoned by the lover of her dreadful husband so distressed Charles that Nell took him and her baby to Newmarket for the distractions of racing and hunting, and the country life he loved.

The summer of 1670 must have been the happiest of Nell's life. Her chief rivals for the king's affection, Barbara Villiers and Moll Davis, were no longer resident in the "royal stable"; her lover depended on her; she had his undivided attention in a place he loved and where he could relax; and she had his son. It would also seem that the "pitiful strolling player," as Barbara Villiers called Nell, pleased King Charles' "Greate Engine"; it was always said that Nell Gwyn was the only woman who could make Charles II jealous, even though she was never unfaithful to him. But he took no chances. During the king's first years with Nellie, Charles Buckhurst was sent abroad on spurious diplomatic missions to keep him away from his former mistress.

In view of the king's persistent interest in "trulls" (though the beauties shown up the back stairs of Whitehall Palace were never professional prostitutes), the people affectionately referred to their king as "Old Rowley"—an irreverent reference to his famously lusty old stallion. Rochester summed it all up with this lampoon:

> *So well, alas! the fatal bait is known,*
> *Which Rowley does so greedily take down;*
> *And howe'er weak and slender be the string,*
> *Bait it with whore and it will hold a king.*

When Nell finally returned to London she immediately began rehearsing in a new play, *The Conquest of Granada,* which appeared in December 1670. It contained wonderful parodies of the French and their fashions, and when tiny Nell appeared on stage wearing a huge cartwheel of a hat, enormous top boots and wide belt, the audience was hysterical, and the king cried laughing. The queen so approved of the play that there were two command performances at court.

Added to the satisfaction of being the capital's darling again, Nell had a new project. Her little house near Trafalgar Square, though comfortable, was small, and perhaps to get her off the stage, Charles offered her the lease of a much grander establishment, 79 Pall Mall. The house had four floors, splendid reception rooms, including a *salle des miroirs,* and backed on to the king's private gardens next to St. James's Park. Nell indulged her love of silver in her new mansion, and with her usual irreverent sense of fun she had a warming pan made in silver to slide between the sheets, inscribed: "Fear God, Serve the King." The king whom she "served" so well had already settled £4,000 a year on Nell, and now willingly met the bills for furniture and the decorations of the new house. Nellie was pregnant again.

> *Our good King Charles the Second,*
> *Too flippant of treasure and moisture,*
> *Stoop'd from the Queen infecund*
> *To a wench of Orange and Oyster.*
> *Consulting his Catzo, he found it expedient*
> *To waste time in revels with Nell the Comediant.* *

While "Mrs. Gwynne" was busying herself with her grand new residence and enjoying her conquest of the monarch and the London stage, Louis XIV and the Duke of Buckingham, each for his own ends, conspired in France to promote a suitable replacement for Barbara Villiers in Charles' affections.† Neither realized how strong an influence the king's little actress had on him, and they decided to reacquaint Charles with the enchanting Louise de Kéroualle.

LOUISE WAS AN impoverished young noblewoman whose innocent beauty disguised her checkered past. As she had no dowry, her parents had trained her to be a courtesan, and brought her to Versailles with the express intention of making her Louis XIV's mistress. But as the Sun King's attention had recently been captured by another lovely

---

* Andrew Marvell.

† The great Duke of Buckingham was said to be "as much in love with wit as with his kinswoman" (Barbara Villiers), and did not therefore object to her new lover, the writer Wycherley, who completely charmed him.

young maid of honor,* Louise failed, though it seems she gave herself readily to a number of other gallants at court. Appointed by Louis XIV to Minette's household, after her death the French king had other plans for Madame de Kéroualle. Her brief was to spy on the English court, but in order to get close to Charles, Louise was urged to show restraint; as a Frenchwoman and a Catholic, she would be instantly suspect, and would only succeed in winning the confidence of the King of England if he believed in her virtue.

Charles was immediately attracted to Louise's childlike beauty and air of fragile innocence—she was dubbed the "baby-faced Bretonne"—and he determined to conquer her. To make the task easier, he instantly appointed his beloved Minette's former maid of honor to the same post with his queen, and gave her a suite of splendid rooms in Whitehall. He visited her each morning, wooed her with gifts and concentrated all his charm on winning her. Charles was so smitten by her feigned virtue and false modesty that in order to possess her he agreed to all her conditions of surrender—her own establishment, household, servants, a generous income, titles for any children she might have with him, and a promise that her own family would be made welcome at the English court. Still Louise continued to play her little game and tease the king.

In September 1671, Charles left with Nellie on his annual visit for the autumn season's racing at Newmarket. But before he could renew his contented domestic routine with Nell and forget the sweet-natured, aristocratic and refined Louise, the French faction hurriedly accomodated *la Belle Bretonne* nearby in the home of Lord and Lady Arlington, who professed that she was far more suitable for their sovereign than his red-headed "lewd and bouncing orange-girl." It was at the Arlingtons' that Louise de Kéroualle finally capitulated and all but publicly gave herself to the king. Thereafter Charles divided his time at Newmarket equally between his new mistress and Nellie, who was heavily pregnant. One can only suppose the king's fiery little actress presumed she would regain her supremacy over Charles once her child was born.

The shared season at Newmarket over, Nell returned to London,

---

* Louise de la Vallière.

and on Christmas Day gave birth to her second son, whom she named James for the Duke of York. Both the king and his brother visited the new royal bastard at once, and delighted in a child born on such an important day.

Charles and James came more and more to Nell's house in Pall Mall, as much for her company as for the knowledge that there no spies could listen. They had good reason to mistrust the corridors of Whitehall. England, in alliance with France, had again declared war on the Dutch, and the palace was riddled with informers. With Louis XIV's money, Charles II had been able to cut himself off from Parliament, but he still needed its consent to move his armies, and secrecy was paramount.

While his victorious navy was being refitted, Charles spent his time with Nell in the country at her house near the Fleet, or at Newmarket or Windsor. She taught the king to fish, but in the beginning he had little patience and despaired when he caught nothing. Once, at the end of an unsuccessful day on the river, Nell had a friend distract the king while she tied several fried smelt to his hook. He laughed uproariously when he pulled in his catch, his good humor restored once again by his Nellie, and for years afterward he would tell the story against himself.

As Louise hated the country, there at least Nell had the king all to herself. At court Madame de Kéroualle did rather better. Ten months after becoming Charles II's mistress, Louise gave birth to a son. As Charles had made Barbara Villiers a duchess,* the mother of the latest royal bastard felt she should become one too. In his usual easygoing way, Charles agreed, on condition that the King of France did so as well—after all, had she not also rendered him a great service? An indignant Louis XIV refused, Louise sulked, and Charles goodnaturedly created her Duchess of Portsmouth anyway, and a lady of the queen's bedchamber.†

Not only Louise, but all the queen's ladies were, in fact, more in

---

* Duchess of Cleveland. Her eldest son was created Earl of Southampton. By September 1671, the French ambassador had written to Louis XIV that Barbara had lost all her influence on Charles.

† Charles later created this their first son Duke of Richmond, as his cousin of that name had recently died.

service to the king than to his wife. Catherine's Portuguese women had been sent home long ago, after enraging the king by refusing to use any bed previously slept in by a man. Charles replaced them with ladies of his choice who were less particular and more accommodating. They all had apartments nearer his than the queen's, and he could visit them without the court's knowledge. Catherine suffered her husband's constant infidelities stoically, and even with a certain humor. Once, hearing Charles was ill with a cold, she anxiously went to his bedroom unannounced. Nellie, who was also comforting the king, just had time to hop out of his bed and hide under it. The queen's anxiety over her husband disappeared when she spotted Nellie's slipper, and she withdrew in haste lest "the pretty fool" who owned the slipper catch a worse chill wherever she was hiding than the one from which Charles was suffering.

Nell's famous wit often extended to satire. She loathed any form of pretentiousness, and loved to ridicule her enemies, especially her rivals. When Barbara Villiers, having mocked Nell as a "pitiful strolling player," drove in a new coach and six to show what a great lady she was, Nell hired a rough farmer's cart and six oxen and drove past Barbara's grand house, cracking her whip and shouting: "Whores to market, Ho!"

Andrew Marvell echoed the people's opinion of this preferment of Louise and Barbara:

> *The Misses take place, and advanc'd to be Duchess*
> *With pomp great as Queens and their Coach and six horses:*
> *Their bastards made Dukes, Earls, Viscounts and Lords,*
> *And all the high Titles that Honour affords.* *

As Barbara Villiers faded from the royal scene, Louise Portsmouth became Nell Gwyn's greatest rival for the monarch's affection and attention, and her pretensions were a constant source of inspiration for Nell's wicked wit. When Louise appeared at court in mourning for her relative the Chevalier de Rohan, Nell also wore black. Asked, in Louise's hearing, for whom she was in mourning, Nell replied, "The

---

* Charles II acknowledged and ennobled a total of seventeen children as his royal bastards.

Cham of Tartary," as "He was the precise same relation to me as the Prince de Rohan was to Madame de Kéroualle!" In fact, Louise was very much a cousin of the Prince de Rohan, but as few of the aristocratic ladies of the court were sufficiently literate to read the almanacs, and the mischievous actress was too ignorant to know or care any better, the joke was a huge success.

Although she had won the king's heart, a grand title and status, the English people mocked Louise. Unable to pronounce de Kéroualle, they called her "Miss Carwell" or "Cartwheel," and lampooned her mercilessly. Nell referred to her as "Weeping Willow" (she knew Charles could never resist a beautiful woman's tears) and "Squintabella" due to her slightly myopic (and very attractive) gaze. The rivalry between Nellie and Louise was public knowledge. To Londoners Nell Gwyn was one of them, someone with whom they could identify, an English girl of humble origins, a popular actress, beautiful, witty and Protestant. Louise de Kéroualle was a foreigner, an aristocrat and, worst of all, a Catholic. As such, she was automatically (and accurately) suspected of spying for the French.

The balladeers were in no doubt about the people's sentiments:

> Portsmouth, the incestuous Punk,
> Made our most gracious sovereign drunk,
> And drunk she made him give that Buss
> That all the Kingdom's bound to curse.

And yet, it bothered Nell that she was still untitled. When Louise implied that Nell gave herself airs, and mocked that her clothes were so fine and beautiful she could be a queen, Nellie retaliated with: "And you, Carwell, look whore enough to be a duchess." Nell's taunts almost landed her in trouble when, rumor had it, the duchesses of Cleveland and Portsmouth joined forces. During a supper party at Barbara's home, Berkshire House, to which they had invited Nell, they tried to get her drunk and then choke her with a scarf. However, as she was seen the next day in the park, the damage could not have been as great as the tale that grew around the "incident."

Nellie used every opportunity to ridicule Louise, but Charles, although amused by the sparring between his mistresses, was clearly very fond of her. Louise was gentle and feminine, cultured, well read and civilized, quite the opposite of the earthy, vulgar actress. Knowing this, Nellie must have been greatly peeved by the favors the king lavished on Louise; the records show that the Duchess of Portsmouth received twice the amount from the Secret Service account as Nell during the period when the king was said to be dividing his time (and favors) equally between them. (However, Nell was also receiving an additional £10,000 a year from the same source as payment for helping to reduce criticism of the king in the Green Ribbon Clubs.)* Much of Louise's extra income came from her judicious friendship with the king's premier ministers Danby and Lauderdale, who had control over the treasury. Nell loathed the Scottish Lauderdale, and once when the king asked her how to appease his Cavalier Parliament, she replied testily: "Hang the Scotch dog and the French bitch!"

Barbara Cleveland had also extracted incredible privileges and incomes for herself and for her children by Charles. In 1674, Charles gave his third son with Barbara the title of Earl of Northumberland,† and the following year he created her first two sons dukes of Southampton and Grafton respectively. In the same year he gave Louise's son the title of Duke of Richmond, establishing Barbara's and Louise's sons as equal in rank with his eldest bastard, the Duke of Monmouth.

As Nell was a common actress, neither she nor her sons had received any titles (though the elder, Charles, had been granted a pension of £4,000 a year), and she minded dreadfully. This attitude was not just due to snobbishness on Nell's part. As well as immense financial rewards, a title offered patronage and protection: Sir Charles Sedley, a friend of Nell's, had an actor cudgelled in the park for no greater offense than imitating his dress. The great and highly respected playwright and poet Dryden was set upon and badly beaten by three rogues thought to be in the pay of the Earl of Rochester or the Duchess of Portsmouth, or both, as they felt Dryden had insulted

---

* A political society founded c. 1675. Its members wore a green ribbon in their hats. Many prominent Whigs, including Shaftesbury, Buckingham, Shadwell and Titus Oates were members. The failure of the Exclusion Bill and the Rye House plot made membership a risk, and in 1688 it petered out.

† Four years later, Charles was to elevate Northumberland to a dukedom as well.

them in verse. Neither the earl nor the duchess was called to account. If Rochester did join forces with Louise to punish Dryden, he himself repeatedly criticized the duchesses of Portsmouth and Cleveland most harshly, and both were his avowed enemies. Only Nell remained his friend and escaped his cruellest jibes.

Rochester felt certain that Dryden was responsible for such lines about him as:

> *Mean in each action, lewd in every limb,*
> *Manners themselves are mischievous in him*

—words hardly worth almost killing a man for: but peers were above ordinary mortals, and Nell wanted the same privileges for her sons as those the other royal bastards had received.

One day in 1676, when the king came to visit her at 79 Pall Mall, he heard Nell calling out to her eldest boy: "Come here, you little bastard!" When Charles reproached her, she asked tartly by what other name she could call him. The king took the hint and created the boy Earl of Burford, while his younger brother became Lord James Beauclerk. Another contemporary story has Nell threatening to throw the neglected little boy out of a top window in Pall Mall, and the king shouting up, "God save the Earl of Burford!"

As the mother of an earl, Nell Gwyn officially became "a lady." She received her own coat of arms, and promptly covered all her plate with her monogram. Nell commissioned some exceptional pieces of silver, including a huge silver bedstead made by John Coques to her own design which weighed more than 2,000 ounces and cost over £1,000. This bedstead, which became quite famous, highly amused the king (though its cost did not), and made both of his duchesses furious. Jacob Hall (the rope dancer) was depicted on it climbing up Barbara Villiers, and Louise Portsmouth was portrayed lying in a tomb with a dusky Eastern potentate. Nell's silver bedstead was the talk of London and considered a wonder of the age.

John Mulgrave, Earl of Sheffield,* another literary peer, wrote of the king's two duchesses:

---

* Later the Duke of Buckinghamshire.

Was ever Prince by two at once misled?
False, foolish, old, ill-natur'd and ill-bred.

If the rivalry between Charles II's mistresses was fierce, the competition between Catholics and Protestants for important posts was just as intense. After the death of Anne Hyde, Duchess of York, James decided to marry the seventeen-year-old Maria of Modena, a Catholic. The king had been forced by Parliament to withdraw his Declaration of Indulgence for Catholics, and now a Catholic bride had arrived in England for his brother. Everyone was concerned about the succession and, to make matters worse, Queen Catherine was seriously ill. Again, Parliament's main complaint against Charles was the cost of his many mistresses. Louise Portsmouth's apartments in Whitehall were said to be so richly furnished they were far grander than the queen's— which prompted another of Rochester's acid couplets guaranteed to delight the populace:

Within this place a bed's appointed
For a French bitch and God's anointed.

The Duchess of Portsmouth further annoyed the Protestant faction by adopting the airs and graces of the queen's imminent successor, though Nell confided in her secretary that she was not unduly concerned as "the nation will never have her." Louise went so far as to have her own medal struck with the image of a Cupid bearing the legendary motto: *"Omnium Victorem Vici"*—I conquered him who conquered all.* When Charles had a magnificent service of plate made for Louise by an eminent London goldsmith, members of the public who saw it on display in his shop protested that it should have been made for Nell Gwyn.

Hatred of the Popish favorite enhanced Nell's popularity, as did public knowledge, and disapproval, of the huge amounts the monarch spent on Louise. But Charles really loved his clever French mistress, and she managed to stand firm against the cries for deportation in Parliament, as well as holding on to her influence at court. Much as

---

* A motto used by Diane de Poitiers. See *The Serpent and the Moon.*

Charles enjoyed Nell's company and valued her friendship, Louise was his unofficial *maîtresse en titre,* and generally considered as the alternative queen.

Daniel Defoe made an interesting observation on the rivalry between Louise and Nell:

> I remember that the late Duchess of Portsmouth in the time of Charles the Second, gave a severe retort to one who was praising Nell Gwynn, whom she hated. They were talking of her wit and beauty, and how she always diverted the King with her extraordinary repartees, how she had a fine mien, and appeared as much the lady of quality as anybody. "Yes, madam," said the Duchess (who had just heard the King had given Nell 17,000 pounds), "but anybody may know she has been an orange wench by her swearing."

When Nellie observed that she really should have the freehold of 79 Pall Mall as she had always "offered her services free *under* the Crown," the Speaker of the House agreed to help as she was Charles' strongest Protestant influence.

Of all Charles II's mistresses, Nell Gwyn was the one least resented by the queen and, after her death, Catherine gave Nell's son Charles an allowance of £2,000 a year. Although Nell acquired a number of houses from the king during her life, as well as an income from an Irish estate and various sinecures and privileges, her acquisitions were relatively modest when compared with the rapacity of the other royal favorites.

To complement her new status, the actress-turned-lady bought a coach and four as well as a sedan chair emblazoned with her arms. Alone of the royal mistresses, Nell took pride in settling her bills promptly—recalling perhaps her own early poverty—thereby endearing herself even more to the common tradespeople, whom she cultivated shamelessly. In terms of avarice, she may have gained less overall than others, but one could not call Nell Gwyn "disinterested," and the distinctions made between her and the more *bien née* of the king's mistresses always rankled with her, and became a recurring theme.

⁂

AFTER ANOTHER FIRE, the King's Theatre reopened in 1674, and Nell massaged her wounded pride with the approbation of her public, taking every opportunity to mock her rivals for the king's affection with her bantering repartee. After Nell's last stage appearance, she was given her own box at the theatre, and King Charles was often to be seen there in her company.

While the foreign Louise Portsmouth concentrated on acquiring riches, mostly portable (Barbara Cleveland generally preferred land), Nellie cultivated well-placed and influential friends to help further her ambitions. As a result, anyone who wished to reach the king was well advised to approach "Mrs. Neslie" (as she was often called), and ambassadors and foreign dignitaries intent on circumventing the spies of Whitehall soon learned to visit the pretty actress at 79 Pall Mall. During her eighteen years' "service to the Crown," no less than five French ambassadors chronicled their fascination with Nell Gwyn and described her positive influence on King Charles. The Venetian and Florentine state archives give the same impression, and Cosimo III de' Medici remarked how impressed he was by Nell's "sound" opinions after meeting her on a visit to London.

Nell (as well as Louise) entertained for Charles, and it was generally agreed that she was an excellent hostess, with the best food and wine in town. Her friends from the theater were regularly called on to perform for her guests, and in this neutral arena in agreeable surroundings the king could meet those he could not be seen with in public. The "orange girl" was said to be "in politics up to her elbows," but only she of all the king's "misses" did not involve herself in political factions. Instead, when Charles asked her for advice on how to solve his problems, Nell encouraged him to "dismiss his ladies and mind his business." Another chronicler claims she "told his Majestie to lock up his codpiece"!

BY 1675 BARBARA Cleveland, looking middle-aged at thirty, her beauty faded, was finding she was having to pay more for her young admirers. As she had fallen in love with England's ambassador to France, she had decided to forsake London and live in Paris. She was further encouraged to leave England by the fact that threats were being made in Parliament to reduce the income of all the king's mistresses. Louise Portsmouth had the pox, and although Charles gave her a pearl necklace and a large diamond to cheer her up, it was not actually certain that she had caught it from the king—there were a number of contenders. Most of her time was spent taking cures and loudly complaining to Charles that her illness was due to his consorting with "trulls."

At twenty-six, Nell was at the peak of her beauty, and felt secure once again in the affection of her king and her public. Charles commissioned the Dutch artist Sir Peter Lely to paint her—one sultry portrait with soft, sleepy eyes, Nell pouting prettily in an open-necked blouse with her breasts exposed, her hand caressing a pet lamb, and another full-length portrait as Venus, for which the lovely actress posed reclining naked. Not surprisingly, the king came often to watch the sittings. Lely became a friend and a frequent visitor to Nell's house, and she was flattered that he had made her appear *"vertuose"* (even naked), whereas his portraits of Louise made her look distinctly sulky.

Nell Gwyn had good reason to be pleased with her achievements: her sons had been ennobled and given the privileges and incomes attached to their titles. She had houses in London, Newmarket and Windsor, and although her income was small by the standards of other royal mistresses, she was still able to pay £4,000 for Peg Hughes' pearls, which she had to sell after Prince Rupert's death.

BY 1675, NELL enjoyed so much of the monarch's favor that she paid scant attention to Louise. *La Belle Bretonne* had grown extremely fat (as well as poxed), and the king teased her by dubbing her "Fubbs" and "Fubbsy" (chubby) and her boat "Fubbs' Yacht." Nell and Louise had more or less settled their differences when a new threat arrived at court.

Hortense Mancini, niece of the late Cardinal Mazarin, came to England in November 1675, intent on challenging Nell and Louise for King Charles's love and bounty. She was the fourth of five ravishing sisters, one of whom, Marie, had failed to marry Louis XIV although she had been his first (innocent) love. At fifteen, Hortense was married to a French marquis, and the couple, heirs to Cardinal Mazarin's wealth, were created Duc and Duchesse de Mazarin.*

Five years after her marriage, the beautiful, spirited and very bored duchess ran away, fetchingly dressed as a young man. A short spell in a convent was not a success and she moved on to Savoy and consolation in the arms of the ruling Duke Charles Emmanuel II. After his death in 1675, Hortense was strongly encouraged to leave Savoy by her patron's widow. A former English ambassador (in disgrace at the time and hoping to line his pockets with the help of a rival to supplant Nell and Louise) advised Hortense to seek her fortune at the English court of Charles II. Hortense was related to her fellow Italian Mary of Modena, the new young Duchess of York, and arrived in London under her protection and as her guest at St. James's Palace. The reputation of this alluring, dark Roman beauty with a Junoesque figure and sparkling eyes of indefinite color had travelled before her, and gentlemen who met her at once professed to have fallen in love.

At thirty, Hortense was still extraordinarily beautiful, cultured, well read, sophisticated and captivating. It seemed there was nothing this passionate woman could not, or would not, do. She could sing, dance, play the guitar (even while dancing), swim, gamble and shoot. Once established in society through the Yorks, Hortense moved into a charming house of theirs in St. James's Park, where she presided over a totally international salon. The Duchesse de Mazarin spoke three languages fluently, entertained exquisitely, and surrounded herself with intellectuals, the beau monde and the literati, patronizing the arts and promoting artists. Although society vied for her invitations, the ladies were consumed with jealousy (she invariably dressed in trousers, and looked superb), while the gentlemen of the court found her frankly irresistible. Her many excesses had left no traces on her,

* Armand-Charles de La Porte de La Meilleraye, whose grandfather was also grandfather to Cardinal Richelieu, France's famous minister. The Duc and Duchesse de Mazarin had three daughters and a son, Guy Paul-Jules, who died without male issue. As a result the dukedom of Mazarin became extinct, but his daughter Armande Félicité married Louis de Mailly, Marquis de Nesle. This couple produced five daughters, four of whom became Louis XV's mistresses. See chapter 2 on Madame de Pompadour.

and the French ambassador said he "never saw anyone who so well defies the power of time and vice to disfigure." Hortense de Mazarin, it was whispered, found women quite as attractive as men, and she continued to fascinate both sexes in society and in the arts long after the other court beauties had been forgotten.

Neither Nell nor Louise realized their predicament until it was the talk of the town that King Charles had stood gazing up at the windows of Madame de Mazarin's house, apparently dying of love. Louise ranted and raved, made embarrassing scenes and lost another measure of the king's regard (though never his affection). Nellie wore black, and said she was in mourning for Louise's dead aspirations. More practical than Louise, she accepted the situation, expecting the infatuation to be short-lived. Charles had enjoyed so many brief diversions that there was no reason to think this one would last. The Yorks were also too late in seeing the danger. When they reclaimed their house in St. James's Park, Hortense promptly received another in Chelsea from Charles, plus £4,000 a year. She had befriended the king's natural daughter the Countess of Sussex, who let her use her suite in Whitehall Palace whenever Charles desired to be with his "Roman whore," as the court called her. Thereafter the king divided his time between Hortense, Louise and Nellie, and the balladeers had a new victim:

> Since Cleveland is fled till she's brought to bed,
> And Nelly is quite forgotten,
> And Mazarine is as old as the Queen,
> And Portsmouth, the young whore, is rotten.

With little choice but to accept Hortense as she had Louise, Nell could still enjoy her greatest advantage over her rivals—sharing her love of the countryside and country pursuits with the king. When autumn came and the court moved to Newmarket, Charles belonged to Nell alone. They were there when the news spread that his new love Hortense was sharing her favors in Chelsea with the Prince of Monaco (among others), and a furious king retaliated by cancelling her income. But, as usual, when faced with a pretty woman in tears, Charles relented. He reinstated the annuity, and expelled the Monegasque prince instead. The king's afternoons with Hortense were reestablished, though he spent most evenings in Nell's company. After the summer of 1676, Louise was no longer Charles' actual mistress, but he clearly remained very fond of her, and continued to attend her supper and card parties.

Gambling was one of the main occupations of the court's ladies, and as there were no banknotes as yet, the stakes were in gold. Lucky in most things, Nell was not lucky at cards, and often lost heavily. At times she even entertained Louise and Hortense at her house; offering them chocolates, she told both how she had despatched Moll Davis with her julap-flavored ones. All three were compulsive gamblers, though Hortense was by far the best cardplayer. In a single afternoon she is reputed to have won £8,000 from Louise and £5,000 from Nell! There is a famous story about Nell at this time discussing Frenchwomen and their amorous skills, as well as the quality and cleanliness of their underwear, with the French ambassador. Comparing her own with that of Louise and Hortense, Nell, who was fastidiously clean, complained that Louise wore dirty petticoats, and that Hortense, usually in trousers, wore none. Then with great pride, she lifted her skirts to enable His Excellency to carry out an inspection. The ambassador reported the sight to his foreign secretary, adding, "I would speak of other things which were also shown." But, in view of his superior's high station, he felt it more prudent not to continue.

IN 1677, NELL told the king that she had definitely decided not to return to the stage, despite tempting offers and the urgings of Dryden (who had a new play), Wycherley (who was in disgrace and needed a new play), Etherege (who needed the money), and the brilliant female playwright, Aphra Behn. Reports that Nell appeared on stage after 1677 are incorrect, though she often entertained her guests at home with prologues and scenes from her past successes. As she was no longer an actress, was there any reason why Charles could not make her a duchess like his other mistresses? The king asked his chief minister Lord Danby whether Nellie might perhaps be made not a

duchess, but a countess, when Greenwich fell vacant. Danby, a friend
and ally of Louise's, was aghast at the idea of "an orange wench" obtaining a title, and strongly advised against it. Nell was furious, which
amused the king, who suggested that she be patient, as Danby would
not be chief minister forever. For the meantime, he appointed her a
lady of the queen's privy chamber. Perhaps at Louise's instigation,
Danby had cleverly planted a spy in Nell's household as nurse to her
sons, and his negative attitude toward her was hardly encouraged to
change when he heard reports of how the cheeky actress mimicked
him and his half-mad wife to the amusement of the king and his
cronies.

NELL GWYN MAY well have cost the country a fortune, as her rivals
claimed, but she spent much of it on others. Her house in Pall Mall
was the social center of London, and there she entertained lavishly for
the king—inviting not only the court, but also politicians, ambassadors and important foreign visitors. Her old friends from the theater
were often included, and whenever any of them claimed to be in financial difficulties, she helped them with money. She gave generously
to the poor, never forgetting her own early poverty. There is no doubt
that Charles II valued Nell's constancy. Perhaps it was because she did
not dare, but she was the only one of all his "misses" who was never
unfaithful to him, and he knew he could count on her complete loyalty. So, indeed, could her friends. Without ever openly taking his
side, Nell championed Charles' eldest son the Duke of Monmouth
time and again, and tried to reconcile his father to him after their numerous disagreements. (Astutely judging his character as a mixture of
royalty and impudence, she dubbed Monmouth "Prince Perkin,"* to
his fury.) Charles felt his son's character was flawed, and blamed his
lack of judgment on his choice of companions. The king loved all his
children, but perhaps none as much as this eldest, about whom Dryden wrote:

* A reference to Perkin Warbeck, a Flemish impostor and pretender to the throne who was
executed in 1499.

Of all this numerous progeny was none
So beautiful, so brave as Absalom.

Buckingham observed wryly that it was a monarch's role to be the father of his people, and that Charles II could certainly claim to be the father of a great many, while Defoe wrote: "Six bastard Dukes survive his luscious Reign." But it could be argued that Charles was merely following the procedure originally established in England and Scotland that dukedoms were intended only for the sons of the king, and he refused to discriminate against them in this regard on account of their illegitimacy. Consistently outrageous, Buckingham had dared try to "fumble Mrs. Neslie," and when a slap did not deter him she had complained to the king. But when Buckingham was later disgraced and sent to the Tower in 1677, Nellie forgot their personal quarrel and petitioned Charles to forgive his old friend.

THERE ARE MANY examples of Nell's generous concern and active help for her friends. In 1673, the conspirator Titus Oates claimed that the Catholics were plotting to rise and massacre the Protestants, burn London, assassinate the king and replace him with his brother James. Panic seized London. Even Pepys and his secretary were thrown into prison in the indiscriminate roundup of Catholics. It was Nell who prevailed on Charles' good nature and persuaded him to strike off the list of possible assassins all those previously known to be loyal. After the Titus Oates plot it was thought prudent for the Catholic Duke of York to leave England until the feelings and tempers of the various religious factions had cooled. James consoled himself in France with his foxhounds, but longed to come home. Through Nell's intercession, Charles transferred him to Scotland, where he was far happier shooting grouse and hunting to hounds. Monmouth, miserable in exile in Holland, bombarded Nell with frantic letters to mediate on his behalf for him to be allowed to come home.

She also helped Dryden, whose parents had been on the side of Parliament during the Civil War. As he had been instrumental in Nell's meteoric rise on the stage, she repaid him later by using her influence at court to have him appointed laureate and historiographer royal.

It was during the period of rabid anti-Catholic feeling that the famous incident occurred when Nell's coach, bearing the royal arms, was mobbed by a crowd at Oxford who mistook it for Louise Portsmouth's. Showing great courage, and with the panache of an accomplished actress, Nell put her head out of the window and, opening her arms as if to her Drury Lane audience, called out: "Pray, good people, be civil. I am the *Protestant* whore."

⁂

NELL'S LACK OF a title of her own still made her rather touchy on the subject of her rank. On one occasion, when she found her coachman had been badly beaten for defending her name and honor, Nell protested to the unfortunate man that, in truth, his attackers had been justified in their slander and that she was indeed a whore. "That you may be, madam," answered her loyal servant, "but I'll not be called a whore's coachman."

⁂

NELL COULD NOT help liking the debauched but brilliant Rochester, and genuinely missed him during his many absences from court. Henry Saville, Rochester's fat, disreputable friend, wrote to him that he should warn Nellie of her folly in good-naturedly including the lovely Jenny Middleton, a potential rival, in her circle. Nell's false friend Lady Hervey, having failed herself to win the king's affection, had promoted Mrs. Middleton into Nell's company "to pimp against herself."

Rochester replied to Saville that his own advice to Nell

has ever been this, take your measures just contrary to your rivals, live in peace with the world, and easily with the king: Never be so ill natur'd to stir up his anger against others, but let him forget the use of a passion, which is never to do you good. . . . Please him with body, head and heart.

Neither Sackville nor Rochester need have worried on Nell's account. Mrs. Middleton, though considered the most beautiful woman in England (and the most expensive), was not to the king's liking.

ANOTHER WHO SANG Nell Gwyn's praises in the theater was Aphra Behn, who dedicated *The Feign'd Courtezans* to her in 1679. The same year, Robert Whitcomb, in *Janna Divorum,* a study of gods and goddesses, somewhat generously claimed that Nell possessed "the primitive wisdom of Apollo, the pristine wit of Venus, and the God-like courage and brave spirit of Hercules." This fulsome praise went some way toward mitigating the effect of those who described Nell as "puddle Nell," the "hare-brained whore."

Nellie did not forget her family. Her jolly, fat mother lived at her expense until she drowned after falling drunkenly into a ditch in July 1679. Far from being ashamed of this and trying to hush it up, Nell, typically, gave her a splendid funeral. Her sister Rose repeatedly turned to her for help, once obtaining a pardon for her convicted criminal of a husband through Nell's intercession. Even the inmates of Oxford Prison, where her father had died, benefited from Nell's kind heart. Rochester wrote:

> *From Oxford prison many did she free,*
> *There dy'd her father, and there glory'd she*
> *In giving others life and liberty,*
> *So pious a remembrance still she bore*
> *Ev'n to the fetters that her father wore.*
> *Nor was her mother's funeral less her care,*
> *No cost, no velvet did the daughter spare:*
> *Fine gilded scutcheons did the hearse enrich,*
> *To celebrate this martyr of the ditch;*
> *Burnt brandy did in flaming brimmers flow,*
> *Drunk at her funeral; while her well-pleas'd shade*
> *Rejoic'd ev'n in the sober fields below*
> *At all the drunkenness her death had made.*

In this same year of 1679, Nellie nearly lost the king when he caught such a serious chill that there was genuine fear for his life. With the queen's permission, she banished his doctors and called in two sensible women who had cured Charles of an infection once before. With their help and Nell's nursing, Charles recovered. During this illness, Monmouth had again tried to establish himself as England's legitimate heir, and his furious father sent him back to Holland.

Nell's generosity to her friends was matched by the king's appreciation of his common little flame-haired mistress. As well as the house he had Wren build for her at Newmarket, her stables at Epsom, 79 Pall Mall, and the Irish estates, he had given her some five other houses around London and land in Chelsea. A new warship had just been named the *Burford* after her elder son, and at the annual birthday party she gave for her younger son Lord James Beauclerk at Christmas, Charles announced he would give Nellie a house at Windsor. Burford House was built just inside the grounds of Windsor Castle, and lavishly decorated at the king's expense, by the same team who had recently completed the work there. A tunnel was built connecting the house to Charles' private apartments in the castle.

Charles II, like all Stuarts, loved hawking, fishing and the chase—all of which he could pursue to perfection at Windsor, as well as holding horse races in the Home Park. Renowned for his extraordinary energy, he loved nothing better than to hunt the wild red deer, and once had a famous run of seventy miles. The king kept otter hounds, and his brother James had what may have been the first pack of foxhounds in England.* No wonder the most important court post at Windsor was Master of Buckhounds.

The king and Nell planted a great many trees in and around Windsor. Charles built a new indoor tennis court near Nell's house—

---

* James' daughters Mary (married to William of Orange in 1677) and Anne were as keen for the chase as their father and their uncle Charles. It was Anne who, as queen, had the gravelled rides made at Windsor so she could follow the hunt when she became too fat to continue on horseback. In 1711, Queen Anne gave a plate of a hundred guineas to the winner of a race to be run "round the New Health at Ascot Common" on Saturday August 11. The following Monday, the Corporation of Windsor gave a plate of £50 for a race, and this was won by Nell Gwyn's son Charles (by then Duke of St. Albans) on his chestnut "Doctor," watched by Queen Anne herself and a large suite. It was the start of Royal Ascot.

he loved the game, and always weighed himself before and after playing; following one exhausting match he recorded a loss of four and a half pounds. Nell built herself an orangery and bowling alleys. She so loved her garden that Charles could not bring himself to finish the Long Walk, as this would have interfered with his Nellie's extensive pleasure grounds. It was not until Queen Victoria's reign that the Long Walk was finally completed.

So that Nell could also have some sport, the king appointed her son Charles Grand Falconer of England, thereby allowing his mother to go "a-birding" in every royal park, chase or warren in the country. She was particularly knowledgeable about hawking and, to please her, Charles made young Burford Master of the Hawks, with a pension of £965 a year.

Domestic dogs also played an important part in Charles' life. His spaniels were always with him, at the council table, and invariably on his bed. To the consternation of his household (and his mistresses), the king even allowed his bitches to whelp in his bedroom. Inevitably, Charles' love of dogs encouraged the lampoonists to liken his mistresses to bitches (or mares in the royal stable), and the wicked wit of Rochester was said to have been responsible for "A Pleasant Battle Between Two Lapdogs of the Utopian Court":

> The English lap-dog here does first begin
> The vindication of his lady, Gwynn:
> The other, much more Frenchified, alas,
> Shows what his lady is, not what she was.

A dogfight ensues amid heavy betting, and although Nell's dog has less quality than Louise's, Rochester, as always the good friend to Nell, so persecuted Louise in his verse that most of it is unrepeatable. Nor did the wicked earl allow Barbara Cleveland to escape the dog analogy:

> [Cleveland] I say is much to be admir'd,
> Although she ne'er was satisfied or tired.
> Full forty men a day provided for this whore,
> Yet like a bitch, she wags her tail for more.

By the time she was thirty, Nell Gwyn vied with Louise Portsmouth as the most important political hostess of the day, adored by the common people as well as by society, politicians and the literati. At the height of her fame, she fell ill for the first time, possibly with a venereal disease caught from her royal lover. Her illness forced her to miss the spring meeting at Newmarket and, too sick to see her new house at Windsor, Nell lay recovering at 79 Pall Mall when she heard of the death of her younger son James in Paris. The cause of death was given as a "bad leg," but Nell was convinced that Louise had somehow arranged to have him poisoned. She was consumed with grief, refused to see anyone, and blamed herself for sending little James abroad for his education, albeit to dear friends. To add to her sadness, the following month she heard that her friend Rochester had died. Very slowly the king, who loved all his children and shared her sadness, coaxed Nell out of her mourning to join him in the autumn at Newmarket.

The following summer, Charles gave Nell a woodland estate in Sherwood Forest. He loved to tease her for being an indifferent rider, and offered her as much of the forest as she could ride around before breakfast. She chose Bestwood Park on the advice of Buckingham, but was forced to mortgage the estate some years later when short of money. Nell was frequently without funds. She was a bad manager, and the income from the Irish estates given her by the king was often blocked or slow in coming. The Duke of York, who had always been very fond of Nellie, redeemed Bestwood for her after his brother's death.

It was during the following Christmas holiday of 1681 that Nell saw Christopher Wren's plans for the Royal Hospital, Chelsea, the king's infirmary for old soldiers. Traditionally, Nell Gwyn has always been credited with encouraging Charles II to enlarge his proposed hospital, and with adding some land of her own to the site in Chelsea. The foundation stone was laid the following spring, and for many years the veterans of the Civil War and the later wars with the Dutch would stand and toast "Good King Charles and our Nellie."

At the beginning of 1682, a charming new ambassador from Morocco arrived in London charged with the delicate mission of prising Tangiers, part of the Portuguese queen Catherine's marriage settlement, from the King of England. The diarist John Evelyn, who had ingratiated himself with the Duchess of Portsmouth, was invited to her apartments in Whitehall as a guest at the magnificent and extraordinary banquet she gave for the ambassador, seating the Moorish suite alternately between the king's concubines and his natural daughters. Louise was so taken with the "civil heathen" (as Evelyn called him) that she promptly took him to her bed. It seems the Moor did not disappoint the duchess, for she encouraged Charles to agree to the withdrawal of the French garrison in Tangiers.

At fifty, Charles II appeared to be aging fast. Following a fire which destroyed his palace at Newmarket, the court was forced to leave for London a few days earlier than planned, and another plot to assassinate the sovereign and his brother was fortuitously uncovered. Charles was deeply shocked, not least because the conspirators implicated Monmouth, and for the next year he more or less withdrew from public life to Windsor. The queen and Louise joined Nell and the king there, playing cards together (Louise was by now too fat to take exercise) and sharing Charles' company in apparent harmony, although Louise's peremptory behavior reduced the poor queen to tears in public on several occasions. Charles no longer rode in races, but he still relished the life of a country gentleman, mixing with the people at cockfights, riding, hunting and hawking with Nell, and most of all, the racing. Politics, however, he left more and more in the hands of his ministers, Lord Halifax and the Duke of York.

At Windsor, Nell busied herself with enlarging Burford House. In an effort to amuse Charles, she invited the Fellows of the Royal Society to stay, as well as their president designate Pepys, who had always remained her friend and admirer. She also had a number of actors and actresses come to Windsor to read to the king, which he much preferred to reading alone. Together there he and Nell heard of the deaths of Charles Hart and Tom Killigrew, and mourned them both.

As new projects usually succeeded in distracting Charles from his troubles or sadness, Christopher Wren was summoned to discuss the building of a new palace at Winchester and a row of houses for the court, including one for Nell. The idea was to move there instead of Newmarket in the autumn for "field diversions." Building began in May 1682, and when Charles came to inspect its progress, he lodged with the bishop, who, to the king's amusement and Nell's chagrin, refused to admit Nell, as "a woman of ill-repute ought not to be endured in the house of a clergyman." Nell solved the problem by finding rooms at the deanery.

Throughout this time of making new plans for buildings and avenues, Charles continued to find Nell's company peaceful and calming. Her constancy to the king had given her a measure of respectability in society, and as her rivals were as usual less in evidence in the country, she felt secure in the monarch's affection. Barbara Cleveland lived in France. Louise Portsmouth had shamed the king by rashly falling for Hortense de Mazarin's nephew, the handsome twenty-eight-year-old Philippe de Vendôme, Grand Prior of France. He needed money, and rightly judged that, at thirty-five and fading, the duchess would make easy pickings. Louise made a complete fool of herself, which enraged Charles sufficiently to expel Vendôme from the kingdom. When Louis XIV heard about his grand prior's behavior direct from an irate Charles, he became most anxious about Louise's preferential status*—with good reason. A number of those close to Charles II felt that the episode with Vendôme may have been the swan song of Louis XIV's star informer at the English court. But she prevailed, and by the following year she was sufficiently in favor to dare invade the queen's privacy dressed as a maid, mockingly waiting upon Catherine at dinner.

Bored with king and court, the lovely Duchesse de Mazarin continued to live in bohemian splendor in Chelsea. When one of her lovers was killed in a duel, Hortense was so distraught she threatened to become a nun—a prospect which hugely amused Charles.

THE WINTER OF 1683 was unusually cold. The Thames froze solid, and Charles and Nell had a colorful pavilion built on the ice in which to entertain. The king would skate with the Duke of Grafton and Nell's son Charles, returning to devour gargantuan meals which she

* In view of Louise's enduring position as Charles's reigning mistress, Louis XIV had made her a duchess, and sent her lavish presents.

had prepared herself. When the old Earl of St. Albans died, Charles bestowed the vacant title on Nell's son (with an upgrading to duke) on January 19, 1684, granting him in addition lodgings in Whitehall and fifteen hundred pounds a year. The king was very fond of this handsome, agreeable boy and kept him near, especially now that his own health was giving cause for concern. With an open ulcer on his leg, he took to rising late, and limited his exercise to short walks in the park. He liked to have his sons around him more often, and once again pardoned and recalled the Duke of Monmouth.

At Nell's Christmas party in London that year, the king appeared cheerful, but could not dance. Five weeks later, on February 2, as he was dressing in Whitehall to attend Nell Gwyn's thirty-fifth birthday party, Charles had a stroke and fell. Despite, or perhaps because of, the bleeding, blistering and other primitive remedies practiced on him by the doctors, Charles II could only linger on for five more days, remaining lucid to the end. Neither Louise, Hortense nor Nell were permitted to visit him, but he did ask to see all his sons. Quietly he asked his brother and heir James to see to the financial needs of his remaining mistresses and children, adding to a list of bequests, ". . . and let not poor Nellie starve." After begging his gentle queen's forgiveness, and expressing his devotion to her and to his brother, he agreed that James should bring him a Catholic priest. There are many accounts of and theories about the way in which Charles II was received into the Catholic Church on his deathbed. Had political considerations restrained him from following an inner conviction until the end of his life? Or did this most agreeable of monarchs simply wish to please his family and acquiesce to the dearest wish of his Catholic mother, wife, sister and brother?

All England descended into deep mourning at the passing of King Charles II, although the stark simplicity of his funeral was totally unexpected for so extraordinarily popular a monarch. It was made known that a Catholic priest had been present at his deathbed at the king's personal request, which so displeased the Church of England that this most beloved of English sovereigns was buried with a minimum of ceremony. Few of his critics had appreciated that for more than twenty years, despite maintaining an image of licentious loose living, Charles Stuart had succeeded in pitting the forces of Parliament, France and Holland against one another to his advantage, and had gained considerable financial support from Louis XIV without bringing about the promised reversion of England to Catholicism. And yet, he passed on his crown to his Catholic brother.

⁂

ALTHOUGH LOUISE AND Nell were not permitted to put their houses in mourning like the members of the royal family, the new King James honored his dying brother's request to care for the Duchess of Portsmouth and his friend Nell Gwyn. He immediately settled Nell's debts, and gave her £500 "bounty" in addition. Nell must have been a very bad manager, as the following year she was again short of money. To satisfy her bankers she sold some of her jewels, including Prince Rupert's fabulous pearl necklace with the ruby clasp, and pawned her plate. Again James came to the rescue, arranging a new, larger pension for her; a year later he repaid her mortgage on Bestwood Park.

Despite James' consideration for her—she was treated much more kindly by the new king than were her former rivals—when Charles II died, Nell lost her own zest for living. She took on his cook but entertained very little, and only occasionally visited the theater. Then Buckingham, her old friend and the cousin of Barbara Villiers,* also died. Fewer and fewer friends were left with whom to share the old life and the happy memories.

A loving and caring father, Charles II had arranged the marriages of all his natural children, and Nell's son the Duke of St. Albans had been betrothed as a child to Lady Diana de Vere, a considerable heiress. Their marriage, like most of those planned by the late king, proved to be a great success.

Nell only survived her "Charles III" by two years, becoming seriously ill after a stroke which left her partly paralyzed. One of the king's favorite doctors attended her regularly, and they shared her last months happily reminiscing about her time in the theater and at

* The Duchess of Cleveland died totally impoverished in 1709, having been ruined by "Beau" Fielding. Ten years older than Fielding, she married him bigamously at the age of sixty-four, and he merrily ran through all her money.

court. His notes give no clue as to the nature of her illness, but it was most probably cancer or venereal disease.

Nell Gwyn died on November 13, 1687. She was thirty-seven. (Louise Portsmouth was to outlive her by forty-seven years to the day.)

In her will Nellie forgot no one—it was full of charitable bequests to friends and servants, and to her sister Rose. All her property went to her son, but she requested that money go to Catholic and Protestant poor and prisoners alike. On the day of her funeral, mourners gathered from all over London and from all walks of life to pay a final tribute to this outspoken girl from the simplest of backgrounds, who had won the heart of a king and of the people of London.

EPILOGUE

NELL GWYN did little to affect the important events of her time; she is not remembered for any great deed or service to her country. She rose from the lowest ranks of society to share in the life of the highest in the land. The love between her and the king was based on friendship and understanding, confidence in each other, and the willingness to share one another's troubles. Unlike so many others, she was not driven by a craving for power, nor by an overwhelming greed for riches. She did not use her influence with the king for political intrigue. It was Nell's zest for life, her warmhearted merriment and her joy in living, which spread to everyone who saw her or knew her, that attracted the king to the spirited redhead. Not least, she gave encouragement to those who took comfort from her meteoric rise, and, like Cinderella, gave hope to any who aspired to the same giddy heights.

Her love for Charles II was honest and genuine, and she brought him joy and laughter.

Coming from her background, perhaps it was inevitable that Nellie would become a whore like her mother, but she pulled herself up out of the gutter for which she was destined by using her wits, her looks and her irrepressible humor to reach out and grasp another world. Any roof over her head must have seemed paradise, and it is

difficult to condemn her for exchanging each protector for a more influential one when the opportunity arose. Nell Gwyn was both proud
and ashamed of her origins—proud to be one of the people, who acknowledged her as a queen among them, at the very least a queen of
the theater. But her shame about her background was also always apparent, and was the cause of the distinction made between her and
the king's other mistresses—even her fellow actress Moll Davis. This
infuriated Nellie, who felt justified in considering herself as good—or
bad—as the other royal "whores," and her lack of a title always distressed her.

No real malice accompanied her move from bed to bed, and once
she had gained the king's she never again looked at another man—admittedly not such a difficult decision when she considered, like so
many others, that the king was the most handsome, kind and charming man in the country. But the fact that these attributes did not keep
Charles II's other mistresses faithful in those days of lazy morality
gives a certain added quality to Nell's constancy.

Unlike other royal mistresses featured in this book, Nell Gwyn
was not honoured as the king's *maîtresse en titre*. Louise de Kéroualle
and Hortense Mancini were both well-bred and cultured, and Barbara
Villiers was a member of the nobility. Nell had none of these assets,
but she had spunk, wit and loyalty, and was rightly valued by Charles
II for these virtues.

When Nell Gwyn died, no voices were raised to condemn her immorality. Her funeral oration was delivered by the famous Dr. Teni-
son, vicar of St. Martin-in-the-Fields and a future Archbishop of
Canterbury, who was not afraid to speak for this best loved of English
royal courtesans.

It seems extraordinary, with hindsight, that the court and the
people of England were quite willing to accept, and love as the mistress of their most beloved king, an illiterate actress, born in squalor
and educated at "Mrs. Ross's house of ill repute." One hundred years
later, at the court of Versailles and in Paris, the French still could not
countenance Louis XV taking as his mistress one of the most accomplished women of the eighteenth century, the cultured and rich
Madame de Pompadour, because she was born a member of the
bourgeoisie and not an aristocrat.

2

La Marquise de Pompadour

1721–1764

MISTRESS OF LOUIS XV OF FRANCE

Sincère et tendre Pompadour
(Car je veux vous donner d'avance
Ce nom qui rime avec l'amour
Et qui sera bientôt le plus beau nom de France)

[Sincere and tender Pompadour
(As I would like to give you in advance
This name, which rhymes with love
And soon will be the most beautiful in France)]

VOLTAIRE (written shortly before the title
was officially granted by Louis XV)

". . . so farewell my friend, remember always the fair goddess, who is no longer either goddess or fair—and who cares not much about the matter."

Possibly apocryphal letter written by Madame de Pompadour
to a friend in 1762. From the *"Collection Bleu"*

*O*n December 29, 1721, Jeanne-Antoinette Poisson was born in the rue de Cléry, in the heart of the overcrowded, bustling Villeneuve district of Paris. A first child, she belonged by birth firmly to the middle classes. Her father, François Poisson, was steward to the influential Pâris brothers—Pâris-Duverney, who was a contractor and army comptroller, and Pâris-Montmartel, who was banker to the king and the court.* Though he had come from humbler origins, Monsieur Poisson was now the epitome of the jolly bourgeois. But his ready smile and bonhomie never disguised his ability to assist the two men who virtually ran the finances of the country.

It was Poisson's efficiency as one of the forage contractors to the Duc de Villars' regiment which had brought him to the attention of the Pâris brothers, and he had not disappointed his new benefactors. When plague struck in Provence, he was singled out for his integrity and prompt action in organizing the necessary supplies. Despite his lack of formal education and manners, he was unusually subtle in thought and expression, and had a talent for resolving the most delicate situations—qualities which soon made him indispensable to his employers.

Louise-Madeleine de la Motte, Madame Poisson, came from the same circles as the Pâris brothers. Her father, like François, was involved in army supplies as well as being a vendor of meat to Les Invalides. Louise-Madeleine, a strikingly beautiful and intelligent young woman, was considered her husband's social superior, and according to rumor, the Pâris brothers arranged her marriage to Poisson to provide Le Blanc, secretary of state for war, with easier access to her. To compensate Poisson, Le Blanc arranged for him and the bride's father to receive official appointments from the regent. In the circles in which she moved, Madame Poisson was considered stunning, witty and clever. What she lacked in social graces, she made up for in ambition. Louise-Madeleine was also more than somewhat amoral.

As marriages were normally arranged and not based on love, infi-

* There were four Pâris brothers, whose lives spanned almost the entire century. At this time the eldest had already died, and the second, Antoine, was to follow in 1733.

delity was commonplace and more or less accepted, provided it was kept within certain limits. Madame Poisson, it seems, well exceeded those limits. Her kinder biographers claim she had at least a dozen lovers, all influential, rich and generous. The most permanent of her many admirers were Monsieur Pâris-Montmartel and a Monsieur Le Normant de Tournehem. A former ambassador to Sweden, Monsieur de Tournehem was a director of the Compagnie des Indes and, as a respected financier, was appointed a *fermier-général.** The Pâris brothers and de Tournehem were also close friends.

Jeanne-Antoinette was named after her godfather, Jean Pâris de Montmartel, and his wife Antoinette,† and the entire Pâris family took the little girl to their hearts.

Opportunities to make enormous profits had always existed for those responsible for equipping and supplying the army. Poisson did well, and the family moved out of the capital's old center into increasingly grander establishments, settling finally in a large, well-appointed house in the rue Saint-Marc. When Jeanne-Antoinette was four, her father was made the scapegoat in a black market scandal involving corn supplied by the Pâris brothers. Poisson was accused of owing an enormous sum and declared a debtor to the treasury. To save himself from prison, or possibly even the gibbet, he fled to Germany. His sanguine comment on leaving his two children, Jeanne-Antoinette and her baby brother Abel, was that as his wife was so pretty, she would surely fall on her feet. And she did, though not before her house and all its contents were sold over her head.

Charles Le Normant de Tournehem was a wealthy bachelor, a connoisseur and a patron of the arts. Above all he appreciated beauty, especially in distress, and he took complete charge of the lovely and destitute Madame Poisson and her family. "Uncle" de Tournehem treated the children as if they were his own—which, in fact, they were not, though given the general immorality of Regency France, and of Madame Poisson in particular, speculation was not unreasonable.

---

* A collector of indirect taxes. These men generally ran the country's finances, making huge fortunes for themselves in the process.

† Her godparents had not yet married at the time of the christening, as Antoinette Pâris was just eleven. As she was the niece of her fiancé, a dispensation from Rome for their marriage had been sought and was granted.

From her earliest years Jeanne-Antoinette charmed those around her, and de Tournehem's and godfather Montmartel's devotion to Madame Poisson was in part due to her enchanting daughter.

LOUIS XV HAD inherited the throne of France in 1715 at the age of five. His predecessor was his great-grandfather, the fabled Sun King Louis XIV, who had outlived his son, his grandson and his two elder great-grandsons, before the sun finally set on his seventy-two-year reign. In the end he was despatched by his court physician, Fagon. This dreadful doctor had almost annihilated the entire royal family within a fortnight by treating their measles epidemic with harsh purges, emetics and prolonged bleedings. The tiny Louis XV only survived due to the quick thinking of his nurse, the Duchesse de Ventadour, who hid the child from the terrible Fagon. Until the little king reached his majority, France was ruled by a regent, his dissolute uncle Philippe, Duc d'Orléans.

To prevent the aristocracy from ever again plotting against the throne and bringing about a recurrence of the horrors of civil war and the humiliations suffered by the royal family which had so affected his childhood, Louis XIV had devised an ingenious method of ensuring the nobles' loyalty. He had an instinctive understanding of human nature, and in particular that of the French nobility. With the help of Cardinal Richelieu he established an absolute monarchy, curtailed the power of the aristocracy and then, to contain them, built an enormous palace complex at Versailles, where he created an irresistible court of pleasure and privilege. As the only occupations open to France's ruling classes at the time were the army or the court, the king enticed them to join him under one roof, at a safe distance from Paris, where he could keep them under his eye. Acting as his own first minister, Louis XIV required cooperation from his people, not collaboration, and the role of the noblesse was to adorn the court to add splendor to the crown. Inspired by the courts of Spain and Bourgogne, at Versailles the king created an exclusive world of powerless privilege, governed by its own rules, customs, idiom, protocol, manner of speaking, punishments and rewards—all within a prescribed routine so complicated and precise that breaches of even the smallest regulation were considered grave offenses. The many changes of clothing required each day, the miles of passages and corridors that had to be covered between one appointment and the next, kept Louis' courtiers under the constant illusion of bustling, important haste.

The *noblesse* with the right of entrée at court were graded, divided and subdivided according to the subtlest shadings of their ancestral quarterings. The slightest inclination of the head, or a minute shift of a shoulder, could denote the exact measure of respect or disdain officially due to one courtier from another. *Le Grand Monarque,* as Louis XIV was called, played on the French weakness for and love of fashion in every aspect of their lives: cultural, domestic and social. At court, fashion was given the same value and consideration as the most important national issues. Versailles was meant to be fun.

Even more than all things fashionable, the French had traditionally loved their kings. It was this devotion to the person of the monarch that enabled Louis XIV alone to pull the strings in his gigantic, exotic puppet theater of Versailles, with the actors obliged and willing to be present for every performance. All honors and privileges stemmed from the king. He was the source and supreme adjudicator in all things: positions, promotions, marriages and betrothals. Any step taken on any ladder, large or small, was in his sole gift. By making himself the fountain and source of power, the king drugged his courtiers with addictive but useless privilege, and ensured that they had almost no effective political power. His family fared even worse, and the princes of the blood were not groomed for any future office.

A framework of intricate protocol underlay an endless program of festivities—fancy-dress balls, card parties and gambling (often involving high stakes), theatricals, fireworks, flirtations. It was an existence dedicated to the pursuit of pleasure, with the tacit approval of the day's society. Moralistic nineteenth-century and later historians often assumed that the courtiers who led such a frivolous and seemingly pointless existence must have been bored and unhappy. On the contrary. Sport, namely hunting, kept the courtiers healthy and well exercised; the official entertainments provided an endless source of incident, gossip, new fashions and distractions; gambling satisfied the need for excitement as fortunes were won or lost overnight; and love (by which an eighteenth-century courtier understood *desire*) was a game which fascinated them all. Marriages between their children were carefully arranged by parents or guardians, not with a view to their possible compatibility, but to the mutual advantage of an alliance of family or fortune. Love or passion was a private matter; couples accepted that their partners had lovers, and it was generally held that a husband and wife could always live together if they were well bred.

There was constant travel as the court moved in ritual succession from one of the king's châteaux to another according to the calendar. There were intrigues and adulteries, alliances made and dissolved, all concealed under a strict code of *politesse* which must never be broken, and subtle insults were delivered by tongues sharp as scalpels. Neither pain nor sorrow had an acceptable face at a court whose members had to appear radiant and smiling at all times. Children were born, christened and married at Versailles and the other royal châteaux, but no one had the right to die under the king's roof. Should such an inconvenience occur, the corpse had to be removed at once from the palace. For all that, court life offered an extraordinarily cheerful and comfortable existence.

Before Versailles became the headquarters of the court, an aristocrat's life could only be lived to the full in Paris, and his estates were used solely for hunting, fishing, and as a source of income. Indeed, there was no worse disgrace for a courtier than to be banished to his estates and so be deprived of the latest gossip, fashion, festivity or scandal at court. No matter how intelligent and well educated, anyone living in the countryside was deemed "provincial"—the equivalent of social death.

Louis XIV had reigned for so long that the energy and vision of his glorious early years had long passed. According to the king's great marshal, Vauban, there was no reason for the country's misery, as he calculated that France could support at least another 5 million people; the peasantry worked hard at tilling their good soil in a temperate climate, and though their taxes were high, they could be afforded. According to Vauban, the fault lay with the clergy and the nobility, who were exempt from paying any taxes, and this burden was unfairly shouldered by the rest of the population. When the Sun King died, the people were ready for sweeping reforms in government, agriculture and society.

PHILIPPE DUC D'ORLÉANS was forty-one years old when he inherited the awesome task of governing France until the little Louis XV came of age. Untrained and unprepared for such an immense task, this capable and intelligent man had dissipated his youth in every possible excess. During the king's last years, the presence of Madame de Maintenon by Louis XIV's side, and the imminent prospect of meeting his maker, had added a stern religious flavor to the end of his reign. His death was followed by an inevitable reaction against the restraints of this royal twilight, and the court, and much of society, reverted to the licentious lifestyle of the new regent. Although Philippe d'Orléans recognized the urgent need for reform, his attempt to involve the aristocracy once again in active government failed. His efforts were further undermined in Paris by the circulation of broadsheets describing his scandalous behavior.*

Because most of the land was owned by absentee nobles who, on the whole, could not care less about their harvests, France's agricultural system was outmoded and inefficient. The vast forests and rivers were teeming with game, all of which belonged to the king, and only he and his nobility had the right to hunt and fish. Poaching, which was rife, was a hanging offense. The lower classes saw their landlords as frivolous, entirely devoted to the pursuit of pleasure, lacking in morals or any sense of their responsibilities, and devoid of religion. Although a strong middle class had emerged in England in the seventeenth century, it was not until the early eighteenth century that the middle class of France reached any great numbers or comparable wealth. As the middle class had no right of entrée at court, their only contacts with the nobility were professional. The aristocracy was gen-

---

* In one poem, unjustly attributed to Voltaire, the regent was accused of conducting an *affaire* with his eldest daughter, the Duchesse de Berry, which seems to have been true. The libertine regent loved women, but none more than his remarkable mother Liselotte, and it was to her that he uttered the famous rebuke when she complained he chose such ugly mistresses: "Bah! Mama, all cats look gray in the dark!"

erally looked upon by all other classes with a mixture of grudging awe and wonder. The French court was envied and admired. Despite the insolent luxury of Versailles, it was slavishly imitated by every other European court.

Louis XIV's legacy to his great-grandson at his death in 1715 bore little resemblance to the achievements of the first half of his reign. A fifth of the population had disappeared due to war, starvation and the expulsion of the Huguenots. For the same reasons much land had ceased to be cultivated. After several bad harvests, bread was expensive and riots frequent. And yet, the overburdened people, whose sufferings were far worse at this time than they were to be in 1789, were still ready to give their hearts to the new king. At last the nation was at peace with its neighbors and within, and among the educated, hope was kindled anew by the dawn of the Age of Reason and the Enlightenment, of Rousseau and the *Encyclopédistes*. But the eyes of the critical world did not look beyond Versailles, and in that exquisite existence they saw only the excess and corruption that misrepresented France.

By the mid-eighteenth century, France was no longer an arid wasteland with a starving peasantry smoldering toward revolution. On the contrary, this was a golden age, during which the quality of life for every stratum of society reached heights it had never known before, and was never to know again. Having recovered from the pointless wars of Louis XIV, and not yet engaged on those of Louis XV, the country prospered. Farmers worked hard and were thrifty, believing fervently in God and the family and, most of all, in their king. The soil was fertile and gave good harvests, with no armies—French or others—pillaging it. The bourgeoisie were industrious, their one aim to improve their lot. Those in commerce and trade applied themselves energetically and diligently. So much money flowed into the capital that it was calculated that more poultry and game were devoured in one night in Paris than in a whole week in London. The craftsmen and artisans, who made up the bulk of the urban population, strove to excel, and succeeded. At no other time has any nation produced such exquisite workmanship in every field of the decorative arts as in France in the fifty years prior to the Revolution.

LOUIS XV WAS a small, beautiful child with large, dark brown eyes and a mass of golden curls. The sole survivor of his family, he was pampered and denied nothing. The regent adored his little nephew, whom he genuinely preferred to his own insipid son. Full of good intentions and determined not to neglect his duty to the crown, this kind, unambitious man brought Louis up as best he could, taking him to council meetings, explaining the complicated politics to the five-year-old with all the solemnity and deference due to his monarch. Philippe d'Orléans was blessed with enough talents to have made him a great prince, but he lacked the ability to use them. His tutor, secretary and chief adviser, the abbé Dubois, succeeded in thoroughly debauching him, and the abbé's corrupting hold over the regent remained firm until the end of his life. Louis returned his uncle's affection, but gained little from his haphazard education. Despite his own avowed scorn for the Church, the regent made a real effort to see that the child had a sound religious education, and this Christian conscience remained with Louis XV all his life.

The boy-king said little, observed much, listened well, and kept his own council. With no mother, father, brothers or sisters, he lacked loving and scolding and the cozy intimacy of family life. All around deferred to him, his every wish was granted, yet his childhood was lonely and unhappy. He grew strong and handsome, but under the veneer of exquisite manners and studied charm he was shy and introverted. In France, the king was everything. His personality was the vital ingredient of the very soul of the kingdom. He set the tone for the entire country throughout his reign. He was the source of inspiration and imitation, not only for his ministers, the civil service and the armed forces, but for the arts and sciences, philosophy, religion, society and family life. To many of his people, the young Louis XV was the handsomest man in France,* dignified, charming, gracious, courageous and intelligent, qualities which mattered a very great deal to them.

---

* On a visit to Paris, Peter the Great remarked that he had never seen a handsomer young man. This was the general verdict of all disinterested visitors. Louis was still handsome enough, at the age of fifty, to charm the fifteen-year-old Marie-Antoinette on her arrival in France.

Philippe d'Orléans died when Louis XV was thirteen, and technically of age. Despite the personal excesses of the king's uncle, his regency was not without success. D'Orléans had had the intelligence to surround himself with capable people, and even Voltaire—never the most forgiving critic—admitted (in the *Henriade*): "Of all the descendants of Henri IV, Philippe d'Orléans most resembled him in his valor, his kindliness and his lack of pose, and he possessed a richer culture."

His place was taken by the Duc de Bourbon, head of the Condé branch of the family, who became known as "Monsieur le Duc." When Louis was ten, the duke had taught him to hunt with the Condé family's renowned passion for the chase, but the boy learned little else through him. Until Louis discovered the thrill and distraction of hunting, he had been an enthusiastic and able student. Following the death of Philippe d'Orléans, the abbé Fleury, tutor to Louis XV and future cardinal, replaced the abbé Dubois as the power behind the throne. Cardinal Fleury was deeply attached to the king throughout his life, and fulfilled his role as First Minister of France with wisdom, skill and integrity for the next seventeen years.

The young king was sexually precocious at fifteen, and his dazzling good looks and position invited easy conquests of both sexes. Indeed, Monsieur le Duc was as anxious about Louis forming a homosexual relationship with one of the young dandies at court as he was about the boy-king acquiring an influential older mistress.

Some years previously, a marriage had been arranged for Louis XV with his cousin, the delightful five-year-old Infanta of Spain. As he was ten years older than his fiancée, the young king was less than enchanted by the prospect of waiting ten more years before consummating his marriage. Clearly, Louis could not wait. The insult to his uncle the King of Spain seemed the lesser of the prospective evils, and the little girl was sent back while another, older bride was found.

The only candidate among the available princesses to whom neither Monsieur le Duc's mistress (who did not relish being outshone in rank or beauty) nor anyone else involved had any serious objection—or too strong an allegiance—was the twenty-three-year-old daughter of the penniless, exiled King Stanislas of Poland, who lived in Alsace, a pensioner of France. King Stanislas Leczinski had been "elected" to the throne of Poland in 1704 under the protection of the King of Sweden, replacing Augustus of Saxony. The Leczinski family had no royal blood in their ancestry. Seven years older than Louis, Marie Leczinska had little to recommend her to the pleasure-loving court at Versailles. She was deeply religious, modest, unassuming, good, plain and dull. She also had excellent health, and was touchingly reluctant to leave her father and her home in Strasbourg for the glorious prospect of becoming queen of the greatest nation in Europe.

Despite cries of *mésalliance,* the marriage took place. Louis fell instantly in love with her, and to the delight of his courtiers (and in their presence) proved his love seven times on their wedding night. Nine months later, Queen Marie Leczinska gave birth to twin girls.

The king was devoted, the queen loved the king, and in the next two years bore him two more daughters. Having never known family life, Louis delighted in his newfound domesticity and, little by little, Cardinal Fleury was left in sole charge of the country. ("Monsieur le Duc" was usurped and banished to his estates. As he was said to possess neither public nor private virtues, he was not mourned.) In 1729 the queen gave birth at last to a son, her fifth child, and France rejoiced in a dauphin for the first time in seventeen years.

By nature a family man, and bored by business, Louis XV was happiest when surrounded by his rapidly increasing brood. He was religious, enormously energetic but domestically lazy, and like most men, a creature of habit. And his habit was the queen. Furthermore, he was shy with women, especially with the dazzling, sophisticated court beauties who vied (in constant frustration) for his attention and favors. As the queen was almost always pregnant, and therefore often indisposed, the king's "needs" were gratified by the young wenches his valet thoughtfully supplied. But these little infidelities counted for nothing. By the time Louis XV was twenty-seven, he had ten children. A doting husband and father, he would have happily continued annually enlarging his family with his worthy queen. But it was not to be. After ten years in which she gave birth to eleven children, ten living, one stillborn (her last child, Louise, was born in 1737), the queen longed, not unreasonably, to stop there and spend the rest of her time in the company of a small group of friends as worthy and uninspiring as herself. Her father, King Stanislas, was heard to remark ruefully that the two dullest queens in Europe were his wife and his daughter.

From the start of her marriage, Marie Leczinska had insisted that she be exempt from the king's attentions on a few important saints' days and religious holidays. With the passing years (and to the growing displeasure of the king), more and more saints crept into the queen's "calendar of restraint." As she complained she was forever "in bed, or pregnant, or brought to bed," Queen Marie Leczinska was rarely able to take part in the court's activities or join in the king's hectic progress from one château to another. Bored by gossip and intrigue, she gradually became isolated from the court and her husband's daily life. She was a truly good woman, always dignified, amiable and charitable, but to hold the interest of a virile young husband whose path was strewn each day with every sort of temptation would have taken a will and feminine skills she did not possess or care to learn. In fact, "trying to corrupt the king" had become one of the favorite games of the courtiers closest to him, and the wonder of it is that Louis XV resisted for so long.

⌾∯∯∾

FRANÇOIS POISSON WAS all too aware of his wife's amoral lifestyle. But as he adored his only daughter, before he fled into exile as a result of his alleged involvement in the corn scandal he made arrangements to ensure at least her moral well-being. Madame Poisson had a sister and a cousin who were both nuns at the respected Ursuline convent in Poissy, and her husband asked them to accept the five-year-old Jeanne-Antoinette a year earlier than usual. From Germany, Poisson wrote regularly to the nuns, begging them to send him news of her progress.

Jeanne-Antoinette was a sunny child, affectionate, well behaved, and popular with both nuns and pupils. She was also bright and intelligent. *"Reinette"* (little queen), as they called her, was pretty and dainty, with chestnut curls, clear white skin, rosy cheeks and a lovely singing voice. Throughout her life everyone agreed that her most remarkable features were her wonderfully expressive eyes of indefinite color.

The Mother Superior's greatest worry was not the increasingly bad reputation of Madame Poisson, but her daughter's health. Reinette was fragile and had a weak chest. Often the victim of colds, flu and bronchitis, Jeanne-Antoinette was to be plagued by this weakness all her life, and it would finally be the cause of her death.

These were happy, secure years at Poissy. Between her bouts of illness, the nuns gave Jeanne-Antoinette a good education. Their pretty pupil became an insatiable reader and began her life-long habit of daily correspondence. Poissy was less worldly than the Parisian convents patronized by the aristocracy. The Ursuline routine was strict, disciplined and caring, and the nuns lavished tenderness and maternal affection on the girls. Above all, they were raised to respect God, their parents and the royal family. (Much later, when her aunt had become the Mother Superior and Reinette the powerful Marquise de Pompadour, she remembered the kindness of the nuns and gave the convent a generous pension and money for repairs.)

Although her father was the more anxious parent, who paid the bills and corresponded with the nuns, when Reinette was eight, her mother sent for her to come to Paris. Despite her earlier neglect, the visit was a success. Madame Poisson was as delighted with her lovely daughter as Reinette was at rediscovering her enchanting, beautiful mother.

Poisson closed his eyes to his wife's *affaires*—in particular with the ever faithful de Tournehem—and continued to write to her and to his daughter from exile. In reply to one of his letters after Reinette's return to the convent, the Mother Superior wrote: "She [Madame Poisson] seemed very pleased with her delightful daughter. . . . So are we, for she is always charming, and, thank God, in very good health."

The following year, Jeanne-Antoinette left the nuns to begin her life as a Parisienne. Madame Poisson had plans for her pretty and talented daughter.

Despite the backwash of bad publicity the Pâris brothers had received over the corn scandal, they survived it and, through their discreet lifestyles and industry, retained their powerful connections. As Poisson had borne the brunt of the scandal, the Pâris family joined their friend Louise-Madeleine to campaign for her husband's recall and pardon. Meanwhile, his children mixed with theirs, and Madame

Poisson carefully began to cultivate fashionable hostesses for her daughter's eventual social debut.

Toward the end of Louis XIV's reign, when the court at Versailles had become as bored and calcified as the aging king, some of the grand ladies began to "receive" small groups of friends and stimulating intellectuals in their town houses in Paris. This exchange of refined conversation, ideas and gossip had evolved by the reign of Louis XV into the Paris salons of the nouveaux-riches bourgeois hostesses. Admittance was not necessarily gained by birth, position, intelligence or even ability, but rather by a sharp wit, brilliant conversation, talent, beauty and, for added spice, a strong whiff of scandal.

No one was better qualified to hold such a salon than Madame Poisson's friend Alexandrine Tencin. A defrocked nun, she had failed in her efforts to seduce the regent, Philippe d'Orléans, but produced an illegitimate child (which she abandoned) with a general of artillery.* She had also been the mistress of the infamous prime minister Cardinal Dubois (for whom she spied), earning herself a small fortune. This she had trebled by astute speculation and the assistance of another lover, the financial wizard and charlatan John Law. After the death of the Marquise de Lambert—one of the last of the grandes dames of Paris—Madame Tencin began a new life as society's premier hostess. She was a *Dauphinoise* like the Pâris brothers, and her romantic career was at last on the wane, but her personality, her fortune, and the memory of her beauty attracted the famous, the talented and the risqué to her salon, where the conversation was considered the most scintillating in the world.

Through Alexandrine Tencin, Madame Poisson had access to the literary circles of Paris—the aged Fontenelle, nephew of the great Corneille; the Montesquieu brothers; the enormously rich Helvétius (who was also master of the queen's household); the abbé Prévost, author of *Manon Lescaut,* who edited a literary paper; and many others. Madame Tencin's brother, the Cardinal Archbishop of Lyons, and her sister, Madame de Ferriol, brought the elegant and fashionable of society to her house, including Richelieu, the most dashing duke in France, and the wise old president of the chamber, Hénault,

---

* The child grew up to become the famous mathematician Jean Le Rond d'Alembert.

historian and *"homme du monde."* Madame Tencin's salon became the meeting place for the worldly and wellborn of all Europe. Few women were invited, but among them were Madame Geoffrin and her daughter Madame de la Ferté-Imbault, who were to preside over the most famous literary salon of the period. Madame Poisson's legendary beauty, which had ensnared so many rich and influential lovers, her personality (described as "possessing four devils") and her quick tongue made quite a stir in her friend's salon, while her exquisite daughter sat at the feet of the learned, the witty and the wise, and stored away every golden moment in her prodigious memory.

When Jeanne-Antoinette was nine, an event took place which came to dominate the imagination of her mother and herself. Clairvoyants and soothsayers were all the rage in Paris at the time, and Reinette was taken by her mother to visit Madame Lebon, a fashionable fortune-teller. She seemed quite taken with the ravishing little girl, dressed like a doll, a miniature version of her mother. After consulting the cards, the woman declared that Reinette would "not be queen, but almost."* In Parisian circles this could mean only one thing. Jeanne-Antoinette's ambitious mother was delighted.

Despite this exciting prospect, it was also a year of sadness for Jeanne-Antoinette. First her La Motte grandparents died, closely followed by her godmother. Then her beloved aunt, whose daughter had been with her at the convent and who had taken her on so many outings—something her mother had never done—died a few months later. It was at this time that she encountered Charles Collin, the remarkable man who was to keep her finances and her meticulous account books in order all her life—as well as undertake the most delicate missions with total discretion. Collin was an attorney who had been tutor to her cousins, and following the death of Jeanne-Antoinette's grandparents, he was appointed trustee for Madame Poisson. Using her considerable La Motte inheritance, Madame Poisson acquired the lease of an even grander house, 50 rue de Richelieu, which she furnished in the latest and most elegant style.

"Uncle" de Tournehem provided for Jeanne-Antoinette, who was

---

* Twenty years later, an item listed in the account books of the Marquise de Pompadour read: "To Mme Lebon, six hundred livres for having predicted, when I was nine, that I would become the mistress of the king."

always clothed in the height of fashion. She dressed with the help of her own maid (a soubrette), who was to remain with her until her death.

For all her faults, Madame Poisson was not a fool. She knew that her scandalous reputation and her husband's flight from the law would make it difficult for her daughter to be received in the best circles, but she was determined to give her every possible advantage. As a beautiful woman herself, Madame Poisson knew from experience that beauty alone would not hold the kind of man she had in mind for Reinette. Her daughter's weak chest might prove another disadvantage, and if her health was poor she would have to learn to hold a man by stimulating his mind. As the Poissons' background was not sufficiently illustrious for them to arrange a great match for their daughter, Madame Poisson set out quite deliberately to educate the unwitting Reinette as a high-class courtesan. To ensure that Jeanne-Antoinette acquired all the accomplishments required by a young lady hoping to enter society, she and de Tournehem engaged the best teachers.

The celebrated Jelyotte, star of the Paris Opéra (five minutes' walk from the elegant Poisson mansion), was engaged to give Jeanne-Antoinette expensive singing lessons. He also taught her to play the clavichord to accompany her clear, rich soprano. The great teacher Guibaudet taught her to dance, curtsy, walk and move gracefully. The actor Lanoue taught her declamation and acting, and the famous old dramatist and poet Prosper de Crébillon taught her how to tell a story, recite poetry and make witty conversation. Reinette developed an enduring love of the theater and learned many plays by heart. She showed a considerable talent for drawing and painting, and took lessons which included engraving. She learned to ride beautifully, dress to perfection and wear her clothes with panache. Exotic plants were arriving in France from the New World, and botany became another absorbing interest of the many-faceted Mademoiselle Poisson.

At home, guided by the knowledge and sure taste of de Tournehem, Jeanne-Antoinette learned about the treasures in the rooms in which she lived. She was surrounded by rare objects of art and beauty. De Tournehem's friends were connoisseurs, and Reinette absorbed and profited from everything she was told.

In 1738 Jeanne-Antoinette Poisson was seventeen, and she had developed into a beauty. A little taller than average, she had a wonderful figure, slender but well formed, with lovely hands and feet. Her face was a perfect oval, framed by pale chestnut curls. Her skin had retained its remarkable whiteness and she would bite her pale lips to redden them. But her best features were her eyes; intelligent, misty and laughing, and of an intensity that changed from light to dark with her mood. When she smiled she showed her perfect little white teeth, and her cheeks would dimple. In themselves, her features were not remarkable, but the combination of her breathtaking coloring, animated manner and bright, expressive eyes made her appear astonishingly beautiful. With such looks and accomplishments, her modest manner and her mother's efforts, it is not surprising that Jeanne-Antoinette Poisson soon graced the most exclusive circles in Paris.

⁂

THE YEAR 1738 was also the year of Louis XV's definitive separation from his queen.

The king was bored. Ennui had always been the main flaw in his character, and his life was spent trying to chase it away. Spoilt since his childhood, he tired easily of people and pursuits. He had loved his fascinating, debauched uncle Philippe d'Orléans, but cared little about the arrival or departure of his successor, Monsieur le Duc. Although described by the diarist the Marquis d'Argenson as "a man of sound sense . . . anxious for the work to go well," Louis XV left the governing of France in the hands of the octogenarian Cardinal Fleury.

The king often interrupted the relentless routine and ceremony of Versailles by private games in the *Petits Appartements*. Dubbed "rats' nests" by the uninitiated, these charmingly decorated small rooms, hidden behind the formal state apartments, were the king's private pleasure domain. The right of entry was restricted to his exclusive group of friends, and as their sole duty was to amuse Louis, he was surrounded by frivolous, witty, entertaining companions, who told him little of value and even less that was original. Gossip, intrigue, gambling and fashion dominated their conversation. Yet even among his closest companions, and in the intimacy of the *Petits Apparte-ments,* strict protocol was observed. The Duc de Cröy wrote in his memoirs that despite the apparent informality, no one forgot they were in the presence of the king. Louis XV knew no other way.

The king's relationship with the queen had become strained; other than their children, they had little in common. Unable to communicate his innermost thoughts and feelings with Marie Leczinska, Louis felt isolated and lonely. As early as 1732 he had raised his glass in a toast to *"L'Inconnue"*—the unknown lady who could steal his heart. After the birth of his second son, Louis became cooler to his wife. She had aged prematurely, and rather bored him. Gradually he began to drift away from the Church's influence and to enjoy the company of the cultured and sophisticated young ladies of the court. The king's valet Barbier stated in his journal that fifteen out of twenty gentlemen at court were unfaithful to their wives and had mistresses, and it was only a question of time before the master did the same.

It is generally thought that Louis XV was first seduced by his beautiful cousin Mademoiselle de Charolais under the influence of champagne and the Duc de Richelieu. One of the most charming men of his time, the duke was an experienced rake with the gift of making the king (and the regent) laugh to such an extent at his wicked, malicious and consistently funny stories that he was forgiven anything. He was thoroughly debauched, and it was almost considered de rigueur in fashionable society to have been his mistress, however briefly. His amorous escapades often ended in duels, which he inevitably won, on several occasions killing his opponent.* He dabbled in the occult (not unusual at this time) and took part in Black Masses. As first gentleman of the bedchamber, this roué was the king's boon companion. In fact Louis was not seduced by the lovely Mademoiselle de Charolais, but it was at her Château de Madrid that he began his *affaire* with Madame de Mailly.

Although many had suspected it for some time, it was not known for certain until 1739 that Louis XV had a mistress. As royal marriages were arranged, and were never result of a love match, Louis

---

* Louis XIV outlawed dueling in the early days of Versailles, as the practice cost him too many of his courtiers.

XV's ten years of public fidelity to his queen were, for the time, an honorable record. It had always been foreseen by the people and the court that the king would one day have a mistress, that she would enrich herself and her family, and that she would exert some influence over him. His first choice did none of these. Madame de Mailly (she had married her father's first cousin) was the eldest of five daughters of Louis de Mailly, Marquis de Nesle, a gambler from an ancient noble family, who had only succeeded in ruining his own. Her mother* was a lady-in-waiting to the queen, and her sisters were all attached to her majesty's household. Having known her all his life, the shy and reserved king felt comfortable with Louise-Julie de Mailly. She was neither pretty nor clever, but she was vivacious, amusing and kind, and she genuinely loved the king. Wholesome and hearty, she avoided her greedy family and posed no threat to anyone.

Sadly, Madame de Mailly was too good to last. She made the fatal mistake of including her avaricious sister, Madame de Ventimille, in her intimate supper parties with the king, and then found herself usurped by her. Madame de Ventimille was no prettier than her sister, but she was ambitious and much bolder. Tired of flattery, Louis was amused by her frank speech and independent manner, and installed her at Choisy on the Seine in a charming hunting lodge he gave her. There she died soon afterward while giving birth to the king's son. Named the Comte de Luc, the boy grew up to be the image of his father, and was always known as the "demi-Louis."

IN 1739, WHEN Jeanne-Antoinette was eighteen and of marriageable age, her father's case was reexamined and, to her great joy, he was able to come home from exile. Twelve years' absence melted into the past and he cheerfully joined his family to live with Monsieur de Tournehem and take part in the search for a husband for his daughter.

Although allowed home, Poisson had not yet been fully exonerated over the corn scandal, and this slur on his character (added to his wife's notorious reputation) would not make it easy for their daughter

---

* See Hortense Mancini in previous chapter.

to make the match she clearly deserved. Once again, "Uncle" de Tournehem came to the rescue. He proposed his young nephew, Charles-Guillaume Le Normant d'Etioles, who worked with him and was to be his heir. Le Normant was extremely eligible. Lord of the lovely Château d'Etioles in the forest of Sénart, he was well educated, charming and cultivated. Though he was not handsome, his appearance was generally considered pleasing. But his parents considered that the Poisson provenance and track record were insurmountable obstacles to the proposed union, and refused. Monsieur de Tournehem persevered, and his generosity proved persuasive, as he offered such excellent terms that finally they could resist no longer. The marriage took place on March 9, 1741, in the church of Saint-Eustache in Paris. The bride was nineteen, the groom twenty-four.

Monsieur de Tournehem had promised to house the young couple in a large furnished mansion he owned in Paris, pay their servants, and provide livery, coach and horses, and a handsome dowry for the bride. Earlier that year, François Poisson had been completely and publicly exonerated of any wrongdoing in the corn scandal, and his confiscated house and possessions had been restored to him. It was this large house in the rue Saint-Marc which he gave his daughter as part of her dowry on her marriage. Madame Poisson used some of her La Motte inheritance to buy the bride appropriate jewels and a trousseau. Added to the large dowry and income from de Tournehem, Jeanne-Antoinette's marriage portion was as substantial as her husband's. To the surprise of everyone, most of all the reluctant groom himself, d'Etioles fell madly in love with his clever, enchanting Jeanne-Antoinette.

Madame Le Normant d'Etioles, while not exactly in love, declared that she was so happy she would "never leave her husband, except, of course, for the king," and her amused entourage considered this remark a typical example of her charm. Jeanne-Antoinette indeed possessed everything that constituted happiness for a lady of her time. In Paris, the young couple lived with the Poissons and their uncle in de Tournehem's beautiful mansion in a fashionable area. Madame d'Etioles paid calls in a carriage emblazoned with her new coat of arms, and was much admired in society. For the summers, she had Etioles, their splendid (though not beautiful) sixteenth-century château in the royal forest of Sénart.

Wealthy and cultured, Madame d'Etioles was in an ideal position to begin entertaining certain intellectuals, *les philosophes* and artists she had met at Madame Tencin's salon or at one or two houses of the nobility with whom she had family connections. Access to even Madame Geoffrin's exclusive salon was assured once Madame Poisson, whose reputation made her impossible to invite, was diagnosed as having cancer, and could no longer accompany her eminently acceptable daughter. Madame Geoffrin and her devout daughter Madame de la Ferté-Imbault were flattered and enchanted that the lovely and cultured young Madame d'Etioles should add her grace and beauty to their salon.

Indeed, the future Marquise de Pompadour has generally been recognized as one of the most accomplished women of her time (or, for that matter, of any other). She was one of the few women Madame Geoffrin admitted to her salon, and on her own select Wednesday evenings, when she entertained mostly scholars and men of talent, *les philosophes* remarked on her intelligence as much as on her pretty manners. In fact, Jeanne-Antoinette never developed a deep knowledge of philosophy, religion or art. Her real skill lay in her flair, her taste, an ability to absorb the essentials and add her wit and intelligence to any conversation. The combination of her beauty, her delightful appearance, her charm, her desire to please, her accomplishments and her social graces resulted in a formidable young woman. Even the king's first mistress, Madame de Mailly, had been so moved after hearing Madame d'Etioles sing and play the clavichord at a soirée that she had spontaneously kissed the delightful newcomer.

Not surprisingly, Madame d'Etioles' list of admirers and acquaintances grew daily. Her former teachers, Crébillon and Jelyotte, brought other writers, poets, scholars and men of talent to her house. In a letter to his mistress Madame du Deffand written in 1742, the queen's friend President Hénault mentioned seeing Jeanne-Antoinette at an elegant evening reception in Paris:

> . . . I found there one of the loveliest women I ever saw: she was
> Madame d'Etioles. She is a perfect musician, sang many songs with
> gaiety and taste, and she acts at Etioles in a theatre as fine as the
> Opéra and well provided with machinery and sets. She has a lovely

complexion, chestnut hair, wonderful eyes and teeth, a fascinating smile, dimples, animation and a perfect figure.

The summers of 1741 and 1742 must have been the happiest of Jeanne-Antoinette's life. Unable to entertain all her amusing and clever new friends at her uncle's house in Paris for fear that they would be bored by his business colleagues, Madame d'Etioles opened to them the doors of her husband's agreeable château near Choisy, not far from Versailles. Voltaire, who called her "the Divine Etioles," visited often and became an intimate friend and adviser. Another new friend was Pierre de Bernis, a secular and very social abbé known for his charm and wit, which he exercised on Jeanne-Antoinette's young friends. These included her cousin Madame d'Estrades and the Duchesse de Chevreuse, among other young ladies to whom she referred as *"mes petits chats."* They all called her "sweet, beautiful, snow-white Pamela" after Richardson's novel which was all the rage, and stayed on at Etioles surrounded by the aura of her special blend of refined elegance.

❦

HER HUSBAND CLEARLY adored her, and had built her a delicious, bijou theater in the park. Intellectuals and writers, including the younger Crébillon, Fontenelle, Montesquieu, Duclos and Marivaux, as well as the neighboring gentry, came to watch or take part in the comedies and operas performed by Madame d'Etioles and her friends.

It did not take long before her name began to be mentioned in aristocratic circles. As the fame of her little theater and the talent displayed there spread, Madame d'Etioles was invited to take part in the rival productions of an elegant neighbor. There she met, as fellow amateur performers, the young ducs de Nivernais and Duras, and found herself applauded by the mighty Duc de Richelieu himself. Soon her name was known at court—but the king had already noticed the lovely châtelaine of Etioles.

Situated in the valley of the Seine, the estate of Etioles was one of several which bordered the royal forest of Sénart, where the king and his courtiers came to hunt around August 20 each year. Straight, wide avenues had been cut through the trees, converging in the shape of stars for the convenience and pleasure of the hunt and its followers. The king's guests would rendezvous with the hunters at the center of these stars, where large clearings had been levelled for magnificent picnics. Only nobility created before the year 1400 were entitled to take part in the king's hunt. The bourgeoisie were totally excluded, but it was an ancient tradition that keys to the gates of the royal avenues were given to the lords of the neighboring estates, who were permitted to follow the royal hunt in carriages. For three seasons, Madame d'Etioles had availed herself of this privilege, and was familiar with every track and footpath of the forest.

To see the king out hunting was to see Louis XV at his best. Love of the chase was in the blood of all the descendants of the Valois and the Bourbons, and Louis was no exception. A man of inexhaustible energy, he rejoiced in the exercise, the traditions, the folklore, and the tales of the hunters at the banquets afterward.

Louis had always encouraged his courtiers to create their outfits for court life, masquerades and for sport. To see them mounted on their superb horses, wearing every shade of velvet and satin, hats trimmed with fluttering feathers, cloaks flying, swords, spurs, brooches, buttons and gold braid all glinting and glittering in the sunlight, the horses surrounded by the staghounds jumping about and barking, everyone laughing and shouting, must have been a breathtaking spectacle.

Since she was nine, Reinette had dreamed of the handsome king and cherished Madame Lebon's prediction in her heart. Here in the forest she saw him in all his glory, relaxed and untroubled by the cares of state, a man in his prime and in his element. She heard his husky voice, strangely high and distinguishable from all the others, calling to the hounds or the hunt servants. Boldly, she had even allowed her eyes to meet that famous velvet gaze. There had never been any doubt in the mind of Jeanne-Antoinette Poisson that there was but one man she could love, and to whom she would dedicate her life. That man was Louis XV, King of France.

When following the royal hunt, Madame d'Etioles, exquisite in coral pink satin, drove herself with panache in a small sky-blue phaeton, her full silk skirts almost covering its high pink wheels. On her head, at a jaunty angle, she set a coral pink tricorne trimmed with pink down; in her pale-gloved hands she held pink silk reins. Flicking a little whip of blue ribbons, she expertly maneuvered her ponies to keep herself in full view of the king. Beside her she had placed a basket of gardenias, and behind, holding a coral silk parasol, sat her young black servant. Impossible for the king and court to ignore, the vision in pink and blue was universally admired and discussed. There were already some who saw in her a possible chance of unseating the reigning favorite, and it was whispered that the little d'Etioles might be a tasty morsel to set before the king. Louis had no such thoughts, but it was noticed and remarked upon, both at Choisy, where the king lodged, and at the Château d'Etioles, that he often sent his pretty neighbor gifts of venison more choice than those despatched to the other ladies of the locality.

AFTER THE DEATH of his mistress Madame de Ventimille in 1741, Louis XV had been grief-stricken. In an effort to console him, and also in the hope that the king would take her back, the faithful Madame de Mailly, who now spent her time working for the poor, adopted her sister's royal bastard. But her gesture was in vain, and the vacancy was filled instead by the youngest de Mailly sister, Madame Marie Anne de Tournelle. Much prettier and far nastier than either of her predecessors, she stated her terms before accepting the king. The official title of *maîtresse en titre* was to be revived, with all the honors, position and power it entailed. Even when she had been created Duchesse de Châteauroux, Marie Anne showed no sympathy for her deposed sister, and had her separated from their little nephew. As gifts, she demanded a grand house in Paris, jewels and a monthly income. Finally, any children she might have with the king must be legitimized. Only then would the alluring Marie Anne de Tournelle capitulate. Louis had fallen deeply in love with this cold, cruel woman, and agreed to everything. In return, the new duchess used and abused the king, and yet she was probably the great passion of his life.

Madame de Châteauroux was a protegée of her cousin the Duc de

Richelieu, who used her to grasp more power through the king's infatuation. Since the age of thirteen, Louis had relied totally on the
brilliant, ambitious Cardinal Fleury to decide France's policies. After
the cardinal's death in 1743 at the age of eighty-nine, the king had
determined to rule himself, as Louis XIV had done, and to head his
council, which governed France. But Louis XV did not have ministers
of the caliber of those of his great-grandfather and he found himself
surrounded mostly by mediocrities. Richelieu wanted control of the
council, and under his management and tutelage the new duchess became so powerful that only a year after her installation she was Queen
of France in all but name. Unfortunately, Cardinal Fleury had never
encouraged the king to develop and trust his own sound political in-
stincts. As a result, his sense of inferiority grew, and he relied totally
on his ministers' advice.

At the instigation of Richelieu, by 1744 Madame de Châteauroux
had persuaded the king to take personal command of his armies'
spring offensive in the War of the Austrian Succession. Louis loved
campaigning almost as much as hunting, and Madame de Châteauroux craved success for her lover, wanting him to shine like a star for
his people, with herself at his side, the inspiration behind the triumph
of France.

As the king had refused to take the queen with him to the front,
his mistress was also left behind. Bored and anxious with Louis out of
her sight, Madame de Châteauroux decided to risk joining her royal
lover, although no summons had been sent. She need not have worried. Louis was delighted to see her, and her position seemed unas-
sailable.

At first all went well, and the French armies won several splendid
victories; then, in August, Louis fell seriously ill at Metz in Flanders.
As his fever rose and his condition grew worse, the nation realized
with alarm that their king might die. Panic seized Madame de
Châteauroux. Although she and Richelieu tried everything to calm
Louis' fears about his condition, finally they had to admit that the end
seemed near. To prepare himself to meet his maker, the king knew he
would have to abandon his beloved mistress and beg forgiveness for
his sins. With deep regret, and only at the insistence of the bishops, he
bade her farewell and sent her home to Paris. Louis then called for a

priest, the queen and the dauphin. Receiving them warmly, he asked God and then his wife to pardon him, reconciled their differences and spoke kindly to his son.

Traditionally, the French disliked their foreign queens, but as no one could deny Marie Leczinska's goodness and charity, she was very popular. Not so Madame de Châteauroux. The Parisians in particular had always hated the king's favorites, and blamed the nation's ills on their sovereigns' "little weakness." Mistresses squandered their hard-earned taxes, were notoriously extravagant, and interfered in politics. Madame de Châteauroux came in for special abuse, not least for her unkindness to the queen.

When the people realized that the reigning favorite had been dismissed, they threw rotting vegetables at her carriage on its way to Paris, jeering and shouting, *"Voilà la putain!"* To add to her shame, the newly deposed *maîtresse en titre* had passed the queen's carriage on the road heading toward Metz and her dying husband's side. Madame de Châteauroux's nerves were shattered. Suffering from the shock of losing her protector and her position, and of witnessing the people's violent hatred, she took to her bed. Mobs surrounded her house screaming abuse, and when once she dared venture out she was almost torn from her carriage.

Before allowing the king the last sacraments, the bishops had forced him to make a public confession. As if that was not sufficiently humiliating for this shy and intensely private man, the document was printed and distributed throughout every parish in France. The following Sunday, there was not a single priest who was not preaching against Louis XV's adulteries from his pulpit.

But the king did not die; his illness passed as suddenly as it had come and he recovered completely. Shamed and enraged by the publicity the Church gave his confession, he returned to Versailles as soon as he was well enough to travel, denied any intention of changing his ways, and sent for Madame de Châteauroux.

It was December and cold when the duchess received the king's summons. Weakened by her long confinement, and frantic to be with him again, she rose too quickly from her sickbed, caught a chill and collapsed with pneumonia. Bled nine times during eleven days of pain and delirium, Madame de Châteauroux died without ever seeing

Louis XV again. She had ruled the king and court for four years, and with her death, the ten-year-long grip of the de Mailly sisters on Louis XV's heart had ended.

By sharing the perils of war with his soldiers, the king had won the love of his subjects. After his miraculous recovery at Metz, his popularity reached its highest point to date, and Louis XV, thirty-four years old, was thereafter called *"le Bien-Aimé,"* the Well-Beloved.

⸎

THE ONLY SAD event in the otherwise enchanted life of the young Madame d'Etioles was the death of her baby son, born a year after her marriage. Unlike her own mother, Jeanne-Antoinette was a devoted parent, and the baby's death affected her deeply. However, in August 1744, as the king lay apparently dying at Metz, she gave birth to her second child, a daughter she named Alexandrine, after Madame de Tencin. Shortly afterward, Madame d'Etioles heard of Louis XV's confession and repentance, his reconciliation with the queen and repudiation of his favorite. She had felt sure that she was already loved by the king, and this news of his return to Church and queen destroyed her hopes. Her distress was so great that she became seriously ill, and almost died.

⸎

MADAME DE CHÂTEAUROUX'S death left the king inconsolable, and he became subject to black moods alternating with bursts of religious fervor. Briefly and unsuccessfully, he tried to relieve his loneliness and fill the gap left by his beloved *maîtresse en titre* with the fourth de Mailly sister, the Duchesse de Lauraguais, but his depression remained.

Jeanne-Antoinette, on the other hand, had reason once again to believe in her impossible dream. She was not alone. In her immediate circle there were others who had good reason to raise the hopes of the accomplished, lovely Madame d'Etioles.

The King of France's official mistress was in a position to make or break political alliances, careers and fortunes. In the hope of subsequent favor, the brothers Pâris and Madame Tencin had used their considerable influence (as accomplices of the Duc de Richelieu) in elevating Madame de Châteauroux to the most coveted and lucrative post in France. A year before her death, her arrogance and intractability had prompted the same group to try to promote another candidate, and the name of Madame d'Etioles had been whispered in the corridors of Versailles. Madame de Châteauroux had taken these rumors of a potential rival seriously enough to stamp hard on the foot of a friend who dared to flatteringly mention the name of *"la dame en rose,"* as Jeanne-Antoinette had become known, in the king's presence. This was a warning Madame d'Etioles realized she could not afford to ignore, and thereafter she declined to join the royal hunt. The king did not see her again in the forest that summer, but his gifts of venison continued.

As well as mourning Madame de Châteauroux, Louis had also just suffered the loss of his dear old governess, Madame de Ventadour, who had saved him from Dr. Fagon, the "killer of princes." She had brought him up, and he had never ceased to call her *"Maman."* Restrained by etiquette from showing his grief in public, Louis had withdrawn in his sorrow to the Trianon Palace. There Binet, Baron de Marchais, the dauphin's chief valet, joined Lebel, chief valet to the king, in trying to console him. Both men, who were in their sovereign's confidence, regaled him with the latest gossip from Paris, and told him of the countless expectant hearts beating faster with desire to replace Madame de Châteauroux. And both men had a candidate it was in their joint interest to promote.

Binet was a cousin of Madame d'Etioles through La Motte, and Lebel had once been a lover of Madame Poisson. Tentatively they reminded the king of the ravishing vision who had caught his eye so often in the forest of Sénart, the goddess in pink who drove her phaeton with such skill and dash in pursuit of the hunt. True, she was from the bourgeoisie, but would not such a naive beauty make a refreshing change from the greedy schemers at court? Perhaps an elegant, refined young woman, without pretensions, powerful connections or involvement in any court intrigue, might amuse the king and make an ideal distraction for a short while? "She has only one ambition, Sire," claimed Binet, a habitué of the Château d'Etioles. "To please the one she longs to please." Of course, it was impossible for a member of the bourgeoisie to be presented to the king, but the public balls during carnival might provide the perfect cover.

There was an added excitement to the usual pre-Lenten carnival season of 1745. In February, the Dauphin of France was to be married to the Infanta Maria-Theresa of Spain, a sister of the little Infanta sent home as too young to marry Louis XV. This was a popular match in both countries, as the union of these two royal houses would help reduce the chances of war. The month-long celebrations included a number of masked balls which the king could attend incognito. Louis XV loved dancing, and the celebrations would create a welcome diversion.

The appointment of a new *maîtresse en titre* was considered so important by the court, by society and by the ambassadors of the great foreign monarchs that it was the chief topic of conversation and speculation. Names of aristocratic beauties reverberated throughout Versailles, the salons of the bourgeoisie and the streets of Paris. During the many public and private balls that February, rumors grew that the king had been seen with the same masked companion and had kept a number of secret rendezvous. On several occasions Louis had returned to Versailles at dawn, but no one name could be linked with certainty to his.

The dauphin's wedding festivities were to reach their climax in a private full-dress ball at Versailles on Wednesday, February 24, and a public fancy-dress ball the following evening, commencing at midnight. It was known among Jeanne-Antoinette's friends that she had received one of the coveted invitations to attend the ball on February 24. It was also common knowledge that there was not an empty bed in the tiniest room or cupboard at the palace that had not been reserved for the wedding guests. Although Madame d'Etioles had not mentioned her plans to her intrigued friends, President Hénault could not resist asking her where she would stay at Versailles. The charming old gossip's ears buzzed when she answered that he need not worry— her cousin, Sieur Binet, would find a bed there for her. Binet's domestic proximity to the king was no secret to anyone.

The royal wedding was celebrated for three consecutive days, and each night the façade of Versailles was lit by countless candles. The formal religious ceremony took place on February 23. The next evening, those privileged to attend the full-dress ball witnessed a memorable spectacle. Thousands of torches lit the avenue de Paris, and when the carriages drew up at the entrance to the palace to deposit their glittering, bejeweled and bewigged passengers, the crush was so great that it took an hour for the guests, clutching hooped skirts and swords, to make their way up the wide, sweeping marble steps.

Sadly, there is no record of the entrance made by Madame d'Etioles into the huge palace riding school, which had been beautifully converted for the occasion. Lit by fifteen enormous crystal chandeliers, it had been decorated with ribbons and swags of flowers under a ceiling painted with putti cavorting in the clouds. After watching a performance of the ballet, the guests looked down from their plush boxes and balconies as the little blond Infanta passed gracefully beneath them in a dress of silver brocade and sparkling with diamonds. Voltaire's nuptial eulogy was drowned by the noise in the vast, crowded room where the guests danced to an orchestra of five hundred musicians.

The following evening, the king opened the doors of his palace to admit the general public for the great fancy-dress ball in the Hall of Mirrors. As long as they were properly dressed and wearing masks, anyone could attend, but no one had expected that so many would. Double lines of coaches, four torches on each, filled the road from the capital and continued in an unbroken stream to the palace glowing in the distance. As the carriages pulled up in front of Versailles, attempts to take down names at the two entrances had to be abandoned as hundreds of masked guests streamed through the doors into the state apartments. The dazzled revellers swarmed through the great halls dedicated to Hercules, Mars, Apollo and Mercury, each with its own orchestra playing, and toward the sagging buffets. As it was Friday morning, only fish was offered, but in many varieties, and the wines flowed freely. Grabbing plates, glasses and cutlery, they stuffed their pockets with anything that came to hand (someone even managed to abscond with a large gold girandole). Much of the exotic fruit was carried away by the guests and reappeared next morning on the market stalls in Paris. Wave upon wave of the public swept on through the state rooms, to the dismay and disgust of the watching courtiers, until they reached their destination, the *Galerie des Glaces*, Versailles' fabled Hall of Mirrors.

No one could have been disappointed on entering this magnificent room. Huge buffets at either end were stacked with mountains of fresh salmon, fillets of sole, trout pâtés and fruits, and there was no shortage of wine. In the *Galerie des Glaces* it was impossible to move. Harlequins and Columbines, Turks, Scaramouches, shepherds and shepherdesses, jostled one another and were reflected again and again in the mirrored walls, making the crowd appear even larger.

The queen seldom attended court balls, considering herself either too old or too pious for dancing, and the dauphin disapproved on principle of anything that might be thought fun. But on her son's wedding night, Marie Leczinska made one of her rare appearances. Suddenly, the double glass doors swung open to admit the forty-year-old queen, unmasked, resplendent in a magnificent brocade dress, the great crown diamonds, the Regent and the Sancy, blazing in her hair. She was accompanied by the bride and groom, also unmasked and charmingly dressed as flower sellers.

An unfortunate incident marred the beginning of French court life for the little Spanish dauphine. She was invited to dance by a tall, elegant, masked gentleman, who spoke perfect Spanish and was extremely well informed about the company and the court. She accepted, and was delighted with her companion. Feeling certain he must be a Spanish grandee, she asked him to reveal his identity, whereupon the mysterious Spaniard disappeared. Later it became known that he was a chef in the household of a courtier. For the little Infanta, educated in a protocol far more constrained even than the French, this was a terrible indignity.

It was quite late when the double doors of the king's antechamber opened. The crowd parted to make way for a curious procession of seven identical yew trees, square-clipped like those in the park, their bodies, or trunks, topped by headdresses of green taffeta leaves. There were two holes in the middle for the eyes. No one doubted that the king was among them, but which was he? The joke had been Louis' idea, to confuse the number of ladies whom he knew hoped to capture him that evening. One such lady of the court, certain she had identified the king, disappeared with her tree into the garden. She returned extremely disheveled but flushed with triumph, only to see the real king standing relaxed and unmasked inside. He was flirting with a beautiful, laughing Diana in a cherry-red domino, who was aiming a silver arrow at his heart. She was the lovely huntress from the forest of Sénart, and Louis had eyes for no one else.

Before leaving the ball, Madame d'Etioles symbolically dropped her handkerchief at the king's feet. He retrieved it, and with a charming mime of adoration, pressed it to his heart for all to see. Instantly, a buzz circled the room: *"Le mouchoir est jeté"*—The kerchief is thrown—muttered the courtiers, who had seen the king pick it up with the traditional gesture. This was the signal everyone had been waiting for, but no one believed it possible for the King of France to have anything but a brief liaison with a member of the bourgeoisie.

The next evening the city of Paris gave a public ball for the bridal couple. The king arrived late, deliberately avoiding the dauphin, who had already left with his bride. Accompanied only by his friend the Duc d'Ayen, and like him wearing a black domino, he entered the town hall as incognito as possible, and immediately found Madame d'Etioles. The meeting was clearly not by chance. Jeanne-Antoinette was also wearing black, which made her beautiful coloring and alabaster skin glow more than usual. The crowd was denser than the night before, and several observers noticed the crushed disarray of the lady in black before she disappeared into a private supper room with the two tall masked men. A short while later, three guests in black dominoes left the ball and flagged down a hackney carriage.

Madame d'Etioles was playing for the highest stakes in the land, and she did not lose her head now. When the king asked where he should take her, she replied: Home to mother! This display of modesty had the desired effect, and excited Louis even more. Louis did not return home to Versailles until nine the following morning. It is possible, but unlikely, that Jeanne-Antoinette succumbed during that night, but throughout the following week her coach was seen on the road between Paris and Versailles, and also several times waiting at the palace.

The queen's friend the Duc de Luynes noted in his diary on March 19, 1745:

All those masked balls have provided opportunities to talk about the King's new *affaire,* and principally about a certain Madame d'Etioles, who is young and pretty; her mother is Madame Poisson. It is said that for some time now she has been constantly here, and that she is the King's choice. If this is true, she can be only a passing fancy and not a permanent mistress.

The Duc de Luynes echoed the prevailing opinion of the court, as no one could imagine their king choosing his *maîtresse en titre* from any other than their own illustrious circle.

During the next weeks, the king failed to appear several times to dine with his usual friends, and it was thought he had supped instead with Madame d'Etioles.

When it became the turn of the ambassadors to celebrate the dauphin's wedding with a number of festivities in Paris, the king did not attend. Again it was rumored he was somewhere with the lovely, graceful Madame d'Etioles. On April 1 she was observed looking ravishing at the palace theater for a performance of the Italian opera, seated in a box opposite that of the king. Tongues continued to wag. The Marquis d'Argenson, a courtier who was to become her bitter enemy, remarked in his generally malicious diary: "She is snow-white, without features, but graceful and talented." Another courtier, the Marquis de Valfons, wrote: "With her grace, the lightness of her figure and the beauty of her hair, she resembled a nymph."

Many speculated whether Madame d'Etioles stayed in Madame de Mailly's tiny apartment at Versailles, which could be reached from the king's rooms by a small staircase, but no one was sure. On several occasions, Jeanne-Antoinette was included among the king's closest friends in the intimate supper parties in his private apartments. On April 10, de Luynes noted that the rumors about Madame d'Etioles continued. "She is very pretty," he admitted in his diary. "Everyone found her extremely polite with never a harsh word for anyone."

When the Bishop of Mirepoix attacked Binet for procuring and assisting his beautiful cousin to divert the king from the Ten Commandments, the valet complained to his sovereign. Although Louis was angry that his private life was again being interfered with by the

Church, he hesitated and insisted that Jeanne-Antoinette continue to keep their relationship unofficial.

Madame d'Etioles was in a difficult position. Her husband, who had been sent on a long business trip by the tactful de Tournehem, knew nothing of his wife's romantic adventure and was due back after Easter in a few weeks. Her situation with Louis badly needed clarification before his return.

It was decided that de Tournehem should explain to his nephew that he had lost his wife to the king. Le Normant really loved Jeanne-Antoinette, and when he was told the news he was so distraught that weapons had to be hidden from him. In despair, he wrote his wife a long, touching letter. When she showed it to the king, to his credit, he observed with some shame that her husband was indeed a gentleman. Madame d'Etioles still needed to know Louis' mind concerning her future; she could hardly return to live with her husband in Paris. With no choice but to force the king's hand, this accomplished actress feigned terror and begged his protection from her desperate husband. Louis XV was always embarrassed by any show of emotion, and immediately offered to accommodate his new mistress at Versailles.

By April 27, the courtiers were saying openly that the king and Madame d'Etioles were in love.

Jeanne-Antoinette Poisson had played her cards to perfection and achieved her life's ambition—she had won the king's heart. But for how long? Keeping the king's love would be more difficult. Luck and timing were both on her side, and Madame d'Etioles was fortunate in the respite fate now gave her.

⁓⁓⁓

BY 1745, THE War of the Austrian Succession was in its fifth year. It seemed as if the rulers of all Europe coveted Austria's crown or some part of its empire, and forgot their pledges to the dying Emperor Charles VI to honor his daughter's birthright. The Archduchess Maria Theresa of Austria was only twenty-three when her father died, and no match for the contenders for her throne. As legitimate male Habsburg descendants, the rulers of Spain, Sardinia, Saxony, Bavaria and, most of all, the twenty-eight-year-old King Frederick II of Prussia, even the Pope, all claimed a right to a part of imperial territory. A complicated system of allegiances had embroiled France in this European conflict. As France already had sufficient territory, Louis XV had made no claim. His interest lay in breaking the Habsburg tradition as overlords of Europe. With the support of France, the weak candidature of Charles-Albert of Bavaria might succeed. Should he be crowned emperor, Bavaria would assume supremacy in Germany. This was just what Louis XV's tricky ally, Frederick II of Prussia, wished to gain for himself—as well as Austria's richest province of Silesia. In 1744, Prussia had failed to come to France's aid, and when Louis XV's province of Alsace was being threatened by Austria's ally, England, France had also declared war on the Queen of Hungary.*

After the appalling defeat of his army at Dettingen, Louis XV had appointed the Maréchal de Saxe to be the commander in chief of his armies. This was a fortunate choice, as Maurice de Saxe was one of the most brilliant military strategists of the time. He was also the bastard son of Augustus, Elector of Saxony, King of Poland.† Under his command France won a series of victories early in 1745. By Easter, the king felt it was time to return to Flanders and show himself to his army. He left with the dauphin on May 6.

The following week, during her husband's absence on business for de Tournehem, the parlement officially granted Madame d'Etioles a decree of separation. The sitting had been arranged for six in the morning, and passed unnoticed. Charles Collin, newly appointed to her household, represented Jeanne-Antoinette's interests. She never saw her husband again.

---

* Maria Theresa of Austria was first known and crowned as Queen of Hungary, then as Queen of Bohemia. She only became empress after the death of her father's successor, the Emperor Charles VII (of Bavaria), when her husband Francis of Lorraine was elected Holy Roman Emperor at the end of 1745.

† The birth of Maurice de Saxe was the result of a tragic illicit love affair. George I of England's wife, Sophia Dorothea, had as her lover Count von Königsmark. When Königsmark mysteriously disappeared, his distraught sister, Maria Aurora von Königsmark, of all things an abbess, searched everywhere for a solution. She even threw herself on the mercy of Augustus of Saxony, King of Poland, with such energy that she became pregnant. The resulting child was Maurice de Saxe. To honor his great marshal, Louis XV invited Maurice de Saxe's niece Josefa of Saxony to marry his son, the dauphin. Maurice de Saxe also produced an illegitimate child through whom he became the ancestor of Aurore Dupin, better known as the French writer George Sand, lover of Frédéric Chopin.

Madame d'Etioles had no wish to tempt fate like Madame de Châteauroux and join the king at the front; instead, she retired to her estates for the summer, accompanied by her ailing mother and a small group of carefully chosen friends. There was much work to be done if the little bourgeoise was to survive at Versailles. Court ritual was so complicated that it would be easy for the envious to make fun of the upstart's origins and ignorance of their ways. Should she fail to comply with the court's procedures, language or code of behavior, she would be ridiculed. That would rebound on the king, and ridicule was something he would never tolerate.

To avoid such a catastrophe, Louis had arranged for the abbé Bernis, a recognized authority on court usage and genealogy, to stay with Jeanne-Antoinette in his absence and instruct her thoroughly. The jovial, entertaining abbé, though only in his thirties, had recently been made a member of the French Academy, and was wise beyond his years. He sensed every potential pitfall and knew every social stumbling block. His consistent good humor, gentle wit and apparent lack of ambition had endeared him to all the factions at court, and made him the perfect choice. Already Bernis had come to like and admire the young châtelaine of Etioles.

After spending this happy summer in her company, the abbé fell totally under Jeanne-Antoinette's spell and became her true, loyal friend and adviser. Bernis was a scion of an ancient noble family, and possessed all the necessary quarterings to enable him to school the king's new love in the complicated litany of the courtiers' genealogy. Years later, he wrote of that summer spent at Etioles:

> I went each week [from Etioles] to Paris, and I made her feelings and intentions known discreetly. I advised her about giving patronage to men of letters, who had bestowed the title of Great on Louis XIV. It was not necessary for me to suggest that she should care for and make friends with honest people: it was one of her cherished principles.*

According to Bernis, Louis had forbidden any other men to visit Etioles except the Marquis de Gontaut, who came to help with her "tu-

* Quoted by Pierre de Nolhac.

ition" and left as another staunch ally. Her family, of course, were welcome, and her cousin Madame d'Estrades stayed with her at Etioles. Brunoy, "Uncle" de Tournehem's beautiful château, was on the other side of the forest of Sénart, within easy reach for Jeanne-Antoinette in her little phaeton or on horseback.

De Tournehem had known and loved Reinette all her life; there was no doubt where his preference lay regarding his nephew and adopted niece. She had charmed him since her earliest childhood, and this fondness for her must have influenced his generosity to the Poisson family. The same could be said for her godfather, Pâris-Montmartel, who was also staying with de Tournehem that summer. Other guests at Brunoy were Madame Tencin and her brother the cardinal. As the godmother of little Alexandrine, Madame de Tencin qualified as family, and all three visited Etioles regularly throughout that summer.

If any of Jeanne-Antoinette's family or friends were surprised at her meteoric rise, they did not show it. All basked in her reflected glory—none more than Voltaire, who wrote immediately inviting himself to Etioles, and sent elaborate poems praising her conquest of the king's heart.

❦

HAPPILY LOUIS ALSO had another victory to celebrate. After the conquest of Ghent, the Maréchal de Saxe and the king had conferred at Versailles and decided on the date and place for the next, hopefully decisive, battle. Louis was buoyant after his army's recent successes, full of conviction that the forthcoming campaign would result in triumph for France—and he was in love. His spirits were high, and he felt invincible. Sensing a great victory within his grasp, he had decided to take the dauphin with him to the front. It was a very long time since a King of France had ridden into battle against the English, much longer since a French king had fought them with his dauphin by his side.

The Battle of Fontenoy, which was waged according to the traditional rules, was a spectacular victory for France, but won at a terrible price. When the French engaged with the English, commanded by the Duke of Cumberland,* they were unaware that the enemy had developed a new system of firing and reloading in quick rotation. The Maréchal de Saxe was a most charismatic leader and was adored by his troops. To his horror and disbelief, and in full view of the royal party, the French infantry was totally annihilated. When the day seemed lost, a distraught de Saxe asked the king and the dauphin to withdraw, as their position was within the enemy's range. De Saxe, too ill to ride, had moved about and commanded from a horse-drawn litter, but the Duc de Richelieu, galloping about the battlefield, had noted the exhaustion of the Anglo-Dutch troops. He urged the king to take advantage of this and to use the last four French cannon and his still-fresh Household Cavalry to renew the attack. Louis agreed, and the sudden bombardment from the French, followed by the unexpected charge of the cavalry commanded by the Earl of Dillon, snatched a victory from certain defeat. Although Dillon was killed in the charge, his Catholic-Irish regiment, in service with the French, seized their chance for revenge on the English after fifty years of persecution, and their ferocious attack won the day for France.

In the face of disaster, Louis XV had shown courage and a cool head; now he taught his son compassion. Orders were given for the hospitals of northern France to treat the wounded of all nationalities.

⌘

THROUGHOUT THE GENTLE summer of 1745, silence reigned in the forest of Sénart, as all the hunters were at the front with the king. Jeanne-Antoinette was surrounded by dear friends; it was to be her last tranquil summer. She received almost daily letters from Louis, written on top of an upturned drum. Addressed to "Madame d'Etioles à Etioles," they arrived via "Uncle" de Tournehem at Brunoy, and Jeanne-Antoinette's replies went by the same route. On July 7 she received Louis' first letter addressed to "Madame la Marquise de Pompadour." It was sealed with the motto: *"Discret et Fidèle."*

Louis XV had decided to revive this beautiful but recently extinct Limousin title to honor and ennoble the woman he loved. He had

---

* "A great ass" in the opinion of his first cousin, Frederick II of Prussia.

bought her the estate of Pompadour, together with its coat of arms (three silver towers on an azure ground), from the Prince de Conti. In the interest of discretion, the king borrowed the money privately from Jeanne-Antoinette's godfather, the banker Pâris-Montmartel. Neither the ennoblement nor the title came as a surprise to the lovely new marquise.

The return of the triumphant king and dauphin on September 7 marked the apogee of Louis XV's popularity. Paris declared a holiday and accorded the victors an extraordinary reception. Shops were closed, triumphal arches erected, fountains spouted wine and balconies were hung with tapestries and flowers. At the town hall, the royal family were fêted with a splendid banquet followed by a magnificent display of fireworks. On an upper floor, a room had been set aside for a private party, whose guest of honor was the Marquise de Pompadour. The dishes served were the same as those presented to the king and his family. Although Louis did not leave his table downstairs, the marquise received the Duc de Gesvres, governor of Paris, as well as the ducs de Richelieu and de Bouillon and the chief of police, all of whom paid her their respects. Madame de Pompadour and her guests, who were mostly from her family, retired at eleven o'clock.

Three days later, the court moved back to Versailles. The king sent a coach for Madame de Pompadour and quietly installed her in Madame de Châteauroux's former apartments. From this day until her death twenty years later, *"la marquise,"* as the king would always call her, reigned supreme over Louis XV's heart and court.

For Madame de Pompadour to be accepted as Louis XV's official mistress, be accorded the title of *maîtresse en titre,* and hold a position of importance at court, she would have to be publicly presented to the king, the queen, the dauphin and the princesses. This tradition had existed for hundreds of years and, awkward and embarrassing as it would be, it could not be avoided. Moreover, she would have to be deemed acceptable to them all by the watching court. That path to presentation was a potential minefield.

Before the dreaded occasion in a week's time, a court post had to be found for her, as well as a sponsor who would make the formal introduction to the royal family. As the queen, the dauphin and the princesses all knew Madame de Pompadour was the king's new love, the sponsor's position was a particularly delicate one vis-à-vis the royal family, especially as the queen was heard to remark: "Which one of our sluts is to present the woman?" In view of the dubious role of a *maîtresse en titre,* no less a personage than a cousin of the monarch was considered suitable as a sponsor. The Princesse de Conti, whose husband had just sold the Pompadour estate to the king, reluctantly agreed when Louis offered to pay her huge gambling debts. The marquise would be accompanied by her cousin Madame d'Estrades and another lady.

By all accounts, Madame de Pompadour looked superb in her presentation gown with short white muslin sleeves, the skirt of heavily embroidered satin draped over wide panniers and trailing a narrow train. The three ladies all wore small white feathers in their lightly powdered hair, held in place by diamond circlets. Under the gaze of a packed court, Madame de Pompadour and her attendants passed from one crowded gallery to another with tiny gliding steps, until they reached the king's council chamber. Looking pale with no makeup except a dusting of rouge, she made her deep curtsies before a visibly embarrassed Louis. Avoiding one another's eyes, the lovers mumbled a few awkward words before the little procession tripped lightly on to the queen's rooms.

The courtiers were even more curious to see Marie Leczinska's reaction to her new rival, and crowded into the Galerie des Glaces. It was traditional at the French court to express "no comment" by making one or two remarks about a lady's dress. Neither the toilette of the Marquise de Pompadour nor her court *révérences** could be criticized, but no one anticipated the queen's generous words to her husband's new mistress, least of all the mistress herself. A stunned court heard Marie Leczinska make a kind reference to a mutual friend, a woman who happened to be the only aristocrat the Poisson family had always known. By this generosity, the queen had officially established the former Madame Etioles, about whose Poisson antecedents such vile stories were circulating, as perfectly acceptable at court in her eyes. Jeanne-Antoinette had expected anything but this.

---

* Formal deep curtsies.

Blushing with confusion, she blurted out that her only wish was to serve Her Majesty, and stammered her profoundest respect.

The queen's attitude is difficult to explain in those days of rigid protocol. Perhaps Marie Leczinska simply enjoyed being contrary on one of the rare moments when she held the court's total attention. She knew with what undisguised glee the courtiers had waited for her to snub the little bourgeoise. Nor had she forgotten the callousness and cruelty of the de Nesle sisters. It may be that she hoped this mistress, with her beautiful manners, might show her some consideration in return. The aristocratic birth of the de Nesles had not prevented them from alienating the queen even further from the king, and if a bourgeoise made her domestic life more agreeable, so much the better. It would have been so easy for Marie Leczinska to have mortified Madame de Pompadour in front of all the court, but by her unexpected graciousness, she earned the favorite's respect and gratitude for life.

In contrast to his mother, the religious, priggish dauphin dismissed Madame de Pompadour with a chilly observation on her dress. The camps had formed.

A little reluctantly, everyone was forced to admit that the king's new love had come out of the ordeal rather well. Her grace and bearing could not be denied, her elegance had impressed many, and most agreed that, apart from her birth, she was a marked improvement on her predecessors.

The dreaded presentation behind her, Madame de Pompadour settled down to life at Versailles. In the early months, Louis almost never left her side. When he did have to leave her, she spent her time studying the secrets of court etiquette and feudal heritage. Her life was made a misery by the courtiers' jealousy, and the one chink in her formidable armor of accomplishments—her bourgeois origins—was seized upon by everyone in their desire to belittle her. Under the daily scrutiny of the courtiers, her smallest mistakes were noted and derided. Minute breaches of ancient, meaningless traditions led to sniggering behind hands wherever she went. Although it seemed to her that Louis did little to protect her from the constant sniping and smirking, her one consolation was his total devotion.

Easily bored, the king appeared much less so since her official installation, which was not surprising. The delicious Jeanne-Antoinette was always ready to entertain and amuse him with a never-ending supply of stories and anecdotes. With the training she had received from Crébillon, she had become a brilliant raconteuse and was very amusing. A natural prankster, the king loved to tease, something neither his wife nor his other mistresses had appreciated. His graceful, witty Pompadour was always full of fun and good humor, as well as being a fountain of fresh and amusing ideas.

She asked a friend, the head of the Paris gendarmerie, to bring her the strangest excerpts from the police reports, and any remarkable or odd letters which the censor had noticed, and then read them to the king in a way that made him collapse with laughter. If he wanted music, she could sing beautifully to suit his mood, accompanying herself on the clavichord. By reciting poetry and soliloquies from plays, she awakened in him a real liking for drama. Jeanne-Antoinette was the ideal hostess, consistently charming, organizing every detail, and never presenting Louis with too many guests or strangers, as he hated new faces. With her light touch and sensitivity, she succeeded in smoothing the shy king's path through any difficult conversation or awkward silence. She was the perfect companion for Louis, and he felt totally at ease in her company.

However, there was a major problem in their relationship, and it gave the favorite great anxiety. Once they had experienced the initial novelty and physical wonder of two people in love, and the urgency of their shared desire had eased, Madame de Pompadour was forced to accept that her capacity for passion did not match that of her royal lover. After nine years of faithfulness to an intensely religious and rather dull woman, Louis XV had discovered his libido in the arms of his various mistresses. A typical Bourbon, he was passionate and physically very demanding, practically to the point of being insatiable. It should be remembered that, in eighteenth-century France, making love was regarded almost exclusively as a gratification of desire, and did not have the emotional overtones of today.

The king was the center of Jeanne-Antoinette's world; near him, she was perfectly happy, but this handsome, sensual man often made her feel inadequate as a lover. Her education had led her to so many other interests: her mind was alive and attuned to every intellectual pursuit; her imagination was geared to the appreciation of every form of beauty, excellence and endeavor. The Marquise de Pompadour was the personification of Renaissance woman, and in her cultivated mind and fragile body, lust did not play a significant part.

Like many unimaginative men, the king needed stimulation and variety from his partner to satisfy his sexual appetite. Madame de Pompadour loved Louis intensely and with all her being, but she was essentially a physically cool woman. Sex was an ordeal for her, and trying to quench the king's desire tested her strength to the point of exhaustion. Yet the thought of losing his love, were he to leave her bed for another, drove her to distraction.

In her attempts to somehow increase her passion, Madame de Pompadour took every sort of aphrodisiac, and tried a variety of quack elixirs. Not surprisingly, she became ill and very thin—at one point her diet consisted of chocolate with triple essence of vanilla, truffles and celery! After the first occasion that the king left her bed and slept on a sofa in her room, she confided her fears to her friend the Duchesse de Brancas. This sound woman gave her good advice, and threw her elixirs into the fire. She urged the favorite to concentrate more on her health, and assured her that men were victims of their habits. Of course she must never refuse the king's advances, but by making herself indispensable to him in every other way, she would find that his natural apathy would counter his roving eye, and he would never leave her.

Madame de Pompadour hated Versailles—*"ce pays-ci"* (this country) as it was referred to by those who lived there. At heart she was a Parisienne, and she missed the capital, but for love of the king, whom she had worshipped for so many years, she would do anything. Her life revolved solely around him, and there was no sacrifice too great to make him love her in return. She followed the advice of her friend, concentrated on her health, took more exercise, applied herself to the king's emotional and psychological needs; and let the rest take care of itself. Anyone who observed Louis XV and Madame de Pompadour in their early years together saw two people in total harmony, a union of spirits, minds and bodies.

Jeanne-Antoinette was used to stimulating company and brilliant conversation, and the king could hardly be described as being the one or capable of the other. Her real interest lay in the intellectual world of *les philosophes,* but there were few if any to be found at court. After their separation during the summer of 1742, Louis had taken his beloved and a small group of courtiers to Choisy. Madame de Pompadour was able to include a few friends of her own, and she added Voltaire, Duclos and the abbé Prevost.

Although he felt at ease with architects and enjoyed the company of painters and sculptors, Louis XV was always uncomfortable with writers, especially the waspish, tactless Voltaire, and Madame de Pompadour did not repeat the experiment. The king was a far shrewder judge of character than his mistress, and he never trusted Voltaire. The philosopher certainly proved a fickle friend, but later in his life, when he had no more reason to curry favor with king or commoner, he wrote (in his *Eloge Funèbre*) that posterity should not listen to "those secret legends which are spread about a Prince in his lifetime out of spite, or a mere love of gossip, which a mistaken public believes to be true and which, in a few more years, are adopted by the historians who thus deceive themselves and the generations to come."

Excepting the presence of the intellectuals, the king enjoyed his stay at Choisy so much he was actually heard singing—slightly out of tune. When the queen heard one day that her husband was unwell and asked if she might visit him there, to her surprise she was made most welcome, and found Louis in good spirits. His brief illness had been the result of merry excess—too much food, drink and lovemaking.

Louis kept Jeanne-Antoinette constantly busy, leaving her no time to herself. Never having known a woman who combined the role of mistress, wise counselor and friend, Louis was entranced by her, and relied on her more each day. She had the gift of keeping him interested and entertained, of knowing when to stop, and when to stop others who were beginning to irritate or bore him. Madame de Pompadour loved the king unreservedly; she understood him and empathized with him. Harnessing her formidable energy, she concentrated on helping him in any and every way. To this end, as well as for her own sake, she set about consolidating her position and establishing a power base at court that could not be challenged. It was not long before everyone realized that Louis XV blossomed in the gentle care of his fascinating new mistress.

Of course Madame de Pompadour knew that the very nature of her position as the official mistress automatically created enemies. These she noted carefully, especially the brothers d'Argenson, the Duc de Richelieu, and the secretary of state and of the navy, the Comte de Maurepas. As foreign minister, the Marquis d'Argenson jealously guarded his proximity to the sovereign. His diary, though strongly biased, is an invaluable source on the lives of those at Versailles. When he was dismissed from the court two years later, in 1747, it was not actually at her instigation, and he was incorrect in blaming her. Nonetheless, he spent the rest of his life pouring out his venom into the diary. His brother, the Comte d'Argenson, remained at court, a thorn in the favorite's side for years. Richelieu, who still chose to think of her as a passing fancy of his sovereign, resented her for his inability to influence her. By the exacting standards of the French aristocracy, the duke was something of an arriviste himself, and he despised Jeanne-Antoinette even more for her meteoric rise. As for the Comte de Maurepas, his wit complemented his poisonous pen. As a childhood friend of the king's and the one Louis relied upon for amusement and distraction, the minister assumed, unwisely, that he could afford to ridicule the Pompadour. The favorite never forgot nor completely forgave anyone who made her suffer, and in the end, in one way or another she avenged herself on them all. She also understood that if she were to succeed she had to cultivate her friends carefully, and form about her a solid circle of support.

During that first year, Jeanne-Antoinette went out of her way to be kind, considerate and thoughtful to everyone at court, especially the queen and the disdainful Richelieu, as well as Maurepas and the d'Argenson brothers. The upright Duc de Luynes reported in his diary that the favorite was thought extremely polite, bright, talkative and not at all arrogant. She spoke ill of no one and forbade anyone in her company to do so. She refused to be ashamed of her origins or her family, and talked about them often, even in the king's presence. The marquise never forgot that her name was Poisson and encouraged Louis to give her fish ornaments. These were often of Oriental celadon porcelain, mounted in ormolu and proudly displayed.

When the entire royal family and the court left for their ritual seasonal voyage to Fontainebleau for a six-week stay, Madame de Pompadour began to establish herself in the recognized mold of a royal mistress. One by one, with the help of the king's architect Jacques-Ange Gabriel, Louis' many houses began to be transformed by her superb taste, but subtly, and without any apparent revolution in style. Her own apartments in all the palaces were connected with the king's, and within her territory, his privacy was secure.

FOR A MAN who lived in a glass cage, whose every thought, word and deed, no matter how trivial, personal or private, was observed, discussed and dissected, these rooms, where he could be alone with the woman he loved and trusted, became a heavenly oasis. No one, no footman, not even his children, had the right to enter without an invitation. If the king was urgently required on a matter of state, a note was sent up by the ministers. Only Jeanne-Antoinette's personal lady-in-waiting and confidante, Madame de Hausset, could remain discreetly in her alcove and attend her mistress. This observant lady wrote in her plain but honest memoirs that the king and the marquise treated her as a pet dog or cat and spoke their minds in her presence.

In fact, the king and his mistress loved animals and had a great many in their apartments, including Louis' fat white Angora cat, monkeys, birds, and Jeanne-Antoinette's little lapdogs, which often appear in her portraits.

At Versailles, Madame de Pompadour had a suite of six medium-sized rooms in the *Attique du Nord,* leading out onto concealed roof gardens. Full of shrubs and flowers, the gardens had magnificent views and housed rabbits, hens, pigeons and aviaries of exotic birds.

To save her the long climb, there was a "flying chair," an armchair which her servants would pull up the stairwell. Her rooms had walls treated in bright, clear, delicate shades of blue, green, pink, and yellow "Vernis Martin," a kind of lacquer or French japanning, and they were filled with small, exquisite pieces of furniture and every sort of bric-à-brac. Her red lacquer study was littered with books, letters, plans and sketches for her many projects, manuscripts, musical instruments, objets d'art, bibelots, clocks, samples of materials, flowers and pets, and it received a never-ending stream of people paying their respects. In the middle of it all, with her little dogs at her feet, sat Madame de Pompadour on the only chair, which meant that every visitor, however exalted, had to stand. "Mistress of the King and of the universe," wrote the Marquis de Valfons, "she was surrounded at her toilette like a queen." To complete the picture, Madame de Pompadour's clothes were designed to tone with her refined and elegant interiors.

The king could reach her rooms on the mezzanine from his, known as the *Petits Cabinets,* by a narrow little passage. His apartment consisted of a principal room reserved for games or cards, separate kitchens, and a gallery which converted into a dining room. In the congenial atmosphere of his private rooms, Louis would often make coffee for his guests himself. The Duc de Cröy, a respected soldier and courtier, was included in one of these intimate *petits soupers,* and noted in his journal how relaxed and at ease the king appeared, as well as "being very much in love with Madame de Pompadour, and without false shame." He describes the favorite's relationship with the monarch rather charmingly as a *"scandale de convenance."*

DUPORT, COMTE DE Cheverny, the former *Introducteur des Ambassadeurs* (Head of Protocol), gave Madame de Pompadour perhaps the ultimate accolade for a Frenchman about a woman:

> Every man would have wished to make her his mistress. She was tall with intelligence and brilliance that I never saw in another woman. She put the prettiest of them into the shade. At Compiègne, the Ambassadors (except the Nuncio), after being presented to the Royal Family, would attend her reception. Nobody understood so well how to treat everyone in a fitting manner. To avoid etiquette she received at her toilette. The arts, the talents, the sciences, paid her homage. The talk was gay and natural though not profound, and her conversation was adapted to each of her visitors.

Before she came to Versailles, Jeanne-Antoinette's life had been dedicated to the study and pursuit of quality and beauty. She had learned well, and in this delicious eyrie in the roof of his palace, Louis XV's mistress was able to create a miniature world of enchantment and peace, an easy, informal atmosphere where her royal lover could learn the meaning of bourgeois happiness. Voltaire saluted her without exaggeration when he said: *"Vous réunissez tous les arts, tous les goûts, tous les talents de plaire"* (In you, all the arts, all taste and all ability to please are indeed united).

⌾⧜⧜~

THIS FIRST YEAR with the king, which had brought her such great happiness, ended on a note of sadness. On Christmas Eve, Madame Poisson died of her cancer. Jeanne-Antoinette had loved her wayward mother, and mourned her sincerely. The king, always embarrassed by any show of emotion, was surprisingly understanding, and suggested that the court's planned *voyage* to his beautiful Château de Marly be cancelled. Madame de Pompadour was aware how much effort had gone into the visit, in general planning and on the cost of the courtiers' new clothes. Cancellation on her account would only cause resentment, and she insisted that the plans remain unchanged. On her suggestion, Louis gave the precious gold and diamond snuff box which he had intended for her mother to the queen. The entire court knew for whom he had bought it, but as the poor queen was moved to tears by her husband's first New Year's gift in a long time, the scurrilous held their tongues for once. According to the Duc de Cröy, Madame de Pompadour was on "excellent terms with the Queen as she had urged the King to treat her with great consideration."

Not unnaturally, the new marquise wished to share her good fortune with her family and friends. Both groups knew they could count on her absolutely, just as her enemies were certain she would never forget them. Anyone who dared to challenge her position or opposed the king in anything earned her lifelong vengeance. The king was her lord and master, and she considered it her vocation to fulfill his every wish.

Her father (who had become inseparable from de Tournehem in their shared grief over the death of Madame Poisson) was ennobled and given an estate. Nonetheless, the old profiteer never ceased pestering his daughter for privileges and titles for his friends. The loyalty and affection Jeanne-Antoinette always showed her family was one of her most endearing "bourgeois" traits.* "Uncle" de Tournehem was given the post of Superintendent of Buildings, in effect minister of works and the arts. As such, he was in charge not only of the king's palaces and public buildings, but also of the royal collections and acquisitions. With his lifetime of experience, knowledge and taste, there could not have been a better choice; the post would pass to Madame de Pompadour's equally capable brother Abel on de Tournehem's death. This handsome, charming and unassuming young man was also ennobled and known as the Marquis de Marigny after his father's death. Despite his dislike of Voltaire, the king agreed to give him several well-paid sinecures. Nor did the favorite forget her old friends the Pâris brothers. They had quarrelled with the king's finance minister, Monsieur Orry de Fulvy, and pressed the marquise for his dismissal. In these early days, the king could refuse her nothing, and Orry, who had been effective and honest in his post, was discharged and demoted. For the first time, the court appreciated the power of France's new "left-handed queen."

When the king left Choisy in the spring of 1749, Jeanne-Antoinette remained behind, apparently ill, most probably due to a miscarriage. Her rest was interrupted by the sudden return of the royal family, who had been obliged to leave Versailles. The little Spanish dauphine had died in childbirth, and according to custom they could not remain under the same roof as the corpse. All the other palaces were either too far away or not prepared for an unexpected royal invasion. The king, who had wanted to be present at the birth of his first grandchild, sank daily into deeper gloom and despondency at Choisy. With no hunting or gambling permitted to divert him during the official period of court mourning, Louis' temper deteriorated further. Madame de Pompadour was so afraid that boredom might drive the king back to the army at Flanders that she wrote in secret to the Maréchal de Saxe (who was to become one of her greatest friends) at the pront. As an old acquaintance and a mutual friend of the Pâris

---

* It was rare for family affection to be shown among the aristocracy, especially as parents at court saw little of their children and less of one another.

brothers, she implored him for friendship's sake to recommend that the king stay at home. Relieved to be absolved of the responsibility of the king, de Saxe willingly obliged and assured his sovereign that there would be no further action that summer.

Not long before, the king had arranged for Jeanne-Antoinette to acquire Crécy, the first of her many beautiful houses. With de Tournehem and her brother Marigny to advise her, and the help of the architect Lassurance, she doubled its size, moved the village, and built a dairy and stables for two hundred horses. Madame de Pompadour personally supervised the Verbreckt and Rousseau paneling, Boucher's paintings and Falconet's sculptures. The gardens were designed by Garnier d'Isle, an apprentice of the great Le Nôtre.

Once his return to the front was cancelled, Louis decided, to the delight of the marquise, to go to Crécy and inspect the progress on the house. The visit was a great success. The king became enthusiastically involved in every detail of the building—its decorations, the gardens, stables, dairy and village. The food was superb, the company, a select group of Louis' friends, well chosen. The king seemed happily occupied with every aspect of the project. A restless man, he thrived on novelty. As a mark of his approval, he allowed the male guests at Crécy to wear an adaptation of Choisy's royal house uniform.

With Louis' good humor restored, his liverish color disappeared, and Madame de Pompadour realized she had discovered another remedy for her constant enemy, his ennui. Until then, the only topic of conversation on which he felt himself safe was hunting. Through the visit to Crécy, his lovely mistress had found him a hobby which fascinated him and which he could freely discuss. This new absorption in projects involving buildings, their surroundings and contents, inspired Jeanne-Antoinette to share her mania for collecting with her lover. In the course of her life, she acquired enough works of art, furniture, paintings, sculpture, vases, bibelots and objets d'art to fill several museums. Here was one of the greatest collections ever made by a single person.

As well as works of art, Madame de Pompadour began to acquire, build and rebuild houses and apartments. After the Château de Crécy came the Château de La Celle, the Château de Bellevue and its summer house Brimborian, the Château de Menars on the Loire, the

Hermitage at Compiègne, the elegant small Hermitage at Versailles (another retreat in which she could be alone with the king), the Hôtel des Reservoirs at Versailles (used more as an overflow for her guests and staff) and, for three years, the use of the Château des Champs. In Paris she owned the Hôtel d'Evreux (better known today as the Elysée Palace) and an apartment in the Couvent des Capucines. As well as all this, Madame de Pompadour had apartments placed at her disposal at almost all the royal palaces—Versailles, Fontainebleau, Choisy, Trianon, Saint-Hubert, Compiègne and others. Furthermore, the king commissioned Gabriel to build the Petit Trianon for her, though she died before its completion.

Installed at Versailles as Louis XV's *maîtresse en titre,* Madame de Pompadour continued to further her dual ambition—to amuse the king and to increase her power at court. The dizzying whirlwind of schemes and expenditure which followed, and which was to cost the nation 36 million livres, gratified her mania for accumulating beautiful and precious things and kept the king stimulated. If the marquise's houses and their contents had survived the Revolution and passed on to become part of the nation's heritage, this huge outlay would have been well worthwhile, as no French patron of the mid-eighteenth century had a more discerning eye for quality, and there was no better place than France to indulge an unlimited budget.

Surrounded by an atmosphere of civilized perfection, the favorite began to entertain, and gave intimate little supper parties in her apartments. As the king was always present, the courtiers vied with one another to be invited. These were agreeable evenings in delightful surroundings, with delicious food and lively conversation. An excellent hostess, the marquise chose the guests as carefully as she selected everything in her life. Here Louis could relax among small groups of familiar faces and, as the favorite went out of her way to be agreeable, her list of friends and admirers at court grew steadily. Encouraged by his mistress, the king became kinder to the queen, and saw more of his children. Madame de Pompadour sincerely tried to win their affection, and saw no incongruity in her desire to be considered as one of the family. It would be too much to suggest that Marie Leczinska liked her husband's mistress for herself, but in time she and the rest of the royal family acknowledged her efforts to please them.

Behind her back, the princesses called her "Pom-Pom." Deeply religious like their mother, they were more shocked by her friendship with *les philosophes* and her distrust of the Jesuits than by her relationship with their father. Madame de Pompadour felt sorry for these girls; she knew the king would surely kill any man who seduced one of them, and as Versailles had enmeshed them in its magic, they had no desire to leave for a foreign *"courette,"* as Europe's lesser courts were dubbed at Versailles. Louis XV only allowed his eldest daughter to marry for reasons of state,* but by the time she was twenty-two Madame Infante, as she was known, was back at Versailles. Her father found her charming and amusing, and sent Richelieu to install her in Parma, so his beloved daughter would have a duchy to rule.

FOR THE PREVIOUS fifty years the court had been entertained twice a week by the Comédie-Italienne or the Comédie-Française at Versailles' own theater. Since leaving Etioles, Madame de Pompadour had longed to perform again in her own amateur theatricals. At Versailles she built a tiny theater within the *Petits Cabinets* which could just seat an audience of fourteen. Boucher, her friend and teacher, was engaged to decorate it and paint the scenery, Perrot to create the costumes, and Notrelle the wigs. From among the courtiers in the king's set she quietly selected those she thought might have some talent, and rehearsed them thoroughly. Then, taking the lead herself, she staged *Tartuffe* before Louis on January 17, 1747.

From beginning to end, it was a tremendous success. The king was enchanted, kissed Madame de Pompadour and in front of everyone declared she was truly the most delicious woman in all France. Named the *Théâtre des Petits Cabinets,* it was to last almost ten years, until public pressure over expenses forced its closure. Together, Louis and Jeanne-Antoinette drew up a set of witty rules which were strictly enforced. Seven tailors from Paris were employed to make the costumes, the company had a large catalogue of props, and there were specially designed and printed tickets and programs.

* She married Filippo, Infant of Spain, son of the Spanish king and his second wife, Elisabeth Farnèse, heiress of Parma.

Perhaps because of his shyness, Louis XV loved fancy dress and al fresco theatricals. With childish delight he would run up the little staircase leading to Madame de Pompadour's rooms, to find his mistress disguised in a variety of costumes—a sultana one day, a shepherdess the next, a nymph or a nun. During Holy Week, to divert the king from his macabre fascination with death, she staged a series of spiritual musical performances. These seven-day operas were an enormous success. Almost everyone in the king's charmed circle sought the honor of performing before their sovereign.

Members of the court rushed to be included, begging to be part of the play, the orchestra or the audience. As almost every educated person of that century had been taught to act, dance, sing and play a musical instrument, Madame de Pompadour discovered considerable talent among the courtiers, and also recruited a number of musical servants. She alone made the casting decisions and, by pleasing the king and having the power to please the courtiers, she became in effect Louis XV's Mistress of Pleasures. The king joined the small audience, sitting in a simple armchair, and for the first time in French history one could clap in the presence of the sovereign.

As director of her own little theater company, Madame de Pompadour at last had a suitable vehicle for her talent, beauty and accomplishments. She always took the leading roles and, as the other actresses were all ladies loyal to her, it was an unspoken rule that no one would try to outshine the favorite. The theater's Monday night performances became a part of the routine of Versailles, but as the audiences grew, so did the expenses. The king's architect Gabriel had been asked to build a larger, "movable" theater actually within the Grand Ambassadors' Staircase. As this was needed each New Year for the ceremony of the Knights of Saint-Esprit, the theater was a complicated and expensive construction in movable sections, which took seventeen hours to dismantle and twelve to re-erect.

Professionals were engaged to instruct the amateurs in acting, stage management and production. The king's choir sang and the court's most distinguished amateur musicians played in the small orchestra. Each performance concluded with a ballet. According to the Duc de Luynes, the marquise was the only one of the court's ladies who danced really well—with as much grace and talent as she acted and sang.

The Duc de Richelieu had charge of a special department entitled *Les Menus Plaisirs,* which organized and financed all palace entertainments, arranging the balls, masquerades, fireworks and so on. His envy of the favorite drove him to sabotage the theater performances and even to ridicule her at her own little supper parties. Madame de Pompadour could not exclude him, as his wicked humor entertained the king, and although she retaliated by subtly mocking him in her plays, his constant tormenting drove her to beg Louis to dismiss him. This the king would not do, but when he pointedly asked *Son Excellence* at his public levée how often he had been in the Bastille, a trembling Richelieu understood it might be prudent to call a truce with the marquise.

As Richelieu hated Maurepas even more than he loathed Madame de Pompadour, under this truce they succeeded in removing perhaps her greatest enemy.

Minister for Paris as well as secretary of state and for the navy, Maurepas had good reason for long consultations with the king. As he was also a childhood friend, he could divert Louis with his witty gossip and malicious anecdotes from the capital. Maurepas loathed the Pompadour for her proximity to the king and for being his most trusted confidante and adviser. He tormented her with his exaggerated imitations of her bourgeois manners, walk and speech, reducing the courtiers to helpless laughter. Maurepas had hated all Louis' mistresses, but to his disgust, this little middle-class nobody was present more and more frequently at his business meetings with the king. Once she had even dared to dismiss him with the words: "Monsieur de Maurepas, you are turning the king yellow. Good day to you, Monsieur de Maurepas." Without a contradiction from Louis, Maurepas had had no choice but to leave.

When the cost of the Pompadour's little theatricals at Versailles escalated, the outraged Parisians were kept informed by anonymous pamphlets and broadsheets written in verse. Vicious and grossly exaggerated, these *Poissonades* were pasted all over the walls of the city. Everyone at court knew or suspected that Maurepas was their author.

They implied that the king's navy was badly equipped because he had spent the naval budget on the Pompadour's theatricals. The favorite was also held responsible for the many expensive building projects de Tournehem was undertaking for the king. Ever since Louis XV had discovered how much he enjoyed constructing buildings, these had increased dramatically in scale and number. So had the list of new pensions being granted by the crown. The taxpayers were already overburdened, and complained loudly.

The scurrilous verses had reached Versailles, and were reducing Madame de Pompadour to a nervous wreck. When a hateful poem suggesting she had venereal disease was found under her napkin in her own apartment at the palace, a distraught Jeanne-Antoinette took to her bed. Still Louis made no move against Maurepas. As a last resort, Madame de Pompadour went to Paris and called on the minister in person, demanding that he stop writing the libels. It was a spirited and courageous move, and she left after a heated exchange. Back at court, Maurepas boasted that her visit would do her no more good than Madame de Mailly's similar pleas had done her; and after all, he added, laughing, everyone knew he had poisoned Madame de Châteauroux! This dangerous quip made the king look a fool; Maurepas had finally gone too far. Without any warning, a curt note banishing the minister was brought to his bed at one in the morning.

But the dirty, hurtful *Poissonades* continued, particularly at the time of the building of Bellevue, Madame de Pompadour's most beautiful house.

The favorite herself had bought the magnificent site, on a steep bank overlooking the valley of the Seine between Sèvres and Meudon, in 1748. Inspired by the beauty of the panorama, Madame de Pompadour set out to create this almost-royal residence as tangible evidence of the love she shared with the king. Conceived as a house of pleasure to enchant and distract Louis XV, Bellevue was the only one of her houses she actually had built, rather than altered. It occupied eight hundred workers for two and a half years and cost 2.5 million livres.

Madame de Pompadour chose her favorite architect, Lassurance, although he may have used plans supplied by Gabriel. A true perfectionist, she personally approved the design of the decorations down to the minutest detail. The greatest artists, sculptors and craftsmen in France worked on Bellevue, including Coustou, Van Loo, Boucher, Falconet, Vernet, Lajoue, Lambert and Sigisbert Adam, and Pigalle. The panelling was by Verbreckt and the Martin brothers applied their delicate vernis in shades of duck-egg blue, celadon green, yellow and white edged with gold. Everything made for Bellevue was unique and specially commissioned, from the fabrics and furniture to the tapestries and door handles. As in all her houses, Madame de Pompadour chose the contents from the stock of the *marchands merciers* Lazare-Duvaux—furniture, furnishings, bibelots and objets d'art. According to their record books, these were of the highest possible quality.

The predominant feature of the house, inside and out, was the abundance of flowers, chosen for their scent as much as for their color and fragile beauty. Bellevue's gardens, the loveliest of all her houses', were terraced down the steep hill from the facade to the Seine below. Gardening became another interest the king shared with the marquise, planning the landscaping, the avenues of trees and the clipped hedges, the formal terraces and the subtly shaded flower beds. In one of his many exaggerations, d'Argenson claimed that Madame de Pompadour spent a fortune blending Vincennes porcelain flowers (carefully scented to match the real ones) into her conservatory and challenging Louis and the courtiers to tell the difference.*

Plants were replaced as soon as they ceased flowering, and guests would wake to find the parterres completely transformed as far as the eye could see. When the *Théâtre des Petits Cabinets* disbanded as a gesture toward economy, Madame de Pompadour continued to indulge her thespian passion by building an exquisite theater at Bellevue, decorated throughout with chinoiserie. *Opéra comique,* ballet and plays were produced there until 1753. The theatre offered *Le Devin du village* for its last performance, with the marquise, as always, playing the lead, fetchingly dressed as a youth.

Bellevue's housewarming party was a disaster. It took place in winter, and everything went wrong; the food was cold, the fireworks

---

* Porcelain flowers from Vincennes were so perfect they were much in demand, and in 1749 they represented four-fifths of the factory's total production. According to the inventory made after her death, Madame de Pompadour owned forty-six pieces incorporating porcelain flowers.

were rained off, and the chimneys smoked so badly that the guests fled to a small pavilion in the grounds. Despite this inauspicious beginning, king and favorite were both very happy at Bellevue. Madame de Pompadour wrote to her brother: *"C'est la plus jolie habitation du monde avec la plus grande simplicité."* Nine years later, she sold Bellevue to Louis for one-tenth of its total cost. This monument to the perfection of Madame de Pompadour's taste incorporated the best craftsmanship available in France in the mid-eighteenth century. After her death, Louis continued to visit this beautiful house, which remained in the royal family until it was completely destroyed during the Revolution.

Possibly more than any other art form, Madame de Pompadour loved porcelain, which at this time was being imported from the Far East as well as from Dresden. There were three royal French factories which all produced beautiful work—Saint-Cloud, Chantilly and Vincennes—but they did not have access to the hard paste used for Oriental porcelain and by the Meissen factory at Dresden. Imported china was very expensive, and Madame de Pompadour felt that far too many French francs left the country for the pockets of the Elector Augustus of Saxony. She patronized all three local factories, particularly Vincennes, but none matched the quality of the work produced at Meissen. Vincennes had been established in 1736 by Orry de Fulvy, the finance minister whom Madame de Pompadour had removed. As she was constantly searching for new enterprises in which to involve the king, the marquise suggested he buy the factory. Then she moved it all to the village of Sèvres near her magical Bellevue and beneath her watchful eye. Under the direction of the marquise and with the help of massive investment from the king, the new Sèvres factory prospered. Largely due to the skill of the chemist Hellot and the gilding of a Benedictine monk, by 1756 the produce of the Sèvres factory rivalled that of Meissen. New shapes were produced in Vincennes' most beautiful colors: lapis blue, turquoise *bleu céleste,* clear fresh green, and the famous pink *"rose Pompadour."** Other wonderful pat-

---

* This was mistakenly thought to be her favorite. The marquise left over three thousand pieces of porcelain in her various houses after her death, and only ten in this color appear in her inventory, the great majority being shades of blue.

terns were known as *"caillouté"* (pebbled), *"vermiculé"* (wormlike) and *"oeil-de-perdrix"* (partridge-eye). Master sculptors such as Falconet, Pigalle and Caffieri often copied their marble statues in Sèvres porcelain.

As it was Louis XV's property, the Sèvres factory carried his cipher of interlaced "L's." Both the king and Madame de Pompadour visited regularly and took a great deal of interest in the production. The early simplicity of the wares, especially the delicate undecorated figures in white biscuit and white enamel, were a reflection of the favorite's perfect taste. Every year at Versailles she would hold a sale of the produce of "her" factory, sometimes acting as saleswoman. Although undeniably beautiful, Sèvres porcelain was rather expensive, and the courtiers bought it under considerable obligation. With her trained eye and shrewd commercial instinct, Madame de Pompadour patronized and bought only the very best herself. Had her porcelain collection remained intact, it would have become another priceless legacy for the nation.

Abel Poisson, now Marquis de Marigny, shared his sister's energy and her love of the arts, but not her ambitious nature. Totally out of his depth at court, he successfully resisted all Jeanne-Antoinette's efforts to push him into a grand marriage. He loved his sister as dearly as she loved him, but the sum of his ambition was to succeed de Tournehem as minister of of arts and buildings. Marigny was only comfortable in the company of artists, and as her matchmaking efforts were heading nowhere, Jeanne-Antoinette sent him off to Italy to further his studies. This was rather a novel move at the time, for unlike the English, French gentlemen did not usually travel abroad for pleasure.

To accompany her brother she chose the abbé Le Blanc, a respected art critic, the engraver Cochin, and the architect Soufflot. Considerably older than Marigny, they were all committed opponents of the rococo, the style with which Madame de Pompadour has always been associated. Indeed, she has often been called the Queen of the Rococo, and certainly her portraits by Boucher in particular epitomize the delicious—almost decadent—frivolity of this indigenous French style. Flounces and frills, swags of roses, ribbons and bows, cherubs and cupids drawing back silk curtains; and Boucher's glimpse of a girl on a swing in pink satin, holding ropes made of flowers in a lush green fantasy landscape; these were the images which character-ized the age. The emphasis was on nature in asymmetrical patterns and the style originated not, as might be thought, from the court, but, like Jeanne-Antoinette Poisson, from the Parisian bourgeoisie.

It is true that Madame de Pompadour loved the rococo, but she always kept abreast with the latest trends. By sending her brother to Rome and in such company, she must have acknowledged the gradual shift toward classicism. Boucher's portraits of her as early as 1756 and 1759, as well as those by Drouais of 1763–64, show her posing with furniture incorporating classical motifs. During her time, the swing to neoclassicism in all the arts included these forms and motifs with so much freedom and warmth of color that the effect was more romantic before than after the Revolution.

Jeanne-Antoinette's regular letters to her *"petit frère"* were full of sensible sisterly advice and concern for his success and future. Recom-mending Marigny to the Duc de Nivernais, her witty and clever friend who was French ambassador in Rome, she warned:

> He is not at all stupid, but he is too frank, so truthful that some-times he seems unsympathetic. Curiously enough, this virtue does not pay at Court. I have suffered from that, and have made a reso-lution never to tell anyone the truth as long as I live.

She need not have worried. Abel was a success with everyone he met. Shortly after the return of the scholars twenty-one months later, de Tournehem died and Marigny, at the age of twenty-six, became min-ister of the arts. At the outset of his journey he had had no clear views on art, but the influence of his three companions (all now close friends) turned Marigny into an excellent choice as de Tournehem's successor. Witty and charming (and rather pleased with himself), Marigny was also learned, cultured and discerning. He was appreci-ated, never inspiring the jealousy and hatred suffered by his sister, and the arts in mid-eighteenth-century France owe him a great debt. Like Jeanne-Antoinette, he had the gift of choosing the right man for the job. During the next twenty years, his sound judgment and shrewd appointments to key positions in the arts enabled him to steer the move away from the curves and scrolls of the rococo toward the classical revival, usually accredited to the next reign.

FROM THE MOMENT Madame de Pompadour arrived at Versailles as Louis XV's *maîtresse en titre*, she assumed the role of supreme patroness of the arts, and cultivated artists. As Madame d'Etioles she had made friends with most of the celebrated painters, sculptors and writers; as the king's mistress, she was able to reward many with official posts in the arts and bestow the accompanying privileges. As well as taste, she had an innate understanding of the artistic temperament and she encouraged, guided, cajoled and, most importantly, *paid* those she commissioned, promptly and in full.

All the artists in France were controlled by Marigny and the marquise. Between them they arranged commissions, materials and sittings, found them lodgings, saw they were paid and, as a result, they worked well and without complaint under the joint administration. Generous and discriminating, Madame de Pompadour's patronage was also a wise investment, as the artists and writers of the day immortalized the king's mistress to her best advantage in their works. By encouraging Louis to have the ban lifted from the *Encyclopédie* she won the esteem and admiration of *les philosophes*. Voltaire wrote to d'Alembert that *"dans le fond de son coeur, elle était des nôtres"*—at heart, she was one of us. Though often less sincere toward others, Voltaire adored her and dedicated *Tancrède* to her, and Montesquieu and Marmontel both had reason to be in her debt.

If there were no limits to Madame de Pompadour's encouragement of artists and writers, there appear to have been several to her own artistic curiosity. During her life she sold houses and jewelry, but never any works of art or objets, so the inventory of her possessions at her death is a true record of her preferences. She left many paintings, but she never formed a real collection. Other than the portraits, almost all the commissions she gave to contemporary French artists were intended to decorate her houses, often as overmantels or overdoors. The majority of her paintings were by Boucher and Van Loo, but works by Oudry, Huet, Coypel and Drouais were also included. Surprisingly, there is no mention in the inventory of the other great contemporary painters: Lancret, Pater, De Troy, Natoire and (other than engravings of his paintings) Watteau. She owned almost no seventeenth-century French paintings, little Italian art and only three Dutch paintings—still lifes by Snyders—plus three copies of Rembrandts. Equally surprising was the large number of religious paintings she possessed, but in their execution there is little to distinguish the Virgin from Venus, or angels from cupids. The architects Lassurance, Garnier d'Isle and the great Jacques-Ange Gabriel all worked on her houses, and among sculptors she commissioned Falconet, Lemoyne and Pigalle to create figures and groups for her. But her paintings and sculptures, the portraits, the Venuses, the nymphs and sultanas, all served only as the carefully contrived backgrounds the marquise arranged for herself within her houses.

Madame de Pompadour's real contribution was more to the decorative arts of the mid-eighteenth century than to the fine arts—in porcelain, furniture and objets. She had a mania for interior decoration, constantly embellishing and ornamenting her houses and apartments. She inspired and created new designs for painted wallpapers and fabrics, and suggested new shapes of tables and chairs for which she used exotic imported woods. As early as the mid-eighteenth century, Madame de Pompadour commissioned furniture "à la grecque," heralding the style known later as Louis XVI. Oeben, Migeon II and his son all worked for her often, as did Godfroy, Tillard and Criaerd, as well as the great Gobelins factory. All her furniture, her wonderful carpets and her vast porcelain collection were of the very finest quality, a quality ensured by the strict annual jury system governing the various guilds before the Revolution.

Another key to Madame de Pompadour's character was her celebrated library. This eclectic collection of books gives an insight into the mind of an intelligent, cultivated and practical woman. Bound in blue, red and lemon-yellow morocco leather and marbled calf, stamped with the three towers of her arms, it included works by the *Encyclopédiste* school as well as classical philosophy, history, political economy and statecraft. Her choice of literature contained all the classics, poetry, romances and novels in French, Spanish and Italian, opera and music treatises, and theatrical works. Books helped to take her mind off her ever present money problems, and she became an insatiable reader. Literature was also a source for finding ways to distract the king.

Madame de Pompadour's archives throw more light on her complex character. She had been educated in the commercial atmosphere of a bourgeois Parisian family, and her papers reveal that she developed a sound head for business, and that her judgments were usually correct. By careful management, she kept her dowry intact, and using her own capital, she founded and ran a successful glass factory near Bellevue. All her purchases are carefully listed; she sued her debtors and paid her bills. Through her many connections in the business world, she kept herself well informed and acted wisely. Perhaps her business affairs would not have been so well organized without the help of the invaluable Collin, but it is clear from her archives that the decisions and initiatives taken were her own. A good psychologist, she chose her staff carefully, and never tried to obtain a post for someone who was incapable of filling it well.

Louis XV, like so many of his predecessors, had no concept of money matters whatsoever. He regarded France as his property, and the country's revenues as his to dispense. Just two years after Madame de Pompadour arrived at court, the amounts the king gave her as an income and as gifts had reached 205,000 livres, as his infatuation and generosity reached its peak. Thereafter her royal income fluctuated, and after 1751 the king gave her no more gifts of money—except once for her courage in allowing the doctor to bleed her for fever using leeches. But as her financial support from Louis dwindled, her expenditure, particularly on her houses and apartments, increased substantially. Listed in her precise account books, between 1746 when she arrived at court, and 1764 when she died, her outgoings of 1,767,000 livres were almost double her royal income of 977,000 livres.

To supplement the revenues from her marquisate, Madame de Pompadour produced and sold her own wine and cheese, and the bottles made at her glass factory; she received rent from a number of her houses, and traded in some privileges. Although she disliked gambling on principle, she often managed to reduce the shortfall in her income by her winnings and, later, by selling her jewels. She also sold Crécy and Bellevue as well as two other châteaux, but cleverly retained the right to live in them for life. Her endless building projects were certainly the cause of her overspending, but the marquise excused herself by saying that she would rather the money went to the hundreds of poor workmen she employed than remained sitting in her treasure chests.*

IN ALL HER commercial dealings, Madame de Pompadour's shrewd business head prevailed, but after five years as the king's mistress her financial circumstances gradually changed when her relationship with Louis moved onto a different plateau.

For some time, Madame de Pompadour's health had been giving cause for concern. She had written to a close friend and to her brother in Rome that the stories of her coughing blood after a series of bad chest infections were true. Several miscarriages had weakened her and she suffered from migraines. Nor could the favorite afford the luxury of a prolonged convalescence. After forty-eight hours spent in bed for a fever, an influenza or a miscarriage, *toujours en vedette*, looking and smelling delicious, she would have to be up and entertaining the king again. The strain of keeping her hold on Louis' heart and juggling the various factions in the power game at court gave her palpitations, and her nerves, which she struggled to control, were badly frayed. When Louis was not away at war, life with him was a perpetual round of activity, lurching in stuffy coaches over dreadful roads, rushing from one icy, drafty château to another. It all wearied her terribly, but she could not bear to be parted from the king and risk losing him through her absence for a much needed rest.

Hours spent at her complicated toilette could not hide the fact that, at the age of thirty, Madame de Pompadour's looks were fading. Worse, the rouge and face paint she used to cover her pallor was full of highly toxic lead, and had begun to poison her. The frills and bows of her elaborate court dresses hid her alarming thinness, and she in-

---

* After her death, only 36 gold louis were found in her desk.

vented the flattering silk ruff to cover her scrawny neck. Hygiene was still virtually unknown, and stale air, tight whalebone corsets, skin diseases caused by dirty hair, and the endless aphrodisiacs, all took their toll of her fragile health. Still, the spiteful d'Argenson records in his journal that "the king by force of habit treats her carnally better than ever. Several courtiers saw him the other day caress her cynically behind a screen."

After a particularly bad bout of flu during which her breathing became more labored than usual, Louis decided to spare her the long climb to her attic apartments—the "flying chair" did not always function. He gave Madame de Pompadour an extremely grand new apartment on the ground floor of the north wing of Versailles, with a secret staircase leading to his suite above. Arranging these magnificent rooms (which had once belonged to Louis XIV's splendid mistress, Madame de Montespan), with their almost royal proportions was the last official undertaking "Uncle" de Tournehem completed before his death.

Madame de Pompadour's move downstairs to her new apartment in 1750 started the gossip at court that she and the king had ceased to be lovers. According to the faithful Madame de Hausset, the physician Dr. Quesnay advised the marquise to cease being the king's "companion of the night" for the sake of her health, and to concentrate on being indispensable to him by day. Contemporary accounts disagree, but the worldly abbé Bernis, who probably knew her better than anyone, claimed that Louis XV and Madame de Pompadour continued to be lovers until some time in 1751. While her enemies hoped this change would be the end of her, the favorite achieved the near impossible; while ceasing to be the king's lover, she managed to retain his sincere friendship.

THE YEAR 1751 had been declared a Holy Year by the Pope, and a wave of religious hysteria swept France. As the nation focused on religion and morality, pressure was put on the king not only to attend the many religious ceremonies throughout the country, but also to complete his "Jubilee." This meant he must take communion by Easter.

The last time the king had taken communion had been at Metz after dismissing Madame de Châteauroux and making his confession. To do so in Holy Year, he would have to dismiss her successor. This put Madame de Pompadour in a very difficult position. She did not relish being castigated as the cause of the Most Christian Monarch's lack of grace in Holy Year. As she watched his religious fervor increasing daily, and her enemies gathering to see the outcome, she trembled slightly.

Louis XV's resurrected piety was so profound that he cut the number of days he hunted during Lent so as not to miss a single sermon by his Jesuit priest. Secure in the dauphin's protection, the Jesuits became a rallying point for the favorite's enemies, who urged the priests to press for her dismissal.

It is difficult for any woman who is constantly ill, no matter how devoted, to feel like making love. Madame de Pompadour was perfectly willing, even eager, to abandon this aspect of her relationship with the king and to let it be known. Then the blow fell. If Madame de Pompadour and the king wished for complete rehabilitation and to regain the right to receive communion, renouncing sexual relations would not be enough. She must quit the court completely. Madame de Pompadour despaired. This time, for the sake of his immortal soul, Louis XV really would abandon her.

She need not have worried. The favorite had become genuinely indispensable to the king, and not just because she was able to prevent his boredom and melancholy. He could trust her completely, and he had no doubt she loved him truly, and for himself. Louis knew he could count on her sound advice and discuss any subject with her, from the gravest political decision to the most trivial domestic detail. For her part, she understood him thoroughly, and could read him better than anyone. The king was troubled and saddened by the Church's conditions, but when his Jesuit confessor advised him to dismiss Madame de Pompadour, he refused. Her presence at court, he declared, was essential to his well-being and state of mind.

Despite this reassurance, Madame de Pompadour was still left in a delicate situation. No longer the king's lover, in the eyes of the public she was still his. To his inner circle, she was the friend who would protect her powerful position by his side at any price.

AS WELL AS her precarious health, the fading of her beauty and the onset of Holy Year, there was another reason for Madame de Pompadour's transition from official mistress to indispensable friend. She craved respectability. Unlike the aristocracy at court, who believed that their rank at birth guaranteed their social superiority, Madame de Pompadour wanted to be accepted by those she admired and respected, in particular the queen. Now that her raison d'être by Louis' side no longer existed, she planned to gain the recognition she longed for by carving a far greater role for herself in politics.

The marquise chose a novel way to underline her transformation. With typical subtlety, she commissioned Pigalle to make a beautiful romantic statue entitled *L'Amour et l'amitié,** depicting Love reaching out to embrace Friendship, for a bower in the garden at Bellevue. She also ordered a portrait of herself by Boucher with the statue in the background to underscore the point.

Strange as it may seem, Madame de Pompadour's loss of intimacy with the king did not diminish her power. On the contrary, the court finally acknowledged that there were two queens of France, and that it was Madame de Pompadour, not Marie Leczinska, who reigned. Jeanne-Antoinette's time as the king's actual mistress had lasted about five years; until her death fourteen years later, Madame de Pompadour helped direct the destiny of France and would prove her dedication as Louis XV's counsellor, political adviser and constant friend.

MORE THAN ANY other illness, Louis XV dreaded venereal disease. Quite unjustly, the vilest and cruelest of the *Poissonades* circulating in Paris and at court hinted that Madame de Pompadour was infected, and that this was the real reason for the end of her liaison with the king. In fact, her love for him had simply developed on another level,

---

* After the death of the marquise, the queen visited Bellevue and remarked to the Duc de Luynes that the bower with the statue had been that of Love, and had become that of Friendship.

and when she felt sure of his devotion and his dependence on her in other respects, Madame de Pompadour was at last able to abandon an aspect of her life she had always found distasteful. The king was used to her and, as her friends had always told her, he would not wish to begin again and install a new *maîtresse en titre* at court.

But the forty-two-year-old king, though heavier and less energetic than in his youth, was not remotely ready to lead a celibate life. Louis XV *did* require female diversions, and these now concentrated predominantly on an establishment known as the Parc aux Cerfs.

In a quiet part of Versailles, at 40 rue Saint-Médéric, the king bought a small house which was equipped for several young girls of "easy virtue." Often the daughters of prostitutes, they were discreetly chosen from brothels in Paris by his valet Lebel, who made all the arrangements. (Louis XV has been castigated by some historians for his known preference for virgins, but this was due to his terror of catching syphilis.) The girls were forbidden visitors or communication with one another, but they were allowed any teachers they wanted and permitted to visit the Comédie-Française, where they had their own screened box. The establishment was in the care of a *gouvernante,* a footman, a maid and a cook. *"Les grisettes"** were told that their patron was a rich Polish nobleman, and not to ask any questions. Madame de Pompadour's detractors have accused her of arranging the "facilities" of the Parc aux Cerfs, as if she had been the madame of a brothel. In this presumption they grossly misunderstand her; nothing would have distressed her more. Of course she knew of its existence, wisely chose to ignore it, and placed her confidence in the safety of numbers. She assured Madame de Hausset that "all these little uneducated girls would never take him from me," and laughed at the extraordinary new expressions Louis picked up there.

Once again, Madame de Pompadour's enemies seized an opportunity of striking at her through the king's little "weaknesses." Among the early occupants of the Parc aux Cerfs was a beautiful fourteen-year-old girl of Irish descent called Louise O'Murphy and known as *"la belle Morphise."* Louis was quite taken with her, and even broke his own rules by bringing her secretly to Versailles a few times. Since

* Working-class girls.

her arrival coincided with Madame de Pompadour's move downstairs to her new apartments, she caused quite a stir. It seems Louise had children with the king, but when a group of courtiers tried to promote her as *maîtresse en titre,* the marquise wasted no time in arranging a dowry and a husband, and had her sent away. Boucher used her as a model and painted her several times,* but most probably only after Madame de Pompadour's death, as he was genuinely fond of his patron, and loyal to her.

⁂

THE PARC AUX Cerfs establishment existed until 1765. There are no precise details of how many girls passed through it, but it was recorded at the time that eight children were born to the inmates. These children were taken to be educated in a convent, given an annuity, and married off to good country folk. Louis XV did not officially recognize any of his bastards.

As Holy Year had failed to dislodge the favorite, her enemies, in particular the Comte d'Argenson, younger brother of the malicious diarist, decided to challenge Madame de Pompadour with a rival. Since coming to court, the marquise had protected and advanced her cousin Madame d'Estrades. Neither beautiful nor accomplished, Madame d'Estrades nursed a secret envy of her patroness which had swelled to an intense loathing. This she managed to conceal under a veneer of friendship and solicitude. When Madame de Pompadour stopped sleeping with the king, Madame d'Estrades fancied that she would replace her in his bed, and attempted to seduce Louis. She failed, but as the king was far too drunk at the time to recall the incident the next morning, it passed without comment. However, Madame d'Estrades did succeed in becoming the mistress of the Comte d'Argenson, and their joint hatred of Madame de Pompadour united them in their ambition to destroy her.

Some years previously, the marquise had lent her lovely Château de Bellevue to a niece of Madame d'Estrades and her new husband, a member of the great Choiseul family, for their honeymoon. As they

---

* She is the subject of one of his best-known paintings.

were lively and attractive, Madame de Pompadour welcomed the young couple into the king's set. Friends of the favorite warned her not to trust the two-faced d'Estrades, and especially not to allow Madame de Romanet-Choiseul to amuse the king too much. This delightful young woman even repeated Madame de Pompadour's own historic avowal that "she would never leave her husband except, of course, for the king." Jeanne-Antoinette noticed nothing.

Through the kindness of the marquise, Madame d'Estrades had wheedled herself into a position of power at court second only to that of her benefactress. She knew exactly how to manage the king, and instructed her niece precisely how best to entice Louis. D'Argenson and d'Estrades advised their pupil to make her final surrender conditional on the expulsion of Madame de Pompadour.

Although the entire court staying at Fontainebleau was fully aware of the Romanet-Choiseul drama being enacted, it was almost too late by the time the favorite realized the seriousness of her predicament. Dr. Quesnay, Jeanne-Antoinette's faithful friend, was in the room with Madame d'Estrades and d'Argenson when their protégée burst in, extremely dishevelled, exclaiming: "I am loved. She is to be sent away." The king had lost his head, and Madame de Pompadour's fate appeared to be sealed.

Also visiting Fontainebleau to pay his respects to the king was the Comte de Stainville, a career soldier of great fascination and attraction. He found himself singularly disenchanted by the court, and particularly by the behavior of his young cousin by marriage, Madame de Romanet-Choiseul. His brother-in-law, the Marquis de Gontaut, had briefed him fully about the effect this affair was having on his old friend Madame de Pompadour, who was in a state of near collapse.

Madame de Romanet-Choiseul was so intoxicated by the vision of her glorious future that she took her dashing cousin Stainville into her confidence. Rashly, she showed him a long letter from the king in which he declared his love for her and promised to dismiss Madame de Pompadour. Most probably Louis would have retracted it all later, but his infatuation at that moment knew no bounds.

This information gave Stainville an extraordinary opportunity, and he needed time to think. He begged his little cousin to allow him to keep the letter for twenty-four hours, with the excuse that then he could best advise her how to reply, and hurried to find his brother-in-law. For years, Gontaut had praised the virtues and charms of Madame de Pompadour to Stainville, and had encouraged the two to meet, certain they would become friends. It surprised and saddened him that when they met, his two favorite people had rather disliked one another. Now, with the king's letter in his possession, Stainville knew he had the power, if he so wished, to rescue Madame de Pompadour from calamity. For Louis to have put his feelings about Madame de Romanet-Choiseul on paper and promised to dismiss Madame de Pompadour was most rash. After so many years, the favorite knew too much about the affairs of state to be discarded so ignominiously. Armed with the king's letter, she could humble him, and force him to retract. When Madame de Pompadour heard that Stainville had a way of solving her problem, she waited for him anxiously. But as he had not been particularly charmed by her, he declined to call on her until she had sent him several desperate messages. He found her in a terrible state, crying hysterically, and with her coach ready to leave at one word from the king.

Even the news that Madame de Romanet-Choiseul's jealous young husband was taking her rival away from court, as she was expecting his child, did little to reassure Madame de Pompadour. Tapping his breast pocket, Stainville repeated continually that he had the means there of her reinstatement. Finally, and only when he felt he had tortured his victim enough, did Stainville produce the king's incriminating letter.

Its effect was electric. For an instant Madame de Pompadour sat stunned, then she completely lost her temper. Her habitual control snapped, and hell knew no fury like hers at that moment.

In the evening, when Louis came for his usual visit, he was totally unprepared for the broadside of magnificent rage that struck him. For the one great scene she threw before the king in her life, Madame de Pompadour combined the perfect timing of the trained actress with the fury of a woman deceived. When her anger had reached its highest pitch, she produced his letter and told Louis how she came by it. The bewildered king turned his shame and anger against Madame de Romanet-Choiseul. That very night the young couple were banished from the court.

A few days after her tirade, Louis appeased the favorite by creating her a duchess. Out of deference to the queen, Madame de Pompadour did not use her new title, only rarely signing herself "Marquise-Duchesse de Pompadour," but she did accept the almost-royal privileges accompanying it—the ducal arms, the use of scarlet livery and the right to sit on a footstool in Her Majesty's presence. To confirm her new status, she was presented at court as before by the Princesse de Conti, accompanied by Madame d'Estrades.

Madame de Romanet-Choiseul died in childbirth a few months later. She was just nineteen.

Madame de Pompadour and Stainville reversed their earlier opinions of one another, and became firm friends. Understandably, the king could not abide the embarrassing presence of the count after this unpleasant episode. All Madame de Pompadour's efforts to reconcile them came to nothing when Louis lost a large sum of money playing cards with her champion. Reluctantly, she agreed that her new friend had to go, and persuaded the king to appoint Stainville as his ambassador to Rome. He was to remain her loyal friend for life, and became an executor of her will.

Although their plans to remove the marquise had been thwarted, Madame d'Estrades and the Comte d'Argenson remained thorns in her side. Louis enjoyed the witty gossip of his beloved's false friend, and could not believe she had been involved in the promotion of Madame de Romanet-Choiseul. Some years earlier, the marquise had arranged for Madame d'Estrades to be given the lucrative post of lady-in-waiting to the Princesse Adélaïde, who also rather liked her. For three more years, Madame de Pompadour had to see her treacherous cousin every day, and behave as if nothing had happened.

Then, one day, Jeanne-Antoinette noticed that an important state paper, written in the king's own hand, was missing from her bedside drawer. It could only have been taken by Madame d'Estrades, and Louis (and Madame Adélaïde) were persuaded of her guilt at last. As those who crossed Louis XV learned to their cost, his retribution was swift and without warning. While Madame d'Estrades sat in her coach on a day trip to Paris, a courier galloped up and handed her a note through the window. With a few curt words, she was banished from the court.

As Madame de Pompadour succeeded in removing her enemies one by one, her importance steadily increased. She began referring to herself and the king as "we," as if they were a couple. Her daughter Alexandrine, who had come to Versailles aged five and a half, was addressed as "Madame Alexandrine" like a royal princess, and signed herself as such by using just her Christian name. The little girl was known to her family as "Fan-Fan," and adored by them as her mother had been. Madame de Pompadour doted on her, old Poisson worshipped her and in her uncle Marigny's eyes she could do no wrong.

The correspondence between the three is full of this enchanting child, her education and her prospects, though her mother's love never obscured her common sense. "She seems to be getting very plain," wrote Jeanne-Antoinette to her old father. "Not that I care—so long as she isn't really hideous I should prefer her not to be a great beauty. It only makes enemies of the whole female sex which, with their friends, amounts to three quarters of the world's inhabitants." She instructed her father never to give Fan-Fan money and wrote to Crébillon, who was in charge of her education: "I don't want her to seem too clever. Molière says that we women are only intended to sew and spin—I don't agree with that either, but I think the learned look and know-all manner simply ridiculous."

It was one of the tragedies of Madame de Pompadour's life that she had never succeeded in having a child with the man she loved. She wanted her daughter to marry one of the king's sons, and at least have their blood joined through their grandchildren, but in this dream she aimed too high. The king flatly refused to sanction a match even between his natural son, the Comte du Luc, and Alexandrine. Oddly enough, Jeanne-Antoinette's next choice was the son of her old enemy, Richelieu. Again she was rebuffed. Finally she settled on another little duke, the son of a friend.

All this matchmaking became immaterial when Alexandrine died suddenly at her convent at the age of ten, probably from appendicitis. The shock was too much for her grandfather; old Poisson died ten days later. Marigny was distraught, and Madame de Pompadour was inconsolable.

The king had also been very fond of the little girl, and showed great kindness to Madame de Pompadour, who buried her grief deep inside her. All her houses and her fabulous collections suddenly seemed meaningless. Without her daughter, there was no future to look forward to, no grandchildren to enjoy in her old age, and, as Marigny had still not found the love match for which he was searching, no prospect of nephews and nieces either.

AFTER THE FAVORITE'S "change of role" in 1751, she modelled herself more and more on Madame de Maintenon, the devout second wife of Louis XIV, studying her life as much as she could, though far less material was available than one might suppose. Madame de Maintenon was forty-nine when she had married Louis XIV. Intellectual and religious, she was also barren. As it was known that she had not been the king's mistress before their marriage, Madame de Pompadour assumed that her physical relationship with Louis XIV had been brief. In fact, at the age of seventy-five Madame de Maintenon had begged her confessor to absolve her from her marital duties, as making love twice a day with the king tired her so. (Her priest felt obliged to refer the matter to his bishop who, while sympathetic, ruled in favor of the seventy-year-old king's conjugal rights.)

Passion appears to have abandoned Madame de Maintenon with age, but religious fervor had not. She had believed it was her vocation to impart her deep devotion to Louis XIV, as well as her wisdom in affairs of state. Inspired by her example, Madame de Pompadour envisaged her own future with Louis XV: cozy in their old age and comfortable in God's forgiveness, they would reminisce on a life of triumphs shared, perpetuated for future generations by *la gloire*.

She began by following in Madame de Maintenon's footsteps to Saint-Cyr, the remarkable convent school Louis XIV's wife had founded for daughters of impoverished noble families. (Madame de Pompadour's dedication and devotion to the school and its pupils so impressed the Mother Superior that she referred to Louis XV's mistress as "that Vestal.") With her thoughts focused firmly on posterity, she embarked on one of her most ambitious and costly projects: the construction of the Ecole Militaire, a project which would glorify Louis XV for succeeding generations.

During the Regency, a plan had been put forward by the Pâris brothers to establish a military academy. A male version of Saint-Cyr, it was to educate and house five hundred boys, the sons of poor officers with some claim to nobility but few prospects. Madame de Châteauroux had also promoted its construction as a means of linking her name to Louis XV for posterity. To convince the king, Madame de Pompadour brought him to Saint-Cyr to see the splendid legacy left by his grandfather and Madame de Maintenon. The enthusiasm of the marquise convinced Louis, and he allowed her to choose a site for the school on the Seine in Paris. Next she pressured her brother Marigny to approve the scheme's outline, and asked Louis' architect Gabriel to prepare some drawings.

Pâris-Duverney, who advanced the money for the huge complex on the favorite's insistence, was to be repaid with the proceeds of a national lottery. She wrote to him: "I was enchanted to watch the King become involved with every little detail; I am burning to see it announced publicly as then there can be no turning back." To another friend she wrote of the beauty of the proposed building, praising it the more as the king had worked on the drawings and details himself without any participation from his ministers. When the plans were posted, to the favorite's annoyance her old enemy, the minister of war d'Argenson, initially received all the credit and praise.

The Ecole Militaire was a project in which Madame de Pompadour believed totally and, during the difficult years that followed, her perseverance never wavered. When funds ran short, she wooed and wheedled more out of Duverney. When that too was insufficient, she offered her own income, pledging 100,000 livres, a sacrifice, Madame de Pompadour told Pâris-Duverney, that she made with great pleasure for the happiness of those poor boys. The marquise wrote that she would not allow a concept to perish which she knew would immortalize Louis XV and, at the same time, establish for posterity her own attachment to his person and to the state.

With extraordinary energy and determination, Madame de Pom-

padour overcame countless obstacles and saw the enormous undertaking through. Five years after its inception in 1751, the first cadets
arrived. Aged from eight to eighteen, they came in forty carriages
from their temporary home in Vincennes to take up residence at the
school. Although the final structure of the Ecole Militaire never
reached its planned monumental size, and the whole project was not
completed until 1770, this beautiful building remains the glorious
monument to Louis XV which Madame de Pompadour had intended.
Gabriel's classical building still stands, though the school itself only
lasted as long as the monarchy.*

Further emulating Madame de Maintenon, the marquise assumed
the role of Louis XV's private secretary. She had never been politically
ambitious for herself, but once she had severed her physical ties with
the king, a genuine desire to help him with everything enabled her to
tighten the bonds of friendship and dependence. As a politician, Louis
XV was astute and involved, but he relied on Madame de Pompadour
to give him the confidence he needed to control his ministers.

AFTER THE DISMISSAL of Maurepas in 1749, Louis had decided to
check the state of his navy and to visit Le Havre in Normandy, where
the fleet was based. While the rest of the royal party travelled by
coach, the king and his courtiers took horses and hounds and hunted
most of the way. They all spent one night at the lovely Château de
Navarre in Normandy, one night in their trundling coaches, and one
night in Le Havre. This was the first time the favorite and most of the
courtiers had seen the coast, and despite the discomfort and fast pace
of the journey, Madame de Pompadour was happy just to be accompanying the king. The entire exercise lasted four days and, although
the Normans felt honored by their monarch's visit, the country complained that Louis' wish to show his mistress the sea and eat fresh fish
had cost the exchequer a fortune.

As usual, money was the country's biggest problem. After the

---

* The fifteen-year-old Napoleon Bonaparte was enlisted as a cadet at the Ecole Militaire in
1784.

Peace of 1748 ended the War of the Austrian Succession, the state's finances had not improved, and taxes were still high. King and favorite were abused for their extravagance by the pamphleteers, and hounded by the mob in Paris whenever Madame de Pompadour was rash enough to go there. By 1754, although France was actually governed by an efficient civil service, the navy still needed a major injection of funds.

Marchault, Maurepas' successor as navy minister, suggested raising the money by levying a new tax on all classes, as well as forcing through a compulsory declaration of property. This tax was particularly aimed at the clergy, who were extremely rich, vast in number, and immune from direct taxation. Traditionally, the Church had always made a token contribution to the state coffers, and the new policy shocked its elders. They realized, however, that public opinion would probably agree that the clergy and Church property should be taxed, and looked for a way to divert the people's attention. For many years, there had been quarrels in France between the various religious groups, Jesuits and Jansenists in particular. A highly organized religious order under the direct authority of the Pope, the Jesuits had caused political trouble wherever possible, and were quick to seize their chance to establish control of the French clergy through this new argument over taxes. Their interference led to a bitter split between the parlement and the Church.

The king was thoroughly annoyed by all the religious haggling which occupied his ministers and caused riots in the streets. In desperation he called on his ambassador in Rome, Madame de Pompadour's friend Stainville, to beseech the Pope to settle the matter. Throughout this endless squabble, it was the marquise's common sense which prevailed. Acting as quasi–first minister, she helped the king establish his will and settle matters between Church and state. Later, the Jesuits were to unjustly hold Madame de Pompadour responsible for their final banishment from France. The order was actually expelled in the year of her death, when the favorite had long made her peace with God and the Church, and had no further quarrel with the Society of Jesus.

Madame de Mailly's sincerely repentant death during Holy Year had helped focus the king's thoughts on religion. The loss of her adored Alexandrine had the same effect on Madame de Pompadour, and became another reason for her to emulate Madame de Maintenon's piety. The fading of her beauty, the deterioration of her health, and the queen's continued resistance to her appointment as one of her *dames du palais** all added to her religious zeal. She wrote to Stainville in Rome: "I worship the Holy Father, and I hope my prayers are efficacious as I pray for him every day." She instructed Lazare-Duvaux to repair her priceless crucifix, and bought a crystal flask for Holy Water from them, instead of her usual trinkets. She threatened to abandon rouge—a sure sign of piety in those heavily painted days—and ordered the little staircase between her apartment and the king's at Versailles to be walled up. She sprinkled her conversation with religious phrases, read the lives of saints, and attended chapel daily—not in her semi-royal box in the gallery, but humbly joining the ordinary parishioners below.

Her ostentatious repentance astonished her friends as much as it amused the court. Not surprisingly, many had their doubts about her sincerity. From Potsdam, home of his new patron Frederick the Great, her old friend Voltaire observed this transformation with an irony not usually directed toward the marquise. After all, as chief patron of *les philosophes* she could hardly have become *une dévotée*. The Duc de la Vallière wrote to Voltaire with the latest news from Versailles:

"A ray of grace has fallen, but there is no intoxication. A few little changes bear witness to it. We have given up going to the play, we fast three times a week during Lent . . . the few moments we can spare for reading are devoted to holy works. Otherwise, charming as ever and quite as powerful, we lead the same life with the same friends, of whom I flatter myself that I am one.

Even some of Madame de Pompadour's closest friends were not convinced, and warned her of her folly should she tire of the holy masquerade and revert to her old frivolous ways. Difficult as it is to believe in Madame de Pompadour's sudden volte-face, it must be said

* The queen's ladies-in-waiting—really her companions, chosen from among the greatest families in France.

in her defense that she was completely frank about herself all her life. According to the court's most observant and relatively impartial chroniclers, the ducs de Luynes and de Cröy, she was never known to have told a lie. But she was also a wonderful actress, and throughout her entire life she appeared to adopt different roles in the same play, thoroughly absorbing them until she convinced herself and the play became reality.

The comedy escalated when she called for a Jesuit priest to hear her confession, so that she could receive communion. Eventually one was found who agreed, on condition that the marquise proved her sincerity by offering to return to Monsieur d'Etioles. Her astonished husband, cuckolded for so many years and living happily with his own mistress, said that he wished the marquise well, but politely rejected the offer of a reconciliation. The priest insisted further. A way of life as public and scandalous as Madame de Pompadour's could only be absolved if she left Versailles. The king, she replied with justification, would never allow it, as he considered her presence necessary to the state. After much negotiation, the favorite finally won her battle and was permitted communion, but only in private—a minor victory, but better than nothing; the queen and the court would at least hear of it, even if they could not witness it.

MEANWHILE, LOUIS XV'S THOUGHTS had briefly abandoned redemption as he pursued a new young beauty at court. Madame de Pompadour was still depressed after her daughter's death the previous year, and this little *affaire* upset her more than usual, especially as she had to welcome the king's new love into her small circle. Like so many before her, the girl overplayed her hand and was soon dismissed from the court. Once again, Madame de Pompadour profited from the king's contrition: Louis appointed the marquise a supernumerary lady-in-waiting to his reluctant but obedient wife.

Until then, Marie Leczinska had been able to use her religious principles as the excuse to prevent Madame de Pompadour's elevation to her household. But when Monsieur d'Etioles refused to take his wife back, it left the onus for their separation with him. Once the marquise had confessed and received communion, she lived within God's grace, and the queen was left with no choice: "I have a King in Heaven who gives me courage to bear my sufferings, and a King on earth whom I obey in all things." Marie Leczinska was understandably vexed that her husband's mistress was raised to a position reserved for the highest ladies in the land, but she was grateful that in Madame de Pompadour she had a rival who was always gracious, generous and kind to her and to all her family.

The favorite's new honor was considered the court's ultimate seal of respectability and approval, and it caused a greater furore among the courtiers than any other she had received. Thereafter, no one could rival her power or position—she reigned supreme beside the king. D'Argenson's rage (and Voltaire's mirth) could not be contained. To celebrate her new status, Boucher's portrait of 1756 presented the marquise dressed to attend the queen for the first time in her new rank, wearing a most elaborate gown and maquillage, and appearing quite the opposite of penitent. A little fatter, and wearing a lace cap in the mornings, Madame de Pompadour looked, according to the queen's friend de Cröy, "quite lovely." When ambassadors called, they found her seated at her embroidery frame rather than her dressing table, and the curtsies made to the Marquise de Pompadour were as low as to a member of the royal family.

DESPITE THE SADNESS caused by the tragic death of Alexandrine, Madame de Pompadour had achieved her every ambition. True, the king still visited the Parc aux Cerfs regularly, but everyone could see that he adored the favorite, the court was obliged to pay her homage and the queen had been forced to accept her. Only d'Argenson remained unpunished and close to Louis XV as his minister of war.

And war was on the horizon. The Peace of 1748 had neatly divided Europe into two well-balanced alliances: England, Austria, Russia, Holland and Sardinia were set against France, Prussia, Spain, Sweden and the Kingdom of the Two Sicilies. As all sides felt little would be gained from a battle between these giant camps, Europe's attention swivelled to the New World, where England had been concentrating on acquiring a colonial empire to strengthen its economy. Louis XV's policies had always been aimed at maintaining peace in Europe, and he had tried to ignore the continued skirmishes between his forces and the English in India and along the frontiers of Canada and Virginia.

In fact, France had paid little attention to its colonial possessions. As it had failed to exploit its rich territory in Canada and Asia, perhaps England's acquisitive attitude was not surprising. Besides, French public opinion, unlike that in England, was firmly set against its holding colonial possessions. Jean-Jacques Rousseau and *les philosophes* cried out for the rights of the "noble savage," while Voltaire denounced Europe's crimes against humanity in the Americas. The high taxes imposed by the French parlement to help maintain the colonial army also had a sobering effect on the people. Besides, most Frenchmen were inclined to believe the description of Canada given in the *Encyclopédie:* "a country inhabited by bears, beavers and covered eight months of the year with snow."

Austria's Empress Maria Theresa, secure on her throne after the Peace of 1748, still flinched at the memory of the loss of Silesia. The jewel in her empire's crown, it had been stolen from her by Frederick II of Prussia. From that moment, this extraordinary monarch set her mind to breaking the powerful Franco-Prussian alliance. By making France its ally instead, she hoped to retrieve Austria's lost territory and humiliate Prussia, the empire's former vassal state. Although one should not exaggerate Madame de Pompadour's role, the favorite had played an active part in France's politics since 1750. A clever woman, Maria Theresa recognized another in Louis XV's bourgeois mistress, and set about winning her confidence.

The first ambassador she sent to Versailles to woo the marquise could not have been a better choice. Graf von Kaunitz was gracious and very charming. He succeeded in cultivating Louis' ministers, the courtiers, the financiers and *les philosophes*. Even more important, he won the favorite's friendship, and sowed the seed of Austria's possible alliance with France in her mind. Louis XV loathed his ally Frederick and had great admiration for Maria Theresa, but his personal feelings were not enough to make him change France's traditional allegiances overnight.

Austria was only to reap the benefits of Kaunitz's efforts five years later in 1755, when the empress sent another charming representative to France. Her new ambassador, the Prince von Starhemberg, informed his sovereign that the Prince de Conti, Louis XV's trusted friend and adviser, no longer had as much influence over the French king in foreign affairs as his powerful mistress. He confirmed that the marquise acted as the king's private secretary and recommended that any approach to reverse France's alliance with Prussia should best be made through her. Here Starhemberg was misled. Louis XV governed through his many councils, and consulted them daily no matter where he was.

In diplomacy, for all her intelligence and wisdom, Madame de Pompadour was an amateur playing in a class of hardened professionals. Her greatest weakness centred on an insecurity over her status— her petite bourgeoise origins never really left her. Imagine her then at thirty-four, the most powerful individual in France after the king, finding herself wooed by the great and virtuous Empress of Austria. It was as if Maria Theresa had placed before her a unique opportunity to help Louis XV outwit the scornful Frederick of Prussia and, by her adroitness, show her king that the hated d'Argenson was superfluous.

Having tempted the favorite with flattery to play politics, Maria Theresa dangled the bait. She gave Starhemberg a secret proposition to pass on to the French king via Madame de Pompadour. Although Louis fully intended to honor his treaty with Prussia, he felt it could do no harm to listen to Starhemberg. To avoid compromising himself, it was agreed that Madame de Pompadour, accompanied by the abbé Bernis, should attend a clandestine meeting with the Austrian ambassador.

Matters as serious as the possibility of involving France in another war should not have been left to Louis XV's mistress and the delightful abbé. A formidable combination in the salon, they were no match for the experienced maneuvering of the Austrian ambassador. His plan for an agreement between their two countries greatly favored Austria, but he convinced the marquise and Bernis of the opposite. In exchange for France's Italian possessions, Maria Theresa offered Louis XV the Low Countries as a throne for his favorite daughter Madame Infante and her husband Don Philippe of Spain. In return for France's help in recovering Silesia, Austria would support the claim of the Prince de Conti to the throne of Poland. Finally, as he knew the Franco-Prussian alliance was due for reaffirmation, Starhemberg played his trump: Prussia, France's slippery ally, was secretly negotiating with England, Austria's ally and France's enemy. This news of Frederick's treachery profoundly shocked the marquise and the abbé. In fact, a possible alliance between Austria and France had been discussed by Louis and his ministers well before Madame de Pompadour had been informed, but on the eve of the Seven Years War, the secret treaty between the two countries was signed by Prince Starhemberg for Austria and the abbé Bernis for France in Madame de Pompadour's pavilion of Bimborian at Bellevue.

In the event of war with France, England was right to fear a French invasion of Hanover, its king's homeland. The thought of Prussia being encircled by Austria, Russia and England panicked Frederick II into opening negotiations with England. But Frederick had miscalculated with regard to France. For some reason he was sure Madame de Pompadour was in England's pay, and that she would oppose any war on land which would take Louis away from home. This may have been the case in the first flush of their love, but ten years had passed, and the marquise thought more of Louis XV's honor than of her loss. Still France hoped to maintain peace in Europe, but when the Convention of Westminster made the Anglo-Prussian alliance public, Madame de Pompadour was proven correct in her support of Austria.

In one guise or another, England had consistently pursued a policy of "divide and rule." The English government coveted France's unexploited possessions in Canada and India, and sought to distract the French at home in order to capture their holdings abroad. Following his treaty with Prussia in 1755, England's King George II sent reinforcements to his American colonies. Despite this strategic buildup, Louis XV continued to hesitate. Neither he nor Madame de Pompadour wanted to accept the inevitability of war.

The English Parliament agreed on a further large subsidy for the protection of its colonies, and approved plans for an offensive on land and sea. While England was so obviously preparing for war, France sent a large, badly equipped fleet to safeguard its Canadian possessions. Most of the ships did reach Quebec or Louisbourg, but when three poorly armed French vessels went astray in fog off Newfoundland, they ran into the English fleet and were fired upon. After weeks at sea, the confused French captain called into the mist, Were they at war? "At peace, at peace," shouted the English captain, and gave the order to fire again.

In France, the people thought the attack on three French ships and the capture of two others by English warships must have been some kind of mistake, and hostilities between the two countries might still be avoided. It was generally assumed that the ships would be returned, but if it did come to war, France and Prussia would, as usual, oppose England and Austria. Louis XV knew better. He recognized that England's naval aggression was an overt act of war. Surprisingly, Frederick II still continued to make overtures to France and to attempt to woo Madame de Pompadour with extravagant offers. The favorite was not deceived. She hated the Prussian king, not least for luring Voltaire away from France, and for naming his greyhound bitch "Pompadour."

As the months of negotiations dragged on, due in part to Louis XV's reluctance to declare war on England, Starhemberg played Maria Theresa's second trump: he let it slip that in order to further weaken France, England had been making overtures to Austria to renew their old alliance. Such a move would leave France totally isolated in Europe and facing England, Prussia and Russia. It was this threat which tipped the scales of Louis XV's indecision. With all the moves on the chessboard of European politics out in the open, the French king saw no alternative. Reluctantly, the parlement agreed with Louis (and Madame de Pompadour) on a formal and public rapprochement with Austria. Louis XV had genuinely tried to avoid war, but once it was inevitable, he was quite attracted to the idea of a Catholic bloc against England and Prussia, who were ruled, after all, by two Protestant German cousins.

All the old treaties were reversed, and on May 1, 1756, the Peace of Versailles was signed between France and Austria. It is true that the marquise supported the Austrian alliance from the beginning with all the force of her personality, but Louis XV had not rushed into the treaty, and had acted with calm and circumspection. Where Madame

de Pompadour could be blamed was in her choice of Bernis as nego-
tiator. A seasoned statesman like d'Argenson would not have agreed
to terms so strongly favoring Austria. In Vienna, Starhemberg and
Kaunitz gave the favorite full credit for bringing about the *renverse-
ment des alliances,* and in Versailles and Paris, Madame de Pompadour's friends and *les philosophes* congratulated her for arranging a
treaty which might help to preserve peace. Her enemies regarded the
Austrian alliance with anxiety, and used it as another pretext to pour
scorn on the marquise. Wicked poems and pamphlets circulated:

> *Versons pour la reine de Hongrie*
> *Tout notre sang.*
> *Donnons pour la Silésie*
> *Tout notre argent*
> *Elle a su plaire à Pompadour.*

(Let us pour out all our blood for the Queen of Hungary,
and spend all our money on Silesia: she has found a way
to please the Pompadour.)

In the same month, and after the French and English navies had
repeatedly harassed one another whenever they met, England declared war on France.

To the surprise of Louis XV, the marquise and parlement, the
French alliance with Austria met with massive national disapproval.
French blood had all too recently been shed fighting its new allies, the
exchequer was empty, and the French people did not want a war they
could not afford, over territory about which they cared very little.
Nor did they relish fighting against their powerful old ally Prussia.
Madame de Pompadour was blamed for everything, although, in fair-
ness, it was the king and his ministers who took the ultimate decision
and responsibility for the treaty and the war.

Two months later, Frederick II opened hostilities against France.
Claiming he was being attacked by Austria, he demanded safe conduct from the French for his troops through Saxony, the home of the
new dauphine. When Louis refused, Frederick marched into Saxony
anyway, occupying Dresden, and Louis had no choice but to come to

the aid of his daughter-in-law's country. The Seven Years War had begun.

At first, France rejoiced in a number of victories over the English. The Maréchal-Duc de Richelieu, with his customary dash and brilliance, captured the strategic island of Minorca after successfully besieging the fort at Mahon and defeating the English fleet. It was a daring feat and gave the French good reason to celebrate—it also gave the world a new sauce made with eggs and oil, all his chef could find after the battle, and thereafter called *Mahonaise,* or mayonnaise.

AT THE END of the year, another kind of disaster struck France. Religious disputes between the Church and the state had divided the country; a very cold winter, high taxation, unemployment, an unpopular alliance, and the people's unwilling participation in an unwanted war, combined to create a tense domestic situation. Nevertheless, the king felt justified in his policies abroad and his decision to tax the Church at home. If his people were disgruntled and dissatisfied, it was because they had the minds of children and were not in a position to understand. Then an incident occurred which shook the nation and, even more, the king himself.

At New Year 1757, the court had moved to the smaller Trianon Palace to escape the cold, drafty rooms and smoking chimneys of Versailles. Everyone had left the main palace for some days, excepting the king's daughter, Madame Victoire, who had remained in bed suffering from flu. On January 5, the king had been visiting her there and was descending the palace steps when a man rushed out from the silent, sullen crowd, bumped into the king and struck him on the chest with a small penknife. At first the wound appeared slight, and a stunned Louis walked back inside to his bedroom—stripped of sheets and all comforts. Although the king lost a lot of blood, the gash was not deep, the assailant had been apprehended and the incident seemed under control.

But Louis continued to bleed heavily and, after fainting several times, he asked for his confessor and summoned his family. Confusion reigned in the empty palace while the king's mattress filled with blood and, one after another, the queen and his daughters arrived and swooned at the sight. After making his confession, Louis publicly begged the forgiveness of Marie Leczinska and his children, and reassured all around him that his kingdom would be safe in the hands of the dauphin. As no one could find the bishop, the last rites were not administered.

No one dared mention the marquise. She had rushed to Versailles on hearing the news and was waiting anxiously and alone, pacing up and down for hours in her empty rooms. At last, Dr. Quesnay came and reassured her; the king was out of danger. But the country was not so well informed. As the churches filled to pray for his survival, crowds gathered shouting insults against the traditional scapegoat, the favorite. "Despite everything," commented d'Argenson in his journal, "the King is loved by his subjects and everyone is moved." Although Louis XV had forgiven Damiens, his would-be assassin, and ordered that he should not be harmed, the man was tortured horribly.

Louis was physically out of danger, but the psychological effect of the attempt on his life was very disturbing. The wound may have been superficial, but the king told his doctor: "It is deeper than you think, for it reaches to my heart." Louis XV had always regarded himself as the benign father of his people, and yet there was one, and perhaps he represented many, who wanted to kill him. For eight days he spoke to no one and brooded in his darkened room.

Madame de Pompadour, meanwhile, had not had one word from the king. Each day a fresh batch of anonymous hate letters and notes were deposited outside her door. Slowly, the king improved, but the marquise received no message, and was so distraught she was near collapse. Her friends advised calm and patience, while her enemies plotted to get rid of her.

Since the appointment of her protégé Machault as navy minister, the marquise had considered him as a member of her camp and a firm ally. To her complete astonishment, the powerful minister failed to respond to her frantic and repeated summons to call on her after he had left the wounded king's bedside. Eventually, when he deigned to come some hours later, instead of giving her news of Louis' condition, he made the curt suggestion that it was His Majesty's wish she quit the court at once.

Madame de Pompadour's head spun, and although she remained outwardly calm, her heart was in turmoil. All her attempts to reach Louis were rejected. As a last resort, she sent her brother, of whom the king was genuinely fond, but Richelieu, first gentleman of the bedchamber, rebuffed him rudely. Mesdames and the dauphin never left their father's side and allowed none of the favorite's friends to see him. This time Madame de Pompadour felt nearer defeat than ever before. She poured out her despair to her friend Bernis and gave instructions for her carriages to be prepared, as well as her house in Paris.

But after so many years of helping others, the marquise was not without friends, and they rallied to comfort her. When the sensible little Maréchale de Mirepoix heard she meant to leave the court, she rushed in exclaiming: *"Qui quitte la partie la perd"* (He who leaves the table loses the game), and urged the marquise to stay put until the king himself told her to go. After all, Louis XV had not received the last rites, and therefore he was not under the same obligation to dismiss the favorite as he had been at Metz. Gontaut, Marigny, Bernis, the Prince de Soubise and the Duchesse de Brancas all agreed that Machault was playing her false. They insisted that the king would be furious if she left the court without his permission, especially as she knew all the state secrets. In the end the marquise agreed to stay, but to delude her enemies she continued with her packing.

Throughout her life, Madame de Pompadour had never lacked courage; now she summoned all she had and sent for her arch enemy, the Comte d'Argenson. The minister of war had been so confident of the favorite's dismissal that he had already written telling Madame d'Estrades to prepare for her return to court. D'Argenson deliberately kept the marquise waiting for hours, something he would never have dared to do before, and when he came, he made no effort to hide his contempt.

The reason for this interview was that Madame de Pompadour had heard that the minister was deliberately showing the king all the hateful letters, threats and seditious matter sent to him through the mail. She realized how it would distress Louis to read criticism of them both at this stressful time, and asked the minister to refrain. D'Argenson had hoped that if the king read it all, he might blame the marquise for the people's attitude and even for Damiens' attack. Madame de Pompadour was certain that d'Argenson was the author of much of it, and told him she found it strange that her friend the chief of police had failed to find any leaflets, while the minister's servants had no difficulty. D'Argenson replied that the king should be kept fully informed of the country's mood, and denied her request. At the end of this short, unpleasant interview, the favorite made her position clear: "Monsieur . . . I see quite plainly that you hope and think I will have to leave the Court and therefore you can say what you like to me. I have not seen the King for five days. It is possible that I shall never see him again, but if I do, you can be quite sure that either you or I will have to go."

After d'Argenson left, Bernis came to cheer the marquise and found her as usual standing in front of the fire, leaning against the chimneypiece with her hands in a muff. She reminded him, he said, of a pensive sheep. Quietly, she replied: "It is the wolf who has made the sheep pensive."*

The days passed. The king was getting up and dressing every morning, but he spoke little, and brooded. Meetings with ambassadors were brief and silent, and the court was numbed by Louis' depression. On the eleventh day, he suddenly borrowed a visiting lady's cloak and disappeared from his rooms.

When the king returned, it was as if the past eleven black days had never happened. He was cheerful, laughing and himself again. Of course he had been to see the marquise. With her sound common sense she had reassured him of his people's love and convinced him that Damiens was a solitary madman. Madame de Pompadour was so happy to be once again in her master's confidence that she wrote to her friend Stainville, now France's ambassador to Vienna† and recently created Duc de Choiseul: "You must not think that present events can lessen my courage. The king's death is the only thing that would do so. He is alive, so I care about nothing else: cabal, insults, abuse, etc. I will serve him, whatever happens to me, as long as I can."

---

* Bernis, *Memoires et lettres, 1715–58.*

† He was an excellent choice, as he had been in the service of Francis of Lorraine, now the Emperor Francis I, husband of the Empress Maria Theresa.

D'Argenson was banished in the king's customary sudden and cold manner. Machault was also dismissed but, unlike d'Argenson, he was allowed to keep his honors and salary. "They have forced me to dismiss him," wrote the king to his daughter in Parma, "a man after my own heart." The ministers' joint disgrace was attributed to Madame de Pompadour's revenge, but as both were opposed to the Austrian alliance, it must be added that their removal also suited the king's foreign policy.

The wretched Damiens, who had made no attempt to flee, had imagined that in wounding Louis XV he would draw attention to the plight of the country's poor. His end was terrible, and came only after hours of public torture witnessed by large crowds, including an English gentleman who had travelled to France to watch the gruesome spectacle.*

On the positive side, the attack on Louis XV had aroused public sentiment in the king's favor and made a reconciliation possible with his rebellious councilors in the parlement. Among them was Président de Meinières, who had called twice on Madame de Pompadour hoping for her intercession on a personal matter. In his account of their conversations, he wrote how impressed he had been with the importance the ailing marquise gave to what she saw as her mission, as well as the clarity of her reasoning: "I must admit I was as struck by her easy speech as by the perfection of her style . . . and I looked at her with pleasure and admiration while she spoke so well."

ON MAY 1, 1757, France and Austria signed their second agreement, "to reduce the King of Prussia's power to limits within which he could no longer disturb the public peace." Although no one protested at the time, the second treaty with Austria confirmed the

---

* This was George Augustus Selwyn, who took such an interest in the proceedings that a nobleman asked him if he was himself a professional torturer. Mr. Selwyn hastened to deny that honor, admitting he was just an amateur. In the eighteenth century, torture was considered a necessary deterrent to crime, especially as the king mixed daily with his subjects at his many public functions. Torture had to be particularly brutal if it were to be more horrifying than the pain which filled an average life. Without anesthetics, all operations were performed on the fully conscious patient, and many suffered as much in the unskilled hands of their doctors as Damiens from his torturers.

first, and was later much criticized for its even larger French contribution. The following June, the abbé Bernis, who sat on the council as a minister of state, was confirmed as foreign minister after performing the post's duties for some time. His immediate preoccupation was to help the marquise find suitable generals. The Maréchal de Saxe had died and no one outstanding had taken his place. In the absence of better candidates, Madame de Pompadour chose her friends, though good friends do not necessarily make good generals. Sadly, her hatred of d'Argenson clouded her normally shrewd judgment, and she refused Bernis' advice to forgive and recall the experienced former war minister.

At last the abbé Bernis was in a position to repay Madame de Pompadour for her years of patronage by interceding for her on a personal matter. Louis had formed a relationship with a beautiful young widow who aspired to the position of *maîtresse en titre*. As foreign minister, Bernis wrote to his sovereign threatening to resign if the widow was installed, as he could not work with a woman whom he did not know, and whom Vienna would not trust. Louis understood, sent the young woman away, and assured his foreign minister that he would never allow Madame de Pompadour to leave Versailles. The king's valet Lebel, who also did not want to see the mistress he knew and trusted replaced, quietly produced a nymphette to distract his master, and no more was heard of the lovely widow.

The Seven Years War totally changed the lifestyle of Louis XV and Madame de Pompadour. Gone were the days of amusing entertainments, and the favorite's glittering carousel ground to a halt. Her charming red-lacquer sitting room became the war's operations center. Maps replaced Bouchers on the walls, and the army's positions were marked by her black beauty patches—a frivolous touch, but practical and near to hand. This was their office, and there, in Madame de Pompadour's presence, the king saw his ministers and discussed every document and detail of the war. With all the nervous energy of someone who feels time running out and a mission to complete, the marquise became a slave to the war effort.

Her health had deteriorated, her beauty was gone and she had never recovered from the loss of Alexandrine. The king's companionship was the only consolation for her deep sadness. She felt responsible in part for the war, and rightly so. Although no battles were fought on French soil, every distant victory was soon reversed by a defeat, and the people blamed and hated her more than ever.

The single constant throughout the Seven Years War appears to have been the confusion and lack of cooperation among the numerous allied commanders. The Maréchal-Duc d'Estrées, who owed his appointment as commander in chief to the favorite, quarrelled with Pâris-Duverney, the army's *munitionnaire*. The result was badly victualed, resentful French troops. He was replaced by Richelieu, who won a number of battles with the luck of the devil he was, but allowed the Grande Armée to rob and ravish the German civilian population. He himself amassed such a fortune by extortion from the defeated towns that his own soldiers, who had lost any sense of discipline, dubbed him *"Papa la Maraude."*

The Empress Maria Theresa was anxious to finish the war quickly, and urged the Franco-Austrian army under the Maréchal-Prince de Soubise to engage in battle, but the French commander knew his badly equipped and undisciplined troops were in no condition to fight. The empress insisted, and the ensuing Battle of Rossbach on November 5, 1757, was a resounding defeat for the allies. Almost every French officer was killed, and a dejected Soubise wrote to tell the marquise of the tragedy. Deserted by the Austrian cavalry, the French troops had been surrounded and slaughtered. "All I can think of are the means to save the army and to put it in a state in which it can make good this misfortune."

Soubise's defeat reflected on his patroness, but Madame de Pompadour refused to desert him. In a letter to Choiseuil in Vienna she demonstrated her grasp of military matters by explaining the battle and its loss clearly and simply. She considered Richelieu the real cause of the shame of Rossbach, but no one at court (other than the king) saw with her vision, and the public continued to blame the favorite.

Although Frederick II had won two further victories by the end of 1757, Madame de Pompadour did not lose heart. But all her energy and constancy could not alter the fact that coalition operations invariably bring problems of command, especially as neither the Austrian nor the French army produced a great leader. The front was far from home and the French people had no sense of obligation or commitment to the war. As foreign minister, Bernis lacked the nerve needed for warfare and opted for peace at almost any price. To make matters worse, Frederick understood the value of propaganda, and had been successfully wooing *les philosophes* and the French intellectuals. As a result, educated public opinion openly supported the enemy. Bernis wrote in his memoirs that there were even ministers and army officers who admitted pro-Prussian sentiments. Public criticism of the alliance with Austria and Russia was more pronounced than ever.

Finally, in early 1758, France's commander in chief Richelieu was recalled. At sixty-two, his face was covered in wrinkles and he was referred to as "the old mummy" by the courtiers. Using his plunder from the German towns, he bought the beautiful Hôtel d'Antin in Paris—promptly dubbed *"Le Pavillon de Hanovre"* to mock the source of its financing. Despite Richelieu's disgraceful behavior at the front, Louis was delighted to see him. *"Son Excellence"* was to continue his amorous pursuits with energy and enthusiasm until his death at the age of ninety-six.

The commander who replaced him, Clermont, a grandson of the great Condé, reported that he found Richelieu's army divided into three different groups: "The first is on the ground; it is composed of thieves and burglars, in rags from head to foot. The second is under the ground; the third is in hospital." With his troops in this state, Clermont had no choice but to retreat, evacuating all the towns Richelieu had won. Demoralizing as this was, the marquise wrote again and again to encourage the commander in chief, who had failed to restore discipline despite hanging the looters and imprisoning the more useless soldiers: "Carry on Monseigneur; do not lose heart because of all the difficulties you are finding."

The French troops in Brittany fared better. Led by their capable governor the Duc d'Aiguillon, they scored a brilliant victory over the English at Saint-Cast, securing the coast and forcing what was left of the invaders to re-embark. Madame de Pompadour had always hated the "milords" and wrote to d'Aiguillon: "I do not know how you could not succeed, with such zeal, intelligence, cool-headedness, and troops who burned, like their commander, to avenge their king."

Further victories by the Prussians and the Hanoverians cast the favorite down again. Still she continued to encourage and comfort the

defeated Clermont. "Who are the fools, Monseigneur, who have led
your troops astray and turned what should have been a fine action
into the worst one possible?" Despite her efforts to ease his bitterness,
he too was replaced, but this did not turn the tide in favor of France
and Austria.

Bernis' nagging pessimism did not help the pervading defeatism
of the parlement or the people either. He bombarded Choiseuil in Vienna with letters low in morale and confidence:

> I die ten times a day. Unless we make peace we shall perish in dis-
> honor. . . . How stupid our generals are! How dull our nation is
> and how little concern there is for the decline of honor and
> courage in France. . . . The Navy is decrepit. Everything has been
> badly planned and thought out. . . . Trade is at a standstill and
> there is no money and no circulation. No Navy, hence no means to
> resist England. . . . What will be the result of this state of affairs?
> The total loss of our colonies; our army cannot even defend our
> coasts. . . .

And much more of the same.

Madame de Pompadour continued supporting her friend Soubise,
and rejoiced in his victory at Lütterberg in the autumn, but this, like
most of the battles won or lost during the Seven Years War, made almost no difference to the eventual outcome. Bernis had lost what little nerve he had and his negative attitude filled his notes to the
favorite: "Canada is lost, Louisbourg in English hands, and above all,
an empty treasury." To Choiseuil he wrote of the marquise: "Her situation is dreadful. Paris detests her and blames her for everything."

Soon the king and Madame de Pompadour regretted appointing
Bernis as foreign minister; he depressed Louis and was really getting
on the favorite's nerves, but none of their other war appointments
had proved much better. There were alternatives among her dismissed
enemies—d'Argenson, Maurepas or the Duc de Nivernais (ineligible
as a relative of Maurepas)—but regrettably Madame de Pompadour
could not forgive them and forget her personal feelings in the interest
of the general good.

Several times Bernis asked to be allowed to step down, claiming his health could not stand the pressure of his post. What he wanted was a cardinal's hat, and to be appointed prime minister: in other words, more power and prestige with less responsibility: "I do warn you, Madame, and beg you to warn the king, that I can no longer be answerable for my post. . . . If the king wants to keep me, I must be given less to do. . . . I owe too much to the king not to sacrifice my life to him, but I cannot sacrifice his affairs." He begged the marquise to have the king appoint Choiseul in his place, while he hoped he could keep his seat on the council and his salary. He wrote to her that he would "look after the Sorbonne and the Parliament . . . and you shall have two friends united at your side."

Louis held back, but Madame de Pompadour had had enough of the fat little abbé's pessimism and complaints about his health. Her own was failing fast, with daily bouts of coughing blood. When only her amazing willpower seemed to be keeping body and soul together, she urged Louis to let him go. The king agreed and wrote to Bernis: "I consent with regret to you transferring foreign affairs over to the Duc de Choiseul, who seems to be the only fit person just now, as I refuse to change the policy I have adopted, or even to discuss it."

By an extraordinary coincidence, Bernis' cardinal's hat arrived from Rome the following night. As yet, the new cardinal had received no guarantee from Louis that he would be appointed prime minister or retain his influential and lucrative place on the council. For some reason, Bernis had imagined he would share the foreign ministry with his successor and form a condominium. "We will discuss matters, perhaps argue, and finally agree—two heads under one hat." But Madame de Pompadour and Choiseul realized that they could hardly be effective with the constant defeatist sniping of the new *Eminence* at their elbows. Kaunitz in Vienna welcomed the change, as all the principals realized their only hope of success lay in a strong and united front.

Two months after Louis had accepted his resignation, Bernis was astonished to receive the king's swift dismissal. He was banished to one of his abbeys within forty-eight hours "without seeing anyone till I order you to return. Send back my letters." Though it would seem the marquise had deserted her old friend of twenty years, Bernis had become a necessary sacrifice to the war effort.* Louis was longing to make peace, and Madame de Pompadour would need all the help her friends could give her to overcome this prevailing attitude of the court, parliament and the country. A triumvirate, instead of Bernis' proposed condominium, thereafter governed France—the king, Choiseul and Madame de Pompadour.

Dealing with Choiseul as foreign minister instead of the whining Bernis was a tonic for the favorite. Choiseul, who was not yet forty when appointed, was short, ugly (resembling a bulldog, according to his friends), and irresistible to women. He continually deceived his delightful, extremely rich wife, and charmed everyone with whom he came into contact. As well as his adoring spouse, Choiseul's household was a ménage à trois which included his sister, the estranged wife of the Duc de Gramont. The king loved her acerbic wit, and she would have been quite willing to step into the role of Louis' mistress if her brother had not forbidden her out of friendship to the marquise.

Madame de Pompadour is often said to have been in love with Choiseul herself and even to have been his lover, but to believe that would be to ignore her condition at the time. Although the marquise was only thirty-eight by the end of 1758, she was physically and mentally exhausted. She relied more and more on the foreign minister, and passed over to him most of her responsibilities. Wearily, she retreated to the familiar area of the arts and the granting of favors, while retaining the outward trappings of power. During the next four years, in addition to foreign affairs, Choiseul acquired an astonishing array of honors and ministries, including war, the navy, the post office and the governorship of Touraine. Quietly he brought about the country's urgent financial reforms, dramatically reducing the foreign affairs budget as well as the expenditure of the king and the court.

Madame de Pompadour, who had disposed of Crécy to Louis at

---

* Madame de Pompadour and Choiseul both felt rather guilty about poor Bernis and helped him financially, particularly as his whole family depended on him. They failed to get a bishopric for him, though they managed to have his exile revoked in 1764. A few years later he was appointed Archbishop of Albi. After Madame de Pompadour's death, Choiseul arranged for Bernis to be sent as French ambassador to Rome, where he later died.

the beginning of the war, also sold him Bellevue. Her diamonds had gone to pay for the completion of the Ecole Militaire, a sacrifice she did not regret, as she never really cared for jewelry. The king and his courtiers had sent their silver to the mint and ate off porcelain instead—which boosted sales at the Sèvres factory and ruined the silversmiths.

The third Treaty of Versailles reaffirming the Franco-Austrian alliance was signed in March 1759. The Empress Maria Theresa was so pleased that she decided to send Madame de Pompadour a gift for all she had done to further the alliance. This was the famous escritoire, made in Paris from two of the empress' own Chinese lacquer boxes which she had chosen and sent from Vienna. The mounts were made of solid gold, not ormolu, and her miniature surrounded by diamonds was incorporated into the design.*

Madame de Pompadour was genuinely delighted by this mark of Maria Theresa's esteem, but as the escritoire was so splendid she hid it, to avoid the court's envy. The gift from the Austrian empress was accompanied by a letter from Kaunitz to the marquise, expressing his sovereign's gratitude for the "constancy and firmness with which, from the very start, you have always favored the system set up by the two Courts." To undermine them both, Frederick had a brilliant forgery made of this letter, reading as if it had been written personally to Madame de Pompadour by the empress, signing herself as the favorite's "friend."

For all his success with internal reforms, Choiseul's appointment did little to alter the course of the war, which had fallen into a regular pattern. Each spring, Prussia would be attacked by the French, Austrian and Russian armies, converging from three directions on Frederick's capital, Berlin. To prevent the allied commanders from joining to form a *grande armée* and presenting a real threat through overwhelming superiority in numbers, Frederick would maneuver between them, defeating each one separately. The tide had temporarily turned in France's favor with victories in 1760, but the public's only interest was in the escalating taxes caused by the war.

---

* The escritoire was missing from Madame de Pompadour's inventory after her death, and seems to have disappeared. The miniature—minus diamond frame—is listed.

The following year, the English navy took Belle-Isle and captured two islands off the Brittany coast, but all Madame de Pompadour's urgent, encouraging letters failed to secure a successful invasion of England by its brave commander in Brittany. Choiseul had brought about the *Pacte de Famille,* a Catholic, Latin union of the Bourbons who ruled over France, Spain, Parma, Naples and the Two Sicilies. The marriages which were to unite these families and bring about the longed-for alliance between France and Spain came too late to benefit the allies in the Seven Years War. Spain was exhausted from its struggles in the New World.

In January 1762, Austria and France's ally, Russia's Tsarina Elizabeth, daughter of Peter the Great, died. The new tsar, her nephew Peter, husband of the future Catherine the Great, promptly made peace with Frederick, his military idol since childhood. Sweden followed suit, and it became obvious that all Europe wanted this long, pointless war to end. The same year there was a change of government in England, whose king, George III, seemed to favor peace. Louis XV realized that his best option was to negotiate with England and salvage what he could of his colonial territory.

An armistice was agreed. Louis sent the Duc de Nivernais to London as his plenipotentiary, but even this famous courtier found the English intractable and determined to fight on to wrench away the last of France's colonies. During the negotiations, Spanish Havana fell to the English, strengthening their bargaining position still further. On February 10, 1763, after five long months of discussions, France signed a disastrous peace, ceding all its colonial possessions other than a few towns in India and Canada, and some fishing rights. It lost Senegal, but managed to keep its West Indian islands. Louisiana was given to Spain to compensate for its losses, which included Florida. Minorca was returned to England.

Although Frederick II managed to keep all his conquests, he had lost the youth of Prussia. The German countryside had been ravaged by the Russians, and the many battles fought on its territory left behind only famine and poverty.

England's losses were minimal, the gains to its empire vast. Choiseul sent Louis XV a memorandum saying: "England is and always will be the enemy of your power and your State. Her commercial greed, her arrogance and her envy of your power should warn you that many years must pass before we can make a lasting peace."*

Nivernais had done the best he could, and what little France retained of its foreign possessions can be attributed to his patience and charm. While he was acclaimed on his return to France, Madame de Pompadour was held responsible for France's disgrace, and was cursed and reviled as she wept with the king.

Seven years of carrying the weight of responsibility for the war, of encouraging flagging generals and supporting pessimistic ministers, had taken their toll. Outwardly she had remained serene and cheerful, but her dream of *la gloire* for the king had eluded her. Her exhaustion was made worse by her depression and the burden of France's shame. The public were not impressed by her efforts, and the hateful pamphlets and verses multiplied. More and more she thought of retiring from the court and living at her château of Menars on the Loire. Twice she had stayed there without the king, causing much speculation. She wrote to a friend: "I ought doubtless to retire from Court, but I am weak and can neither endure it nor quit it."

To cheer her, Louis had commissioned his architect Gabriel to draw up plans for the Petit Trianon to be built in the gardens of the main palace. This would enable them to spend more time on their lovely farm without having to open up the Trianon. The project proved a welcome diversion and they enjoyed working on it together, but Madame de Pompadour did not live to see more than the outer walls of the Petit Trianon completed.

TO ADD TO the favorite's depression over the shameful end to the Seven Years War, that same year Louis had formed a relationship more threatening than any previously. Anne Coupier de Romans came from the minor nobility and was the daughter of a respectable provincial

---

* Although France and England were often at war during the eighteenth century, there was little animosity between the peoples of the two countries. Voltaire wrote glowingly of his visit to England, and described London as *"La Ville Lumière."* While French visitors admired England for its religious tolerance, independent judiciary and free institutions as much as for its wealth, English intellectuals such as Horace Walpole and Edward Gibbon, who spoke fluent French, were admired in Paris.

lawyer. She had refused to live in the Parc aux Cerfs, and when she found she was expecting Louis' child, she insisted that a house be bought for her near Versailles. Very tall and strikingly beautiful, with black hair as long and thick as a cloak, she plagued the king with letters concerning the baby until he wrote to her himself, a rare occurrence: "I wish him (or her) to be called Louis (or Louise) Aimé, son (or daughter) of Louis LeRoy or Louis Bourbon, whichever you prefer. I also wish the foster parents to be poor people or domestics." Madame de Pompadour heard that the child, a boy, was as beautiful as his mother, and could not resist an incognito visit to see them both.

The sight of this lovely young woman swathed in black lace, her wonderful hair caught up in a diamond comb, sitting in the park feeding the king's blond son, totally demoralized her. Loyal, sensible Madame de Mirepoix set her mind at rest: "Be assured that the King troubles mighty little about the boy. He had enough of it and would not wish to have mother and child on his hands." She reminded the marquise how little Louis had bothered with his bastard son the Comte du Luc, who was his father's image. As usual, the mother (badly advised, it was rumored, by Casanova) made too many demands on her royal lover. She was dismissed and separated from her son. Some time after Madame de Pompadour's death, an attempt was made to establish her as the king's official mistress, but it failed and she was married off.* Hers was the only bastard child Louis XV legitimized. The boy became known as l'abbé de Bourbon, and died of smallpox as a young man.

◦≶≶≶∽

THE PEACE OF Paris was celebrated in February 1763 by the inauguration of a statue mounted in the future place Louis XV (now the Place de la Concorde). Designed by Gabriel as early as 1748, the square had been left unfinished. Bouchardon had begun the equestrian statue of the king, intended to stand on a plinth by Pigalle,

---

* Mademoiselle de Romans married the Marquis de Cavanac in 1772, and later the Baron de Meilly-Coulonge. She lived at Passy.

which was retrieved from the sculptor's studio and erected in the middle of the square. The four allegorical female figures around the base, representing Force, Prudence, Justice and Peace, were immediately dubbed Ventimille, Mailly, Châteauroux and Pompadour by the crowd. The festivities celebrating the peace and the inauguration of the statue marked the last public appearance of the marquise.

DROUAIS PAINTED HER in her last years; although he made her radiant and plump, at forty-one she looked like an elderly lady. By this time she was suffering from the last stages of tuberculosis. Bernis' recall and visit cheered her, as did seeing her old friend Madame de la Ferté-Imbault, daughter of Madame Geoffrin. "I found the marquise beautiful and serious," the younger woman wrote,

> looking well, though she complained of insomnia, bad digestion and difficulty in breathing if she had to walk upstairs . . . She assured me she only remained with the King because of her great devotion to him, that she would be a thousand times happier living quietly at Menars but that he would be lost without her. Then she opened her heart to me, as she could do, she said, to nobody else, and told me all she had to put up with. I have never heard a finer sermon on the nemesis of ambition. She seemed so wretched, so proud, so violently shaken and so suffocated by her own enormous power that I came away after an hour's talk feeling that death was the only refuge left to her.

Madame de Pompadour did not have long to wait.

Soon after, at Choisy, she collapsed with a violent headache and hovered between life and death for several days. Her doctor diagnosed severe congestion and inflammation of the lungs with very high fever, as well as heart trouble brought on by stress and anxiety. The king, who cancelled his return to Versailles in order to stay with her, was affectionate and attentive, but he wrote to his son-in-law in Spain that he feared the end of "a debt of almost twenty years and a sure friendship" was near. But the marquise rallied, and was brought back to Versailles. It was a damp, cold, wet spring and her condition soon grew worse again. She sent for the faithful Collin and added several bequests to her will, which is forever stained with the secretary's tears.

During the last days Louis hardly left her. Her congested lungs made breathing so difficult that she could not lie down, but had to be propped up on pillows. Still she did her best to look attractive in a brocade dressing gown spread over white taffeta petticoats. Thin and emaciated, her beauty gone, she never complained, kept smiling at everyone and wore rouge to relieve her deathly pallor. Cosmetics could not hide the disillusion of her life which was mirrored in those huge expressive eyes. The end was plainly near, but Madame de Pompadour knew well that once she had made her confession she could never again see the king, and refused to call for the priest until the last moment. With tears running down his cheeks, Louis knelt, embraced and kissed her, then left the room without turning back.

Before granting the marquise absolution, the priest insisted that she be reconciled with her husband, and wearily she sent for him. Only when he had sent word excusing himself was she given communion and the last rites. The next day was Palm Sunday. The king remained in church all day, and Madame de Pompadour's three great cavaliers, Choiseul, Soubise and Gontaut, stayed at her bedside. When at last she felt the time had come to bid them all farewell, she asked them quietly to leave her to her women. This they did, and as the priest turned to go as well, she called to him: "Wait, Monsieur le Curé, we will leave together," and died.

As it was getting dark, and by law her body could not remain under the king's roof, her servants did not wait for her carriage, or even to dress her. Covering her body with a sheet, they brought her the short distance to her Hôtel des Réservoirs, next to the palace, in a handcart. For two days, Madame de Pompadour lay there in state in her bedroom facing the garden.

With all the bells tolling at Notre Dame de Versailles, the obsequies were first celebrated with a funeral service on April 17. The coffin was brought to the church in a magnificent procession of one hundred priests and twenty-four choirboys chanting and carrying candles. The entire interior of the church had been draped with black cloth, and her catafalque was placed in the center on a raised platform, hung with black velvet studded with ermine tails. After the service, her cortège left the church for her burial beside her daughter in the Convent of the Capucines in Paris.

At six o'clock on that windy, freezing, wet evening, without a hat or coat, the king stood on the balcony of a corner room of the palace. As he watched the procession pass below, he let the raindrops mingle with the tears running down his cheeks, and without turning his head he whispered to his valet: "And this is the only homage I am allowed to offer her. Think of it: to a friendship lasting twenty years."

EPILOGUE

NEWS OF the death of the marquise travelled throughout the courts of Europe as swiftly as had word of her installation twenty years before. As so often before in history, when the object of a nation's criticism dies, suddenly she was mourned and missed.

The dauphin, who openly disliked her, wrote: "She is dying with a courage rare for either sex." The dauphine added to the same letter: "We have lost the poor marquise. . . . The King is in great affliction, though he controls himself with us and with everybody."

The queen wrote to Président Hénault: "Nobody talks here of *what is no more,* it is as if she had never existed. There's the world for you, worthy indeed of love!"

The Duc de Cröy noted in his journal the feeling at court: "Broadly speaking, she was regretted, for she was kindly and helpful to almost everyone who approached her. . . . Her death was almost the greatest event one could imagine."

Voltaire, sincere or otherwise, wrote (as well he might): "I mourn her out of gratitude. It is quite ridiculous that an old scribbler like me is still alive, while a beautiful woman dies at forty, in the middle of the finest career in the world."

Madame de la Tour-Franqueville wrote to Rousseau: "It [does not] surprise me that she is now as much mourned as she used to be despised or hated."

The British ambassador, Lord Hertford, wrote: "She saw the approaches of death with great courage . . . and I think, is generally regretted. She has died poor which wipes off the imputations of rapacity that popular clamour had thrown upon her."

The day after Madame de Pompadour's death, her brother Marigny offered Louis XV his resignation as minister of works. The fat and amiable Marigny's effectiveness had often been underestimated, but not by the king, who had always liked him and appreciated his work. Louis refused to let him resign and insisted that Marigny continue in his ministry as before. He remained as Directeur Général des Bâtiments du Roi until 1772.

AS FOR MADAME de Pompadour's influence on the private life of Louis XV and the court, it was undoubtedly beneficial. The stiff pomposity and discomfort of life in the state apartments was replaced by the cozy intimacy of the *Petits Appartements;* through her inventiveness, hideously formal court entertainments were replaced by the fun of the *Petit Théâtre* and her witty little supper parties. Gently, and with a sure hand, she created for Louis XV a world in which he was surrounded by her own particular brand of civilized perfection, unequalled at that time or any other. Her greatest talent was her innate understanding of the essence and quality of life; it was her dedicated ambition to share it with the king. Her total commitment to this single aim guaranteed its ultimate success. A good judge of character, Louis appreciated her qualities and never ceased to be grateful to her.

Only after Madame de Pompadour's death did the court fully understand her contribution to their daily life, and regret the loss of her positive effect on the mood of Louis XV. His brooding, melancholic ennui returned and cast a shadow of gloom and grayness over Versailles until it was relieved by the jolly Madame du Barry, natural daughter of a seamstress from Champagne. Only then did the court regret the loss from their midst of the cultivated bourgeoise they despised for her origins. And yet it was the qualities of her class, as well as her culture, knowledge and accomplishments, which she brought to the court. Qualities of judgment, a good head for business, scrupulous honesty in financial matters, and a desire to earn the respect and affection of those whose lives touched hers.

Whatever their personal feelings about her career, her contemporaries agreed on her contribution to the arts in France, and on her control of that difficult stratum of society with delicacy, charm and intelligence. She became the arbiter of taste and fashion in all things—a smile or a frown from Madame de Pompadour could make or break a new play, a musician, a painter or sculptor—but she handled this power without caprice or rancor when crossed or thwarted by artists she admired. Her interest in their work was intense, dedicated and stimulating, her loyalty as unwavering as it was to her friends, her family, poor relations and even strangers. She commissioned generously, paid promptly, and provided work for an army of craftsmen. Most of their creations reverted to the crown and, but for the Revolution, would have remained in France.

Her critics have louder voices than her friends, but that does not mean they outnumbered them. Incidents of her spontaneous generosity are legion, and in her genuine kindness to artists and writers she reaped a worthy harvest. Whether on canvas, in marble or in print, her celebrity was assured, and her image remains forever fresh, delicate, sensitive and beautiful—a true Queen of Rococo. By cultivating writers and artists to promote her image positively for posterity, Madame de Pompadour was also able to stem the upsurge of hostility encouraged by the cruel, anonymous *Poissonades,* the product of the Parisian gutter press. The effect these vile pamphlets and verses had on her cannot be underestimated.

Whatever the verdict on her obvious ambition, Madame de Pompadour lived and died working for France through the person of the king, and not only as the supreme patron of the arts. Once her role as Louis XV's mistress ceased to include making love, she had the wisdom and foresight to make herself indispensable to him in his political life. As his impartial counselor and trusted adviser, her influence was longer lasting than any other. In a court of rapidly changing allegiances, Louis could always count on her loyalty, her total devotion and discretion as well as her sound opinions. The king and his interests were her first concern, a fact Louis XV never doubted and rightly valued. She was the fourth of his five official mistresses and the only intellectual among them, a woman of unquestionable ability and infinite resource.

Because she was pretty and decorative, and had raised frivolity almost to a refined art form, Madame de Pompadour's detractors have often failed to recognize her clear political vision. Whether her influence was politically beneficial to France, however, will always remain open to debate. Her policies were simple but definite: peace at home must lead to strength abroad. Religious quarrels only distressed the honest, gave opportunities to the troublemakers, and pointlessly divided the nation. When the parlement assumed too much power, members were reminded that it was *the king* who ruled. She instantly saw Frederick II of Prussia's ambition as a danger to France and to Europe; it had to be curtailed. She thus plunged France into the disastrous Seven Years War. But the political theories she advanced were totally supported by Louis XV and Choiseul (also Bernis, though only in retrospect), and would probably have been proven correct if France had been blessed with better leadership at the time.

She wrote that she wished she had been born a man: "I would have preferred a big part and have to make do with a small one. It does not agree with me at all." France's tragedy was that such intellect, courage and sensitivity, totally dedicated to Louis XV, was not found more often in his statesmen or generals; had it been, France's history later in the eighteenth century might well have taken a different turn.

Traditionally, the foreign wives or the mistresses of France's kings were singled out as the cause of the nation's ills. Marie Leczinska was undeniably a good woman, but a saintly bore makes a poor scapegoat. Madame de Pompadour did not escape wicked calumny, but she braved the hate around her with "sweet audacity" and furthered her ambition to share and improve the king's life with a single-mindedness bordering on the naive.

Voltaire wrote after her death, "Born sincere, she loved the King for himself," and this devotion killed her. Madame de Pompadour was the fourth mistress of Louis XV to die before him. If she had lived to grow old with the king, Louis XV might never have sunk to the degradation and dissipation of his later years. The standards she set for herself and for the king she idolized were of the highest, and would have been maintained. In time, Madame de Pompadour would be acknowledged as one of the eighteenth century's most accomplished, cultured and influential women.

3

Marie Walewska

1786–1817

MISTRESS OF THE EMPEROR NAPOLEON I OF FRANCE

"The man who lets himself be ruled by a woman is a fool!"
THE YOUNG NAPOLEON BONAPARTE

"Be patient. Because of you, your country is very dear to me now."
NAPOLEON to Marie Walewska

"Close to, the man struck terror into my heart. What an extraordinary man! He was like a volcano. The passion which dominated him was not love—which, though violent, was transitory—but ambition."
MARIE WALEWSKA, *Memoirs*

"She is a charming woman, an angel. There can be no doubt that her soul is as lovely as her face."
NAPOLEON to his brother Lucien about Marie Walewska

*B*y the end of the year 1806, following his victory over Prussia, Napoleon, Emperor of the French, was the acknowledged conqueror of Europe. France's triumph over Russia and Austria at Austerlitz the previous year had effectively brought an end to the domination of the Habsburg Empire, and taught the young Tsar Alexander of Russia the humiliation of retreat. Austerlitz was Austria's third defeat by Napoleon, and after each victory more and more of its empire was absorbed into his. Istria and Dalmatia were annexed; "Italian" Austria, renamed the Kingdom of Italy, became a state within the French Empire; and the Tyrol was given to France's ally Bavaria. Out of sixteen German kingdoms, Napoleon created the Confederation of the Rhine as a vassal of France. Only England and Russia still opposed the conqueror.

In October 1806, Napoleon rode through Berlin's Brandenburg Gate after his victory at Jena over Frederick William's Prussian army, but even such a triumph could not erase the defeat of his Franco-Spanish fleet at Trafalgar exactly one year earlier. England, he knew, would not be easy for the Grande Armée to crush, but he could start by destroying its trade, and through it its economy. In order to bring its banking system to ruin, Napoleon formed a policy he called his "Continental System." From Berlin he announced a total blockade of England, barring its merchant ships from entering Europe's ports. No English travellers, no parcels, letters or merchandise were permitted to enter any Continental harbor. Without a market for its unique and inexpensive exports—woolen and cotton fabrics from its mills, silver plate and steel cutlery, scissors and razor blades, as well as coffee, sugar and spices from the Far East—England might be forced to submit to France. But Europe's greatest military genius since Roman times failed to reckon with the influence of the housewife used to these luxuries, which at this time only England could provide. It has never been easy to enforce a blockade; in the face of the European demand for these products, the French domestic shortages spurred on the English blockade-beating initiatives. Napoleon found it more difficult than he expected to bring England to heel, and English gold continued to help his enemies. He turned his attention to Russia.

THE TSAR'S ARMY had not suffered the same fate as its coalition partner Prussia, forced to retreat after the decisive rout at Jena. Russia absorbed the defeat; the young tsar refused to sue for peace and withdrew his armies into Poland. Encamped on the banks of the Vistula, he waited for winter—and for Napoleon. Tsar Alexander could afford to wait.

Poland had suffered partition three times, first in 1772, when Russia, Austria and Prussia annexed a quarter of its territory. The largest country in central Europe, Poland was rich in natural resources and inhabited by an enterprising people. Its rivers and canals, crisscrossing the land, connected the Baltic to the Black Sea, and carried the produce of its rich soil and great forests. And yet Poland had long been crippled—by the accident of geography and the ineptitude of feudal lords. With no natural boundaries to the east and west, and little protection offered by the Carpathian Mountains to the south, Poland was the natural victim of its neighbors. With undisguised interest they watched the country slide into helplessness, abetted by the incompetence of its leaders.

This land of 32,000 square miles of plains and a population of 15 million was ruled by a feudal landed gentry. As the kingdom was elective, the 200,000 nobles whose deputies had the right to sit in the Diet and vote for their monarch could also thwart any reform he might propose by just one veto. This law of total acceptance, called the *Liberum Veto,* successfully prevented Poland's rulers, no matter how well intentioned, and their ministers, no matter how capable, from accomplishing anything.

Through the Diet, the nobility also controlled the treasury and the armed forces, but as the veto was invariably employed on any proposed budgets for the military and the foreign service, the army and the diplomatic corps were all but eliminated. Another of the nobility's ancient privileges was tax exemption, so the rich grew richer and the treasury remained empty. As a result, there were no ships and hence

Pretty, witty Nell Gwyn, in a portrait by Lely.

Nell's reputed birthplace in Hereford, photographed in 1858.

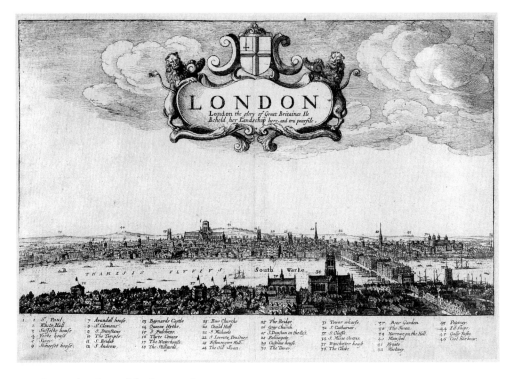

London at the time of the Restoration.

The Restoration of Charles II in 1660.

The Palace of Whitehall.

Londoners fleeing the plague, 1665.

Charles II, the "Merry Monarch."

Charles' queen, Catherine de Braganza, who learned to tolerate his infidelities.

An orange wench, like Nell Gwyn.

Louise de Kéroualle, Duchess of Portsmouth,
Nell's greatest rival for the king's heart.

Barbara Villiers, Duchess of Cleveland.
Charles II found her irresistible for
many years, but her behavior eventually
distanced her from the king.

Jeanne-Antoinette Poisson, marquise de Pompadour, possibly the most cultivated woman of eighteenth-century France.

Louis XV, "the Well-Beloved." He was considered the handsomest man in France.

Marie Leczinska, Louis XV's saintly queen.

The Nesle sisters, each of whom was in turn Louis' mistress.

Louise O'Murphy, an incumbent of the Parc aux Cerfs.

Madame de Pompadour at the age of forty-two, at her needlework frame. She is wearing the toilette she chose for her presentation to the queen.

Portrait of Marie Walewska by David. She was described as having a particularly sweet expression, making one think of an angel or a wood nymph.

Emperor Napoleon in his prime.

The Empress Josephine.

Marie and Napoleon.

Marie, painted by Gérard after her return to Paris with Napoleon's son.

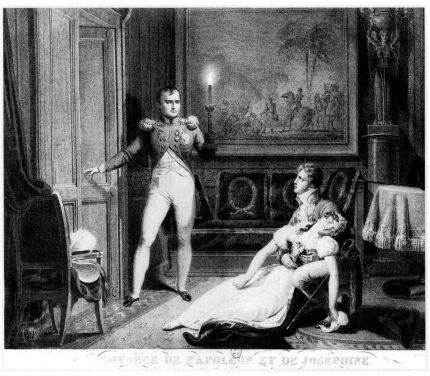

DIVORCE DE NAPOLÉON ET DE JOSÉPHINE.

Napoleon divorces Josephine after Marie's pregnancy proves to him that he can sire a dynasty.

The Empress Marie-Louise, the "womb"
Napoleon married to found his dynasty.

MARIA WALEWSKA
mal. Jacquotot Marie-Victoire

2 50 ZŁ POLSKA

A Polish postage stamp, issued in 1970,
honoring Marie Walewska as one of the
country's great patriots.

Lola Montez. Ludwig I of Bavaria commissioned this portrait by the court painter Stieler for his Gallery of Beauties in Munich.

King Ludwig I of Bavaria. Amiable and intelligent, he dedicated his life to the pursuit of beauty in art and art in beauty.

Queen Thérèse of Bavaria, Ludwig's long-suffering wife.

"Europe Farewell! America I come." A caricaturist's view of Europe's monarchs bidding Lola Montez a tearful farewell.

Lola "enthusiastically" received by American audiences.

Portrait of Lillie Langtry in oils by Sir Edward John Poynter. This was the only portrait of herself that she owned.

Edward VII as Prince of Wales. He fell in love with Lillie and became her lover in 1877.

Oscar Wilde met Lillie at her first appearance in society and was instantly smitten by her beauty. He became a staunch ally and friend.

This portrait of Lillie Langtry was painted by Sir John Everett Millais and exhibited at the Royal Academy in 1878, where it had to be roped off from the press of people. The painting, in which Lillie wore her signature black dress, caused a sensation. In her hand she holds a species of amaryllis that grows on Guernsey. Millais mistakenly titled the painting *A Jersey Lily.* It made her name.

no trade. Without trade there was no gold and, even worse, no exchange of ideas or culture. The key to trade was transportation, yet in both its water systems and its roads Poland faced impossible obstacles. The great river Vistula, which should have been a lifeline, was poorly maintained and only partially navigable. The same was true of the canal system. The only highways were the old caravan route from Kiev, through the medieval capital Cracow, and on to Prague and Vienna, and the major road between Warsaw and Berlin. The remaining roads deteriorated quickly into quagmires, impassable for up to half of each year.

In the law courts, corrupt judges found in favor of the highest bidder, and there was no mechanism for law enforcement. Serfdom was illegal, but the peasants were so poor that they were little more than slaves, though loyalty to landlords was common and often warranted. Their feudal lords may have been irresponsible in government, but they were not lacking in paternal feeling for the thousands of souls living on their domains. The clan chieftains and scions of great families employed vast numbers of the peasantry in their personal armies and splendid "courts," and looked upon their poor or distant relations as brothers, and many of their employees as members of their extended families.

Masters of estates of more than half a million acres of fertile land, the most powerful magnates often owned several towns, and modelled their huge palaces on those of France and Italy. Having made occasional visits to Paris and Vienna and sent their sons on the Grand Tour, the Polish nobility considered themselves cultured "Western" Europeans. But many were far more Oriental in outlook, ruling their estates like independent little kingdoms. Among the powdered periwigs of the courtiers one could count as many potentates with dark flowing mustaches and clean-shaven heads. Their love of ostentation in the decoration of their palaces spread to their clothes and the uniforms of their soldiers, courtiers, staff and retainers.

All the splendor, color, glitter and flair of the neighboring Ottomans and Magyars could be found in Poland: the gypsy music, strong spices, bright hues and textures, rich silks, soft velvets trimmed with fur, the glittering jewels; their prancing Arabian horses with gem-encrusted saddles and bridles, manes plaited with silver and gold, as proud and vain as their riders. More than anything it was in their character that the Polish magnates showed their Oriental connections; in spontaneous laughter or sudden tears, wild generosity or inexplicable cruelty, extreme happiness or darkest melancholy, passion or frigidity, all without restraint. Often reckless, they were blind in devotion and uncompromising in loyalty—love of their country dominated everything. And yet, whether through arrogance or ignorance, by time-honored tradition this love did not prevent them from living for the moment, and thereby they lost all that they held most dear.

In eighteenth-century Poland, the king, deprived of any power, could only watch the decline and rape of this land so blessed by nature. Two further partitions of Poland took place in 1793, when Russia took the eastern provinces and Prussia swallowed central Poland, and two years later, when Austria joined its former partners Russia and Prussia in taking what was left. Poland's King Stanislas Poniatowski, the Tsarina Catherine II's former lover, abdicated, and the name of Poland disappeared from the map of Europe.

Thereafter, only one thought dominated the mind of the Poles—how to regain the independence they had so wantonly lost through neglect and misrule.

Educated Poles had always looked to France as their spiritual and cultural home. French was the language of the court (the educated classes also wrote Latin), and in the capital's drawing rooms French philosophy and Parisian fashions dominated. Since the disintegration of their country, the Poles had found a hero in France's great general, Napoleon Bonaparte. By fighting for "Liberty, Equality and Fraternity" in his army, the Poles firmly believed they would eventually drive out their joint enemies—Russia, Austria and Prussia. Twenty thousand men enlisted in the French forces, forming separate Polish legions. Their motto was "God is with Napoleon and Napoleon is with us." Renowned as skillful horsemen and brave soldiers, the Polish legionnaires in the Grande Armée were highly valued by its commander in chief.

The celebrated French statesman Talleyrand had always resisted Poland's partition. France had gained nothing from the dismemberment, which had led to a distinct shift in the balance of power in Europe. Talleyrand reasoned that a strong Poland would help stabilize

Europe by acting as a buffer between Austria and Russia's expansion to the west. Although Poland's partition had been sanctioned by the Ancien Régime, he urged Napoleon to reunify the country. Europe's conqueror was never convinced of this strategy, but neither could he defeat Russia without Poland's help. He knew he had to make promises, no matter how vague. In their desperation, the Poles were prepared to clutch at any straw. For this reason, they put their faith in the gentle, blond, twenty-year-old Countess Marie Walewska.

MARIE WAS BORN at the small village of Brodno on December 7, 1786. Her father, Matthias Laczynski, came from an old but impoverished family from central Poland, a family with an impressive record of gallantry, courage and service to the state over the centuries. The Laczynskis had flourished until the first partition of 1772, when most of their estates were incorporated into Prussia.

Marie's childhood was happy. The family lived on their farm in Mazovia, twenty-five miles from Warsaw, situated on an endless plain, covered with flowers to gather in spring, dusty sweet-smelling crops in summer, and snow blown by icy winds from distant Siberia in winter. Summer to Marie was one long picnic, and winter a never-ending sleigh ride shared with her family, cousins and neighbors. She was one of seven fair, blue-eyed children who filled the pleasant white country manor of Kiernozia with boisterous laughter, her secure little world revolving totally around the figure of her father.

In 1794, a year before Poland was totally absorbed by Russia, Austria and Prussia, Matthias Laczynski enlisted in the Polish Volunteer Army. United by their desperation about their country's plight, the gentry, civil servants, merchants and peasants alike armed themselves with picks, scythes and axes, and tried to stave off national annihilation by defending all that remained of Polish territory. The Battle of Maciejowice, a popular insurrection against the occupying Russians, was fought before the outer gates of Warsaw. Few escaped the slaughter as wave after wave of Cossacks charged the volunteers in that legendary confrontation. Matthias Laczynski was cut down trying to help a wounded friend.

As they marched on the capital, butchering men, women and children, the Russian soldiers met no further resistance. The streets of the Warsaw suburb of Praga were piled with corpses and awash with blood. Observers claimed the carnage made the recent Terror in France pale by comparison. Poland would long remember the Russian massacre of its innocents.

Marie was not yet eight when her father's body was brought home and buried in the family crypt. Her childhood had ended. His death marked for her the birth of a deep hatred for the Russians and an intense desire to help her country.

Matthias Laczynski's widow Eva, though young and energetic, was left with seven children and a debt-ridden estate; she was hardly in a position to restore the family fortunes, which predictably declined even further. The harvest deteriorated year by year, and the friendly advice of neighbors could not take the place of Matthias Laczynski in running the estate. Steady decay crept over the charming manorhouse of Kiernozia. The roof leaked, paint peeled off the walls inside and out, bats dive-bombed the candles at night, and weeds invaded the courtyard.

Of Matthias and Eva's seven children, two sons and three daughters survived childhood. Tradition and custom, rather than circumstances, dictated the pattern of their education. Already heavily in debt, Eva borrowed further to send the eldest, Benedict, to the military academy in Paris. He was nine years older than Marie, and she saw little of him. Theodore, one year Marie's senior, who was to become her life-long trusted friend, was sent to a smart boarding school in Warsaw. The three girls, Honor, Marie and Catherine, were initially educated at home by a remarkable young man.

In 1790, Nicholas Chopin, future father of Frédéric Chopin,* left his village in Lorraine for Warsaw, as the business aide of a Polish friend long established in France. As the Revolution gathered momentum, travel was restricted and young men were being conscripted into the French army. Nicholas Chopin was nineteen, and not prepared to die for the Revolution.

The Poles welcomed the many émigrés who fled from the Terror,

---

* Marie never met Frédéric Chopin, who was born in 1810, seven years before her death.

including Nicholas Chopin. He learned Polish and quickly found work as a family tutor. Nicholas felt great sympathy for his new country's political plight, and willingly joined the Polish Volunteer Army. Like Marie's father, he fought in the Battle of Maciejowice, in which he was wounded, and was fortunate to survive. He recovered from his injuries and in the same year entered the Laczynski household as a tutor.

FOR THE NEXT six years Nicholas Chopin remained at Kiernozia, and Marie became his devoted, admiring pupil. The studious, intense young Lorrainer taught her excellent French, history, geography and a thorough appreciation of music. But most of all, having found a worthy cause for himself, Nicholas Chopin encouraged her ardent patriotism, until it assumed almost mystical proportions.

Despite the worry of her mounting debts, Eva Laczynska allowed her children to grow up in a relaxed atmosphere, without burdening them with her financial anxieties. It was decided shortly before Marie's fourteenth birthday that, regardless of expense, she should finish her education at a convent in Warsaw. A neighbor's son described her at this time as "very beautiful, with incredibly blue eyes, blond hair which she wore down to her waist and a particularly sweet expression on her face. She made me think of an angel or a wood-nymph."

Warsaw was the first city Marie had seen, although there was little opportunity to explore from her convent. In all there were about thirty-five girls living in, and Marie enjoyed their company. She had always been a conscientious reader at home, but here she had access to new works by the sudden wave of romantic novelists from France. She made a lifelong friend in Elizabeth Grabowska, daughter of Poland's last king, Stanislas Poniatowski, and his morganatic wife Eva Grabowska. Together they would sigh over their romantic heroes, none more than Napoleon Bonaparte, whom they saw as the future liberator of Poland. Marie's intense patriotism focused on this one dream, and she absorbed everything she could read about him, and even scratched his name in the ice on the windowpanes of her room.

She was not alone in her hero worship. Since her father's death and the final partition of the country in 1795, Polish boys had been brought up to fight and die for the restoration of Poland, and girls learned to live and pray for the nation's deliverance. Marie saw her duty as loving God and her country—the one through the other.

At sixteen and a half Marie returned home, her formal education completed. To her hard-pressed mother's joy and relief, she had developed into a beautiful young woman, a suitable consort for a wealthy "liberator" of her debt-ridden estate. Such an idea would not have shocked any of Eva Laczynska's daughters. A great marriage to a wealthy landowner, perhaps a neighbor, was the natural ambition for a girl of their background, and it would also save the family from certain ruin. They all knew that the boys' military careers could never produce the wealth needed to save Kiernozia.

Marie was under no illusion that, as the beauty of the family, she would become the virgin sacrifice. "When I returned home from school," she later wrote in her memoirs, "my mother, busy as always with the affairs of the estate, hardly had time to examine me properly. Her first impression, though, must have been favorable, for she patted me under the chin and said: Marie has grown very pretty. God help her find a husband soon; it would be a big help for all of us." Although deeply religious, Marie doubted that God was involved in the choice of Anastase Walewski.

Count Anastase Colonna Walewski, chamberlain to the last King of Poland, was the largest landowner in the district. Rich and cultured, he lived in an impressive stone mansion about an hour's carriage-drive from Kiernozia. He had been widowed twice, and was sixty-eight years old. His second wife had died ten years earlier, and one of his granddaughters had just become engaged to be married. Slim, and of medium height, the count had bright blue eyes that still twinkled and he was renowned in Warsaw as quite a dandy in his beautifully cut French clothes. He was also rather pompous and a snob, pontificating endlessly on his days at court and boasting of his successes in the boudoirs of fashionable Parisiennes.

After the last partition, Anastase Walewski felt he could do no more for his king and his country. He retired gracefully to his country seat and the pleasures of his excellent library and equally fine cellar. When he needed distraction, he moved to his elegant town house in Warsaw and called on the city's fashionable hostesses or attended the French theater—all suitable diversions for a gentleman of his age. What persuaded him to woo a girl fifty-two years his junior, when even his youngest grandchild was six years older than her, can only be imagined. Perhaps arrogance or conceit led him to believe that this shy, beautiful girl would care for him; all they had in common was their sincere patriotism.

At first Count Walewski visited Kiernozia to advise the widow of his friend Matthias Laczynski. When he saw Marie, transformed from a shy girl in braids to a ravishing young woman fresh out of the convent, his heart, his vanity, or simple lust prompted him to take her and show her the world. The old Casanova began by offering to give a ball in honor of his slain friend's daughter, the first ball she had ever attended.

The evening was a success. Anastase dazzled in his elaborate grand chamberlain's uniform and decorations. For some reason he decided not to wear his peruke, and his bald head shone, incongruously naked, above his finery. A young officer caught Marie's attention, a foreigner whom she guessed was Saxon or Swedish. They danced, and it seems he even called on her several times in the following days. It was her first inkling of love. Then she learned he was Russian, and of the family of Field Marshal Suvorov, commander of the bloodbath at Praga.

It must have come as a severe shock to a romantic, impressionable young girl to find her first love one of the hated enemy, even though it was quite commonplace among the Polish and Russian upper classes to intermarry. But Marie's sensitivity, the memory of her father's death and of the Cossack horrors at Praga, made her young admirer repellent to her. At the same time her brother Benedict, on leave from Napoleon's army, joined Eva in urging Marie to accept Walewski, as only she could save her family home. The realization that she could not escape marriage to her old neighbor panicked her mind and body to seek oblivion in illness.

It was some months before Marie recovered from her "pneumonia" and Anastase was able to continue his courtship. Resigned to her fate, she married him on June 17, 1804.*

The unhappy little bride was nonetheless exquisite. Small, with a perfect figure, she now wore her long flaxen hair in a high chignon of loose curls, as befitted a young lady, which bared her elegant neck for the first time. Her alabaster skin had always attracted admiring comments, as had her large, gentle, cornflower-blue eyes, which failed to sparkle on that sad wedding day at her parish church.

For the rest of the summer the child bride remained with her husband at his country estate of Walewice, and in the autumn they left for a combined honeymoon and Grand Tour. They travelled south, through the beautiful old medieval capital of Cracow and on to Vienna and Bad Gastein, then through the Brenner Pass to Italy. Stopping in Verona, Bologna, Florence and Lucca, the Walewskis made their leisurely way to Rome, arriving in January 1805.

From Rome, Marie wrote to Elizabeth Grabowska, now married to Frank Sobolewski, a future justice minister. She described her travels and her contentment with her kind old husband, and her intention to enjoy all that he had to offer. She told Elizabeth of her joy at experiencing so many beautiful sights and of her relief at knowing that all her family's debts had been settled by Anastase. She also revealed that she was pregnant.

Following a visit to Naples, they returned to Rome for Easter before travelling back to Walewice to await the birth of Anthony Basil Rudolph Walewski, born exactly one year after their marriage. According to local custom, the sickly child was immediately taken from the mother and handed to a healthy peasant wetnurse.

When Marie left her convent, the Mother Superior had written in her report: "She may be a little too introspective for her own good: though shy and reserved by nature, she has strong and even passionate feelings, particularly in matters concerning religion and the tragic present state of affairs in our country." Condemned to a loveless marriage, Marie poured her passionate heart into her patriotism and looked for comfort in Catholicism.

---

* According to Christine Sutherland, Marie had the date on the marriage certificate altered to 1803 at the time of her divorce, to add weight to the argument of coercion, as she would then have been just sixteen (*Marie Walewska, Napoleon's Great Love*).

"IT IS IN the interest of France, in the interest of Europe, that Poland exists," Napoleon had said as he marched eastward from Berlin toward Warsaw. But despite his bold rhetoric, the emperor's policy regarding Poland's future was ambiguous. Though defeated, Tsar Alexander had refused to make peace with France, and by the end of 1806 Napoleon knew that he might find himself coerced into a winter campaign. The news of the Russian Army's sudden westward advance into East Prussia and Poland forced Napoleon's hand. His troops were neither trained nor equipped to fight in deep snow and freezing conditions. To supply his 300,000 men with food, remounts, accommodation and reinforcements he would need substantial Polish help; but for this he would have to make promises.

By 1806, nothing remained of Poland that could be recognized as a sovereign state. After his total victory at Jena, Napoleon could have insisted that Prussia return its Polish territories. To antagonize Austria at this time with a similar demand might jeopardize its neutrality in the coming conflict. Nor did he want the Poles, encouraged by French promises of liberation, to stage uprisings in Russian-occupied territories and force France into war prematurely. But without the Poles' help, he could not hope to defeat Russia. When he sent his marshals Davout and Murat to precede him into Poland, he instructed them that they should arrive not as conquerors, but as liberators. The nearer Napoleon came to Warsaw, the more vague his promises became, and the louder his demands for supplies and men.

Far from trembling at the advance of the Grande Armée, the extent of the emperor's demands, or the absence of any guarantees in return, the majority of Poles still saw Napoleon as the Messiah. They welcomed the prospect of receiving the man they had long regarded as their future liberator, the only man capable of restoring to them their beloved country. By defeating Austria and Prussia, Napoleon, crowned little over a year before, had dissolved the empire of Charlemagne and begun to realize his dream of a new empire and a united Europe. The Poles had no doubts that he would also re-create a strong and autonomous Poland under the protection of his eagles, the standard for whose glory so many of their countrymen had fought and died.

When it became known that the French were coming, Warsaw was thrown into a frenzy of excitement and preparation. The capital's Prussian military governor hastily packed and left with his troops, followed by a hail of stones and abuse from the citizens. Some marauding Russian detachments met the same reception. A citizen's council of prominent Poles was formed to present the keys of a free Warsaw to Napoleon's representative, his brother-in-law and Marshal of France, Prince Joachim Murat.

Benedict Laczynski, Marie's brother, had been quietly sent by his regiment to recruit volunteers for the French army in his home district, and Marie and her husband visited Walewice that autumn to see him. Their house had been occupied by the staff of the French Guards Brigade, and they moved to the adjacent home of their factor. While trying to cross the muddy road to the main house, Marie was literally swept off her feet by a charming young officer, and deposited safely on the dry steps opposite. A lieutenant attached to the Imperial General Staff, Count Charles de Flahaut was the son of France's great statesman Talleyrand and his mistress, Adélaïde de Flahaut. The aging foreign minister was himself struggling to Warsaw over Poland's impossible roads, to prepare for the emperor's arrival and to hear what news and gossip his son had gathered. It was Talleyrand who had secured this posting on the Imperial Staff for his son, and it would also be Talleyrand, the omnipresent schemer, who would present (some would say procure) Marie to Napoleon.

⚜

As a young man, Napoleon Bonaparte had recognized only one love—his homeland Corsica, for which he was prepared to die. All other forms of love he despised, and said so in a treatise on the subject: "I regard love as injurious to society and as destructive to the individual's personal happiness. I believe that it does more harm than good. We could thank the gods if the world were quit of it!" He pitied friends smitten by love as if they had some ghastly disease, and considered human love debasing. When every refinement of the old regime was being swept away during the Revolution by the new liberty, Bonaparte noticed that ladies in general remained steadfast to the old social conventions, and he mocked them for it: "The women are royalists almost without exception. No wonder for that, seeing that Liberty is fairer than they, and eclipses them."

And yet, for all his cynicism, Napoleon had many mistresses. Women did play a part in his life, but only on his terms. He used women for relaxation, a temporary necessity. As a young man he wrote: "Woman is indispensable to man's animal organization; but she is even more essential to the satisfaction of his sensibilities." With no time to devote to cultivating and refining these sensibilities, he often appeared rude and brusque in conversation with ladies in society, making gauche and personal remarks almost calculated to embarrass. His manners were those of a conqueror, who had no time to learn the art of seduction, and no desire to flirt or to flatter. As a young soldier on campaign Napoleon had no leisure time to acquire the skills of the successful lover. Women, he wrote, "misuse certain advantages in order to lead us astray and to dominate us. For one who inspires us to do good things, there are hundreds who bring us to folly."

Napoleon was educated more as an Italian than a Frenchman, which showed in his attitudes to love and morality, and to women as lover, wife or mother. At his court, ladies were to be ornamental and moral. "In women," he said, "chastity is what courage is in men; I despise a coward just as much as I despise a loose woman." His was a serious rather than a frivolous court, its female members natural and unspoilt. What the young ladies lacked in sophistication they made up for in freshness and joie de vivre. The emperor was totally inflexible about the court's moral code: mistresses, no matter how exalted their breeding, were not admitted. His own infidelities he excused as weaknesses, not vices.

Almost as much as women "with a past," the emperor detested intellectual women, especially those who tried to interfere in politics. "States are lost," he said, "as soon as women interfere in public affairs. . . . If a woman were to advocate some political move, that would seem to me sufficient reason for taking the opposite course." And, in a bulletin to the Grande Armée: "How unhappy are those princes who, in political matters, allow themselves to be guided by women." Intellectual women he considered bossy and meddlesome, and the women closest to him, epitomized by Josephine, were very feminine.

The one woman above criticism in Napoleon's eyes, and against whom he measured all others, was his mother, Letizia Bonaparte. Married for twenty-one years, she bore thirteen children, of whom eight survived. Strong, loyal and honest, she was Napoleon's ideal of a housewife and mother, and she ruled her children with a rod of iron. They always obeyed her and dreaded her displeasure. "She knew how to punish and to reward; and, detesting all our baser feelings, she knew how to nip them in the bud." His concept of family loyalty, each member supporting the other, came from his Corsican childhood, and he regarded his brothers' and sisters' children as if they were his own.

From his mother he learned to respect marriage, and to consider its only purpose the procreation of children. That his own marriage was childless was the source of his greatest disappointment. An energetic matchmaker, he promoted marriages among his general staff, at his court and among his own family.

In his early love affairs, Napoleon did not open his heart to a woman before Josephine, although it seems his temperament craved love. Only with Josephine did he discover the depth of his own sensuality, and he sanctioned it with their marriage. Certainly his letters to her burned with desire. All his posturing against women, all his hurt and rage at Josephine's many infidelities, melted at the sight of her tears, and he forgave her everything. Such a man could not be immune to love, but he never lost sight of his ultimate goal; his actions were always dominated by his ambition.

THE CITIZENS OF Warsaw waited en masse in the cold and rain to welcome Prince Joachim Murat, Marshal of France, victor of Auerstadt and brother-in-law of Napoleon. Riding at the head of his troops on a Lipizzaner stallion, its mane plaited with silver and jewels, Murat, darkly handsome, was a dazzling figure. He wore a flamboyant green velvet uniform of his own design, its cape lined with sable. A green velvet hat with sweeping white ostrich plumes (for all the world like a pantomime musketeer), which he swept from his shoulder-length hair and flourished at the crowds and the Polish delegation, completed the picture.

Prince Joseph Poniatowski, the forty-year-old nephew of Poland's last king, a charming, cultivated man possessing great qualities, who was later to be described by Napoleon as "the natural king of Poland," led the delegation. He was handsome, popular, loved by men and women, and a patriot. Since the partition, Poniatowski had tried to avoid politics, but now, by popular request, he headed the citizens' council.

Murat was welcomed as Poland's new king—which indeed he hoped to become. The populace vied for the honor of housing the soldiers, and the city gave a memorable reception and ball to honor the marshal, his staff and officers, at the recently restored royal palace.

Marie was just twenty, and loved to dance. Each year since her marriage, she had spent the winter months in Warsaw attending receptions with her husband. Anastase had aged, and appeared older than his seventy-one years. While he remained socially as indefatigable as ever, he did little to earn the appreciation of his hostesses, and tended to neglect his wife. Marie would have enjoyed these evenings had it not been for her husband's jealousy if she so much as danced twice with the same partner, or spoke with any man for more than a moment. As a mother and the wife of a senior citizen of Warsaw, her place, according to Anastase, was with the other dowagers on the sidelines.

Count Colonna Walewski considered that he knew more about court etiquette than anyone, but to his intense chagrin he had not been invited to join the citizens' council to prepare the festivities for the emperor's arrival. His affectations had annoyed too many people, though naturally the Walewskis were invited to the reception for Prince Murat. A contemporary source noted that Marie danced with the delightful Charles de Flahaut, who presented her to his father, Talleyrand, Prince de Benevento. Father and son were heard commenting on the charm and elegance of the Polish ladies, and of Madame Walewska in particular, as a pearl of beauty and intelligence.

Talleyrand was one of the most complex, brilliant characters of the age. A master of foreign policy, he was a product and disciple of the Ancien Régime. While he considered Napoleon a parvenu, he admired his genius and the glory he brought to France. Talleyrand was opposed to the Revolution and determined to destroy it, and with it Napoleon, who had risen through its ranks. While Talleyrand despised his master, he enjoyed his favor and was delighted to have been made a prince of the new empire. Napoleon was aware of Talleyrand's secret treachery, and the two were locked in a mental game of chess. Talleyrand was obsequious, yet he mocked the parvenu's obsession with etiquette; Napoleon, for his part, enjoyed tormenting his old grand chamberlain by summoning him to attend him in full dress in the middle of the night.

There are many dissenting accounts of Talleyrand's ambivalent relationship with Napoleon, but most agree that he was an excellent judge of quality in all things. He was very taken with Marie, and if he used her for his own ends, they coincided with hers and with Poland's. He knew his master too well to imagine that Napoleon would be influenced by a girl of twenty, albeit a pretty, intelligent one, but he saw to it that the Walewskis were included on all the lists for the various entertainments planned for the emperor. Besides, he liked Marie, and throughout their acquaintance he never denied her his advice.

If Murat's arrival caused a fever of excitement in the population, Napoleon's was to have been a sensation. Bonfires were to have been lit across the country as he approached the capital through decorated, illuminated triumphal arches, accompanied by torch parades. But it was not to be. War was on the horizon, and the "liberator" had work to do. The Russian armies were combat-ready and encamped not far from Warsaw. Accompanied only by a small cavalry escort and Berthier, his chief of staff, Napoleon arrived in Warsaw unexpectedly on horseback late on the night of December 18, 1806. In the next four days he reviewed his troops and refused to see anyone except his chiefs of staff. As suddenly as he had arrived, he left for the east with his Imperial Guard and a regiment of Polish Lancers.

The mood in Warsaw changed overnight from festivity to that of a city on the front line, and throughout Christmas week cannon boomed from the east. Wounded soldiers rapidly filled the hospitals.

Cold, hungry and far from home, they spoke of the dreadful conditions at the front, where they lost their boots in the rivers of mud unless they were tied to their waists. Moved by the plight of these poor French soldiers fighting, in their eyes, for Polish freedom, the people of Warsaw closed their schools and opened their houses to give them room and beds. The harsh weather and terrible road conditions made it impossible for the French to take advantage of their usual speed of attack. The Russians withdrew, and the Grande Armée found it too difficult to follow them through the mud. By New Year's Eve Napoleon issued orders for the army to go into winter quarters, and he returned to Warsaw.

Since her marriage, Marie had moved like a sleepwalker through her days, numbed by the prospect of her future by Anastase's side. Her mother noticed a depression in her daughter, "a sort of suppressed lament that betrayed a hidden strain of melancholia." Nor did Marie find much consolation in her child, as she was allowed so little say in his care. Unlike many of her contemporaries, she longed to have her son with her, not whisked away to be smothered by too much attention from Anastase's old sisters at Walewice. Marie's confidante, Elizabeth Grabowska, was disturbed by her friend's attitude of resignation. But since the arrival of the French in Warsaw everything had changed, and Marie's eyes began to shine with a new fire. Elizabeth watched with growing concern what she referred to as "Marie's patriotic exaltation."

Elizabeth and Marie had joined the ladies of Warsaw who were working long hours in the hospitals tending the wounded soldiers. More worldly than her friend, Elizabeth expected more concrete evidence of Napoleon's gratitude for Poland's sacrifices for him over the past ten years, and had less faith than the idealistic Marie in the emperor's promises.

Shortly before the Battle of Jena in October, Napoleon had learned that Eléanore Denuelle, who had been placed in his bed by his sister Caroline Murat, was pregnant. Napoleon's brothers and sisters hated Josephine, and did all they could to torment her. Caroline hoped that if Eléanore could give her brother a child, so proving that Josephine's childlessness was her fault and not his, he would divorce his wife and remarry. Eléanore was a friend of Caroline's from school and had just the right qualities to amuse Napoleon. She was also greedy, and prepared to accept the "stratagem," as Caroline's plan was called, in exchange for money.

Napoleon was always remarkably tolerant of his bickering siblings, who hated one another almost as much as they loathed Josephine. He had placed them on several of Europe's thrones, but he knew that unless he created his own dynasty, his system of government and his empire could die with him. His enemies would simply continue to force him into one war after another until his strength was exhausted.

A dynastic marriage into one of Europe's great families would placate some of his enemies, but if the union was childless they would all just wait until he died to return Europe to the old order. If he produced a son from such a marriage, his family would be firmly established and recognized, and his empire's future secure.

Josephine had been with Napoleon at his headquarters in the Teutonic palace at Mainz when he had heard the news of Eléanore's pregnancy. As a desperate ploy, she implied that she knew all about this little *affaire* and insinuated that Murat, Caroline's husband, was also Eléanore's lover. By casting doubt over the unborn child's paternity, Josephine was able to destroy Caroline's "stratagem." This defeat hurt Napoleon as much as any in battle. Josephine knew her magic was losing its effect on her husband, and was terrified that he would set her aside. Napoleon sensed that she would stop at nothing to avoid divorce, and even suspected that his wife had encouraged Murat with Eléanore.

Throughout November and December, Josephine remained at Mainz. Waiting anxiously for Napoleon's summons to join him at his winter quarters, she bombarded him with pathetic letters to which he replied kindly, promising to send for her soon.

On December 31, the day he heard of the birth of Eléanore's son,* Napoleon wrote to Josephine: "I have had a great laugh over your last letters. You idealize the fair ones of Great Poland in a way they do not deserve."

Returning to Warsaw, Napoleon decided to remain there in winter quarters for the month of January 1807, and the unending round

---

* The boy grew to look remarkably like Napoleon, and was certainly his.

of receptions and balls could at last begin. The emperor had yet to meet the "fair ones" of Warsaw.

A number of Napoleon's biographers relate an incident concerning Marie which was said to have taken place outside a posthouse at the little town of Bronie. It was known that Napoleon was to stop there briefly on his way into Warsaw, and a small crowd had gathered to greet him. According to a number of accounts, Marie was carried away by patriotic fervor and, wishing to welcome her hero herself, she went to Bronie in her carriage with a friend. Veiled and simply dressed, the two young women waited, and when Napoleon's carriage stopped to change horses, Marie is said to have given him a bouquet and a charming message of welcome. The emperor was enchanted, and on his arrival in Warsaw he asked to have the young lady (whose name he had discovered from the arms on her carriage) presented to him during his reception. (Constant Wairy, Napoleon's personal valet and a meticulous chronicler, does not mention the incident in his diary, and Sutherland found no verification either, but the story has been handed down and believed by Marie's Ornano descendants.)

When the invitation to the first great reception for the emperor arrived, Marie's shyness at the thought of meeting her childhood hero, her country's deliverer, overcame her, and she begged Anastase to refuse. But if Talleyrand had had a special mission for her, he could not have prepared the ground better. After meeting Countess Walewska at the reception for Prince Murat, Talleyrand had flattered Walewski by pretending to remember him from years before at Versailles. After that, nothing would persuade the vain old courtier to give up the honor of meeting the emperor, and in the company of his beautiful young wife. Marie was to order an elaborate new dress and wear the family sapphires. Walewski even arranged for an old friend, Henriette Vauban (Prince Joseph Poniatowski's mistress), who had spent many years at Versailles, to instruct his wife on the finer points of court etiquette.

At the time of his arrival in Warsaw, Napoleon was thirty-seven and in his prime, fit and hardened by tough campaigning. His mind was alert, and no one of his staff could keep pace with his energy or capacity for work. He was five foot seven (the average height for Frenchmen at the time), broad-chested yet slim, with fine olive skin, about which he was very vain. His gray eyes could pierce the soul of a man, or melt with tenderness at Josephine's tears, though of late those tears had moved him less than in the past.

Since his coronation, the emperor had withdrawn into himself, as if all his great achievements had made him even more alone. After ten childless years with Josephine, and endless tragicomic dramas over infidelities exposed and forgiven, his only remaining unfulfilled dream was to found a dynasty—and this seemed impossible with his wife. On the other hand, his empress was French, and popular with the people.

Napoleon had not sought out a mistress while on campaign for a number of years. In Berlin, his valet noted how very much absorbed in his thoughts he appeared, and a new note of bitterness crept into his comments about women: "They belong to the highest bidder. Power is what they like—it is the greatest of all aphrodisiacs. . . . I take them and forget them."* The episode with Eléanore Denuelle may have been partly to blame—he knew Murat would have been only too willing to seduce a young temptress conveniently living under his roof. Joachim Murat was irresistible to women, and Napoleon knew he had not even restrained himself from conquering his empress. Ten years of the faithless Josephine, whom in a sense he would always love, had shrivelled Napoleon's heart. As he returned to winter in Warsaw, the last thing he expected or desired was to fall in love.

At the age of twenty, Marie Walewska had given herself only two goals in her short life: Poland's "renaissance" and Heaven. Then she met Napoleon.

⚜

WARSAW WAS *EN fête*—the emperor who was to restore their country to the Poles was to be their guest for a month, and he would not find the city inhospitable.

On the night of January 7, 1807, a heavy blanket of snow covered the Polish capital, muffling the sound of hundreds of horses and carriages winding their way in a well-lit procession up the escarpment to

---

* Constant.

the royal palace high above the frozen Vistula. The ball which the capital gave for their hero was the greatest event in the lives of most of its citizens. At Napoleon's request, not only society but also representatives from the arts and prominent merchants were invited. The old castle of Poland's kings was brilliantly lit as the glittering company progressed between two rows of the Imperial Guard, resplendent in scarlet uniforms, to be received by Prince Joseph Poniatowski.

The walls of the principal drawing room had been re-covered with yellow damask, and a thousand candles flickered in the huge Venetian chandeliers. As Poland's past kings gazed down on the assembly from their portraits on the walls, the scene would have reminded them of the splendor of former times. Deep green, scarlet, black, pale blue and white uniforms, heavy with gold braid and medals, embellished with colorful sashes and decorations, vied with the rustle of silks and satins and the sparkle of the ladies' jewels in the candlelight. Spurs jingled up the grand staircase, heels clicked, swords gleamed and ostrich plumes fluttered as hats were swept off in greeting.

Most of the ladies dressed in the French fashion as a compliment to their guests. They wore narrow Empire ballgowns, small sleeves coming from wide, deep décolletés, their heads framed by high, stiff lace collars. Hair was worn up in chignons pinned with flowers or jewels.

Marie arrived with her two aging sisters-in-law and Anastase, who wore his full-dress uniform from his days as court chamberlain. In her slim dress of velvet in a blue that matched her eyes and the Walewski sapphires, golden hair piled high with little curls escaping and framing her delicate features, Marie looked more like Walewski's granddaughter than his wife. Taking her place in the receiving line between husband and sister-in-law, she trembled with nerves and expectation. It was happening: soon the hero of her childhood, the savior of her country, would be standing before her.

Countess Anna Potocka, whose husband had graciously given the main floor of his palace over to Prince Murat, described the atmosphere of nervous excitement which pervaded the room. "We waited for quite a long time on the evening of the presentation, and admittedly our curiosity was mixed with apprehension." Word of the emperor's capriciousness, even rudeness, at social gatherings had spread, and the longer they waited the greater the tension throughout the ballroom became. "Suddenly a rush of sound broke the silence, the doors burst open, and M. de Talleyrand advanced declaiming in a loud, clear voice the magic words which cause everyone to tremble: 'The Emperor!'"

Unlike his marshals, who dressed like peacocks, Napoleon chose simple uniforms which stood out for their plainness among all the gold braid and feathers. Followed by his faithful friend Marshal Duroc, Master of the Imperial Household, the emperor proceeded down the line as Talleyrand presented the guests one by one. In her memoirs Madame Anna Nakwaska, who was standing near Marie as the emperor reached her, describes Napoleon's initial preoccupation. Then

> as he looked around, his face gradually softened, the powerful brow relaxed . . . as he surveyed us with evident approval. *"Ah, qu'il y a des jolies femmes à Varsovie!"* I heard him say as he stopped in front of Madame Walewska, the young wife of the old Chamberlain Anastase, who happened to be standing next to me.

Marie must have been a delight to the eyes, so young and fresh, her cheeks flushed. In his memoirs Constant refers to her "skin of dazzling whiteness" and her "charming and beautifully proportioned figure." Napoleon was seen to hesitate before her, then he passed on. Later in the evening he was noticed looking in Marie's direction; Talleyrand, his old procurer, was briefing him about her and her situation.

The guest of honor's comment about the beauty of Warsaw's ladies had swept around the ballroom; as had the fact that it had been directed at the lovely Countess Walewska. The feelings of the other guests were mixed. Pride that a national flower such as Marie appealed to the Great Deliverer mingled with envy of the shy country girl with no ambition or aspirations who had been singled out. The only person unaware of the sensation she had caused was Marie herself.

IT HAD BEEN decided that the carnival season for the year should be launched by a ball given a few days later by Talleyrand, Prince of Benevento. The foreign minister had occupied a splendid palace, which he transformed into a fairy-tale setting for an evening the city would never forget. The emperor's personal *chef d'orchestre* came from Berlin by fast sled, together with his wife, a famous singer, and countless delicacies, vintage wine and flowers. All the great conjurer's experience concentrated on creating a remarkable mise-en-scène to help win the emperor's affection for Poland and her cause.

Of course Talleyrand had noticed the effect of the beautiful young countess on Napoleon; more than likely he had even planned it. No one knew his master's domestic situation as well, or could better anticipate his needs, than the foreign minister. He was anxious to find a way to inspire Napoleon to honor his promises to the Poles and so to protect Europe from Russia. In winter quarters, far from home and without his wife looking over his shoulder, Napoleon might lose himself in the spirit and passion of a people ready to worship and even die for him. If the little countess fitted the emperor's current needs, Talleyrand would deliver her to him.

AGAIN MARIE HAD begged her husband to decline the invitation, and again he admonished her and accepted. No matter how much Anastase urged her to hurry and finish dressing for Talleyrand's ball, her nerves and excitement slowed her toilette. To see and speak to her hero twice within a few days was almost too much for her.

The narrow, winding streets of the old town leading to Talleyrand's palace were lit by barrels filled with burning tar, and crowded with people watching and hoping for a glimpse of the emperor. As the Walewski carriage approached, the music told them the dancing had begun, and that therefore Napoleon had arrived. When their carriage came to a halt opposite the Imperial Guard of Honor on the palace steps there was a flurry of excitement, and Louis de Périgord, aide-de-camp to General Berthier, greeted Countess Walewska on behalf of the emperor and bade her follow him.

Napoleon had given orders to find Marie the moment she entered, as he wished to honor her as his partner in the contre-dance.

As Anastase watched his wife's graceful movements on the dance floor, he was astonished at her overnight rise to prominence. There was Marie, together with three of Warsaw's great beauties, dancing with the emperor and his two brothers-in-law, Prince Murat and Prince Borghese, the chief of staff General Berthier making up the eightsome. Walewski was aware of the general interest in Marie, and had noticed the whispers and furtive glances in her direction, but instead of scowling with his customary jealousy, he beamed and absorbed the admiration as if it was directed at him, preening and bowing around the ballroom. Constant recorded his impression of Walewski that evening: "an old noble of exacting temper and extremely harsh manners, more in love with his titles than with his wife, whom, however, he loved devotedly, and by whom he was more respected than loved."

All the beauty and glamour Poland had to offer was present that evening, but the eyes of the Conqueror of the West were fixed on the shy young woman with whom he insisted on dancing—for which he had no talent at all. That night, Marie wore a high-waisted dress of white satin lined with gold and pink, her only jewelry a coronet of golden laurel leaves on her blond curls. To Napoleon, who knew all her circumstances by now, she appeared a sacrificial virgin, given to an old man for the sake of her family.

The dance over, the emperor, touched and charmed by her shyness, tried hard to put her at her ease with questions about her family and her home. He then admitted that he disliked her dress: white tulle on white satin did not become her beautiful white skin. Constant says the emperor "immediately began a conversation [with Marie], which she sustained with much grace and intelligence, showing that she had received a fine education, and the slight shade of melancholy diffused over her whole person rendered her still more seductive."

If Napoleon found Walewski's young bride seductive, as Constant claims, Marie was not consciously to blame. Every contemporary account describes the sweetness of her expression, her innocent, unspoiled nature and her lack of any kind of coquetry or sophistication. And yet, to attract Napoleon initially, Marie Walewska must have had a passionate personality beneath her placid temperament. She also spoke and argued well, and was particularly convincing and articulate on her one great theme—the liberation of Poland. Thanks to Nicholas Chopin, her education was thorough—indeed, for a young Polish woman, quite exceptional—but she was not remarkably gifted or highly intelligent. Napoleon was more drawn to her pale, fragile beauty than to anything she said. When she spoke, it was the expression in her wonderful blue eyes as much as her words and her gentle modesty which he found irresistible. Completely natural and ingenuous, Marie represented a kind of woman he had not experienced among all the worldly, bold faces of the sophisticated beauties scattered throughout the courts of Europe.

Not only the emperor was taken with Marie at Talleyrand's ball. General Bertrand and Louis de Périgord were also smitten, and made the grave error of showing it. Many years later Napoleon was to recall how, to his annoyance, they had "danced attendance on her and were constantly under foot, dazzled by her beautiful eyes, no doubt."* They paid dearly for their folly. Napoleon immediately ordered poor Bertrand to rejoin his brother Jerome's army on the Baltic—"he never knew what hit him"—and de Périgord was despatched to East Prussia.

Marie returned home that night intoxicated with the events of the evening, aware she had been singled out and honored in some way but confused as to the reason for her meteoric success. In the eyes of the other guests she had seen a disturbing mixture of envy and admiration, but she could not quite grasp the reason, or the cause of her own disquiet. In the morning, when the Master of the Imperial House, Marshal Duroc, called with a huge bouquet of flowers and a thick parchment letter with the green imperial seals attached, it all became clear.

After the ball, Napoleon had spent a restless night. He could think of nothing but the sweet, innocent beauty of the evening before. Even when not standing by her, he had continued observing her across the room, enchanted by her grace, her gentle, accented voice, her discreet musical laugh. He became obsessed with the idea that she

* Montholon.

had been sacrificed to that ridiculous old husband, and must be dreadfully unhappy. Constant claims that this idea inspired his master to be "more interested in her than he had ever been in any woman," so that he found it almost impossible to dress his master in the morning. It was as if the conqueror chose to imagine himself as a mythical knight errant, determined to rescue a distressed damsel from the old dragon.

"I saw no one but you, I admired only you," he wrote. "I want no one but you; I beg you to reply promptly to calm my ardor and my impatience. Napoleon."

Marie was stunned. This larger-than-life hero of her childhood, for whom she would gladly give her life, had asked her for what she could not, would not, give. If Napoleon saw himself in a romantic quest for Marie, she knew all too well what he really wanted from her. She was a patriot, a Catholic, a wife and a mother—not a courtesan! Hurt pride and shame suffused her. The marshal was informed he need not wait; there would be no reply.

Duroc had often played messenger for his master, but this was the first time he had failed on such a mission. Napoleon was bewildered; how could any woman in Poland, or elsewhere, refuse him? Surely the lady was not in love with that pompous old bore. "He considered himself irresistible to women, and I really believe his *amour-propre* had been hurt," wrote Constant. For once, the conqueror was nonplussed; young girls who married rich old men for their money, even if it did save their families, had to have a certain amount of ambition, be somewhat calculating, and not a little unscrupulous. He had watched Marie enough to know that she was not in love with her husband, and that to Walewski she was just another decoration, like those on his chest. In Napoleon's experience women, even when loved as he had loved Josephine, were not faithful to their husbands for long. Although she was six years older than Napoleon, Josephine had constantly betrayed him, and with men even younger than he was. Napoleon did not imagine that Marie loved him already, but she clearly admired him, and he knew very well the attraction power had for women. Why did she refuse him?

The conqueror tried again. In the evening, Duroc called on Marie with more flowers and another letter:

Did I displease you, Madame? Your interest in me seems to have waned, while mine is growing every moment. . . . You have destroyed my peace. . . . I beg you to give a little joy to my poor heart, so ready to adore you. Is it so difficult to send a reply? You owe me two.

Napole.

Marie's shame deepened. It was true she had not wanted to marry Anastase, and her sensitive nature had sought refuge in months of illness and fever before she had consented to be his wife. But she had given her word to her husband and to God. She had borne a son, and she had remained faithful. Marie Walewska had known only one man's touch, and he was over seventy. It is unlikely that she had known the beauty or the pleasure of physical love, and it may even have filled her with revulsion. She had built up Napoleon's image for so many years, but now her hero's pedestal was rocked by his explicit love letters. Again the marshal returned to the royal palace without a reply. According to Napoleon's valet, this made his master "even more obsessed by the lady."

Some time before, Talleyrand had arranged for the Walewskis to be present at a dinner and concert in Napoleon's honor to be held at the castle on the night after his ball, and it was too late now for Marie to decline. At dinner she was placed next to the charming, kind Duroc, directly opposite the emperor. Although Napoleon did not speak to her, his eyes never left her as he discussed politics with his neighbors, and she noticed that he communicated with Duroc in a private sign language. At one moment Napoleon placed his hand on his heart, and immediately Duroc asked her why she had not worn the emperor's flowers. Piqued and affronted, she replied that she had given them to her son. But after dinner, according to Madame Nakwaska, Napoleon was seen talking to Marie "with an almost tender expression on his face," and he left before the concert. The next morning, Marie received another letter:

There are moments in life when to be in an elevated position constitutes a real burden, and I feel it now most acutely. How can a heart, so very much in love, be satisfied? All it wants is to throw itself at your feet; but it is being restrained . . . my deepest longings are paralyzed. . . . Oh, if only you wanted it! You and you alone can remove the obstacles that separate us. My friend Duroc will tell you what to do. Oh come, come . . . all your desires will be granted. *Your country will be so much dearer to me if you take pity on my poor heart.*

N

Marie was at such a loss what to do that she shut herself in her room.

Neither the emperor's letters, nor their content, had remained a secret from Anastase or his friends. Any matter which concerned the emperor concerned Poland, and this third letter had made it clear that the country's fate now rested with Marie. Her brother Benedict, as head of the Laczynski family, gave her his blessing to go to Napoleon, his eye no doubt fixed firmly on his military career. Her husband, a genuine patriot, indicated his willingness to sacrifice his honor for his country. There are also a number of contemporary accounts of a document from prominent Poles, Prince Joseph Poniatowski among them, urging Marie to accept Napoleon despite her principles. In the letter, they likened her position to that of the biblical Esther, who "gave herself for the salvation of her people; for that reason her sacrifice was glorious."

Nothing would have moved Marie to succumb to Napoleon's desire to see her alone, but for that one phrase: "Your country will be so much dearer to me." She became even more confused. Her patriotism was at odds with her pride, with her religious beliefs, and with the added fear of dishonoring her family.

Henriette de Vauban, mistress and companion of Prince Joseph Poniatowski, had lived at Versailles during the reign of Louis XVI, and was therefore considered Warsaw's expert on etiquette. The golden rule—the only rule that could never be broken at the French court since the Sun King Louis XIV had set the rules of etiquette at Versailles—was the king's code of good manners. Manners served for, and replaced, both morality and spirituality at the French court. For the emperor to take an official mistress, a *maîtresse en titre*, was perfectly natural, and in the best French tradition. It was also a compliment to Poland and to the charm of Polish women that Napoleon wished to do so now. When Madame de Vauban heard that the lovely, innocent Madame Walewska was refusing the emperor's attentions out of duty to her marriage vows and her religion, risking her country's future by causing him displeasure, she decided that it was time to teach her a little about the ways of the world, and of rulers in particular.

Henriette de Vauban's looks might have faded, but her wits had not; to keep the handsome Prince Joseph Poniatowski happy, she had filled his palace with ravishing (if rather risqué) young women. In Warsaw they were known as Prince Joseph's *cour d'amour*, in effect his harem. They adored him unreservedly and, by all accounts, with good reason. Madame de Vauban knew that one of these beauties, Emily Cichocka, who was known as "the siren with the face of an angel," had formed a friendship with Marie through their shared ardent patriotism. Emily, a tall, fiery girl with black hair and eyes and the air of a gypsy, accompanied Madame de Vauban to call on the virtuous Madame Walewska.

Warsaw was not Versailles. Adultery was frowned upon in society and usually concealed by all concerned, including the injured party. A shrewd judge of women, Madame de Vauban knew that Marie was more likely to listen to the advice of a contemporary whom she knew and liked, despite her dubious reputation, than to the sophisticated mistress of Prince Poniatowski. While Henriette charmed and flattered Anastase, it was Emily who spelt out to Marie the consequences of refusing Napoleon. Did Marie realize she had been chosen to fulfill a sacred mission? Surely Poland mattered more than anything else? Who was she to put her feelings and her pride before the fate of her country? The emperor had begged her to come to see him—this was an opportunity to convince him, when they were alone together, of his duty to Poland. "Go to the emperor," Emily urged. "Talk to him about Poland. Nothing need happen."* Like so many young, inexperienced girls before her and since, Marie clung to this straw, and actually believed in it. "Nothing need happen," she repeated over and over, and finally agreed to go.

So that she would not change her mind, the two ladies remained

* Contemporary social chronicler Françoise Trembicka, quoted by Sutherland.

with the terrified young woman until after dark, when Duroc came to fetch her. Hidden under a dark cloak and hat, Duroc walked with Marie, heavily veiled and shaking, to the emperor's carriage a little distance from the house, and brought her to a concealed entrance of the royal castle.

Napoleon was pacing up and down, and was quite unusually agitated while he waited for Marie. "At last Madame W. arrived but in a terrible state. . . . Pale, trembling, her eyes full of tears . . . she could hardly walk unaided and kept clinging on to her escort's arm. . . . Later, while she was with the emperor, I heard her sobbing . . . my heart ached for her." Duroc did not think Napoleon "had any satisfaction out of her," and that they only talked. At about 2 a.m. the emperor rang for Duroc, who took the weeping girl home.

Next morning, Marie confided in Emily (and Emily told Madame Trembicka, who told everyone) that Napoleon had spared her. Emily had said, "Nothing need happen," and she had been right. Marie was reassured, her weeping over. The emperor's gentle and caring questions about her family, her marriage and its circumstances had soothed and calmed her. He had listened patiently as she had repeatedly expounded her patriotic theme as the only reason for her visit. Full of sympathy, Napoleon consoled her and called her "his gentle dove." After she had promised she would return to see him, he let her go home.

When a large red leather jeweler's box arrived during the morning enclosing another letter with the green imperial seals, her composure was shaken.

Marie, my sweet Marie—my first thought is for you—my first desire of the day is to see you again. You will return, won't you? If not, the eagle will fly to the dove. . . . I will be seeing you at dinner tonight—I am told. Please accept this bouquet, as a secret link between us among the surrounding crowd. Whenever my hand touches my heart, you will know what I mean, and I want you to reciprocate the gesture at once. Love me, my sweet Marie, and don't let your hand ever leave your heart.

N

This time, the bouquet was of diamonds.

Marie was incredulous and angry. All her tears had meant nothing. He had not heard a word she had said last night. That evening she did not wear the brooch, but as soon as she saw the thunder on Napoleon's face, her courage left her and her hand flew to her heart. Its violent beating only subsided when she saw that her gesture had succeeded in soothing his anger. When Duroc came with the emperor's message that he wished to see her again that night, she was too frightened to refuse; perhaps once again, *nothing need happen . . .*

In her memoirs, written shortly before her death, Marie described how that night Napoleon had lost his temper with her and made a terrible scene. He pulled off his pocket watch, and throwing it on the floor he shouted, "If you persist in refusing me your love I'll grind your people into dust, like this watch under my heel!" If this is true, Napoleon's performance may have been deliberately calculated to terrify her into, as she put it, "the final surrender." How irritating all this patriotic talk, when all he wanted was her.

Certainly his patience was at an end, but it seems hard to believe the claim of a number of his biographers that he simply raped Marie. Forceful words are as much a part of a man's armory of seduction as gentle ones and pleading glances belong to a woman's. Marie wrote that she fainted and became that night the "unwilling victim of his passion." Whether that is true or not, she was certainly willing enough thereafter. Napoleon, on St. Helena, told one of his aides that Talleyrand had procured Marie for him, and boasted that "she did not struggle overmuch."

TALLEYRAND WAS PLEASED with the progress of his little scheme. If Napoleon would not listen to his reasoning on the subject of Poland, he might yet be moved by the pleas of this delicious, patriotic young woman. Marie had resisted as long as she could, but her will and her strength gave out against the magnetic force of Napoleon. Initially she had hoped for some kind of platonic relationship based on her "sacred mission," and she was still very much in awe of Napoleon.

Marie stayed with him until early morning, and "after that night she came to see him every day," noted Constant. Napoleon was still young and handsome, and his air of authority was irresistible to her. She resigned herself to him, and fell in love. Her innocence made him tender, her evident pleasure delighted him, and the usually impatient lover discovered a new dimension to his libido. The eagle had spread his wings over the gentle dove.

Had Marie's surrender made her country "so much dearer" to Napoleon? On January 14 he formed a provisional Polish government and named Prince Joseph Poniatowski minister for war. This was not exactly a triumph for Marie; Napoleon had promised much more. Joachim Murat had set his heart on the Polish crown, and wooed the Poles (and Prince Joseph) accordingly, but the emperor would not commit himself. The hopes of Poles, and of Talleyrand, still rested on Madame Walewska and the influence they prayed she had.

Marie was in love, and Napoleon could not see enough of her. Josephine's pleas to join him were dismissed with excuses about the state of the roads and other discomforts. The emperor insisted that Marie be included on every occasion, and be placed near him at every social engagement. The poor girl was dismayed at the amount of attention she received wherever she went, but Napoleon made it clear he needed her. It was as if, through this enchanting girl of twenty, Napoleon was reliving his youth and discovering love again. For Marie it was the first time, and her lover was the man she had idolized since she was eight years old.

The emperor's infatuation with the Countess Walewska could not be kept secret. Even when Marie was at home there was no escape from her new fame, and distinguished visitors began to call on her. Walewski, who had not received this much attention for years, was delighted. His behavior toward Marie changed to that of an indulgent grandfather, and she went to the castle each day with his compliance and the blessing of her mother and brother. To her embarrassment, she became increasingly aware of the new respect with which she was treated by all Warsaw. In the whole capital, it seemed that only she was troubled by the moral question of the relationship. She concentrated on her "sacred mission" for Poland, but her lover would gently place his fingers on her lips and tell her, "Be patient. Because of you, your country is very dear to me now."

Often she would join the crowds watching Napoleon reviewing his troops in midmorning. His little notes to her from this time show a tender caring unknown in him since the early days with Josephine. "You were so beautiful yesterday, that for long in the night I could still see you in my mind. . . . I reproached myself for having insisted you come to the parade . . . it was so cold."

◈

NAPOLEON HAD AN apartment set aside for her next to his own quarters, and when he was not attending some function in his honor, Marie spent most of her time with him there. But her happiness did not last. Russian troops, hardened to the winter weather, had concentrated in East Prussia and launched an offensive against the ill-prepared French. Promising Marie that he would be back with her soon, Napoleon hurried to join his army.

A week later, on February 8, his ambition resulted in the murderous slaughter of the Battle of Eylau. In freezing temperatures, twenty-two degrees of frost and a blizzard, Napoleon continued his war of attrition with the Russian commander, Benningsen. Napoleon's inconclusive victory did not warrant the terrible cost of fifteen thousand French lives, and Eylau remains a considerable blot on his military reputation. Unable to pursue the enemy through the deep and continually falling snow, the emperor moved his headquarters to Osteröde.

Just as he had wanted Josephine with him on campaign in the early days of their love, now he wanted Marie by his side. "Would you really be willing to brave the discomfort of the journey?" he wrote to her. Her letters have not survived, but she must have agreed to go. This truly represented a crossroads for her: certainly the *affaire* had become the talk of Warsaw society, but were there not extenuating circumstances? Had she not sacrificed herself for "the Cause," with the tacit agreement of her husband? If her life were to resume its normal pattern after the departure of the French, there would be no slur on her reputation—it might even be enhanced. Marie would be considered a patriot. But were she to join Napoleon in East Prussia, her "patriotic mission," no matter how much she believed in it, would appear a somewhat flimsy excuse; she would look like a married woman running after a married man, which in essence was the truth. The *affaire* would become international gossip from the highest circles to the lowest. Walewski was a proud man, but if the Conqueror of the West, who had the power to restore his country, demanded his wife as the price, then up to this point he had seen it as his patriotic duty to comply, and hers to make the sacrifice. However, for her to join Napoleon at the front could only be seen as proof of her infatuation with the world's most powerful man.

For Poland, little had in fact been achieved. Napoleon's formation of a provisional Polish government hardly guaranteed the country's restoration. The emperor had not kept his promises, and his army's needs over the past five months in Poland had cost the people more than they could afford. Nor were all the most powerful Polish families behind Napoleon. Many whose estates bordered Russia had more to lose than to gain from a French victory. Just as society had united to urge Marie to surrender to the French emperor for the sake of her country, it would condemn her for leaving her family in Warsaw to follow Napoleon to East Prussia. She would bring dishonor on her family; she would lose her husband and all that went with being his wife, possibly including her young son. Army headquarters were no place for a lady, and Marie had two months in which to make her decision.

Since the charming Hanseatic town of Osteröde had been devastated by the war, there was no question of Marie joining Napoleon there; besides, his quarters were quite unsuitable for his "gentle dove." The winter of 1807 was particularly severe, and all February and March Napoleon remained with his army in Osteröde, ruling his European empire from its most distant point. Bonaparte was as effective at his desk as he was on the battlefield. *Estafettes,* as the imperial couriers were called, arrived several times a day with dispatches from Paris, Rome, Milan, Naples and Amsterdam, and left again with his intructions for his far-flung empire. As the French capital was almost a thousand miles away, over thirty changes of horses were needed for the many dispatch riders to bring him his cabinet boxes. The care and attention he gave to the trivial as well as to the most important details is astonishing: changes to the laws; recommendations for the school curriculum; advice to one brother on how to rule, to another on how to cure piles; suggestions for setting up a boys' career guidance service; instructions to his chief of police on how to deal with foreigners plotting insurrection or, just as bad, undermining his monarchy with ridicule, like Madame de Staël.

Nothing escaped him, including the private movements of his wife. Napoleon's letters to Josephine from this time are stern and cold. He felt she was too much in the company of the young Prince Metternich, the ambassador of Austria, France's enemy. Metternich was a friend of Madame de Staël, daughter of the famous Swiss banker Necker, and the most wicked tongue against Napoleon in Paris. When the emperor banned Madame de Staël from the capital, she set up court at Chaumont, the royal château in the Loire Valley which Diane de Poitiers had received from Catherine de' Medici in exchange for Chenonceau. There she filled her salon with admiring liberals who joined her in undermining the empire. Napoleon had heard of Madame de Staël's unlawful return to Paris, and that Josephine had entertained her and Prince Metternich at Malmaison. Germaine de Staël was a thorn in Napoleon's side; her money gave her independence and access to circles where her sharp wit and poisonous pen had the greatest effect. An ugly, brilliant woman, Madame de Staël considered Josephine frivolous and unworthy of Napoleon. Having tried, and failed, to become his mistress herself, she had no alternative but to become his enemy, since "she could not remain indifferent to such a man." Talleyrand, who fathered her first child, described this domineering woman as "such a good friend that she would throw all her acquaintances into the water for the pleasure of fishing them out again." Napoleon warned Josephine from East Prussia: "Live as you would do if I were in Paris; greatness has its inconveniences; an Empress cannot go where a private individual may." And he used the formal *vous* instead of the familiar *tu*. Between late March and mid-May, the emperor wrote to his wife very little.

It was early April before Napoleon moved his headquarters to the splendid castle of Finkenstein in East Prussia.

⌘

AFTER SUCH A brief romance, the two long months of waiting for better travelling weather must have seemed an eternity to Marie. Josephine was also waiting. She had left Mainz on Napoleon's instructions and returned to Paris. Her sadness, fear and anger soon disappeared as the city and its carnival festivity seduced her back to her old habits and acquaintance. A clever, intuitive woman, Josephine had guessed from the tone of her husband's letters, and from the fact that he had not sent for her, that he might be having an *affaire*. She also had her spies.

Meanwhile, Napoleon wrote to Marie: "I would like to see you. . . . It's up to you. . . . Never doubt my feelings for you." For the sake of Marie's reputation, it was imperative that Josephine did not learn of her presence at Napoleon's headquarters. "Trust me—my gentle dove . . . you will be safe with me here . . . come . . . hurry." Marie needed no further encouragement.

The plans for their tryst had been carefully laid. Marie left Warsaw in early April with only her brother Benedict to accompany her for the ninety-mile journey over treacherous roads. They travelled in a splendid *berline,* a large heated carriage with a separate compartment for cooking pots and chamberpots. But neither her furs nor the excellence of her carriage did much to relieve the discomfort or the danger of travelling in northern Poland in winter. East Prussia's log roads, covered in slimy mud, were no better.

French mounted patrols halted their carriage several times, but Benedict's travel papers guaranteed a swift resumption of their journey. Exhausted after ten hours bumping and sliding on each of the two days since leaving Warsaw, Marie reached Osteröde to be met by an imperial courier welcoming her on the emperor's behalf. Finally, at midnight, they arrived in heavy rain at the castle of Finkenstein. Marie almost wept with fatigue and relief when Constant met her at a side entrance.

The next six weeks were the happiest of her life. At least a hundred staff officers lived in the main castle, and as many again in the outer buildings, but apart from Napoleon, Marie saw no one except

Constant and Ménéval, the private secretary. Not even Benedict could be relied on to hold his tongue and resist boasting. When Marie arrived, a rumor had flashed around that a mysterious beauty had come to the castle in a *berline* and was installed in the emperor's apartments, but as no one saw her the story died.

This was the time of their closest companionship. The days began early with breakfast in bed served by Constant. While Napoleon reviewed his troops in the mornings, Marie would watch him, discreetly hidden, from his bedroom window. While he worked at his desk or dictated to Ménéval, she sat quietly over her embroidery or read.

"During all this time, she never ceased to show affection of the deepest, most disinterested kind for the Emperor. He, for his part, seemed thoroughly to appreciate the lovable qualities of this angelic woman whose sweet, unselfish nature I can never forget," wrote Constant, who clearly adored her.

Marie's rooms in the castle were very comfortable: deep carpets, thick curtains, tall porcelain warming stoves, wide open fireplaces, and a large, curtained four-poster bed. Throughout his life, Napoleon suffered from the cold and liked to have great log fires burning day and night. Marie was often left alone while her lover attended to his duties, and as the rain lashed at the windows the crackle and hiss of burning logs kept her company in her cozy nest. At about eleven Constant would serve them lunch, and then dinner at seven, always on a little table by the fire.

Napoleon enjoyed gossip and was curious about the smallest details of other people's lives. He loved to quiz Marie about everyone she knew, members of Warsaw society and her country friends and neighbors. He taught her his secret sign language to help them communicate in public, and she told him about Poland's legends and heroes. He dissected her country's history, explaining the faults of the past so that she could better understand his policy for the future. One evening he scolded her for wearing black, and she replied, "When you have restored Poland, I promise I'll always wear pink." The emperor reassured her, but urged her to be patient. "Politics is a slow business, it is not as easy as winning a battle. . . . You must give me more time."

Marie did not exactly lose sight of her "special mission" in these golden weeks, but she succumbed so totally to her lover's powerful presence that her fighting spirit was dulled by her dreamlike existence. "Her noble character, her serenity and her amazing lack of self-interest enchanted the Emperor. . . . Each day he became more and more attached to her," wrote Constant. Very occasionally Napoleon left her to play cards with his generals—he invariably cheated—but most evenings of those rainy weeks of April and May Marie spent alone with the most remarkable man of the time.

EVEN BEFORE JOSEPHINE'S infidelities had hardened Napoleon's heart and poisoned his romantic nature, he had felt a creeping fear of impotence. He was a passionate man, yet aware of his lack of virility—which he described as *"la faiblesse dans le déduit d'amour."* Anxious to please, he had always been afraid of failing to satisfy his women, and Josephine's cruel jibe, *"Bonaparte—bon à rien,"* did not help, any more than did her blatant infidelity. And yet this great conqueror was not ashamed to let his soldiers observe his physical shortcomings, stripping to wash outside his tent in their full view every morning. His men adored him, and it did nothing to diminish his stature in their eyes, although inevitably it led to the usual coarse jokes.

Jaded and bitter, he had once shouted at Josephine: "I'm not interested in women, nor in gambling—in none of these things. I am wholly a political being." Through her betrayals, he had grown to despise women. Naturally he was aware of the attraction of his power and position and, as his bitterness grew, his approach coarsened until he ceased to care if he pleased or not. As women were either too flattered, too ambitious or too afraid to refuse him, Napoleon took what he wanted when he wanted, and was even content to pay. By the time he agreed to the heartless "arrangement" with Elénore Denuelle, he had completely lost faith in women and in the existence of a pure love. Before and after his marriage, there had been a number of liaisons in Napoleon's life, but there had never been a child; hence his acute disappointment at having to doubt his paternity of Elénore's son.

At a time when his cynicism about women was at its height, Marie changed everything. In Warsaw, Napoleon had been attracted by her beauty and excited by her rejection. Winning her had presented him with a challenge. Her reluctant surrender and shy lovemaking during his Polish sojourn had surprised, charmed and delighted him. It was only during their stolen weeks alone together at Finkenstein that, for the first time in his life, Napoleon experienced simple domestic happiness. Her love was so unselfish, so disinterested, that she gently restored his confidence, not only in women, but in himself as a lover. Marie was in no position to make comparisons; she sensed his anxieties and was able to reassure him through her tenderness and understanding. Besides, for this conqueror of men to show a weakness only led her to love him the more. Marie, as Napoleon makes clear in his memoirs, was his one true *affaire du coeur*.

Whatever feelings of guilt she may have had in Warsaw about her religion, her husband or her son, all melted in the warmth of their love at Finkenstein. "I really felt I was married to him," she later told Elizabeth Grabowska; and he called her his "little Polish wife."

Marie was Napoleon's ideal woman. She was beautiful, graceful, gentle, quite intelligent, well bred and well educated. She was warmhearted, a tender companion who loved him for himself. She listened attentively and was content to sit at his feet and devote her life to making him happy. Marie was what he had always searched for—with the sweetness and gentleness of Josephine, but in every other way her exact opposite.

There was only one cause for unease in their relationship. After several months as Napoleon's mistress, Marie had not become pregnant, while she had previously borne a son to a man of seventy.

While Napoleon was at Finkenstein planning the coming campaign against the Russians, he learned of the death of his little nephew, Napoleon-Charles. The son of his brother Louis, King of Holland, and Josephine's daughter Hortense de Beauharnais, the little boy had died of croup at The Hague. It was a terrible blow. Napoleon loved children, and he particularly adored this nephew, on whom he had looked as his provisional heir. When, as General Bonaparte, he had married Josephine, Hortense and her brother Eugène were very young, and he brought them up as if they were his own. He had always been as devoted to his stepchildren as they were to him, and they never gave him reason for complaint. At once he wrote to his "daughter" Hortense, and to Josephine—the first letter since his admonishments of March.

The sudden death of her grandson was a double blow to Josephine. Everyone had loved this child and she mourned him sincerely. But there was another consequence of his death, which made her frantic. Although the little boy was not Napoleon's, he was the son of his older brother, and a Bonaparte. As the grandmother of the emperor's heir, Josephine felt that her own position as empress was a little more secure. Without this nephew to ensure that all Napoleon had fought to achieve would continue under a Bonaparte, Josephine realized it was only a question of time before her husband divorced her and took a new wife. Divorce had been discussed before, and Napoleon still did not know if he could father a child, but he was in love, and when he learned of his wife's latest *affaire*, this time he might not forgive her. Of course, Josephine had found out about Marie and knew everything—the Polish ladies she had met at Strasbourg on her way home from Mainz, as well as those resident in Paris, could not resist boasting that the emperor had taken a new mistress from their country. Her only consolation was that, as yet, his "Polish charmer" had not become pregnant.

By mid-May, spring had come at last to East Prussia, and with the drier weather Marie knew that hostilities would soon begin again. The idyll at Finkenstein had to end. Just as she had become resigned to her marriage, as she had accepted the pressures of her countrymen and yielded to the conqueror, Marie now accepted her uncertain future. The only thing of which she was sure, from the bottom of her heart, was her love for Napoleon. He had insisted that she follow him to Paris next winter, and she had promised to do so. Then, with Benedict as her escort for the return journey, she left the castle where she had known happiness. Her departure, like her arrival, was at midnight and in total secrecy, but this time the great *berline* headed for Kiernozia, her childhood home.

ONE MONTH LATER, on June 14, Napoleon underscored his earlier costly victory against the Russians at Eylau by winning a decisive battle at Friedland. It was a devastating defeat for the Russians, their army routed. But Napoleon knew it was one thing to defeat Russia, quite another to conquer it. Besides, he needed it as an ally if France's Continental System, the trading blockade against England, was to succeed. A truce was declared so that Tsar Alexander, ruler of the East, could meet personally with the Emperor Napoleon, ruler of the West, to negotiate the peace treaty at Tilsit, on Russia's frontier.

Count Molé, in his memoirs, described Napoleon at Tilsit:

> His head was superb, and unlike any other. In the depth of his skull, the formation of his splendid forehead, the setting of his eyes, his sculptured lips, the droop at the corner of the mouth, the beautiful proportions of his face, and the regularity of his features, but above all in his glance and his smile—in all this I thought I could recognize the qualities which raise a man above his fellows, and make him fit to rule over them.

Talleyrand wrote that the setting at Tilsit "was so romantically conceived and so magnificently arranged, that Napoleon, who saw it as a brilliant episode in the romance of his life, accepted it." The two emperors were to meet on neutral territory—a barge in the middle of the Niemen River, which marked Russia's border. French engineers erected a magnificent pavilion on a raft moored midstream, flying the French and Russian flags and topped by interlaced, crowned "A" and "N" monograms. Both emperors left their respective shores simultaneously, were rowed to the splendid pavilion, met there and embraced.

Whether enemies or allies, all the world's rulers were fascinated by Napoleon, not least the thirty-year-old Russian tsar. Alexander was a blond giant, with extraordinary insight into human nature. He was also an incurable romantic. The theatrical mise-en-scène at Tilsit was his idea, and its splendor and romantic setting had a marked effect on Napoleon. By flattering him and treating him as a brother sovereign, and by offering his friendship, the vanquished Tsar Alexander gained more than he had lost in battle. After two successful meetings, unrecorded and alone on the barge, the emperors decided that the raft could be dismantled, Tilsit declared neutral and discussions continued on shore. Despite the efforts of his wife, the lovely Queen Louise, the Prussian emperor, a despised nonentity, was completely ignored throughout their discussions. For more than a week Alexander and Napoleon spent their days talking and riding in the countryside, then dining together in the evenings. As the strange camaraderie between them developed, there was even talk of Alexander offering Napoleon his sister Catherine as a wife. The French emperor had become so mesmerized with the Tsar of all the Russias that he wrote to Josephine, "If Alexander were a woman, I would make him my mistress."

Meanwhile, his mistress was at Kiernozia, sharing Poland's anxiety about this new friendship. Her fear, and that of her countrymen, was that Napoleon's terms for peace would be far too generous to Alexander, and at the expense of Poland. They were right. Frederick William of Prussia lost half his kingdom—everything west of the Elbe became Westphalia, and the following year it was given to Jérôme Bonaparte as his kingdom. Russia was obliged to agree to join Napoleon's Continental System, but kept its Polish territory, annexed by Catherine II. In addition, Alexander was granted Bialystok, a prosperous Polish town province. With Prussia's Polish territory, Napoleon created the Duchy of Warsaw, a small semi-independent state to be ruled over by his friend and ally the King of Saxony. For the Poles, it was something, but not very much, and hardly worth the lives of the thousands of their young men who had died fighting for France. The provisional Polish government was not even consulted during the negotiations at Tilsit, and Talleyrand stalked around town "sarcastic and vaguely embarrassed."

Throughout the past campaign Talleyrand, as foreign minister, had remained in Warsaw trying to bring about an alliance with Austria. He reasoned that if Austria were to give up its Polish territory, France would compensate by returning Silesia, seized by Frederick of Prussia seventy years earlier. With Austrian Poland added to Prussian Poland, Talleyrand's scheme for a Polish state would become viable and secure a useful alliance with Austria. But if Napoleon defeated Alexander and began negotiations for an alliance with Russia, the Austrians realized that they might find themselves at the mercy of both emperors. Speculation and negotiation ended with Napoleon's brilliant victory at Friedland, which cancelled Talleyrand's hopes for Poland, as well as the argument for an alliance with Austria. He would not remain as France's foreign minister much longer.

AT HOME IN Kiernozia with her mother, Marie was embarrassed and bitterly disappointed for other reasons. Initially, her virtue had been the price of her country's independence. In that respect, her surrender had been in vain. Despite all her best intentions, she had fallen in love with Napoleon. She had given him her trust and her heart, and believed in his pledge to restore her country's independence. This was her "sacred mission," and she had failed. After the Peace of Tilsit, she needed Napoleon's reassurance concerning Poland, as well as herself, more than ever. Throughout the spring campaign his letters had been short and crisp, and she had understood, but when she learned of his return to Paris after Tilsit at the end of July, she awaited his summons anxiously.

Napoleon had been absent from his capital for ten months. During this time he had succeeded in establishing his Continental System from the Baltic all the way to the Black Sea, and he rewarded himself on July 27, 1807, with the title of Napoleon the Great. He ruled over most of Western Europe and a mixed population of 70 million. But despite the glory and the achievement, all France prayed that after Tilsit the fighting would end, and their emperor would settle down to governing his extended empire. After two days in Paris, Napoleon wrote to his "little patriot," "you who so dearly love your country," a tender letter from a man who missed his beloved. Name days in Poland take precedence over birthdays, and Marie shared hers—August 15, the Feast of the Assumption of the Virgin Mary—with Napoleon's birthday, his thirty-eighth. He sent her a sapphire bracelet, which meant nothing to her, and a locket with his portrait, which meant everything, and she wore it each day.

"The thought of you is always in my heart and your name often on my lips," he wrote, but still he did not send for her. Marie had fully expected Anastase to ask for a divorce on her return from Finkenstein, but instead he left for Austria to take a cure, and then continued on to Italy for the rest of the summer. Before leaving, he made financial provision for her, and had their son Anthony brought to Kiernozia. Marie remained quietly waiting at her mother's house throughout the summer and autumn of 1807, while Benedict, who was then attached to General Berthier's staff, kept her informed of Napoleon's movements. The emperor spent the summer and autumn with the court at his favorite palace, Fontainebleau.

Meanwhile, the English had been using their men-o'-war to escort their merchant ships into Italian ports, breaking France's blockade. Napoleon had retaliated by putting pressure on the Pope, which made the devout Marie uneasy. At Christmas, she received the message for which she had waited since Tilsit. On his way home from Italy, Napoleon sent her his greetings for the New Year and a request that she join him in Paris in February.

POOR MARIE HAD to travel in winter again, but this time she took her maid. It was ten days before they reached France, but the thrill of seeing new places mingled with her excitement at seeing Napoleon again. At the last change of horses before Paris, to her great joy, Benedict and dear, kind Marshal Duroc had been sent to meet her. Duroc had taken a house for her at 2 rue de la Houssaye, a small eighteenth-century town house in a fashionable quarter. It had been rather haphazardly furnished, but the marshal had seen to everything himself and had installed a team of discreet, carefully chosen staff.

NAPOLEON HAD STUDIED the history of France's kings carefully and, like so many rulers before him, as well as his hero, Frederick the Great, he recognized the influence of the arts on society and the people. He cultivated writers, painters and musicians, and generously sponsored the theater and ballet. But the emperor was much more than just a patron. By his extraordinary deeds, he also influenced taste and style. His victories on the battlefield inspired a whole generation of artists and influenced the themes of musicians such as Beethoven,

dramatists, painters, architects and decorative artists. Teams of archaeologists, scientists, writers and draftsmen followed his campaigns, returning with their findings and, like the soldiers, laden with the spoils
of conquest. In the euphoria of glory the craftsmen and builders of
France incorporated each victory into their grand designs. A new style
called "Empire" emerged, and the emperor's patronage encouraged
such intense artistic activity that Paris became the intellectual and cultural capital of Europe once again.

Like most women arriving in Paris, especially for the first time,
Marie went out shopping at once. Napoleon was very particular about
women's clothes and always noticed and commented on whatever
Marie wore. (On his return to Paris after Tilsit, he had sent the Emperor Alexander a trunk full of dresses which he had chosen himself as
a gift for the tsar's mystic mistress Julie de Krudener.) Napoleon had
established his empire less than ten years after the execution of Louis
XVI, and he quickly saw to it that his new court would not be dis-
credited by society's ladies appearing in the skimpy, transparent, semi-
naked fashions of the day. Ladies' court attire, he decreed, was to be
sumptuous and in good taste. During the years of the Consulate,
fashion followed the classical ideal in the same way as did philosophy
and the arts. Parisiennes dressed as caryatids, in slender diaphanous
muslins, ribbons or cords tied high under the breasts, exposing deli-
cately rouged nipples. This fashion did not allow for any underclothes
whatsoever, and the accompanying shoes were no more than light
sandals with thongs crisscrossing and tied over the ankle. The adop-
tion of the thinking and style of the Roman republic was hailed as
proof of deliberate opposition to the concept of monarchy and the
Ancien Régime. But ancient Rome's fashions were hardly suited to
the climate of France, to its filthy streets or to the shape of its matri-
archs.

High waistlines had remained in style, and admirably suited slender young beauties with masses of hair like Marie. She visited the famous (and contrary) designer Leroy, who fortunately liked her—he
had been known to keep very important clients waiting endlessly, and
simply refused to dress others. His salon offered a complete service to
beauty—not only a new outfit, but a makeup artist and hairdresser as
well. Marie was twenty-one, and her natural, unadorned looks re-

flected her youth; but with Leroy's guidance and a few little touches of makeup she was transformed into a beauty even by the standards of fashionable Parisian society.

Napoleon saw her when he could, often late at night or between appointments, and Marie really spent more time with Duroc during this visit to Paris than with her lover. Tall and elegant, Duroc was three years older than the emperor and had known him since the first Italian campaign. As Master of the Imperial Household, he was in charge of Napoleon's social life, his food and entertainments; as one of the emperor's closest friends, he was entrusted with the care of Marie. Together they visited the theater several times—and the Opéra, where Duroc's box was exactly opposite the emperor's. Napoleon did not attend, but Madame Walewska observed his elegant empress, and Josephine raised her opera glasses to study her lovely young rival better. Marie declined Napoleon's suggestion that she be presented at court; she had no wish to embarrass Josephine, although the empress had let Duroc know she would receive the Countess Walewska "most graciously."

Shy and unused to Parisian society, Marie saw few people other than her compatriots, including the young officers of the Polish Lancers. These scions of noble Polish houses, who equipped themselves at their own expense, worshipped Napoleon. Soon they were to make good their boast that they would follow him to Hell and back.

The previous fall, Napoleon had invaded Spain in his ongoing struggle with England, and by March the war was progressing so badly that he was needed at the front. With her lover gone, Paris lost its appeal for Marie, and she returned home to Poland.

SIXTEEN MONTHS WERE to pass before Marie saw Napoleon again. Few letters survive from that period, but she most probably received the same brisk, businesslike notes she had in the past when he was on campaign.

During the protracted Peninsular Wars, an incident occurred which epitomized the Polish people and their devotion to the French emperor.

With hindsight, Napoleon should never have invaded Spain. It was a war he could not win. Anxious to recapture Madrid and reinstate his brother Joseph on the Spanish throne, Napoleon added another 150,000 troops to those already there. At the beginning of winter, three regiments of Polish Lancers had arrived in Spain, seeking glory in Napoleon's army. These volunteers had marched all the way from Warsaw to Paris and then on south to join the Grande Armée at Bayonne. Inexperienced and young, these officers represented the flower of Poland's youth. Napoleon was their idol and they were ready to die for him to prove their courage and loyalty. This was their chance.

In a series of swift, brilliant engagements throughout the spring, summer and fall, Napoleon had driven the Anglo-Spanish army south until only the wild, stark peaks of Guadarrama stood between him and Madrid. The way through that savage chain of mountains was the pass at Somosierra.

There was only one way through: a narrow track defended at the top by some thirteen thousand Spanish troops dug into carefully prepared positions, supported by massed artillery. The defenses appeared impregnable, with overlapping fields of fire from three sides. Any assault had to be frontal: four abreast up that track. To attempt it meant certain death. Even with a total disregard for loss of life, the task was surely impossible. But with the capital so tantalizingly close, Napoleon could not turn back. The campaign had ground on for months, winter would soon be upon them again, and the soldiers wanted to go home. Besides, the emperor was needed back in Paris.

When Napoleon chose the Polish Lancers to make the charge, it seemed like pure madness; not even seasoned veterans would have stood a chance in that valley of death, let alone these inexperienced cavaliers. But he knew the spirit of the young Polish officers and their burning desire to show him their mettle. Not only Poland's youth but also its future, its statesmen and leaders-to-be, rode among the Lancers; and they rode with their faith in God, their only hope in the luck of the devil.

Two miles separated them from their goal. Captain Niegolewski's memoirs bring the scene to vivid life:

We re-formed and hurriedly moved uphill on the narrow pass, four abreast, gathering speed as we went, unsheathed sabres in one hand, pistols held in the other, reins between the teeth . . . we flew toward the amphitheater with the speed of the wind shouting *"Vive l'Empereur,"* oblivious of the murderous enemy fire from above.*

Incredibly, a handful reached their goal: the gun emplacements were overrun, the line was breached and the enemy driven into chaotic retreat.

Napoleon had observed the terrible carnage, and was overcome by the extraordinary courage of the Lancers. The charge of Somosierra was a glorious, crazy, reckless gesture; it was also in vain, for Poland gained nothing from staining Spanish soil with the blood of a generation of the country's potential leaders. A few days later, Napoleon captured Madrid.

Marie was proud of her countrymen, but mourned the loss of so many friends in the Lancers; the leader of the charge, Hipolithe Kozietulski, a near neighbor, survived despite multiple wounds. During the Christmas and New Year season which followed, Napoleon remained in Spain, pursuing his elusive adversary. In January 1809 he hastened back to Paris, leaving his army to continue the futile quest.

During the emperor's absence, Talleyrand, no longer foreign minister, and Fouché, former head of police in Paris, had been plotting to make Murat King of France should Napoleon be killed in battle. Fouché was an admirer of Caroline Murat, Napoleon's sister, who sanctioned the plot. France longed for peace, but if the emperor remained at the helm and continued with his current foreign policies, many foresaw only a future of endless conflict. To prevent what they considered Napoleon's warmongering, the conspirators approached Tsar Alexander. They hailed him as the "Savior of Europe" and proceeded to undermine the Franco-Russian alliance.

Although the Austrians had lost three decisive battles against France, in the three years following Austerlitz, they had rebuilt and reorganized their army. They had also been secretly negotiating with their enemies the English, who had promised to create a second front

* Quoted in Sutherland.

in northern Europe once Austria declared war on France. As well as having the advantage of England's support, Austria would only have to face half the French army; the other was still engaged in Spain. Nor had Russia, as a result of Talleyrand's cabal, definitely committed itself to supporting France in a war with Austria. At last the Austrians felt the timing was right for a final confrontation with Napoleon.

Early in April 1809, Austria invaded Bavaria, France's ally. Certain that Russia would not intervene, another Austrian army of thirty thousand newly equipped and trained troops marched toward Warsaw. As most of Poland's troops were scattered within the French regiments in Spain, Germany and France, all that the war minister, Prince Joseph Poniatowski, could muster to defend the duchy's capital were fifteen thousand untrained volunteers and older men. After a fierce battle outside Warsaw, the Austrians, led by Archduke Ferdinand, defeated Prince Joseph's soldiers and occupied Warsaw. Following a truce, Prince Joseph evacuated his army, and the duchy's government fled to Thorn, a small town in the northwest of Poland. Among the citizens who left to join the government-in-exile as their pro-French sympathies made it dangerous for them to remain in Warsaw was the Countess Marie Walewska.

Napoleon had not forgotten her. A number of dispatches passed between the foreign minister in Paris and the French minister in Warsaw giving instructions, as a matter of "great urgency," to care for Marie's welfare. By mid-May, Napoleon was victorious and Vienna had capitulated to the French. "My enemies," he wrote to Paris, "are defeated, beaten, utterly routed. They were in great numbers; I have dispersed them." He set up his headquarters in the imperial summer palace of Schönbrunn outside Austria's capital, and a few days later he wrote to Marie: "Come to Vienna. I want to give you new proofs of the warm affection I have for you . . . Many tender kisses on your lovely hands and just one on your beautiful mouth. Napole."

Marie longed for nothing more than to join her lover, but Archduke Ferdinand's army was still in Warsaw blocking the routes south. For two more months she could not leave Poland. As Austria occupied Warsaw, Prince Joseph led his forces south to seize Cracow, the ancient Polish capital annexed by Austria during the partition. Although the Polish population had never really suffered under Austrian rule, Prince Joseph was welcomed enthusiastically throughout Galicia, Poland's former southern province. To his surprise, his troops found the Russians, France's supposed allies, blocking their advance from the east. Despite the Franco-Russian alliance, the tsar had not yet honored his commitment to Napoleon, but nor had his troops received any orders to engage the Austrians. As the Poles raced toward Cracow, the Russians hurried to arrive there first and stop the Polish army from meeting up with Napoleon on the Danube. Prince Joseph and his Poles won the race by two days, and entered their ancient capital.

On July 7, Napoleon won a great victory over Austria at Wagram, near Vienna. It was only after a truce had been signed that the Archduke Ferdinand and his Austrian army left Warsaw. The road was clear for Marie to travel to Vienna. Accompanied by a cousin of Anastase, Josephine Witte, and her husband John, Marie was among the first to leave Poland. They arrived in Vienna four days later.

A charming villa had been taken and furnished for her in the Viennese suburb of Mödling not far from Schönbrunn, where the emperor was supposed to be resting—*"le repos du lion."* At thirty-nine, Napoleon looked older, pallid and heavier. But after Marie's arrival he was transformed, and appeared in the best of spirits. Those near him at headquarters soon knew the reason why. Every evening, Constant was sent in a closed, unmarked carriage to fetch the Countess Walewska and escort her the short distance to the emperor's private entrance to the palace. But Schönbrunn was not like beautiful, secluded Finkenstein, and offered little privacy. An encampment of the Imperial Guard was stationed in the lovely pale ocher palace, there were daily official deputations, and innumerable staff sorting and dispatching to Paris the mountains of booty Napoleon had gathered there.

Like so many royal palaces built in the eighteenth century, Schönbrunn was inspired by Versailles. A classical central block with extended sides, and wings set at right angles like arms, enclosed a parade ground with enough space for eight thousand troops to maneuver. A massive black and gilded wrought-iron gate opened onto this vast courtyard, with huge obelisks topped by golden eagles on either side. Fountains played in the courtyard. Outside the other facade of the palace, formal gardens were laid out to a plan by Le Nôtre, Versailles' famous garden designer, which led up to a classical colonnade on the skyline called the Gloriette. That was the view from Napoleon's windows in the "Japanese Apartment," a luxurious suite of rooms decorated in red and gold lacquer, which he had also occupied in 1805, after Austerlitz.* Schönbrunn also boasted a small private zoo in the park with kangaroos, elephants and a lion.

As in Paris, Duroc was Marie's support and link with Napoleon, and he organized her visits to the emperor as well as her social life. Countess Walewska never appeared in public with her lover and continued her discreet, supportive role in his life as before. At Mödling she lived a peaceful domestic existence, entertaining only the Wittes and other visiting Poles, as well as several of the Polish Lancers stationed nearby. Most people, especially in society, were aware of Marie's real role, but as she was always accompanied in public by her husband's relatives the Wittes, and as she insisted on keeping up the pretence of her imminent departure for Bad Gastein to take a cure, an air of respectability always surrounded the dignified young Polish countess. Contemporaries spoke at that time of her special aura, a blend of glowing beauty and a remarkable modesty given the circumstances.

Constant in his memoirs recounts many instances of Napoleon's concern for Marie's welfare. The emperor asked him daily if the coach was in good condition, whether he was sure of the coachman, and to beware the potholes and the slippery road after rain. On one of Marie's short journeys to the palace, the carriage did overturn as the coachman tried to avoid a large hole.

> Luckily it tilted on the right side, so I was able to act as a cushion for Madame W., who escaped unhurt. She thanked me with that unique amiability and charming grace which was so characteristic of her. Though I was slightly concussed, any pain I might have felt disappeared as a result of her kindness, and we were both able to

---

* The same lovely rooms were to be the sad prison of the King of Rome, Napoleon's son. He would die of consumption there twenty-three years later, transformed into a German princeling known as the Duke of Reichstadt.

laugh at the accident. As soon as we arrived at Schönbrunn, Madame W. told the emperor what had happened and he thanked me for protecting her.

Napoleon used this mishap as an excuse to have Marie spend most of her time with him at Schönbrunn. She continued to keep her house in Mödling and retired there when Napoleon really had no time for her, but more often than not she slept at the palace.

Ever since Somosierra, Napoleon had attached the Polish Lancers to his personal bodyguard, and their devotion to the emperor was matched only by their adoration of Marie. When Napoleon could not resist taking her driving in an open carriage along the banks of the Danube or through the Prater, the great park where the Viennese would gather on the long summer evenings, the mounted Lancers, all fiercely protective of the Countess Walewska, would be their guard. A honeymoon atmosphere filled Schönbrunn. Napoleon and Marie were clearly in love, and all who knew wished them well. Everyone acknowledged the unselfish devotion of this beautiful, discreet young woman, and no one doubted her feelings for Napoleon. Marie asked for nothing and gave her lover everything.

Throughout the protracted peace negotiations following Wagram, Marie was in Vienna at Napoleon's side. Although he hated women to interfere in politics, he always asked for her views and opinions. He knew she was totally dedicated to his interests, as much as to her country's, and that her judgment was sound. She also understood that Napoleon could not afford to antagonize the unpredictable Tsar Alexander; the survival of his Continental System depended to a large extent on Russia's alliance with France. Yet, when the treaty was finalized, she was heartbroken that Poland was only to keep Austrian Galicia and not the Russian part, especially after the Polish army had conquered it all.

THROUGHOUT THE SCHÖNBRUNN summer, Josephine had remained in Paris; all hope of Napoleon sending for her to join him in Vienna had long faded. She was right to be anxious about her future, despite the reassurances of her son Eugène de Beauharnais that as long as Countess Walewska showed no signs of pregnancy, she need not fear divorce. Napoleon's letters to his wife had become more and more indifferent and cold. Hortense, Josephine's daughter, wrote:

> A young Polish countess, whom the emperor had known in Poland, came to Vienna during the armistice. My mother knew that she was hidden in the Palace of Schönbrunn, unseen by anyone, and the infidelity of a husband to whom she was still tenderly devoted filled her with despair.

Josephine had tried to play the injured wife, but to no avail. As summer drifted into autumn, Marie looked even lovelier. Each day, her life with Napoleon had more the feel of a marriage than just a love affair, and he referred to her often as "his Polish wife." In September, Marie realized that she was pregnant. To know she would have the child of the man she loved fulfilled her completely. Her happiness, and his, knew no bounds. This was the greatest gift she could give him, and it provided the reassurance he had craved for so many years. He was not sterile; he could have children. Now that he could establish a dynasty, his dream of the Continental System enduring and guaranteeing peace in a united Europe could continue after him. Napoleon summoned his own doctor from Paris, who confirmed Marie's hopes.

No effort was too great for the emperor's beloved. "I could not even begin to describe the loving care the Emperor lavished on Madame W., now he knew she was pregnant. . . . He was reluctant to let her out of his sight, even for a short time."* Throughout September, as the trees turned golden and the mists rose in the valleys of the Danube, other than telling Constant, Marie kept her secret and her joy to herself. On the advice of his doctor, Napoleon had insisted that she should return with him to Paris once the peace had been signed in October. Although she had been away from home and her son Anthony for some time, Marie wanted to remain near the father of the child she was carrying. And yet she was still married to Anastase. How

* Constant.

would he view this development? No letters survive that describe her state of mind over her delicate situation.

Napoleon had often spoken of his desire to divorce Josephine, and Marie knew he had left instructions that the secret staircase between their apartments was to be walled up. It is very likely that she knew of the confidential memorandum Napoleon had sent to his court chamberlain in Paris, giving instructions for the machinery to be set in motion for the divorce to be finalised after the emperor's return.

When she was sure of her pregnancy, Marie in her happiness had told Constant, "I belong to him now, my thoughts, my inspiration, all come from him and return to him . . . always." Could she have imagined Napoleon belonged to her, as she did to him? She knew that Napoleon's plans to divorce Josephine had gone ahead following the confirmation of her pregnancy. Could Marie have dreamed that she would become Napoleon's wife, and that they would bring up their child together? We have no evidence of her thoughts, but there was never a place for her in the dynastic chessboard about to be set up. From Schönbrunn the emperor had written to his brother Lucien: "Yes, I am in love, but always subordinate to my policy. And though I would like to crown my mistress, I must look for ways to further the interests of France." And a legitimate, acceptable heir to Napoleon's vast empire was essential. He was not the only one conscious that all depended on him. Napoleon alone, with the support of his army, controlled the destinies of 70 million people. Should he die, the whole carefully constructed empire would disintegrate.

IN EARLY OCTOBER 1809, after the peace was signed, the emperor was ready at last to leave for Paris. The treaty was a disaster for Austria and its ruler. The aftermath of Austerlitz was the effective dismemberment of the Holy Roman Empire. Francis II, Holy Roman Emperor, became Francis I, Emperor of Austria. His humiliation did not end there; the defeat at Wagram led to the further loss of enormous tracts of territory as well as a huge cash indemnity to the French, and the pillage of much of Austria's cultural heritage. In a witticism which captured their emperor's continued diminution, the Viennese dubbed him "Francis Zero."

When she left for Paris in mid-October, a few days before Napoleon, Marie was happily ignorant of his plans for their future. Travelling at a leisurely pace with the Wittes through Munich, Stuttgart and Strasbourg, she reflected on her three months in Austria. It had been such a happy time, and she enjoyed the journey, certain her intimacy with Napoleon would continue once she reached Paris. Could Marie have had some inkling that the honeymoon of Schönbrunn might not continue? Before leaving she had given Napoleon a gold and enamel ring entwined with strands of her blonde hair. Engraved on the inside was the message: "When you cease to love me, remember that I love you still."

SHORTLY BEFORE THE emperor was to leave Vienna, something happened to make him even more conscious of the need for an internationally recognized heir. A young German had been spotted in a crowd carrying a knife with which he admitted he intended to assassinate Napoleon. The son of a Lutheran pastor, he said he had travelled to Vienna with that aim, for "without him Europe would finally be at peace." He had acted from his own conscience, and was an agent of no party. Although Napoleon wrote to his chief of police in Paris that the incident meant nothing, he was shaken, and more eager than ever to ensure his life's work would survive him. If he was to give his line legitimacy, and forge a bond with one of his enemies (or an uncertain ally), his bride had to be a sovereign's daughter. "I want to marry a womb," he declared. "It matters not what she looks like, as long as she comes from royal stock."

Deep in thought, the emperor left for Paris. As always, he travelled fast in a lightweight green carriage, preferably drawn by four sturdy Limousins. Escorted by his Polish Lancers, whose "spirited singing" he enjoyed during breaks in the journey, Napoleon sat on the right, Duroc on the left. The seat opposite them was piled high with dispatches, which the emperor perused rapidly and ejected in a continual stream. As one of the escort later recounted, "we travelled in a blizzard of paper flying out from both sides of the carriage."*

When Marie arrived in Paris, her happiness was short-lived. Napoleon was at Fontainebleau, and too preoccupied to have any time for his pregnant mistress. He was determined to proceed with the divorce, yet he allowed a month to pass before he found the courage to tell Josephine and end her anxious misery. Repudiating his wife was more difficult than Napoleon had imagined, for despite everything an enduring affection for her remained. But ambition ruled his heart. The French foreign minister was sent to St. Petersburg to ask for the hand of the Tsar Alexander's sister, Grand Duchess Anna Pavlovna. In return, Napoleon offered a prize he hoped was irresistible—Poland. His ambassador, the Marquis de Caulaincourt, Duke of Vicenza, told the tsar that, for the hand of the Grand Duchess Anna, "His Majesty was prepared to see the words Poland and Polish people disappear from all current political transactions." Napoleon would also agree that "the kingdom of Poland will never be restored."

No wonder Napoleon had no time for Marie Walewska! After Josephine's repudiation in December, Marie soon learned of her lover's plans for a dynastic marriage. Sensitive, intuitive and shy, she understood that her presence in Paris had become an embarrassment and could possibly even jeopardize the emperor's plans. It is unlikely that Marie was aware of Napoleon's treachery to Poland or of her country's key role in the negotiations for his Russian bride. She simply sensed that she did not fit into his dynastic schemes, and when Duroc gently confirmed her fears, she quietly returned to Poland. In her aching heart Marie realized that it was the miracle of the child she carried, her one real political contribution to Napoleon's life, which had lost her the man she loved.

TSAR ALEXANDER WAS quite content to exchange his sister for Poland. Discussions had begun a year earlier about the possibility of

---

* Quoted in Sutherland.

Napoleon marrying his older sister Catherine, but his mother the Empress Dowager so disliked Napoleon she married her off to the Duke of Holstein instead. As Grand Duchess Anna was only fourteen and not yet nubile, her mother insisted that she wait for two years before being sold to that parvenu and reputedly impotent tyrant. Napoleon could not wait three years for an heir and, as the Russian marriage discussions dwindled to an embarrassing silence, Prince Metternich, Austria's brilliant young ambassador to Paris, saw his chance. He offered Napoleon the daughter of the vanquished Emperor Francis. By this alliance, he managed to save something from the ashes of Wagram for his country. Napoleon instructed Josephine's son Eugène de Beauharnais, of all choices, to make the formal offer to Metternich for the hand of the Archduchess Marie-Louise. Then Eugène signed the contract "in the name of the Emperor and with the approval of the Empress, my mother." Josephine and Marie had both lost Napoleon to his ambition.

THE NEW EMPRESS OF the French was nineteen years old and, with her long face and Habsburg lip, no great beauty. But she had a pleasing figure, pretty hands and feet, and masses of chestnut hair. Napoleon was blind to everything but the dazzling prospect of a union with the great house of Habsburg and its reputation for fecund daughters. (He did, however, send instructions for his bride to have her teeth cleaned!) Following a proxy wedding in Vienna with her brother the Archduke Karl standing in for the French emperor, Napoleon married his Austrian bride at Saint-Cloud on April 2, 1810, amid great pomp and ceremony. At her mother's house near Warsaw, Marie Walewska learned about the marriage from the newspapers.

SINCE DECEMBER, MARIE had been back home at Kiernozia awaiting the birth of Napoleon's child, unsure if she had any prospects left at all in her lover's orbit. The emperor had written inquiring about her health and urging her to "chase away the black thoughts—you must not worry about the future." Although he signed himself "Napole," he had addressed her as "Madame." That one word confirmed everything she feared about their future relationship.

Unbeknown to Marie, the emperor had entrusted his minister in Warsaw with a very delicate mission. So that his child would not be born illegitimate, Count Walewski was to be flattered into granting "a personal request from the Emperor" to give the child his name. Just as she had helped in arranging Marie's capitulation in Warsaw, Henriette de Vauban, Prince Joseph Poniatowski's *maîtresse de maison,* was once again brought in to resolve a difficult situation between the Walewskis and Napoleon. The seventy-three-year-old chamberlain, who dreaded a scandal, was indeed flattered, and agreed. So too did his eldest son, who now ran the great house. To the delight of his sister and nieces, Anastase asked Marie to return to Walewice, as it was "the right place for a Walewski child to be born."

As cold, gray winter settled over Kiernozia, Marie's heartbreak steadily declined into depression. She was twenty-three and carrying the child of the man she loved above all else, to whom she had given her heart and soul. She should have been the happiest of women, and indeed had been until so very recently. In February, Napoleon had written again, addressing her as "Madame," and referring to her "black mood." In all, it was a kind letter, but it could hardly have eased her pain: "Never doubt the pleasure I will always feel at seeing you and my tender interest in everything that concerns you. Adieu Marie, I confidently await your news. Napole."

The move to Walewice at the end of winter was a blessing, as Marie was in a state close to nervous breakdown. Almost in her seventh month, she was ready for the warmth and cosseting of her in-laws. They all adored her unreservedly and shielded her from their curious neighbors: Anastase had tactfully gone abroad. The long winter was at last over and, as spring brought sunshine and life back into the bleak countryside, Marie gave birth to Napoleon's son. Alexander Florian Joseph Colonna Walewski, born on May 4, 1810, was a strong and healthy baby. Years later he wrote: "Thunder and lightning accompanied my birth—a good omen, my mother was told, and an indication that my life would be far from ordinary." Anastase came home for the christening, acknowledged the child, and left again shortly afterward to take the waters at Bad Gastein. Honor and face had been saved by all concerned.

Apart from a little kidney trouble, Marie recovered quickly from an easy labor. Her emotional recovery from Napoleon's rejection took much longer. Every mention by acquaintances or the newspapers of the emperor's wedding, and of his obvious happiness with his new wife, was a knife thrust deeper into her heart. With time her pain eased into a dull numbness, and she consoled herself by caring for Napoleon's Polish son, the product of their love. The baby brought her joy, and a measure of her former serenity returned. The emperor had written as soon as he heard the news—happy to hear the child was a boy, he wished Marie well and sent gifts. In the months of silence that followed, Marie knew his mind was focused on his new wife, and that she and her son had been forgotten.

Not until September, three months later, was there further word from Napoleon. During the golden months at Schönbrunn a year before, he had appointed Marie's younger brother Theodore to Duroc's staff, and through him they kept in touch. Napoleon's letter to Marie included an affectionate summons to Paris for late autumn.

To judge from the amount of luggage which accompanied Marie, her sons, Anastase's two charming nieces, as well as three maids and two cooks among other staff, they intended to remain in the French capital for some time. The escort for this exodus from Walewice for the ten-day journey was Marie's beloved brother Theodore, her best friend and adviser.

DURING THE THREE years since her idyll at Finkenstein, Marie had seen herself playing a principal part in Napoleon's private life. Following her return to Paris with his son, this role became merely supportive in the great epic about to unfold.

By November 1810, Paris had lost the gloom of the preceding two years. The emperor's staggering building program was transforming the city, and the Arc de Triomphe rose at the end of the Champs-Elysées to remind the citizens that theirs was the capital of the conqueror of Europe. There were daily parades of French, Italian,

Polish, German, Dutch, Portuguese and Spanish troops, all part of the new Grande Armée of the great French Empire. As travel to all these countries was both safe and easy, Paris had become a truly international capital.

The emperor had given instructions that, following her arrival, the Countess Walewska should be received at court and should lead a life appropriate to her rank. At her presentation she was sponsored by the lovely Duchesse de Montebello, widow of the emperor's friend Marshal Lannes and a lady-in-waiting to the Empress Marie-Louise. The duchess had met Marie in Warsaw and was the ideal choice to help her through this embarrassing official interview. Marie-Louise had heard all about Marie, and stiffly managed the required ritual remarks. The emperor said nothing, and Marie's reply to the new empress is not recorded, but it seems she executed her three deep backward curtsies with the same grace she brought to all her movements, despite the awkward long train on her dress. The ordeal over, Countess Walewska could now be referred to in the court circular as a "distinguished acquaintance of both the Emperor and the Empress."

Napoleon's appearance had changed. His skin had turned an unhealthy yellow color, he was considerably fatter, and his movements had become slow. Although known to be happy with his new wife, he was said to be often irritable and depressed, and he had lost his renowned concentration on his work. He was forty-one and not well.

The emperor gave orders that Marie should be installed in Paris with "dignity and style," and her house in the rue de la Houssaye was redecorated most elegantly à l'Empire. The days of living in Paris in secrecy and waiting for the moment of Napoleon's summons were over. He also bought her a country villa near Boulogne, not far from his official residence in Saint-Cloud, and apparently chose the furniture himself. Marie would have preferred their relationship to have resumed its former status, but as this was not Napoleon's wish for the moment, she consoled herself with his solicitude.

A box at the Opéra and another at the Théâtre Français were provided for the Countess Walewska, and she had the right of free entry to the new museums, which were the exclusive domain of the sovereign, with access limited to a select few. Sutherland recounts a delightful anecdote from a contemporary Polish memoir of a visit Marie paid to Vivant Denon, director of the Musée Napoleon (now the Louvre). Denon was an aristocrat, connoisseur and collector, who had been introduced by Josephine to General Bonaparte and went with him to Egypt, where his taste and knowledge of objets d'art were much appreciated by the future emperor. Napoleon later appointed him to head his museum, with the authority to select for its collections from the booty gathered after French victories. Denon, a bon viveur who delighted in the company of beautiful women, invited Madame Walewska to lunch at the museum. As Marie was leaving, her path was blocked by a guard, who explained: "Madame, I am here to guard the Venus and to prevent her escape."

Countess Walewska was offered an income of 10,000 francs from Napoleon's privy purse, which she accepted. Mother of the emperor's son, Marie had to adapt to her new role as Napoleon's friend since his love now concentrated on his pregnant wife. At Schönbrunn, when she learned that her love for Napoleon would result in having his child, Marie had experienced the ultimate physical fulfillment for a woman. In giving him everything she had to offer, she had made it possible for him to achieve his greatest ambition. In her unselfishness, she now rejoiced for him. But, at twenty-three, Marie was at the height of her beauty, and the man she loved with all her heart, whose son she had borne, had ceased to be her lover.

Although that part of her life had abruptly ended, Marie knew she could still help Poland through her friendship with Napoleon. Her house became a center for the Polish community in Paris. The Poles had always considered France their spiritual home; French was their second language, and traditionally they had absorbed French culture as if it were their own. By assuming a leading role in Parisian society, Countess Walewska was able to remind the emperor of his obligation and promises to her country. Countess Anna Potocka was also living in Paris. Not noted for her kind remarks, especially about beautiful women, she wrote of Marie at this time:

> Madame Walewska has become an accomplished woman of the world. She possesses rare tact and an unerring feel of proprieties. She has acquired self-assurance but has remained discreet, a combination not easily arrived at in her sensitive situation. Conscious of

Marie-Louise's jealousy, she somehow managed to conduct her social life in such a way that, even in this gossipy capital, few suspect
that she still remains in close touch with the emperor. It does not
surprise me at all that she is the only one of his loves that so far has
survived the test of time and of the Emperor's recent marriage.

Countess Potocka visited the fashionable portrait painter Gérard's studio as "everyone" was "rushing there" to view Marie's portrait, which
caused a sensation. In 1811 the Poles were all the rage of Paris, particularly the beautiful Madame Walewska who, it was rumored, had
borne the emperor a son.

Shortly after Marie's arrival in the capital, Napoleon had called to
see little Alexander. He was enchanted with the blond, curly-haired
boy, and his visits continued. At a reception that winter at the Tuileries Palace, the emperor told Princess Jablonowska, one of Anastase's nieces who had come to Paris with Marie: "Don't worry about
the little boy. He is a child of Wagram and one day he will become
King of Poland."* Despite this reassurance, Marie saw Napoleon in-
frequently in society. It was only when he came to visit Alexander, or
when she brought him to the emperor's study at the Tuileries, that
she could be with the man she had come to love so much.

Although she had been brought up as a strict Catholic, Marie
Walewska understood the semi-Oriental attitudes to women held by
her countrymen such as Prince Joseph Poniatowski. Equally, she understood Napoleon's dynastic ambitions; even so, it must have been
difficult for her to accept his happiness with Marie-Louise and his intention to remain faithful to her. Marie loved him so much, she would
have tolerated the existence of a "political wife" on the throne to provide the dynastic Bonaparte heir, and through him peace for France, if
only she could still have remained Napoleon's "Polish wife" in secret.

THE FOLLOWING MARCH, Marie-Louise gave birth to Napoleon's
son and heir, to whom his delighted father gave the title King of

---

* Quoted in Sutherland.

Rome. The writer Stendhal, then living in Paris, described the mood of jubilation as the cannon boomed 101 times: "A young prince had been born. All around us people went wild with joy. . . . It is a happy event for us all, for it spells peace." To Josephine the emperor wrote glowingly of his new heir, adding kindly that he was still very pleased with her own son Eugène, as "he has never given me an hour's anxiety."

The French had not welcomed their new Austrian empress with much enthusiasm—it was only twenty-odd years since they had cut off the head of the last Austrian archduchess who had come to France as a king's bride, well within living memory. But they welcomed this child whose birth could be expected to guarantee peace for the next generation. Marie-Louise was what the Viennese describe as a *knoedl,* a dumpling, all pink and blonde. If she was appreciated at all in France, it was for her fine childbearing figure, and precious little else. On the other hand, Josephine—elegant, graceful, generous and kind-hearted—had always been popular. Since Napoleon's first Italian campaign following their marriage, the Parisians had called her *"Notre Dame des Victoires"* and *"Josephine la Bonne."* When he divorced his wife after Wagram, the general feeling of the population was that "he shouldn't have left his old girl. She brought him luck."

During the glittering Parisian season of 1811–12, Marie entertained the most prominent celebrities and influential personalities of Napoleon's France in her houses on the rue de la Houssaye and the rue de Montmorency in Boulogne. She had met a number of Napoleon's marshals and ministers in Warsaw and in Vienna, and they joined the ever faithful Duroc at her gatherings, as did politicians, artists and members of the Polish community. Although the Poles treated Marie with a reverence bordering on obsequiousness, she managed to remain detached from the intrigues for which her countrymen were renowned. Marie was aware that Napoleon kept her under police surveillance, and that her every move was reported to him. Even if she had wanted it, a new romance would have been impossible to keep from the emperor. Perhaps she felt that as long as he watched over her and her son she was, in a sense, still close to him. Marie met Napoleon's sisters, Caroline Murat, Queen of Naples, and Pauline, Princess Borghese, whose husbands she had known during

Napoleon's stay in Warsaw, as well as his stepdaughter Hortense de Beauharnais, Queen of Holland.* They all liked the Countess Walewska, and acknowledged her disinterested feelings for Napoleon as well as her modesty and honesty. It was clear to *le tout Paris* that Madame Walewska's life revolved around her dedication to her son, her country and the emperor.

During the summer of 1811, while France was enjoying the prospect of peace following the birth of the King of Rome, Napoleon realized he would have to wage war again with Russia. His differences with Tsar Alexander centered on two main areas—the Continental System and Poland. The alliance with France concluded at Tilsit had seriously damaged Russia's economy. The trade blockade against England, to which it had agreed, deprived Russia of the cheap English manufactures it needed, and prevented it from exporting its agricultural produce, which England lacked and for which France had little use. Russia, on the other hand, offered only a very small market for French luxury goods such as wines, cheeses, scents and silks, which were cheap to import after the treaty.

As well as the economic pressures on the tsar, there was the problem of Poland. Ever since the creation of the Duchy of Warsaw, Alexander had been accused by the powerful Russian nobility of harboring pro-French feelings and of allowing French principles to infiltrate Russia from its Polish neighbor. Poland had adopted the Code Napoléon, France's excellent new legal system, as well as many other social improvements such as civil rights for Jews, women (including easier divorce laws) and peasants. The tsar was warned that, should such revolutionary ideas take root in Russia, he might suffer his father's fate. He was strongly advised that the only way to prevent his people from aspiring to the Poles' new freedoms was to annex that country and have himself crowned king.

Throughout 1811, Russia reorganized its vast army, opened its ports to neutral shipping and imposed huge taxes on French goods, actions viewed by France as highly provocative. Tsar Alexander also

---

* Hortense had two more sons before finally leaving her husband, Napoleon's brother Louis, following her mother's divorce. When she was granted a separation Hortense lived openly with her great love, the dazzling son of Talleyrand, Charles de Flahaut, who had admired Marie in Warsaw.

wooed England, Prussia and Sweden with some success, and hoped Austria would remain neutral. But victory in the forthcoming confrontation would depend on Poland, over whose territory the war would once again be fought.

France and Russia both "promised the Poles resurrection, provided they died for their cause" (a wry contemporary comment, quoted by Sutherland). No one in Poland wanted a war which would only drain their economy further and again strip and lay waste the land. Many of the powerful Polish magnates, particularly those whose estates bordered on Russia, genuinely felt that their country's best prospects lay in an alliance there, or even with Austria, rather than with distant France. They argued that despite all his promises, Napoleon still refused to give the Polish government any guarantees concerning their country's future if they continued to support France. But the decision really lay with Prince Joseph Poniatowski, commander of the Polish army and his country's foreign minister. He had given his oath as a soldier to Napoleon, as had his troops; and the Poles were men of their word.

⁂

THROUGHOUT THE BRILLIANT Paris winter season of 1811–12, rumors circulated of a "second Polish war" to be fought in the spring. As France's huge polyglot Grande Armée began to gather and march eastward, equally large numbers were making their way across Russia toward the western border. To add to the international unease, a comet was seen in the European sky from Moscow to northern Scotland and as far south as Portugal. Glittering white and with a long, blazing, uplifted tail, "Brook's Comet," like comets throughout history, was seen as a portent of doom.

In late April 1812, Tsar Alexander had sent the French emperor an ultimatum which he knew was unacceptable. War became inevitable, and for the first time Napoleon did not appear confident of the outcome. On May 5 at the palace of Saint-Cloud, four days before his departure for the front, he signed a detailed, carefully constructed legal document in Marie Walewska's presence, amply providing for their son's future and for her. Its twelve articles bestowed property near

Naples on Count Alexander Florian Joseph Colonna Walewski—sixty-nine farms with an annual income of about 170,000 francs—and set out precise conditions pertaining to the grant. Until Alexander came of age, the income was to be Marie's to use as she wished, with no obligation to account for it. When her son reached his majority, Marie was to receive an annual income of 50,000 francs from him. The estates were to be inherited by Alexander's direct male descendants, and if these died out, provision was made for the title and estates to be passed on through the female line. Should Alexander die without issue before his mother, she was to continue to benefit from the settlement until her death. Marie was to remain in sole charge of their son—Napoleon realized that no one could bring up the boy better—but he appointed Prince Cambacères, the arch chancellor, as Alexander's guardian. Napoleon never ceased to admonish Josephine and Hortense for their extravagance, and Constant mentions that the Bonapartes were all "stingy" with money; but this was not the case with the endowment made to Alexander and Marie.

Not only was it a very generous legacy, but the document is remarkable in the attention it gives to safeguarding the mother's welfare, and shows how much Napoleon cared for her. (The original decree is still in the archives of the Walewski family.) The following month Napoleon signed the letters patent creating Alexander a hereditary Count of the Empire with a new family crest combining the Walewski and Laczynski insignias.

ALTHOUGH THE WAR had begun, Marie left her family in Paris and travelled to Poland at the end of June 1813. The official reason given for her trip was to help France's new minister in the duchy, Monseigneur abbé de Pradt, Archbishop of Malines, generate enthusiasm for the war effort. In fact, she went to ask Anastase for a divorce. For some time, the Walewice estates had been making a loss, the result of bad management and the country's depressed economy. Under the new Napoleonic law adopted in Poland, Marie could be held equally responsible for her husband's debts. This put Alexander's inheritance in danger, particularly as Marie had taken the decision to make Paris their home.

On condition that his wife agreed to be financially responsible for their son Anthony and to make a trust fund for him out of her marriage settlement, Walewski, who was by now almost senile, agreed to the divorce. He signed a statement that Marie had been coerced into the marriage by her family when she was ill and under age, as well as signing an extraordinary declaration that he had an understanding with his wife absolving her from marital fidelity. It took only six weeks for the Polish courts to dissolve the Walewski marriage, thanks to the new laws and pressure from the French government, in this case the abbé de Pradt.

Napoleon showed a serious lapse of judgment in sending Pradt as his representative to Warsaw at this crucial time. He was pompous, new to politics, and lacked perception and finesse. The appointment of an ecclesiastic may have been necessary to explain to the Poles the emperor's difficulties with the Pope and his reasons for annexing the Papal States. Poland was a deeply religious country, and the support of its priests and bishops was vital if Napoleon was to keep the loyalty of its people. And their loyalty and support were needed more than ever: Napoleon was asking the Poles once more for the near to impossible. *"Toute la Pologne à cheval!"*—Let all Poland mount and ride with me!

Pradt succeeded only in alienating every group with whom he came in contact. Politically and socially, he was a disaster; personally as well, as far as Marie was concerned. Anna Potocka was back in Warsaw, and described how his Excellency "treated Madame Walewska as if she were the Empress herself." At functions he insisted that she be placed on his right, taking precedence over any other guest. The abbé then proceeded to ignore the room while hanging on Marie's every word, "much to the fury of old dowagers and to the intense amusement of the younger set, who watched with great merriment the lecherous old archbishop ogling, through his lorgnette, Madame Walewska's splendid shoulders and her shapely white arms." His Excellency had been instructed to show Madame Walewska every consideration, but he so embarrassed Marie that she had to flee to

Kiernozia to escape his attentions. There she waited anxiously with her mother for news from the front.

ONCE AGAIN POLAND had given its sons to Napoleon, this time for the decisive campaign against Russia, and forty thousand of them joined his huge army, including his personal escort of Polish Lancers. "Destiny must run its course. We are still the soldiers of Austerlitz. Let us march beyond the Niemen and carry the war into her territory. . . . Our victory this time will guarantee peace for at least fifty years." Napoleon had remained vague on the subject of their independence and gave the Poles no guarantees, yet they greeted his Order of the Day proclaiming "the Second Polish War" with the same enthusiasm they had shown for the past fifteen years of marching under his standard. His veterans had not forgotten the hardship and horror of the last winter campaign of 1807 in Russia—the never-ending blanket of snow which swallowed everything in minutes—yet surprisingly the troops' spirits were high as they assembled from all over the huge empire.

THE GERMAN POET Heine, who had watched Napoleon review his troops before they left Germany, immortalized their dedication:

> Forever I see him, tall on his horse, the eternal gaze fixed in the marble of the imperial face as, with the calm of destiny on his brow, he watched his Guards march past. He was sending them to Russia, yet still the old grenadiers looked up to him with such overwhelming devotion, such sympathy and earnestness, and with the pride of death: *"Ave Caesar, morituri te salutant!"* [Hail, Caesar, we who are about to die salute you!]

The story of the Russian campaign has often been told. In brief, as the Army of the West advanced, so the vast Army of the East retreated steadily toward Moscow, refusing whenever possible to engage the French. There were battles: Smolensk was fought in the blistering heat of August 1812, and although on September 7 the French won Borodino, the battle was both savage and indecisive, with heavy losses. Napoleon wrote that the Russians' retreat was disorderly, their soldiers discouraged, but at this stage it is unlikely he was aware of the strategy of their withdrawal. More important, as the Russians pulled back toward Moscow they laid complete waste to the country, killing all livestock and burning everything. The extent of the wanton destruction horrified Napoleon, leaving "600,000 families to beggary," as he wrote to Tsar Alexander from Moscow. His Grande Armée now had to supply itself.

As the distance between the French troops and their depots lengthened, the greatest problem facing the Grande Armée was the staggering difficulty of getting food and supplies to the men and horses. Foraging parties either came home empty-handed or were set upon by the Cossacks and slaughtered. As their need grew desperate, unauthorized units searching for food would fall into Cossack ambushes. But as they came nearer Moscow, their spirits rose. A battle was certain—the Russians would surely stand and fight to defend their capital, and with Moscow theirs the emperor would have all he needed for the army.

When it became known in Warsaw that the Grande Armée had reached Moscow, there was general rejoicing. It was October, and it seemed certain that Napoleon would remain in the Russian capital for the winter. Anxious for news, Marie had returned to Warsaw from Kiernozia. She occupied herself working in the hospitals while waiting for word from the front, keeping in touch with Napoleon through the French minister's office. No letters have survived, but a number of contemporary sources indicate that Marie thought of joining Napoleon in Moscow, just as she had in Finkenstein and Schönbrunn. It is improbable that she would have considered such a bold move without some encouragement from the emperor, either in May when Alexander's settlement was being planned before Napoleon left for the front, or once the campaign had begun.

It was mid-October before the news reached Warsaw of the burning of three-quarters of Moscow by its own population, by Russian troops and even by pillaging French soldiers. Since the beginning of the month, Napoleon had waited among the smoking, charred ruins for the tsar to reply to his offer of a truce, but by the third week of October none had come. With winter closing in and a shortage of food and firewood in the capital, the emperor decided to abandon Moscow and return home. The great, unwieldy army of Babel, cold, hungry and weighed down with plunder, began the slow march back. The story of the annihilation of the Grande Armée during Napoleon's tragic retreat from Moscow in 1812 is military history. Freezing and starving, all their horses eaten, the soldiers were forced to abandon their plunder, their cannon and even their shoes in the boggy ground. Stragglers either perished under an instant blanket of thick snow, were slaughtered by the invisible but ever present Cossacks, or attacked by wolves. On December 3, the remnants of France's mighty army finally reached the Lithuanian-Polish border; only nine thousand men remained in formation. In all, of the 600,000 troops who had marched so proudly into Russia, hardly 50,000 returned. The emperor had left Murat in charge of the main retreat, but he had deserted and returned to his warm Kingdom of Naples.

ON DECEMBER 10, Marie was at Kiernozia when Napoleon arrived unexpectedly in Warsaw to try to raise another ten thousand cavalry. His halt was brief, a short rest and a meal before his sleigh sped off again toward Paris in a temperature of minus 23°C and a blizzard. There is a popular story that he stopped at Kiernozia or Walewice to see Marie; but in fact when the emperor suggested that they make the detour, Caulaincourt, who was travelling with him, dissuaded him. With so much suffering among his troops, Napoleon could not be seen attending to personal matters. Was his wish to visit Marie merely nostalgia, or was he missing her as much as she yearned for him?

In a few days, the Russian army would be in Warsaw. Poland was left defenseless to face the barbarian hordes. For all its sacrifices, that tragic country had gained nothing and lost everything by following Napoleon's star. Marie had received instructions to leave for Paris at once—Napoleon's mistress must not fall into Russian hands and become a hostage. Before leaving, she called on Prince Joseph Ponia-towski for the last time. The great man had returned with what was left of his Polish army—less than one thousand of the forty thousand who had set out in June so full of hope. Wasted, ravaged by fever, in-capacitated by a serious leg wound, he remained loyal and willing to continue his support of the emperor. It was a great pleasure for Marie to be able to advance Prince Joseph a large loan from Alexander's set-tlement toward the refit of the Polish army. (Years later, that loan was repaid to Marie's heirs by Prince Joseph's estate.)

Back in Paris, Marie continued living as before, leading a discreet social life centered around her family—as well as her children, she had brought her younger sister Antonia and her brother Theodore with her—and the interests of her country. In the spring of 1813, she was surprised to receive a request from the former Empress Josephine to visit her at Malmaison with Alexander. The invitation was probably the idea of Josephine's daughter Hortense, former Queen of Holland, who seems to have been on friendly terms with Marie as well as with Napoleon's new empress. During the tense Russian campaign, Marie-Louise had shown Hortense the emperor's letters, knowing that Hortense would pass on any news to her anxious mother. Although she had been refused permission to see Napoleon's son and heir, Josephine had engineered it, and now she wished to meet Marie and hold Napoleon's other son in her arms.

At forty-nine, Josephine was still graceful and lovely. Curiosity, perhaps even a premonition that she had not much longer to live, made her want to know her former rival. Reluctantly, Marie agreed to come, and brought the three-year-old Alexander with her.

Josephine had a passion for flowers, especially tulips, hyacinths and carnations. After her death, Pierre-Joseph Redouté, a protégé of Josephine's, published his famous book *Les Roses*, which made her name synonymous with the flowers of which her garden at Malmaison had over two hundred varieties.*

This unlikely meeting among the flowers of Malmaison brought together the two women whose lives had been most closely touched

---

* From the roses Josephine had sent from Persia she developed first the tea rose and then the hybrid perpetual. Most garden hybrid tea roses have their origins in the Empress Josephine's experimental garden at Malmaison.

and shaped by Bonaparte: the dark-haired, effortlessly elegant Creole—the great love of the young general, for whom he had won his famous victories—and the petite, blond, twenty-six-year-old woman with the striking blue eyes who had been the emperor's "Polish wife."

The meeting was a success, and according to the memoirs of her lady-in-waiting Madame Avrillon, Josephine liked Marie very much. "She often talked of her unusual qualities and went to great lengths to stress that this woman, so essentially kind and good-natured, had never caused her any pain." Little Alexander reminded her of Napoleon, and she sent regular gifts to both mother and child.

During this spring Marie also came into regular contact with Philippe Antoine d'Ornano, a cousin of Napoleon's from Corsica. They had first met in Warsaw in 1807, when he was one of Napoleon's aides-de-camp, but had not seen each other since. Now a general, he was one of the wounded heroes who had returned from Moscow. It seems Napoleon approved of the friendship, and the handsome, charming d'Ornano, only two years older than Marie, became her escort in Paris while Napoleon spent the remainder of the 1812–13 winter reorganizing his forces.

SINCE THE HUMILIATION of 1807, Prussia had totally transformed and modernized its army, and in February it joined Russia in declaring war on France. Napoleon knew that the tsar was involved in secret talks with his father-in-law, the Emperor Francis, but he trusted in the dynastic bond of family to keep Austria loyal to its treaty with France. In Sweden, Madame de Staël had the ear of Bernadotte, the king's adopted son, which she filled with anti-Napoleonic propaganda.* When Sweden betrayed Napoleon and signed a treaty with England joining the Allies, Germaine de Staël was largely responsible.

* Bernadotte was an ambitious soldier in Napoleon's army who married Desirée Clary, the young Napoleon's love and the sister of his brother Joseph's wife Julie. The Clary girls were the daughters of a rich textile merchant from Marseilles, and to the impoverished Bonapartes, recently arrived from Corsica, they represented a luxury well beyond their means. In these extraordinary times, the "upwardly mobile" soldier Bernadotte became a Marshal of France. Adopted by the King of Sweden as his heir, he made Desirée, the merchant's daughter, his queen. Their descendants are the current royal family of Sweden.

The enemy was gathering its strength for a mighty conflict, and the entire world seemed to oppose France.

BY THE END of April 1813, Napoleon had mobilized a new army of 300,000 troops, but they were young and untried and, apart from the Poles, the foreign soldiers could not be relied on completely. Leading his army personally, Napoleon managed to win a series of victories, but they gained him little and cost him dear. A sniper killed Marshal Bessières, Duke of Istria, his beloved cavalry commander second only to Murat in brilliance. And Duroc, the emperor's closest and dearest friend, was disemboweled by a shell as he rode alongside his master, dying shortly afterwards in a nearby farmyard. Napoleon was so affected by grief that he called off the action and refused to see anyone. Géraud Duroc, Duke of Friuli, had been with him since his first campaign in Italy. He was Napoleon's only real companion, and the one man with whom he shared all his secrets. Marie had been one of those secrets, and she mourned the gentle friend who had been her closest link with the man she had loved since that first evening when he had brought her sobbing to the conqueror's feet.

Unsure of Austria's continued support despite his recent victories, Napoleon tried to negotiate a truce, hoping that this would give him time to dissuade Metternich from joining the Allies. But the Austrian chancellor's terms for non-intervention were uncompromising. "There is no end to the insolence of Austria . . . These people are mad and hopelessly out in their reckoning. No Court could be more treacherous," Napoleon wrote on June 2 to Eugène in Italy. By appointing Marie-Louise regent in his absence, he had hoped to retain Austria's loyalty. On June 7 he found time to write to the regent ("Madame and darling") admonishing her for receiving the French chancellor while she was reclining in bed: "You shall not, under any circumstances, or on any pretext, receive anyone while you are in bed. It is improper until over the age of thirty."

On June 4 an armistice was arranged which was to last until July 20. Austria used the time for secret talks with England, while Metternich, negotiating on behalf of all the allies, was pressing Napoleon to agree to give up most of the territory he had conquered since 1800. Although the emperor had won most of the spring encounters, both he and Austria knew the strength of the allies and the weakness of the Grande Armée. Due to Metternich's unreasonable demands the talks failed, and Austria joined the allies against the French, declaring war on August 12. Bavaria too had deserted Napoleon, and in Spain the Duke of Wellington defeated King Joseph Bonaparte's army.

Finally, on October 14, 1813, at Leipzig, the Battle of the Nations began, and continued for four days. The combined Russian, Austrian and Prussian armies badly defeated the Grande Armée, inflicting losses of 73,000 men.

MARIE WAS CAREFUL not to encourage General d'Ornano by answering too many of his letters, but she was grateful that he kept her abreast of events. She was at Spa taking a cure to improve her delicate health when she received Ornano's letter telling her of the tragic death of Prince Joseph Poniatowski at Leipzig.

Little of his Polish army had remained after the dreadful retreat from Moscow, but Poniatowski had managed to raise another, made up mainly of peasant boys mounted on the fast ponies from the Cracow area. Napoleon had just named him a Marshal of France and detailed his "pygmy cavalry," as he called them, to cover the French armies' withdrawal from Leipzig. The Poles had had their own escape route cut off by an overzealous French engineer who had prematurely blown up one of the pontoons over the Elster River. After his horse was shot from under him, Prince Joseph, wounded three times and bleeding heavily, had still refused to surrender. As he could no longer stand, another horse was found to carry the commander in chief who, witnesses said, had "death on his face." Ignoring the murderous enemy fire, the Poles fought their way to the banks of the river. As the enemy infantry advanced and enclosed his men, Prince Joseph spurred his horse and leapt into the river.

Prince Karl Schwarzenberg, the field marshal in command of the Austrian forces, watched in sadness from a nearby hill as the Elster's muddy waters swallowed up his childhood friend, whom the French had justly called *"le chevalier sans peur et sans reproche."* With Prince Joseph Poniatowski's heroic death, his country's hopes died too. Marie had admired him all her life, and joined the whole Polish nation in mourning him.

LESS THAN A month later, on November 9, Napoleon was back in Paris trying to hold together his collapsing empire. Added to his territorial losses, there were no more than sixty thousand men left in his army, many of them raw recruits of sixteen or seventeen, and very few cavalry. France's satellites—Italy, Holland and the German states of the Rhine Confederation—were tired of the Continental System and their economic isolation, and demanded their independence.

Following Leipzig, the allies, on the advice of Metternich, had offered Napoleon terms which would leave France with its "natural frontiers": the Rhine, the Alps and the Pyrénées. In addition, it would keep Savoy, Nice and Belgium. The offer was not unreasonable, but Napoleon procrastinated, the allies changed their minds, and both sides prepared for another confrontation. France was sick of war, its treasury was empty and its young men were evading conscription.

As the situation worsened for Napoleon's empire and the stock exchange plunged, Marshal Murat, King of Naples, was considering defecting to Austria to save his throne. As such a move would endanger Alexander's inheritance in Naples, Napoleon sent for Marie in December to discuss an alternative financial arrangement.

Later the same month, the Russian and Prussian armies crossed the Rhine, the Austrians advanced through Switzerland, and Wellington approached with his armies from the southwest. The combined strength of Napoleon's enemies was more than half a million troops.

As renewed war became inevitable, Napoleon still made time to think of Marie and Alexander's future. Early in January 1814, he had arranged for a new house to be bought for his son at what is now 48 rue de la Victoire. It was a spacious, two-storied south-facing villa, with a courtyard, stables, a garden and a porter's lodge. He also had a document prepared giving Alexander an income of 50,000 francs derived from his personal property and gilt shares.

On January 25, 1814, as the emperor left Paris to meet his enemies in the field, Marie wrote to Ornano: "The Emperor left this
morning. I did not have a chance to say goodbye to him . . . I wonder
whether he noticed . . . my nerves are in a very bad state." Marie felt
sure it was the beginning of the end.

Despite the allies' overwhelming numerical superiority, Napoleon
fought a campaign of such brilliance that there were moments of ela-
tion and even hope for France. But it was not to be. Napoleon had
once remarked to Goethe that "politics are destiny," and the politics
of the European powers had sealed his own. While the Cossacks raped
and pillaged in the French countryside, the last of several battles was
fought on March 30, outside the French capital. By evening, Paris
had capitulated.

The next day, as the emperors of Prussia and Russia rode down
the Champs-Elysées, Napoleon waited at Fontainebleau, the wonderful Renaissance palace of François I, the Salamander King, to sign his
abdication. He had tried to impose his vision of equality through his
laws, his hopes for peace and trade through the Continental System,
his progressive administration and government on the world, and the
world had spurned him. Neither England nor Russia had been prepared to yield to Napoleon's domination of the globe, and in reject-
ing him they rejected his enlightened reforms as well. The old order
had defeated the new.

Two weeks later at Fontainebleau, Napoleon tried to kill himself
by taking poison. Somehow, he had always retained his optimism even
in the face of defeat, but when he heard that Marie-Louise was taking
their son, his hope for the future, back to Austria, he finally despaired.
Three days earlier, he had signed a treaty at Fontainebleau renouncing
his vast kingdom and accepting the tiny island of Elba as his sovereign
principality for life. Naturally he had expected his wife and son to join
him. Their departure for Vienna led him to fear that he would never
see them again.

Napoleon's powerful constitution rejected the poison and, as he
lay exhausted and semiconscious throughout the next day, Marie arrived in secret at Fontainebleau. Constant, faithful to the last, found
her wandering through the deserted château and brought her to
Napoleon's small library adjoining his bedroom. She had felt his

need, sensed his despair, and came to comfort him in whatever way she could. All that day and night she waited outside Napoleon's door for his call to enter. When the dawn still brought no word from the ailing emperor, and as Marie did not want to be discovered there, she left quietly for Paris without seeing him. Constant records that less than an hour after her departure Napoleon appeared and asked for her. When told of the circumstances of her visit, he was distressed. "Poor woman," he said, "she must have felt humiliated. I must tell her how sorry I am." According to Constant, Napoleon went on to say, rubbing his forehead, "I have so many problems here."

Marie's letter written that day does not survive, but Napoleon answered it immediately:

> Marie—I have received your letter of the fifteenth and I am deeply touched by your sentiments. They are worthy of your lovely soul and the goodness of your heart. When you have settled your affairs in Paris and decide to take the waters at Lucca or Pisa, it would give me the greatest pleasure to see you and your son again [on Elba]. My feelings for you both remain unchanged. Keep well; don't worry. Think affectionately of me and never doubt me.

On March 20, Napoleon left for Elba, accompanied by a thousand of his guard who had volunteered to share his exile. Marie had tried to reach Fontainebleau with Alexander to say goodbye, but the Bourbon troops had barred the road. Two weeks later, on May 3, Napoleon arrived on Elba.

In April, Marie had sent her brother Benedict to Naples to try to dissuade King Joachim Murat from abolishing Alexander's entail along with all the other Napoleonic donations being cancelled. When the only hope seemed for Marie to intervene personally with her friend Napoleon's sister Queen Caroline, she packed up her family and departed for Italy. Passing through Bologna, she called on another Bonaparte sister, Elisa, Grand Duchess of Tuscany, now living in retirement but full of useful information about Napoleon's agents in Italy.

After a brief stop for her health at Lucca, Marie, together with Alexander, her sister Antonia, brother Theodore and two maids, arrived at their rented villa in the hills above Florence toward the end of July.

It did not take Napoleon's agents long to send him news of Marie's arrival. On July 27 the emperor instructed Bertrand, still chief of a considerably reduced Imperial Household, to "deliver a message for the Countess Walewska at the address in Florence given to you by Cipriani [Napoleon's agent in the city]; you will tell her that we have learned with pleasure of her arrival in Genoa, and subsequently in Florence, and you will ask her to send news of herself and her son . . . she should address her letters to you."

In early August, Theodore travelled to Elba, returning to Florence after a few days on the island with a letter for Marie from Napoleon. Dated August 9, 1814, the letter urges her to go to Naples to settle her affairs:

> I will see you here with the same pleasure as always—either now or on your return from Naples. I will be very glad to see the little boy, of whom I hear many nice things, and look forward to giving him a good kiss. Adieu Marie.
>
> > Your affectionate
> > Napoleon

At the same time, Napoleon also entrusted Theodore with a letter for the Empress Marie-Louise, who was taking the waters at Aix. It was a difficult mission for Marie's brother. Napoleon's letter begged his wife to join him on Elba and to bring their son, just as he was encouraging his "Polish wife" to visit him with Alexander. At Aix, Theodore saw for himself that the rumors concerning Marie-Louise's friendship with the dashing Austrian general Count Neipperg were true. The Emperor Francis had himself nominated the handsome count to "keep the Empress company," and ordered him to prevent his daughter from joining her husband on Elba.

Marie had been fully briefed by her brother about his visit to Aix when she embarked from Livorno for Elba with Alexander, Antonia and Theodore on August 31. As she knew the empress had no intention of ever joining her husband in exile, Marie had made tentative arrangements before leaving Italy to remain on Elba indefinitely if

Napoleon wanted her. To help him financially she had brought what money she had and all her jewels.

In just a few months, Napoleon had transformed the lovely, mountainous island. His enormous energy, attention to detail and capacity for organization were now channelled into the improvement of the lives of his new subjects—through innovations ranging from tree planting to halt soil erosion, to the development of a range of industries and even the eradication of flies.

The prospect of seeing Marie excited him, but as he still hoped his wife would come and share his exile, he did not want any word of Marie's visit to get out. *"Madame Mère,"* Napoleon's mother, had come to live with him, and despite her sensible attitude to most things, she would have disapproved of the arrival of her son's mistress if there was a chance of his wife joining him. Then there were the island's inhabitants to consider. Napoleon felt that "his children," as he called the staunchly Catholic Elbans, would not understand his passing the time with his mistress while awaiting his lawful wife.

High in the mountains, an hour's steep walk above Marciana Alta, the nearest hill village, there is a shrine dedicated to the Madonna del Monte, a small church, and a hermitage housing six monks. It was here, surrounded by ancient chestnut trees, a prevailing aroma of Mediterranean herbs and a breathtaking view, that Napoleon prepared to receive Marie Walewska.

The travellers landed in a secluded bay at nine in the evening and were met by Bertrand, who settled them in Napoleon's coach and four. After a drive of some two hours, Napoleon held up their coach like a highwayman with four guards carrying flambeaux, and took Bertrand's place in the carriage. As the road became rougher they changed into a smaller carriage, then to mules for an hour's steep climb. They reached the hermitage, exhausted, at one in the morning.

The weary group was revived by supper *al fresco*, lit by flaming torches under a great chestnut tree and prepared by Napoleon's renowned chef Louis Etienne Saint-Denis (Mameluke Ali). He recalled that the emperor "carved the meats and poured the wines," taking "great pleasure in serving the ladies himself." During the entire meal, Napoleon was "very gay, gracious and charmingly gallant. He was happy." Marie had changed into a pretty gray taffeta dress and, while the chirping of the cicadas sent little Alexander to sleep, she sat and talked with Napoleon.

Theodore was lodged in the village below, and Alexander, Antonia and Marie stayed in the spartan cells of the hermitage. Napoleon had a tent erected under the trees nearby for himself. Saint-Denis recalled how the emperor "came out of his tent wearing a dressing gown and went to her room where he stayed until daybreak. It was obvious to all what was going on. . . . Even the most humble of his subjects would have been more skillful at conducting a secret love affair than the Emperor."

The next day was spent exploring, and when the sun was high they rested under the trees where, as Alexander Walewski was to recall in his memoirs, "only the murmur of the stream and the bell of a restless goat broke the silence"—a family reunion in magical surroundings, and unforgettable for Alexander. The little boy called his father *Papa l'Empereur,* and Napoleon played with him, rough-and-tumbled on the grass, and carried him about on his shoulders. Saint-Denis again: "The young boy looked a bit pale and his features were very like the Emperor's; he was rather serious for his age."

That night Napoleon went once again to Marie's room.

Just when she might have thought that this paradise would never end, on the following day Napoleon received word that the whole island knew of the arrival of a young blond lady and a fair little boy. Naturally the islanders concluded that the Empress Marie-Louise and the King of Rome were with him, and the elders asked to pay their respects. Napoleon was alarmed. If Marie's presence was discovered, it could cause a public scandal and give the empress more reason not to join him. He did not hesitate. Marie and her family must leave at once, and he sent an order for his boat to be prepared.

While Napoleon wrote a letter to Murat about Alexander's Neapolitan estates, a heartbroken Marie packed. She felt unable to tell him about his wife's betrayal with Neipperg—he had suffered enough betrayals already—but this last rebuff was the hardest of all for her to bear.

In a gathering storm Napoleon escorted the little group down the mountain path to his carriage. Marie had offered him her jewelry; she knew he was short of money, but he refused. As their words of farewell were whipped away by the wind, Marie and her family left on a nightmare journey through the storm, and only reached the sheltered port, now called Porto Azzuro, on the other side of the island at midnight.

Despite the pleas of the harbormaster and the Polish commandant of the port, who had accompanied Napoleon to Elba with 120 of the Lancers, Marie obstinately refused to wait out the storm. The emperor had wanted their presence and their departure kept secret, and their orders were to leave at daybreak. The frightened little group set sail in a dangerous sea, and were too far away to recall when Napoleon's messenger arrived. He had ridden all through the treacherous night with the order that Countess Walewska was to wait until after the storm before embarking.

It was a week before Napoleon heard that they had arrived safely, but he received no word from Marie. After the Elba sojourn, she was physically and emotionally spent. She had offered to give up everything and remain with the man she loved, and again her sacrifice had been rejected. Just as before, Napoleon's ambition had shattered the dream.

But Marie still had business with the Bonapartes—her son's estates had been confiscated, and if possible she intended to reverse that decision. Joachim and Caroline Murat were energetic and dedicated sovereigns, conscious of the people's rights after living so long with Napoleon's reforms. They knew that Napoleon's era was over, and devoted their considerable skill and energy to saving their thrones.

Another of Napoleon's sisters, the delicious, fun-loving Princess Pauline Borghese, was also staying in Naples. She genuinely loved her brother and planned to spend the winter with him on Elba. Murat, Caroline and Pauline were all very fond of Marie, and welcomed her and Alexander with real warmth. The sisters doted on Alexander, "so like Naboulione at that age—only fair," and spoiled Marie. Whether it was nostalgia for Napoleon, Marie's charm or family feeling that prevailed is not certain, but on November 30 the decree confiscating Alexander Walewski's entail was cancelled. Marie was given two years' back payment with interest and an advance on the first five months of 1815, almost 1 million francs. Napoleon had written to Murat thanking him for restoring Alexander's estates, and entrusted him with the care of Marie and Alexander, "who is very dear to me."

With little to entice her to return immediately to Louis XVIII's Paris, Marie remained in the pleasant winter sunshine of Naples, while the victorious European powers divided the spoils of Napoleon's empire at the Congress of Vienna. In January 1815, she had heard of Anastase's death, and it is likely that, through her friendship with the Murat court, she was aware of Napoleon's plans to quit Elba. Louis XVIII had refused to honor the Treaty of Fontainebleau and pay the defeated emperor his annual indemnity. Napoleon was so short of money that he could not pay his soldiers or even his household on Elba, and he knew from his spies of the French people's dissatisfaction with the restored Bourbons.

☙

ON MARCH 1, having evaded the English warships cruising the Mediterranean, Napoleon landed at Fréjus near Antibes with a thousand men. The heroic tragedy of the Hundred Days had begun. Three weeks later, on March 20, Napoleon was carried on the backs of his veterans into the Tuileries and installed in the palace. The Bourbons had fled.

Napoleon's old magic worked again on Marie, just as it had on his soldiers, and by early April she was back in Paris, communicating with Napoleon through Hortense, who acted as his hostess in the Tuileries. The emperor's return lifted the spirits of the nation; suddenly the people remembered only the glory, and forgot the pain and hardship of the wars.

But this time the allied forces were determined to crush Napoleon forever. Wellington gathered together the English, Dutch, Belgian and Hanoverian forces, as well as the Prussians under Blücher. The Russians and Austrians were also on their way. The eagle would be trampled under the massive onslaught of Europe's combined forces.

On June 11, the eve of his departure for the final conflict, Napoleon summoned Marie to the Elysée Palace. They talked for a long time, and he gave her excellent financial advice, for which Alexander had reason to be grateful later.

On Sunday, June 18, 1815, Wellington's immense army crushed the ailing Napoleon at Waterloo. For those who had witnessed this extraordinary man's star blaze more brightly than any other conqueror's since Alexander the Great, the dream was over, the epic had ended. The allies would see to it that there would never be another glorious Hundred Days.

◦∮∮∼

THREE DAYS AFTER Waterloo, Marie and her son were back at the Elysée Palace. While Alexander played with Louis Napoleon, Queen Hortense's younger son and the future Napoleon III (whom he would one day serve as foreign minister), Marie helped with the packing. The next day, Napoleon abdicated for the second time.

On June 28, ten days after Waterloo, with the roses in Josephine's lovely garden in full bloom, Marie Walewska and Alexander came to Malmaison for their last parting from Napoleon. Alexander later recalled that "the atmosphere was very sad. I can still see the Emperor. . . . He took me in his arms and I remember a tear ran down his face." Marie spent an hour with Napoleon; when she had to leave, "she fell into his arms and remained there for a long time" (Marchand).

Marie was twenty-eight, and her son, the image of his father, was five. She had offered to join Napoleon in his new exile, and he had refused her. He had been the center of her life for nine years, and now she felt as if something had finally died within her. Without her realizing it, her fatigue was being compounded by advanced kidney problems. She continued to live quietly in Paris with Alexander; Theodore and Antonia had returned to Poland. For some time she had maintained her correspondence with General d'Ornano. Following Anastase's death and her brusque, hurtful dismissal by Napoleon from Elba, Ornano had written asking her to marry him, but it had been too early for her to decide.

In January 1816, General d'Ornano was arrested for denouncing the shameful trial and execution of Marshal Ney, Napoleon's heroic cavalry commander known as "the bravest of the brave." Although Ornano had joined the Bourbons after Napoleon's first abdication, he had returned to the emperor's standard for the Hundred Days, missing Waterloo due to a bad wound, the result of a duel fought the day before. After Waterloo he had joined the Bourbons again, but he still felt sincerely loyal to his old comrades-in-arms. Talleyrand refused Marie's pleas on his behalf, but he was finally released and strongly advised to leave France.

A number of Napoleon's biographers suggest that he encouraged Marie to marry Ornano, as she was alone and he was worried for her and for their son. Whether or not this was the case, Marie finally gave General Count d'Ornano her promise. They were married on September 7, 1816, in Brussels. On June 9, 1817, she gave birth to Rodolphe Auguste d'Ornano, a strong healthy boy, but her fragile health never recovered. She had just enough strength to dictate her memoirs for her children and posterity throughout the summer. In the autumn, the condition of her kidneys and her acute toxemia grew worse and she begged to be allowed to return to France, her adopted home.

On December 11, 1817, Marie Laczynska Walewska d'Ornano died at her house in Paris, surrounded by her three sons and her husband. She was thirty-one years old.

ON ST. HELENA, Napoleon had heard of Marie's marriage and was glad for her. He had always kept her portrait, together with that of Josephine, on his bedside to remind him of the lovely "little patriot" he had found in Warsaw. He never learned of her death. By the time Ornano's letter, diverted by the winter storms, reached St. Helena, the emperor, who had loved his little "Polish wife" in his own way, was dead. The ring with a twist of golden hair, which she had given him so long ago at Schönbrunn, was still on his finger:

"When you cease to love me, remember, I love you still."

EPILOGUE

AS HE stipulated in his will, Napoleon wanted Alexander Walewski to join the French army or spend his life somehow in the service of France. Alexander did not disappoint his father, serving as French ambassador to the Court of St. James's and with distinction as foreign minister under his cousin, Napoleon III.

Marie Walewska was one of the few who loved Napoleon the man more than the emperor, but she was seduced by the legend as well as the myth. Balzac wrote that Napoleon "could do everything because he wanted everything." When he wanted Marie, she fell under his spell like the soldiers, painters and writers of the day. His memoirs, written by Las Cases from Napoleon's reminiscences on St. Helena, were the greatest bestseller of the nineteenth century. Such was the fascination of Napoleon. Even on Elba, when he no longer resembled the slim conqueror who had arrived in Warsaw, his gaze was still penetrating, and the smile Chateaubriand described as "affectionate and beautiful" managed to captivate Marie.

Marie Walewska's role in the drama of Napoleon's life is perhaps not important in historical terms. Her love for the emperor, no matter how patriotically inspired, gained little if anything for her country. Napoleon's policies were certainly not influenced by her (or by any other woman). Her one great political deed was to prove to Napoleon that he could sire a dynasty, and for that he cast her aside. At the time of their romance, she probably did mean something to him, but not enough to change the course of events for Poland as she had hoped. She may have had a humanizing influence, restoring his faith in women, but his personality was so overpowering that the dove became another of the eagle's victims.

Of all the arts, Napoleon preferred tragic drama because it exalted honor and courage. He felt that "the hero, in order to be interesting, must be neither completely guilty nor completely innocent." Most of all, a good drama in his view had to have a tragic ending. All these things applied to his life and to Marie Walewska's. Once she fell in love with Napoleon, she knew she was acting against the rules of the Catholic Church, hence her guilt; but her innocence also cannot be denied, and her early death was a tragedy for her children and for all who knew and loved her. It is not surprising that Marie Walewska is still looked upon by the majority of the Polish people as a heroine whose virtue was the price of her patriotism.

Napoleon said, "There are only two powers in the world, the sword and the mind. In the long run, the sword is always conquered by the mind." And yet the Napoleonic legend, which he did so much to foster himself through the bulletins of the Grande Armée, turned his epoch into a Romantic era. Marie had hero-worshipped Napoleon from childhood, and this feeling never left her. Her love for him was even more single-minded than her love for her country, which in a sense it supplanted. For a young woman of Marie's background and religious scruples, to become the mistress of any man was alien to everything she had been brought up to value and believe in.

Placid by nature, constant in her beliefs, Marie was loyal to her cause. Her sense of duty led her to accept without question her destiny as it was thrust upon her: marriage to Anastase Walewski, a man fifty years her senior; mistress to Napoleon, having been offered to him as one of the spoils of the conqueror; the hope of her country; and, finally, being abandoned in favor of a dynastic marriage.

"L'amour est l'histoire de la vie des femmes; c'est un episode dans celle des hommes."

MADAME DE STAËL

4

Lola Montez

1818–1861

MISTRESS OF KING LUDWIG I OF BAVARIA

"It has been my fate to be pursued, from the very beginning, by calumny. It has besmirched my origin even as it has besmirched my whole life."

LOLA MONTEZ

"When you met Lola Montez, her reputation made you automatically think of bedrooms."

ALDOUS HUXLEY

"Courage—and shuffle the cards"

Motto of Lola Montez

*M*arie Dolores Eliza Rosanna Gilbert was born in Limerick, Ireland, in 1818. Her father was an officer in the King's Own Scottish Regiment who had earned his commission for courage during the Napoleonic Wars. Her mother had been the beautiful Miss Oliver of Castle Oliver. According to Lola's memoirs, her mother was descended from the Count of Montalvo, an impoverished Spanish grandee who had brought his family to Ireland during the reign of Ferdinand and Isabella. It was this cherished belief in her Spanish antecedents which prompted Lola's choice of a professional name in later years.

Little more than a child when she was obliged to marry, the lovely Mrs. Gilbert gave birth soon afterward to a frail, dark-haired girl. Four years later, Captain Gilbert, accompanied by his wife and their tiny daughter, rejoined his regiment at Dinapore in India. Like most army stations, Dinapore was infested with cholera and other diseases, and it was feared the weak child would not survive. Instead she thrived, and the gallant captain succumbed. The little girl, known as "Lola," the diminutive of her second name, Dolores, became the darling of the regiment; passed from lap to lap, she invariably settled on the general's knee. Her dying father had bequeathed his young wife to his best friend, a Captain Craigie, who was as much under the child's spell as her mother's. Six months later he married the young widow.

In less than two years, Craigie had been promoted to colonel; his lovely wife ruled the station and her daughter assumed the mantle of a princess. Surrounded by adoring soldiers, the pretty child with huge blue eyes and thick black curls learned a great deal more about manipulating men than she did about schoolwork.

When Lola was eight years old she was sent "home" for her education. Her first stop was with her stepfather's Calvinist relations in Montrose, Scotland, who spoilt her and totally failed in taming her. As part of her education, she was sent in the traditional manner from one respectable family to another, in London, Perth and Bath. It seems that all these places made much less of an impression on her than she did on them.

She was a mischievous child, who exploited her exotic past to great effect in front of other children. India's magic and color—the sounds, noise, scents and smells—were all to stay with her, and her wish to recapture the adventure of her early childhood there fired her imagination all her life. Her formal education was completed at a finishing school in Paris.

◦ℱℱ◦

LOLA AND HER mother had the same volatile character, and were perhaps too alike to form strong natural bonds. In the ten years they were apart, neither had missed the other. But Mrs. Craigie had received regular reports on her pretty, wilful daughter and decided, when Lola was eighteen, that it was time for her to marry.

In 1837, Lola returned from Paris to join her mother in Bath. The reunion was not a success, but Mrs. Craigie pleasantly surprised her daughter with the vast amounts of shopping she did for her. Accompanying her mother was a handsome young Irish officer, Lieutenant Thomas James, who had travelled on the same boat from India as Mrs. Craigie. Lieutenant James was as kind and attentive to the daughter as he was to the mother, and it was to him that Lola turned in her wretchedness: these clothes were intended for her trousseau—her mother had arranged for her to marry a rich sixty-year-old judge of Calcutta's Supreme Court. Lieutenant James was full of sympathy and, to the fury of Mrs. Craigie, solved Lola's dilemma by eloping with her himself.

The young bride looked so small and fragile when she appeared in Dublin society that she was described as "the married child." After six months spent at his family's grim castle, to the couple's relief James was recalled to his regiment in India. Both husband and wife flirted with fellow passengers on the voyage out; the marriage was in essence already over. James drank and was indifferent to Lola, whereas every other man who saw her wanted her. More than anything, Lola feared boredom, and her indiscretions often resulted more from this than from any genuine passion or desire.

Lola's excitement at the prospect of returning to India was dampened by the dreaded prospect of meeting with her mother, who never forgave Lieutenant James. But Craigie, who was now a general, adored his stepdaughter, and welcomed the young couple. As the station's social life was as abundant as the lush vegetation, Lieutenant and Mrs. James were invited everywhere. Before long, Lola became the belle of Calcutta and Simla. She danced, she teased—remembering all her admirers by their initials—and immersed herself once again in her fascination for the exotic: the vibrant colors, varied cultures, religions and animals of India. Meanwhile, James alternated between boredom and jealousy of his wife's success. He was posted to Afghanistan, where Lola was so miserable that she wrote pleading with her stepfather to arrange a reconciliation with her mother so that she could join them in Simla.

At nineteen, Lola was stunning. Vivacious and witty, she looked more like a fragile girl than a young married woman. Mrs. Craigie was not yet thirty-five and at the peak of her beauty; together, mother and daughter turned every head. James followed Lola back to Simla and briefly all went well. Emily Eden, the governor-general's sister, wrote home about Lola at this time:

> [She is] very pretty and a good little thing apparently, but they are
> poor, and she is young and lively, and if she falls into bad hands she
> would soon laugh herself into foolish scrapes.

Lola's mother, on the other hand, had money and an important social position; her daughter was a rival she did not need. After a month in Simla, Captain and Mrs. James returned to Afghanistan, where Lola could only share her mother's glamorous life through the descriptions in her letters.

While Mrs. James dreamed, her husband dallied with other women, finally running off with the older wife of a fellow officer. Mrs. Craigie refused to take back her jilted daughter, and paid her passage to England instead. With tears in his eyes, General Craigie bade his stepdaughter farewell, and pressed a check for a thousand pounds into her hand.

Lola, who was now twenty-four (although she claimed to be eighteen), had been put in the care of the ship's captain and his wife for the voyage home, but she clearly preferred to be consoled by a

Captain Lennox, an aide-de-camp to the governor of Madras. Although she was to write in her memoirs that theirs was purely a friendship of like minds, shocked fellow passengers claimed they had seen Mrs. James through the open door of her cabin, sitting on her bunk and slowly rolling on her stockings in front of Captain Lennox.

On her arrival in London, Lola moved into Captain Lennox's lodgings, which outraged society. When James heard of her behavior, he started divorce proceedings at once, on the grounds of adultery with Lennox. In December 1842, Lola was divorced from her husband's "bed and board." They were absolved of any responsibility toward one another, but neither could remarry as long as they were both alive.

From this pointless and indecisive judgment, Lola began her clash with the law and her career as a maverick. Never again would she fall victim to a man unless he had qualities she could admire. Now that she was alone in the world, she decided that she could only live as an *artiste*. Divorce took Lola beyond the pale of Victorian society—and going on the stage firmly closed its doors to her forever.

The relationship with Lennox was short-lived. Although the lovely Mrs. James could have chosen any one of a dozen rich and influential "protectors" to provide for her, she decided to study acting. From her brief and unsatisfactory marriage she had learned to know what she needed from a relationship, and most decidedly what she did not. "Runaway matches," she wrote later, "like runaway horses, are almost sure to end in a smash up." For a woman with a mind as independent as Lola's, to be a man's pawn solely for financial security was unacceptable. There were obvious advantages in taking a rich and powerful lover, but she would only do so on her terms. Lola always wanted to be someone in her own right, and not just exist as the appendage of a great man.

THE MUTUAL DISLIKE between Lola and her mother may have stemmed from their closeness in age and their instinctive sense of female competition, first for Gilbert's love and then for Craigie's and that of the entire regiment. This need for attention and applause in

Lola later grew into a craving for publicity. She knew she was beautiful, and enjoyed the envy of her audiences as much as their admiration. Her personality required approbation, not so much out of insecurity but rather to confirm her self-esteem. Throughout her life she played the roles of her choice and device. As a natural actress she saw opportunities to assume the leading part in the scenes she had created since her childhood. Her drama teacher recognized the valuable assets of her appearance, temperament and presence, but had to admit failure in teaching her the formal techniques required at the time for acting on the stage, and suggested that she try learning to dance instead.

Mrs. James took the advice and left for Spain to study the language and dancing under a famous instructor. Four months later she reemerged in London as "Lola Montez," related to Spain's most illustrious bullfighter, and a descendant of the Montalvos. The impresario of Her Majesty's Theatre, Benjamin Lumley, billed his new star as "Donna Lola Montez, première danseuse from the Teatro Real, Madrid."

A journalist who met her backstage before her first performance in June 1843 was captivated by the twenty-five-year-old Spanish dancer, and her notices were good. But her debut was not a success. Lord Ranelagh, a rejected suitor, recognized her, and the hisses and cries of "impostor" from his box and from his friends drowned the sighs of admiration for her face and figure from the stalls and gallery. The audience had liked her, but the spurned lothario, influential and vindictive, succeeded in ruining her chances.

All her life Lola would complain about bad or unfair publicity, but even this was infinitely better than no publicity at all. If she could not become a success as a dancer, Lola Montez would became a succès de scandale. Foolishly, she began a lifetime habit of answering the press with fanciful explanations of incidents involving her. Following the termination of her contract at Her Majesty's, this letter was sent to all the newspapers:

> I am a native of Seville . . . until the 14th of April when I landed in England I have never set foot in this country and I never saw London before in my life.

When her mother heard this latest news, she declared her daughter dead and went into mourning. Lola was consistently unapologetic—if the facts did not fit, she invented new ones. She convinced herself that she was being persecuted and, driven by a desperate need to be thought innocent and right, she became a compulsive liar.

IT WOULD HAVE seemed natural for Lola at this point in her career to try her luck in Paris, as both an *artiste* and a courtesan. But, in her practical way, she recognized the French king as bourgeois and mean (as well as totally faithful to his dull wife, as his sons the princes were to theirs), and she saw no point in trying for one of them. She opted instead for King Leopold of the Belgians, who was known to be susceptible to pretty women, but she ran out of money before she could get to him. Lola was reduced to selling her clothes, singing in the streets and who knows what else to make money. A kind but not rich German took her on his travels and helped her obtain an engagement at the opera in Warsaw. The management told her she could not dance, but the audience appreciated her visible assets, and so for two months she was kept on "for ornament."

Lola's next stop was Dresden, where she claims in her memoirs that she created a furore; certainly the Spanish dancer was thought sufficiently interesting to be invited by the king and queen to their summer palace, either for her dancing, her beauty or her wit. This visit must have been a success, as the queen gave Lola a letter of introduction to her sister, the Queen of Prussia, ensuring a welcome in Berlin.

By nature a rebel, Lola was instinctively drawn to those who made their own rules and lived by them. Similarly, the more she mixed with international aristocracy and even with royalty, the more readily she adapted to their ways—her "aristocratic bearing" was always remarked upon. She also found the looser morals of some in the circles in which she moved admirably suited to her temperament.

In Dresden, Lola met Franz Liszt; hauntingly beautiful, sensitive and talented, he was the idol of music lovers, the toast of the salons and adored by the ladies of society. Liszt was captivated by Lola's physical perfection. They shared a mutual fascination and for a brief period became lovers. He even wrote a sonata in her honor. One day Richard Wagner saw her waiting for Liszt in a theater. Far from being stunned by her beauty, he recoiled and fled from the "painted woman with the insolent eyes." Years later, when Wagner had come to obsess Ludwig II, he was to be reminded of that face. The Munich mob would ridicule him as "Lolus! Lolus!," in memory of the beauty who had captivated Ludwig I.

As both Liszt and Lola were spoilt and temperamental, the *affaire* could not last. Quarrels between them grew more frequent and stormy. The composer tired first. He escaped by locking Lola in his hotel bedroom, paying the bill in advance and arranging for the door to remain locked for twelve hours to give him time to get away. Just as he had feared, Lola totally destroyed the room in her fury. Somehow, when next they met, they became and remained friends. Certainly Lola never bore a grudge against a former lover. Later, when she controlled the King of Bavaria, she tried in vain to lure Liszt to Munich with the promise of high honors.

The *affaire* with Liszt in Dresden had brought the lovely Lola out of obscurity and gained her a certain international notoriety. She moved on to Berlin, where King Frederick William IV invited her to dance at a reception for his brother-in-law, the Russian tsar. Here, as in Dresden, Lola triumphed and made a number of powerful and influential acquaintances among members of the tsarist court. However, an unfortunate incident occurred at a private party following Lola's command performance at the royal palace of Sans Souci. Six drunken young gentlemen made determined advances upon Lola and five other lady guests. Always armed, Lola brandished her knife and successfully defended herself and her companions. Lola's favors were hers to give, and no one's to demand or take.

Shortly afterward, a military review held in honor of Tsar Nicholas became another notorious episode in the dancer's stay in Berlin. Lola's horse became uncontrollable, probably at the volleys of salutes (or at a sharp jab from her spurs), and bolted straight into the royal party. Although she was an expert rider, taught by the Indian army, Lola appeared helpless, and had it not been for the quick thinking of a young soldier who grabbed her reins and tried to remove horse and rider from the group, Lola might have fallen into the arms of the king or the tsar. Thwarted or rescued, her instinctive reaction was to raise her whip and give the interfering young guard several lashes. Such was the power of Lola's charm and beauty that the wretched soldier was obliged to call on her to beg pardon.

But there were too many such incidents involving pistols, knives and whips, and a reluctant Lola accepted her royal patron's suggestion that she leave his domain.

ON THE STRENGTH of her success in Berlin, and with a handful of useful introductions, Lola returned to Warsaw. This time she had an overwhelming reception at the theater. There was no doubt her fame encouraged the Poles to a greater appreciation of her ravishing face and figure, and concern about the obvious limitations of her choreography diminished accordingly. One journalist was so overwhelmed, he eulogized:

> Of the three times nine attractions held requisite by a Spanish poet* for perfect feminine beauty, the danseuse Lola Montez has all except one. Twenty-six of these essentials of highest bodily beauty she possesses in most perfect degree, and as far as the twenty-seventh is concerned, the very lack of it, in my opinion and certainly in that of my readers, constitutes the crown of her beauty.

> Three white: the skin, the teeth and the hands.
> Three black: the eyes, the eyelashes and the eyebrows.
> Three red: the lips, the cheeks and the nails.
> Three long: the waist, the hair and the hands.
> Three short: the teeth, the ears and the feet.
> Three broad: the bosom, the forehead, the space between the brows.

* Often quoted since the fifteenth century. The prophet Mahomet has also been named as the author.

Three narrow: the mouth, the waist and the ankle.
Three soft: the fingers, the hair and the lips.
Three small: the nipples, the nostrils and the head.

All these charms are Lady Lola's in the most excellent proportions
excepting only the color of her eyes, which are not black but blue.
Hair as soft as silk, rivalling the gloss of the raven's wing, cascades
luxuriantly down her back. Her beautiful, noble head rests upon a
slender, delicate neck whose dazzling whiteness shames the swan.
How, then, am I to paint Lola's bosom, if her other charms leave
me at such a loss for words?

Lest I fall short of the truth, which my pen is too feeble to express, I must have recourse to another. [etc. etc.]

Undeniably, Lola's most beautiful features were her extraordinary
eyes, described by the smitten Polish journalist as possessing all the
shades of blue of the sixteen varieties of the forget-me-not. "This
lady," he gushed, "wherever she casts her magical glance, must be a
Conqueror."

Her repertory at this time included "El Olle" (a sailor's horn-
pipe), the Swiss dance from *William Tell,* and the audiences' favorite,
her own invention, the "Spider's Dance." More music hall than classical, it featured black rubber spiders attached by webs to her dress.
After much wriggling and feigned expressions of horror, they fell to
the floor, to be crushed under her dainty foot in time to the music.
When one of her silk garters burst during an energetic Spanish number, Lola elegantly kicked it into the auditorium. The resulting scrab-
ble for the trophy nearly caused a riot.

Among the audience was Poland's Russian viceroy and brutal op-
pressor, Prince Paskevich. After seeing Lola dance, he wanted to possess her at any price. Small, round, old and ugly, he demanded her
presence at his palace the following morning. Lola, on the urgent advice of her Polish friends, reluctantly obeyed. But she rebuffed the
aging regent's advances and, according to her memoirs, spurned his
offer of a country estate, a title and priceless jewels. Lola was proud
but not foolish, and considering her dwindling resources, if Paskevich

did make extravagant offers, he must have been utterly repulsive for her to have refused him. Humiliated and furious, the viceroy retaliated by threatening Lola with imprisonment or deportation.

As the theater's director was also a colonel of the gendarmes, he had to obey the viceroy, and mingled his staff among the audience with instructions to hiss at Lola. Forced to stop her performance, the "enraged and fiery" little dancer rushed down to the footlights. With her famous eyes flashing, she told the Polish audience about the threats and tactics of the hated Russian viceroy and her refusal to accept his repellent offers. Lola's tongue was a weapon as dangerous and effective as her beauty, and the audience was hers. Cheered and applauded, a large crowd of Poles escorted her home. This incident coincided with one of the many uprisings in Warsaw against tsarist rule, and by chance or design, the following day Lola found herself at the center of a potential popular uprising. Ignoring the danger, when the viceroy's police came to arrest her, Lola was ready, appropriately dressed and armed for another starring role. From behind her locked door she informed them calmly that she would shoot dead the first man who broke in. While the officers retreated, no doubt to draw lots, the French consul (presumably smitten) rescued the "Spanish" dancer by claiming her as a French subject.

With her beauty and her talent for histrionics, Lola had no difficulty in conquering the romantic, sentimental Poles. The young, rich and eligible Count Owinski fell so in love with her that he proposed marriage. After an ugly scene ensued with his family, adding to her difficulties with the viceroy, Lola decided that the time had come to move on again. The city was in ferment, with rioting in the streets and hundreds of arrests being made, so she wisely slipped away to conquer new hearts and horizons.

ACCORDING TO LOLA, Tsar Nicholas I himself had invited her to Russia after their meeting in Berlin at the court of King Frederick William; true or not, she certainly had an introduction from the Queen of Prussia. Lola went further and claimed in her memoirs that she was in Russia on a diplomatic mission for the British government.

Although this would seem highly unlikely, there were a number of occasions in Lola's career when British consuls and officials suddenly appeared and rescued her from awkward situations. She was intelligent
and had a great facility with languages,* and her profession as a
dancer would have given her access to every level of society. As a
beautiful woman, men would confide in her, perhaps even reveal their
political secrets.

Whatever the case, she enjoyed the confidence of the tsar. There is
a story that when their secret political discussions were interrupted by
the sudden appearance of an important official, the tsar hastily shut
her in a wardrobe in the Winter Palace. It seems he then forgot to release her, and felt obliged to pay Lola handsome compensation.

Despite her alleged success in Russia, Lola's restless search for her
destiny drove her to move on. "The only place for a woman of spirit,"
she announced, "is Paris," and she left to conquer the French capital.

PARIS IN 1844 was Europe's most sophisticated city, its cultural center and the capital of joie de vivre. The boulevards, cafés and theaters
were full of energy and life. Good living was cheap, and talent and
beauty were universally worshipped. Lola had known Paris as a girl
and probably visited the city several times on her travels with various
"protectors." This time she planned her Parisian debut as a dancer.
She arrived with a reputation enhanced as much by her own exaggerations as those of others. Mystery surrounded her origins, and Lola
did nothing to discourage the amazing stories that inevitably circulate
about a woman of extraordinary beauty, spirit and daring. Some
claimed she came from a noble Spanish family and was stolen by gyp-
sies, others that she was an illegitimate daughter of Queen Christina,
or of the Spanish toreador Montez. It was gossiped that her desires
were insatiable but that she would grant her favors only to kings,
princes or men of genius; that all men who cast eyes on her were forever enslaved, and that she was more dangerous than a tigress if

---

* The journalist A. D. Vandam, author of *An Englishman in Paris*, claimed she spoke nine
languages, including Hindustani—all with a foreign accent.

thwarted. Her various escapades in royal circles had not gone unnoticed, nor had her courage and her ability to handle knives, pistols and whips.

The name of Lola Montez was known throughout Europe—but Lola, though famous as a *danseuse,* had remarkably little experience on stage, certainly not enough to warrant the overwhelming attention she received from the public and the press. Her combination of beauty, arrogance and physical courage attracted the curious and appealed to the imagination of the sophisticated Parisians.

Liszt appeared in Paris at the same time, though they may not have arrived there together. According to her memoirs, she did see the composer in Paris, but soon he left for his tour of the south. Although their relationship could only have been brief, thereafter Lola had a yearning for men of rare talent, sensitivity and culture.

It may well have been Liszt who introduced Lola to the intellectual bohemian circles she immediately frequented on her arrival in Paris. She soon met the notorious Marie Duplessis, immortalized by the younger Alexandre Dumas as *"La Dame aux camélias."* It was said she kept the nightshirts of her seven lovers in seven separate drawers in her bedroom. The pale and fragile Marie was Lola's perfect foil, and together they were invincible. The ravishing lady of the camellias was to die young, a victim of love and consumption.

Years later, in her "Lectures on Beauty," Lola would recount how every Parisienne who could afford such luxury would bathe in milk. This custom became so commonplace that "while hundreds of fashionable women were swimming in milk every morning, thousands of families were obliged to dispense with the use of it in their chocolate and coffee." Milk became almost unobtainable for domestic purposes, and the police discovered that the vendors were in the habit of buying back from servants milk which had been used in the bath, and reselling it.

Lola met George Sand,* the celebrated writer and mistress of Chopin, and Alexandre Dumas *père et fils.* The elder Dumas, famous as the author of *The Three Musketeers* (*The Count of Monte Cristo* was published the following year), was instantly smitten with Lola. She

* See footnote on the origins of the Maréchal de Saxe on p. 84.

met Balzac and Victor Hugo, the brilliant religious philosopher
Lamennais, the poets Joseph Mery and Alphonse de Lamartine, and
Théophile Gautier, the writer and critic. Alfred de Musset, another
writer and former lover of George Sand, and the novelist Eugène Sue
were also among the group, as was Joseph Samson, head of the
Comédie Française and teacher of the great actress Rachel,* and many
more. These boulevardiers made the Café de Paris their headquarters,
and an unwritten rule excluded anyone from their company who did
not excel in some form or other. Lola dazzled them all with her
beauty, her wit and her intelligence, and was often the only woman
admitted to join this group of Olympians. From the "liberal" philoso-
phers in the group Lola learned about the oppressed masses and the
manipulative power of the Jesuits; how they eased the reins of government into their hands and, by governing on behalf of uninterested
or illiterate rulers, successfully resisted progress. The endless discussions in the Café de Paris encouraged her growing fantasies of political power.

   In the company of these literary giants Lola absorbed the writers
Gautier and Sue's prevailing concept of the "Fatal Woman," a type established in a number of their romantic works. *La belle dame sans
merci* and the Byronic hero merged in Lola's fertile imagination and
from this time colored her self-image to include the femme fatale. For
this role she even invented a costume for herself of black silk and lace,
trimmed with blood-red roses. She saw herself as a splendid untamed
creature, "a free, independent being," she wrote, "subject to my
whims and sensations alone." At other times she smoked cigars, wore
men's clothes (magnificently) and swore eloquently. She described
herself as "better than a devil, which the ladies have frequently called
me, and worse than an angel, as the men have so often christened
me." She was a magnet for men, yet she liked them to keep their distance. It had to be her decision to take a lover or to discard him—another of her more masculine traits, but one totally in keeping with her

---

* Rachel, whose full name was Elizabeth Rachel Felix, had affairs with "Plon-Plon," son of
Jérôme Bonaparte, and with Alexandre Walewski, son of Marie Walewska and Napoleon Bonaparte. In 1844 she gave birth to Alexandre Antoine Colonna Walewski, and the present-day
Colonna-Walewskis descend from her (Napoleon and Marie's son Alexandre Walewski only
produced two daughters from his first marriage, and the line from his second marriage died
out).

own philosophy and that of the women she admired in Paris. These women, who often wore men's clothes and insisted on keeping their financial independence, openly rebelled against society's custom of confining women to the home. Since leaving her husband, Lola had determined to be independent, and she only used men in financial desperation or to gratify her whims. She saw herself as a George Sand, a flag carrier of reform for the role of her sex. Her misfortune was to be a woman, "a target placed in a conspicuous position to be shot at by all unenlightened human beings, who may have peculiar reasons for restraining the progress of the mind."

Nor could Lola ever take as a lover a man who did not attract her physically. As actresses were a byword for immorality on the boulevards, men casually took liberties Lola would not tolerate. She used a fan to create a natural barrier between herself and others, and wore dresses with high Byronic collars to discourage the gallants from kissing her on the nape of the neck as they did other actresses. If she wore décolleté in the evenings, she added a Spanish headdress with lace to protect her shoulders and hair.

Under the patronage of the great cantatrice Madame Stoltz (another who usually wore men's clothes), Lola secured an engagement at the Paris Opéra for March 30, 1844. As always, her notoriety and reputation guaranteed her a full house. When the curtain rose on her first night, the audience gasped in admiration. She stood quite still in center stage, wearing a dress of white satin trimmed with gold and scattered diamond studs. Every line of her figure was accentuated by the tight-fitting bodice. Her white skin glowed, her rich mane of black curls rested on her shoulders, and Lola knew she had won her audience before the music began. Her critics agreed that she could not dance in the technical sense, but her debut performance at the Opéra lacked nothing in fiery tempo and passion. Somehow, as the music reached its climax, her satin slipper came off; unperturbed, she recalled the effect her garter had had on the Poles, and elegantly flicked the shoe into the audience with her toe. The French scrambled for the slipper as energetically as the Poles had for her garter.

Though the audience cheered and applauded, the critics were less appreciative of her performance and she was not engaged by the Opéra again. On one thing, however, the reviewers all agreed—her stunning beauty far outshone the quality of her dancing. "We suspect," wrote Théophile Gautier, present that evening as a critic, and correctly grasping her essential masculinity, "after the recital of her equestrian exploits, that Mlle Lola is more at home in the saddle than on the boards." But he admitted that she "redeems her imperfections as a dancer by a voluptuous abandon, and an admirable fire and precision of rhythm."

Gustav Claudin, whom Lola asked to write her memoirs, called her "an enchantress. There was about her something voluptuous which drew you. Her skin was white, her wavy hair like the tendrils of the woodbine, her eyes tameless and wild, her mouth like a budding pomegranate. Add to that a dashing figure, charming feet, and perfect grace. Unluckily," he concluded, "as a dancer she had no talent." A. D. Vandam, with his somewhat jaundiced eye, was less charitable. He found her education wanting, her speech (in every language, including English) full of grammatical errors, and her wit, especially when she was angered, often more suited to "the pothouse." And yet even he, who mostly transcribed hearsay, wrote that "Men of far higher intellectual attainments than mine, and familiar with very good society, raved and kept raving about her."

As Lola always went out of her way to woo journalists in the hope of favorable notices, there were many who fell under the spell of those magnificent blue eyes. One was Alexandre Henri Dujarier, part owner and literary editor of the influential newspaper *La Presse*. Dujarier was twenty-nine, handsome, rich, highly accomplished, engaging and full of mischievous good humor. When he met Lola she had spent several months in the circles of the Parisian intellectuals, and the natural sharpness of her mind had been finely honed in their company. Already in awe of her physical perfection, Dujarier was not disappointed with her intellect.

They were instantly attracted, but Lola approached the relationship with uncharacteristic caution. Dujarier, for all his bravado, was by nature reticent with women, and had reluctantly acquired a mistress almost for the sake of form. He quickly understood that Lola's notoriety, her exquisite clothes and her flirtatious manner were all cultivated to help secure theatrical contracts. He noticed that she withdrew from intrusive approaches, and set out deliberately to win her friendship. Their courtship began with long evenings of discussions at the Café de Paris. They shared a fascination with politics, and as Dujarier was one of the leaders of the French Republican Party, Lola became an avowed Republican from this time.

Lola Montez appreciated her own beauty, and often used it as a weapon to ensnare or destroy. In common with many beautiful women who take their looks for granted, she longed to be admired and appreciated for her mind. Dujarier sensed this, and wooed her slowly but ardently. He taught her the joy of trifling pleasures—a bunch of violets bought from a street vendor, a walk in the park in pale autumn sunshine.

Their love grew steadily through tenderness and mutual respect. Lola's arrogance, and her defiance of a world she imagined relentlessly hostile, melted in the warmth of Dujarier's unconcealed adoration. They became lovers, and for the first time in her life Lola knew contentment. Although each kept their own residences, the two became inseparable; every moment he was not at his desk, Dujarier spent with Lola. She joined his group of close friends, "liberals" like her lover— Dumas the elder, Balzac, Mery and Emile de Girardin, Dujarier's partner at *La Presse*. Girardin's scathing replies to the attacks of his competitors, in particular *Le Globe*, had resulted in his fighting a number of duels, in one of which he had killed a man. Dujarier's own pen was said to drip acid, and the sarcasm and irony of his writing earned him the hatred of his rivals.

With the help of Dujarier's friends in the press, Lola had received some favorable notices, resulting in a booking for March 1845 at the Théâtre de la Porte Saint-Martin. Although it was said that the society of the boulevard *"se fiance mais ne se marie pas"* (become engaged but never marry), in the fall of 1844, Lola and Dujarier decided they would wed the following spring when she had completed her contract. Dumas and Mery were invited to travel with them on their honeymoon tour through Spain, an ambitious plan full of literary possibilities.

Dujarier's devotion had tamed Lola and succeeded in making her almost "respectable," yet even he knew better than to attempt to prevent her from appearing on the stage. He always tried to accompany her to rehearsals and refused to allow her to associate with other actresses. One such actress invited them both to a dinner in a fashionable restaurant together with all their literary friends. Lola longed to go, but Dujarier forbad her to mix with these demi-mondaines and went alone.

Heavy drinking, wild spirits and bravado inevitably led to gambling for high stakes. Like his beloved, Dujarier had a sharp tongue and an uncontrolled temper. When his reason was dulled with drink, it was easy for an enemy from *Le Globe* to provoke him to insults. Dujarier fell into the trap; he returned home committed to receiving "satisfaction" and fighting his first duel. He could not explain the cause of the argument to his friends the next day; he simply accepted it as an extension of the rivalry between *La Presse* and *Le Globe*.

De Beauvallon, his antagonist, was a famous swordsman and an excellent shot, whereas Dujarier had no skill or experience with either sword or pistol. His friends tried everything to extricate him from an impossible situation, but Dujarier saw the duel as a matter of honor. Lola was not told the identity of his opponent, but she was assured that he was a genial friend of all the group, and felt sure the affair would end honorably without injury to either. The night before the duel, Dujarier sent Lola home to her apartment, promising to call on her the next morning. He then sat down to write to his mother, to Lola, and to prepare his will. For several hours that night, his friend Alexandre Dumas remained with him and tried in vain to dissuade him from fighting.

March 11 dawned cold. At seven Lola sent her lover a message, and Dujarier replied that he would come soon. Instead, accompanied by his seconds and a doctor, he drove to the Bois de Boulogne. There they waited in the freezing cold, stamping their feet in the snow. Two hours later, de Beauvallon's carriage arrived. Pistols were chosen, and despite his opponent's assurances to the contrary, one of Dujarier's seconds noticed that the muzzles were lined with black powder, as if they had just been tried.

Dujarier's hands were shaking so badly with cold and fear on the hair trigger of his pistol that he almost fired into one of his friends. When all final attempts to halt the duel had failed, the opponents paced away from each other, turned and advanced the required six steps. Through cold or nerves, Dujarier fired at once and wildly, then stood frozen to the spot, facing de Beauvallon. His enemy raised his pistol slowly and, taking careful aim, shot Dujarier between the eyes.

When her lover did not come to take her to the theater as promised that morning, Lola was gripped with misgivings. Dujarier's servant arrived at nine as instructed with the letter he had written the previous night:

> My dear Lola,
>
> I am going out to fight a duel with pistols. This will explain why I wanted to spend the night alone and why I have not come to see you this morning. I need all the composure at my command, and you would have excited too much emotion in me. I will be with you at two o'clock, unless—Goodbye, my dear precious Lola, the dear little girl I love.
>
> D.

Lola's carriage raced the short distance to Dujarier's house, where she found his valet in despair, certain his master had been killed. She rushed to the apartment of Alexandre Dumas and learned from him that her lover's opponent was de Beauvallon. "Oh my God, then he is a dead man!" she cried. Dumas refused to tell her where they had gone to fight. Having once accompanied Lola to a shooting gallery, he knew how well she handled a pistol; he recognized her courage and knew she was sincere when she said she would have prevented the duel had she known it was to be with de Beauvallon. He had no doubt she would either throw herself in front of Dujarier or grab the pistol and shoot de Beauvallon herself. In great agitation, Lola returned to Dujarier's apartment to wait.

When she heard the carriage, Lola flew down the stairs and out into the street. As one of his friends opened the door, Dujarier's body rolled out and fell to the ground at her feet.

Through the Frenchman, Lola had come to know love; now she understood sorrow. He had become her reason for living, and had brought out all that was good and honest in her. Until he had come to dominate her life, she had only thought of the world and everyone in it in relation to herself. Dujarier had taught her self-respect, given her stability and helped her both to develop and refine her mind and to listen to her heart.

In an attempt to console her, Balzac ventured that "Heaven was not meant to be found on earth." Lola was quoted as answering: "Heaven I have just left, now I must return to Purgatory."

A month later, after the magnificent funeral, Lola had to fulfill her contract with the Théâtre de la Porte Saint-Martin. Not surprisingly, she danced without her usual passion, and the audience responded with hissing and catcalls. Lola answered them from the footlights with her unique rhetoric, and thereby ended her dancing career in the French capital.

Dujarier had left her 20,000 francs and, freed from financial restrictions, Lola joined his friends in a quest for vengeance. It was clear to them that de Beauvallon had sought Dujarier's death and that he had practiced with the pistols, a criminal breach of the laws of duelling. The case became such a cause célèbre that it had to be heard outside Paris. Twelve months later, de Beauvallon was tried in Rouen for murder.

The trial caused a sensation, with Alexandre Dumas and Lola Montez, wearing black velvet and ruffles of lace, the stars of the proceedings. Although Lola had very little evidence to give following "the murmur of admiration which ran through the gathering" when she entered the witness stand and lifted her veil, she was satisfied she had done all she could for her dead lover. She did not wait for the final outcome. It was not until October 1847, more than two and a half years after the duel, that de Beauvallon and his principal second were found guilty of conspiracy to murder Dujarier. By that time Lola had left France.

Vandam claimed they had all forgotten Lola Montez within six months, and that only Alexandre Dumas occasionally spoke of her. "She has the evil eye," he is alleged to have said. "She is sure to bring bad luck to anyone who closely links his destiny with hers, for however short a time. You see what happened to Dujarier. If ever she is heard of again it will be in connection with some terrible calamity that has befallen a lover of hers."

WHAT LITTLE SENTIMENT Lola had, died with Dujarier. She had been powerless to prevent the loss of the only man to whom she had ever given her heart. That heart now turned to stone; whether it was revenge or an inner rage that drove her, from this time Lola Montez courted danger and adventure with a greater abandon than ever before. Recalling her motto, "Courage—and shuffle the cards," she left for Spain. But the visit to her "fatherland" could not replace the dream voyage she had planned with Dujarier and his friends. After a brief interlude during which, she claimed in her memoirs, she was almost carried off by the dashing, infamous bandit Madras, Lola gathered her formidable inner resources and moved on to Germany.

IN 1846 THERE were some thirty-six principalities in Germany, and ample opportunity for Lola to succeed in her ambition "to hook a prince." Five years spent circulating within Europe's centers of power had given Lola Montez a taste for controlling destinies. If fulfillment through love had been snatched from her, then why not use her influential connections to find another stage and play a leading political part? Lola had realized long ago that all most men required of a woman was physical beauty. Intelligence and courage may have appeared to be admired, but in reality they presented a threat, and any woman who possessed them inspired more fear than admiration. After Dujarier, she decided that no man would again rule her life or her heart. She would use the power of her beauty and the force of her personality to succeed in a man's world. Having buried her heart with Dujarier, she was ready to face any challenge. A born gambler, she would risk everything for what she believed in at that moment, and no one would be allowed to stand in her way. Change and variety were essential to recharge her energies and inspiration. Her ambition was more than mere survival; Lola wanted to triumph on her own terms and against all the odds.

TOURING THE FASHIONABLE spas and watering places of Germany, Lola met the ruler of a tiny principality in Thuringia, Heinrich LXXII von Reuss, an eligible bachelor. Although Lola considered his domain as little more than a toy, Heinrich von Reuss would have been a prince worth "hooking." But as marriage to the beautiful dancer never crossed his mind, she amused herself briefly by having her every whim gratified. Dubbed "the fair impure" by his disapproving subjects, she was soon bored by the minuscule court's stiff protocol, the more so in a country that had little to entertain a woman like her. The people objected to her capricious demands and easy use of her whip, and she infuriated their ruler by taking short cuts across his precious flowerbeds. This stage was too small for Lola. Prince Heinrich called her a "she-devil" and presented her with a deportation order. Lola retaliated with a considerable bill for "expenses." Only when it was paid did she quit his domains. Her next stop was Munich.

ON THE THRONE of Bavaria sat the amiable sixty-year-old Wittelsbach king, Ludwig I. His family had ruled the country for almost a thousand years, and its members were so interrelated that the frequent telescoping of the family tree resulted in some of its members suffering from a hereditary madness—although "mad" to the Germans would have passed as merely eccentric among the English aristocracy. Despite his age, the king had never lost his sparkle, and his energy and contagious enthusiasm made him appear ten years younger.

Ludwig was born in Strasbourg in 1786, while his father, who was the brother of the hereditary Duke of Bavaria, was serving in a French regiment. To demonstrate their loyalty to their commander, the officers of his father's regiment shaved off their precious mustaches to make a pillow soft as down for the new prince. He was named after his godfather, the luckless Louis XVI of France. Too young to have felt the effects of the French Revolution, the boy was sent away to a famous tutor to be given a solid German education. He grew up hating Bonaparte, whose victories consistently humbled the Germans and Austrians. In 1805, the Emperor Napoleon created Bavaria a kingdom and appointed Ludwig's father, Max Joseph, as its king. Napoleon made every effort to befriend the new crown prince, but Ludwig made no secret of his loathing of the French emperor. Obliged to join the Bavarian Regiment in Napoleon's army, he fought with distinction and courage, but without enthusiasm or pride. His obvious hostility made Ludwig a thorn in Napoleon's side, and the emperor decided that Bavaria's crown should eventually bypass her truculent prince and go instead to one of his own family. But this was not to be.

Due to the careful strategy of its king, Bavaria emerged from the Napoleonic Wars intact, unspoilt, prosperous and loyal to the Wittelsbachs. After Waterloo, Crown Prince Ludwig was free at last to devote himself to his life-long vocation of pursuing beauty in art and art in beauty. As a young man he had been considered pleasant-looking, though never handsome, with a fine figure. Like many admirers of Lord Byron, he favored velvet jackets with large white collars tied at the neck by a generous bow, and narrow trousers. He also subscribed openly to Byron's obsession with beauty and belief in sin, and became famous as a lover of poetry and the arts.

With peace restored, the Crown Prince of Bavaria travelled Europe to see the great monuments and collections. He found his aesthetic ideal in Italy, particularly in the ancient ruins of Rome. His son Otto had been offered the throne of Greece some years before Ludwig himself became king, and there he had studied at first hand the classical application of the golden rule of proportion, employed in architecture since the age of Pericles. Prince Ludwig did not confine his love of the arts to the visual. He sought out and befriended the great scholars, writers, composers and artists of the day and commissioned their works. He himself was a poet, composing verses on almost any pretext and allowing them to be published for the pleasure of his subjects.

WHEN LUDWIG INHERITED the throne of Bavaria at the age of forty, he was in the enviable position of realizing his dream. Already as a young man he had decided to make his capital, Munich, the most beautiful city in Europe. Not only did he devote himself to art in every manifestation, he was also a supreme patriot. As king, he had the opportunity as well as the means to combine his love of art with love of his country. After so many years spent training his eye by study and observation, he had the knowledge and the taste to direct his architects.

Under King Ludwig's careful direction, quaint old Munich was transformed into a city of wide boulevards and imposing classical buildings. The new avenues were lined with trees, and parks were made for the people's recreation. No matter how much Ludwig may have loathed Napoleon, something of the emperor's transformation of Paris slipped into his artistic subconscious and was reborn in Munich. He built the Pinakothek to house the fabulous Wittelsbach picture collection, the Glypothek for the countless statues his archaeologists dug up in Italy and Greece. At Ratisbon, he built the Valhalla, a massive copy of the Parthenon, in which he honored the greatest men of Germany—all except Luther. As well as filling his magnificent new buildings with works of art, the king offered his patronage to artists from all the world to come to his city and embellish it.

Ludwig of Bavaria's admiration of art did not stop at inanimate treasures. His worship of beauty extended quite naturally to the loveliest women in his realm. Regardless of social position or class, the chosen ones were offered a place in his *Schönheits Galerie* (Gallery of Beauties), and their exquisite features, whether countess or shepherdess, were preserved by the court painters. Although he spent hours alone in silent meditation of the beauties in the *Schönheits Galerie,* it was opened at certain times for the appreciation of his subjects.

The king's patronage also included modern improvements to his domain. Ludwig built his country's first railway, inaugurated its first steamboat and constructed a canal linking the Danube with the Main River which gave ships access to the North Sea and the Black Sea. To pay for all these artistic and progressive projects, he scrimped and saved from his public and his private purse. Having been deafened as a child by French guns, he loathed anything to do with the military and drastically reduced the army and the civil service. Any luxuries in his palaces that were irrelevant to their artistic embellishment were curtailed, and his devoted wife and seven children simply went without. Despite his many romantic indiscretions he was usually a good husband to his kind, long-suffering Queen Thérèse, and a devout Catholic.

⁂

WHEN LOLA ARRIVED in Munich, Ludwig had reigned for twenty years. His obvious dedication to his people and their needs made him an extremely popular autocrat whose little idiosyncrasies were overlooked. Watching him walk home exhausted after a day spent on a building site, hatless and covered in dust, or peeping under ladies' veils in his endless search for beauty, the good burghers of Munich, their caps in their hands, would simply smile and shake their heads as he passed. Politically, the king espoused the concept of freedom and progress, but as he truly believed he ruled his people far better than they could ever rule themselves, little progress was actually made.

In the latter part of his reign, when Ludwig was devoting more of his time to his artistic pursuits, he allowed his government to slip into the control of the reactionary Ultramontane Party of Bavaria. "Religion" became confused with "right" in the king's mind, and he became convinced that his God-fearing subjects needed God's ministers to help him govern them. As a result, Catholic orders of priests and nuns flocked to Bavaria and established their religious houses. The politically minded Jesuits took advantage of the king's growing indifference to government and became so influential that they virtually ruled Bavaria through the ministry of Baron Carl von Abel, the Catholic prime minister.

Lola Montez arrived in Bavaria in September 1847 and installed herself in Munich's best hotel, the Goldener Hirsch. Armed as usual with useful introductions, she had no difficulty in meeting the jeunesse dorée of the town. She applied for an audition at the Court Theater, long recognized as the citadel of quality, excellence and taste in opera and dance throughout Germany. The director, influenced as much by the opinion of his principal dancer as by his own scruples, rejected the lovely Spanish señora as lacking talent and expertise. Undaunted, Lola sought the help of Count Rechberg, a dashing young courtier and an aide-de-camp to the king.

At twenty-seven, Lola was at the peak of her perfection. To add to her arsenal of seduction, she had carefully studied how to dress her wonderful figure to its full advantage. She understood the sensuous appeal of dark velvets against her skin, the seductive power of rustling silk skirts and the allure of pure white Byronic collars lighting her face and innocently showing off her slender neck. Lola's mass of thick black curls and those famous gentian eyes were as nothing compared to her greatest asset: she knew herself. She was fully aware of the impact of her stunning beauty, and had learned how to use her power. Few women of her time had her experience of foreign courts and societies, had travelled so extensively or had been as closely involved with so many men.

When Lola asked Count Rechberg to help her gain an audience with the king in order to persuade him to reverse the decision of his theater's director, he readily agreed. Lola was not without contacts—it was Ludwig's sister, the Queen of Prussia, who had sent her to another sister, the tsarina in Russia—and she knew when to drop the right names. Oddly enough, Ludwig was not so eager to meet the "Spanish dancer"; he had heard of her dubious reputation, and his aide-de-camp seemed rather too insistent.

Every incident concerning Lola Montez always has a number of versions, and her first meeting with Ludwig I of Bavaria has more than most. Some sources claim she rushed into the king's audience chamber on the heels of Count Rechberg; another that she forced the door when she heard the slightly deaf king repeat loudly that he would not see her. The truth was probably that the king was intrigued to meet the famous beauty, as he considered himself the greatest expert on that subject, and wanted to judge her for himself.

When Lola stood before him, the dazzled king asked Rechberg to withdraw. Later it was alleged that Lola watched Ludwig's eyes as they followed the contours of her tight black velvet bodice. Seeing his open admiration, as well as a hint of disbelief, she unsheathed the dagger she always carried and slashed the laces to prove nature's perfection. Another account claims that she grabbed the shears from his desk to cut her bodice, and another that the king then commanded her to dance for him at once without music in his chamber.

All this is, of course, nonsense. Lola was capable of unlimited histrionics, but she knew that Ludwig I of Bavaria had the same reverence for decorum and good taste as he had for beauty. He found the lovely Señora María de los Dolores Porris y Montez lacking in neither.

Just as he had studied Italian to read the works of the great Renaissance writers, the king had also learned Spanish and had read some works by Calderón. Not only would he allow this breathtaking and noble apparition from Andalusia to dance at his theater, he would ask her to indulge his love for her country and language, and come to the palace to converse with him in Spanish.

The king's unabashed delight at meeting Lola can be better understood when it is remembered that there can have been few women of Lola's beauty, education, sophistication and wit in Munich. In the many European capitals she had visited, Lola Montez had been acknowledged as one of the most beautiful women living. In the eyes of this ruler who had spent his life in pursuit of beauty and filled his capital with the fruits of his life's quest, the ravishing Lola appeared before him as the greatest work of art in his kingdom. All his classical temples and palaces were empty and lifeless without this most perfect of all hetaerae.*

It was arranged that the Spanish dancer's debut would take place the following month, on October 10, at the Court Theater. The previous day a schoolgirl saw a lady coming toward her in the street,

veiled and wearing a black gown, a fan in her hand. Suddenly something seemed to flash across my vision and I stood quite still, completely dazzled by the eyes which for a moment held mine. They shone from a pale countenance that lit up with delighted laughter at my bewilderment. Then she swept past me; and I, forgetting what my governess had said about looking round, stared after her until she disappeared. Fairies in nursery tales must have looked like that, I told myself. I returned home breathless, and told

* Female courtier as opposed to "courtesan."

them of my adventure. "That," said my father disapprovingly, "must have been the Spanish dancer, Lola Montez."*

It was typical of Lola to delight in playing the enchantress even for a moment to a little stranger. Every day of her life was a performance and any appreciative audience always gave her pleasure.

On the next evening the theater was packed for *The Enchanted Prince,* billed as "a Farce in three Acts by J. von Plotz. During the two entr'actes Mademoiselle Lola Montez of Madrid will appear in her Spanish National Dances." Munich was full of gossip about the Andalusian dancer who had turned the head of their king at their first meeting; how her audience had run well past the usual time allotted, and how those waiting outside had heard their king talking loudly and cheerfully to her in Spanish of his admiration for her country, its art and literature. Just four days after this audience, Ludwig had presented Doña Lola Montez to his ministers as "my very best friend," and was quoted as declaring that he was "bewitched."

Meanwhile, Munich was humming with stories about her past: in Paris had she not caused a man to be killed in a duel? In Berlin had she not whipped one of the king's gendarmerie? In Warsaw had she not incited the city to riot against the viceroy? The curious, the envious and the disapproving all rushed to see the notorious Spanish beauty. Not only scandalous, she was already known as a liberal, and staunchly anti-clerical.

As well as being quite a liar, Lola was also impulsively frank. It was one of her greatest faults and, at the same time, one of her more endearing but self-damaging habits. Women with overwhelming charm and beauty often achieve all they want without bothering too much with dissimulation or guile. Lola was playing for the highest stakes, and to succeed she would need friends. Too often and without hesitation she spoke her mind, regardless of consequences and feelings. "I talked to the King as I do to everyone, openly, frankly, and without concealment." Time and again she flaunted her confrontation with convention and the establishment, and for this she would never be forgiven. For every conquest, Lola Montez made ten or more ene-

---

* Louise von Kobell, *Unter den Vier Ersten Königen Bayerns,* 1894.

mies, all too ready to accept hearsay and condemn the foreign she-devil. The Jesuit press christened her "The Apocalyptic Whore."

Louise von Kobell was present at Lola's debut on October 10, 1846:

> In the pit they clapped and hissed; the latter, explained my neighbor, because of the rumors circulating that Lola was an emissary of the English Freemasons, an enemy of the Jesuits—a coquette, too, who had had amorous adventures in all parts of the world, according to the newspapers [the Jesuits and the clerical party were evidently leaving nothing to chance]. Lola Montez took the center of the stage. She was not dressed in the customary tights and short skirts of a ballerina, but in a Spanish costume of silk and lace, with here and there a glittering diamond. Fire seemed to dart from her wonderful blue eyes and she bowed like one of the Graces before the King in the royal box. She danced in the manner of her country, swaying on her hips and alternating one posture with another, each exceeding the former in beauty.
>
> While she was dancing she held the attention of all; their eyes followed the sinuous swaying of her body, now indicating glowing passion, now a light playfulness. Not until she ceased her rhythmic movements was the spell broken. The audience went mad with rapture, and the entire dance had to be repeated over and over again.

Emulating Byron, whenever Ludwig was greatly moved with joy or sorrow, he wrote poetry. That evening, intoxicated by Lola's performance, as if in a trance he wrote:

> *Happy movements, clear and near,*
> *Are in thy living grace.*
> *Supple and tender as a deer*
> *Art thou, of Andalusian race!*

Four days later, Lola appeared at the Court Theater for the second and last time, dancing a cachucha and a fandango during the entr'acte of two plays. Louise von Kobell was again in the audience:

In order to drown any manifestations of displeasure, the pit was occupied by an organized claque of policemen in plain clothes and theatre attendants. The precaution was unnecessary, as Lola Montez exercised a universal charm.

Forced to bow before audience opinion, the Court Theater director offered Lola his apologies and a contract. A triumphant Lola scorned the offer and left the theater with the king. She knew she would never again have to dance for her living in Munich.

BEFORE MEETING LOLA Montez, Ludwig had not had a mistress for a number of years, and had sadly resigned himself to an old age devoid of the rapture of love. If it is true that the great events of one's life are governed by timing, then Lola's timing with Ludwig was perfect. Seeing the king's zest for life return, his eminent court physician encouraged the friendship and urged Ludwig's family to do the same. Not only Count Rechberg, but another aide-de-camp, Lieutenant Nussbaum, became the dancer's devoted slaves. Queen Thérèse, gracious and tolerant, had long accustomed herself to Ludwig's peccadilloes, and contented herself with her grandchildren, the country's affection and the sure knowledge of her husband's devotion. Ludwig at sixty had few teeth, not much hair and a cyst in the center of his forehead. This did not stop his sisters from accusing him of always having *"le feu aux flancs,"* and his purple poetry left no one who read it in any doubt of his passions.

Despite his unprepossessing appearance, the king still cut quite a dashing figure, and his regal manner suited his status, despite the shabby clothes he treated like comfortable old friends. He was known by sight to every inhabitant of the capital, and they doffed their hats to him as he walked unaccompanied each day from his palace to call on Lola Montez. Every citizen acknowledged that Ludwig had turned their provincial city into one of the great capitals and centers of learning in Europe.

Shortly after her arrival, Ludwig commissioned the court painter Josef Stieler to paint Lola for his *Schönheits Galerie*. During the sittings, dancer and patron conversed in Spanish on every possible subject, the king daily falling more under Lola's spell. That an aging monarch, aware of entering the autumn of his life, should surrender his heart to a stunning beauty of twenty-seven—she told Ludwig she was only twenty-two—with fire in her eyes, intelligence and experience, is not surprising. It would be wrong to assume that this captivating siren must inevitably have become the king's mistress. Lola did not need to give the king more than the pleasure of her radiant company—his cup was full just from looking at her. Their true relationship was a meeting of minds, each gaining from the other, and no one who knew the king had ever doubted his formidable intelligence or learning, despite his eccentric ways.

Politics had been one cause of the mutual attraction between Lola and Dujarier, and with King Ludwig it was the same. Lola had learned her lessons well from Lamennais in Paris, and now she reminded Ludwig of the liberal policies he had espoused as a young man before the Jesuits had taken control. This lovely creature not only restored his youthful emotions, she rekindled in the king his desire to reform the restrictive policies of the Abel ministry. Ludwig fell in love with Lola's beauty, her mind and her *esprit fort;* and Lola delighted in the company of this amiable, intelligent monarch who allowed her to flex her political muscle and to taste the heady wine of power. She knew what so many great beauties before and after her have learned, that power is the greatest aphrodisiac of all, and that to control one man in the boudoir is cat-and-mouse play compared with controlling the destinies of a nation.

There are many accounts of King Ludwig's fascination with the dancer, but few make an honest attempt to explain Lola's feelings for the king. The assumption that her only interests were venal does both dancer and king an injustice. Ludwig was an easy man to like, and in some ways his temperament was very similar to Lola's. As well as being very learned, the king was a tremendous enthusiast who carried along with him anyone willing to listen and learn. Lola understood this and declared: "His soul is always fresh and young." He was gracious, kind and excellent company; nor should the particular glamour and appeal of absolute monarchy be underestimated. Was it so extraordinary that this lovely, sophisticated and erudite charmer should

delight as much in the king's company as he did in hers? The queen
certainly did not object to Lola's regular presence at the palace, and
was reported to be in sympathy with her theories and ideals—she addressed her as "my dear." Lola understood her own sex just as well as
she understood men, and never had any difficulty in winning the regard of an honest woman.

A sixty-year-old's infatuation with a beautiful dancer less than half
his age could easily be dismissed as the product of his senility and her
scheming. This was not the case. The king was an enamored with
Lola's mind as he was with her beauty. Many a sane man has bought a
woman he admires flowers each day—Ludwig's daily bouquets for
Lola were poems:

> *By thee my life becomes ennobled,*
> *Which without thee was alone and empty:*
> *Thy love is the food of my heart;*
> *Without it, it would surely die!*

Their conversations regularly turned to politics, and Lola had no difficulty in assessing the state of Bavaria's government. In the aftermath
of the 1830 revolutionary movement the king had abandoned his initial pursuit of liberal ideas. Since then, the power of the Jesuits and
their control of the government had grown to such an extent that
Ludwig preferred to ignore the problem and concentrate on the cultural life of his subjects. Lola's arrival changed all that. Suddenly a
young, energetic creature had appeared who reminded the king of his
youthful convictions and his intentions to increase his people's political freedom.

As a young prince, Ludwig had met the ex-priest and philosopher
Lamennais in Munich. The Frenchman had tried to make him see the
harm a government controlled by the clergy could inflict on the people. Although Ludwig was sympathetic to his views, he did not become a disciple. Lamennais had found a more attentive pupil in Lola
during her time in Paris. Surrounded by the Parisian intelligentsia, she
had learned her lessons well. Now that Lola knew she and the king
were of the same mind, she eagerly seized her chance to help Ludwig
put Lamennais' principles of fraternity into practice. She wrote:

I told him of errors and abuses in his government, I told him of the perfidy of his ministers. Honest and unsuspecting, he did not believe it, but I proved it to him. I exposed to him especially the art, duplicity and villainy of his prime minister, Baron Abel, a Jesuit who had wormed himself into his confidence.

Lola's intention to help bring down the Abel ministry was soon common knowledge—her frankness was a double-edged sword.

Abel turned to "Metternich in Vienna for help in ridding Munich of this monster. Lola was aware that the Austrian prime minister was opposed to the spread of liberal ideas in his own country, and that he had been responsible for the Jesuits entrenching themselves in Bavaria. When Ludwig's sister, the Dowager Empress of Austria Karolina Augusta, offered Lola money to leave Bavaria, she guessed correctly that the bribe had been Metternich's idea. Ludwig confronted his prime minister, who told him furiously that it was clearly Lola Montez, and not the king, who ruled in Bavaria. Ludwig, it seems, happily concurred.

While political influence and the king's adoration were gratifying, they did not give Lola security, and Dujarier's money would not last forever. Ludwig, who was renowned for his parsimony in every respect except where art and women were concerned, had promised her anything she needed. Like the great courtesan she was, Lola sensed her opportunities and persuaded Ludwig that she remained in his capital solely for his sake. She had decided to make her home in Munich; that the king should provide for her seemed to Lola a fair exchange for her advice and her company.

There is a story that Lola, who preferred to speak French while shopping in Munich, would exclaim when handed the bill: "You know me, my Louis will pay!"—"Louis" being the currency as well as the king's name.

Within a month of their meeting, Ludwig had added a codicil to his will, bequeathing 100,000 gulden to Lola Montez on condition that she was neither married nor widowed at the time of his death, as well as an income of 2,400 gulden per year payable by his heir. He bought her a small house in the Barerstrasse and had his own architect Metzger almost totally rebuild it to Lola's specifications. This charming villa has often been described as a "palace" built by Ludwig for his favorite, and as Lola was able to move in within a few months, the architect did well to complete the substantial alterations in such a short time. Throughout her life, Lola was known for her taste, not only in her clothes and magnificent jewelry, but also in the decoration of her residences. In India she had witnessed luxury, in England, comfort, and in France, style. The rest was a combination of her own talent and observation on her travels. The house on the Barerstrasse combined the best that Ludwig's money could buy with Lola's sense of color, style and comfort.

Lola's house was called a bijou, a small manor, two stories high. George Henry Francis, an American journalist living in Munich at the time, described it:

> Elegant bronze balconies from the upper windows, designed by herself, relieve the plainness of the (Italianate) exterior; and long muslin curtains, slightly tinted, and drawn close, so as to cover the windows, add a transparent, shell-like lightness to the effect. . . . The interior surpasses everything, even in Munich, where decorative painting and internal fitting has been carried almost to perfection. . . . Such a tigress, one would think, would scarcely choose so beautiful a den. The smallness of the house precludes much splendour. Its place is supplied by French elegance, Munich art, and English comfort. . . . Books, not of a frivolous kind, borrowed from the royal library lie about, and help to show what are the habits of this modern Amazon. Add to these a piano and a guitar, on both of which she accompanies herself with considerable taste and some skill, and an embroidery frame at which she puts to shame the best of those exhibited for sale in England.

Lola, he said, liked plain food, "cooked in the English fashion; [she] drinks little, keeps good hours, rises early and labours much." Her visitors came from all over the world,

> ministers *in esse* or *in posse,* professors, artists. . . . As is usual with women of an active mind, she is a great talker; but although an egotist, and with her full share of the vanity of her sex, she under-

stands the art of conversation sufficiently never to become wearisome . . . she can be, and almost always is, a very charming person
and a most delightful companion. Her manners are distinguished,
she is a graceful and hospitable hostess, and she understands the art
of dressing to perfection.*

With her taste, reputed extravagance and political influence on the
king, it was inevitable that Lola would become known as "The German Pompadour."

"Whatever Lola wants, Lola gets" was the cry in the streets of
Munich, as treasured items left the Pinakothek Museum to adorn
Lola's house. A carriage trimmed with gold and lined in ermine stood
ever ready outside her door, and it seemed no favor was too great for
the king's new friend.

Lola was extremely well read, and it is probable that she had absorbed the life of Madame de Pompadour. Her next request for a private chapel and her own confessor would almost appear to be
modelled on the Pompadour's progress and quest for respectability a
century earlier. Unlike Madame de Pompadour, in this request she
was denied, as no cleric would accept the post "for fear of their
virtue."

When bribery failed with Lola, her enemies resorted to scandal
and slander. The foreign dancer was such an easy target. She could be
arrogant, spoilt, irritable. Anyone who disagreed with her or defied
her was immediately accused of being a Jesuit. According to George
Henry Francis:

> Everyone whom she does not like, her prejudice transforms into a
> Jesuit. Jesuits stare at her in the streets and peep out from the cor-
> ners of her rooms. All the world adverse to herself are puppets
> moved to mock and annoy her by these dark and invisible agents.

Her moods and her temper often destroyed the effect of her charm
and intelligence. And Lola relied too much on her beauty to compensate for her willful behavior.

---

* *Fraser's Magazine* (January 1848).

⊘§§~

AS WELL AS exerting her influence over men, Lola enjoyed controlling powerful, even wild animals—horses, dogs and, later, in her
American life, wildcats and a bear. In Munich, she kept an English
bulldog and often walked through the streets with only this animal by
her side, carrying a whip with which to control him. She often
failed—it was rumored that he had an instinctive loathing for Jesuits;
more likely he could not resist their fluttering black cassocks. Unfortunate incidents followed.

The more the pressure of opposition increased, the more irrational Lola became, throwing temper tantrums, plates and books. Her
little whip lashed out indiscriminately and her bulldog snarled at Jesuits and attacked tradesmen. She was as quick to apologize as she was
to show anger, but as her influence over the king grew, the stories
about her became increasingly vicious. Baron von der Tann, the
king's old friend and confidant, faithfully reported to Ludwig, at his
own insistence, all the stories in circulation. Ludwig would only sigh
and repeat:

> *But the heart's goodness shows itself;*
> *Thou hast a highly elevated mind.*

Ludwig was right in discounting much of the gossip as wicked in-
ventions: that Lola was an emissary of Satan; acting as a spy in the pay
of Disraeli; an agent of the Freemasons engaged to destroy the Catholic Church . . . The tears and protestations of his adored one
never failed to move him, but Lola did not help matters with her
temper and fanciful embroideries of her own. She not only told Ludwig, but had written to the editor of *The Times* on March 31, 1847,
that she was "born at Seville in 1833; [the daughter of] a Spanish
officer in the service of Don Carlos. I beg leave to say that my name
is Maria Dolores Porres Montez, and I have never changed that
name." Lola had told this lie so often that she had begun to believe it
herself.

THE INHABITANTS OF Munich were quite accustomed to their king having a favorite, and had never objected on moral grounds. With Lola it was different, especially as no one could be quite sure of the true nature of her relationship with Ludwig, who continued to maintain that they were not lovers. She was amoral, ambitious and a coquette capable of anything. And yet the king was not prone to lie, and had freely admitted to his other liaisons. When he was called to task by the Prince Archbishop of Breslau, Ludwig composed a declaration of the purity of his relationship with Lola, which he had read from every pulpit in his kingdom. "Stick to your 'stola,'" he wrote to the archbishop, "and leave me my Lola."

Closing his ears to all criticisms of his beloved, the king lavished gifts and privileges on her in gratitude for all her advice and promises to stay by him and help him in his work. Lola's box at the theater was adjacent to the royal couple's, and whenever the dancer appeared, her presence always caused a stir in the audience. In a country of large-boned, well-rounded blond women, Lola's delicate, small frame, flashing eyes and clouds of gleaming black hair made her beauty even more conspicuous, especially when she wore the exquisite gowns and fabulous jewels the king had given her.

MUNICH WAS A university city, and as most of the senior academic posts were occupied by clerical appointees, these professors were vehemently opposed to Lola. Like students everywhere, Munich's were intensely involved in politics. They were divided between the followers of the clerical party and those who supported more liberal ideas such as Lola's. For some time, King Ludwig had been aware that the extreme Catholic views of his ministry under von Abel would lead to conflict in a country with so many religions. Soon it became clear that the clerical party was agitating the students (as well as the populace) against the dancer and pinning the country's grievances on her. A

small group of students loyal to the favorite formed a fraternity, calling themselves the Alemannia (those for Germany), and its members
met regularly at her house. The king granted them the same recognition and privileges as the traditional, old established fraternities, which
caused even more friction among the Catholic students.

Lola was finding it more and more difficult to appear in the
streets of Munich without the danger of a fight between the Alemannia, who acted as her personal bodyguard, and other student fraternities. Lola was undisciplined and hot-tempered, but she felt secure in
Ludwig's devotion; although she was guilty of extravagance and
breaches of Bavarian protocol, she would never have risked losing the
king's protection by flagrantly committing the excesses of which she
was accused.

Efforts to separate Ludwig from the dancer continued. Anonymous letters listing grievances against her arrived daily, caricatures and
slanderous pamphlets were circulated. The king became more stub-
born in her defense, and angrily refused to listen to anyone who spoke
against her:

> *The ties of love will tie us so much closer*
> *If the world attempt to tear thee from me.*

Lola was accused of every kind of immorality, of taking all the Alemannia as her lovers, of undressing in front of her open windows and
of forcing her dressmakers to fit her clothes to her naked body. The
king commissioned Kaulbach to produce a new portrait of his beloved
"Lolita"; he portrayed her as a victim, her hair loose, mounting a scaf-
fold, a snake around her waist, a cup of poison in one hand, a riding
whip in the other. Ludwig rejected the portrait.

Finally, at the urging of the Jesuits, Pope Pius IX wrote to Ludwig
admonishing him for "straying from the paths of virtue." The king's
anger against the Jesuits grew, and he would not be moved.

Although Ludwig had asked her to remain in his country, Lola
had no papers, so in return for her loyalty to him, the king proposed
to make her a Bavarian citizen. Prime Minister von Abel was so vio-
lently opposed to this that he and his entire ministry sent a memorandum to the king threatening to resign en masse rather than allow the

naturalization of Lola Montez. Further, were she subsequently to be rewarded with a title, as was to be expected with a royal mistress, this would constitute a public affront to the nobility as well as to the people. "National feeling is deeply wounded," the memorandum stated, "because Bavaria considers she is being ruled by a foreigner, who, on account of her reputation, is condemned by public opinion."

When the document was leaked to the press, it was universally denounced by the foreign ministers, especially the French. The English minister wrote to Lord Palmerston: "A more melancholy picture of the manner in which the government of this country has been conducted, or more commendatory of their own system by the ex-Ministers themselves can hardly be drawn."

The king accepted the government's resignation and wrote to his friend von der Tann on February 15, 1847: "The Jesuit rule is broken . . . [they are] spreading the report that Lolita is in league with the devil and has given me a love potion. . . . The Queen continues to behave admirably."*

Unfortunately, although the Abel administration had been almost unanimously condemned, its removal appeared to be the work of the dancer and not due to the wisdom of the king. After such a short time in the country, Lola had scored a remarkable triumph over the clerical party. Her enemies further despaired when neither the admonishments of the Pope and an archbishop, nor bribes and slanders had been able to dislodge the favorite.

Ludwig appointed new ministers, and his choice of a strongly liberal cabinet was welcomed with great enthusiasm by the majority of his people as well as by foreign governments. Throughout Germany, Lola was regarded as the standard-bearer for liberalism, and Ludwig as the most enlightened monarch of his time. The Prussian minister reported to Berlin: "I welcome the consequences [of Abel's downfall] with all my heart, for they are of the greatest importance, not only for Bavaria, but for the whole of Germany." The English minister wrote to London echoing these sentiments; both stated that the Jesuits' downfall had been achieved by Lola Montez. Although Lola was hailed as the country's liberating angel by most of Germany and Eu-

* Tann family archives.

rope, Ludwig's ministers insisted that they had implemented the reforms and had acted independently of the favorite. In this they were correct, but as the cabinet could only act on the king's instructions and the king consulted daily with Lola, it was indeed she who ruled. The queen and the crown prince* were in full agreement with the change of government. As well as the royal family, Lola automatically had the support of the Protestants and the republicans of all creeds. A cry of "Lola and Liberty" rose in many parts of Bavaria. Looking back some years later on the events of this time in Munich, Lola wrote in her autobiography:

> There was as much truth as wit in the old writer who said that "the woman of extraordinary beauty, who has sufficient intellect to render her of an independent mind, ought also to be able to assume the quills of the porcupine in self-defence." At any rate, such is the social and moral fabric of the world, that woman must be content with an exceeding narrow sphere of action, or she must take the worst consequences of daring to be an innovator and a heretic. She must be either the servant or the spoiled plaything of man; or she must take the responsibility of making herself a target to be shot at by the most corrupt and cowardly of her own sex, and by the ill-natured and depraved of the opposite gender.

In Vienna, Metternich watched events in Munich developing in direct opposition to his policy. Afraid to oppose Palmerston and England openly, he did his best to destroy Lola's influence by secretly financing any plan to turn the people against the person who had freed them from ten years of oppressive clerical domination.

Although the Ultramontane Party was out of power, Jesuit and Catholic exiles from France, Poland and Switzerland had increased their numbers, and they still possessed significant influence in the Bavarian capital, particularly within the university. Munich's students, unlike those in most other European universities, were traditionally conservative. When a popular Catholic professor publicly admonished

---

* Letter dated 1847, Tann Family archives.

the king on moral grounds, Ludwig obliged him to resign. A demonstration of Catholic students in favor of the professor developed into a riot outside Lola's house.

As the crowd swelled into an ugly mob, throwing stones and breaking windows, Lola defiantly toasted them with champagne from her balcony and tossed them sweets. Always inclined toward dramatic gestures, her cavalier attitude succeeded in taunting the students into a frenzy. Ludwig heard of the disturbance, and hurried to her house. When they saw their beloved king arrive on foot, the crowd relented and serious trouble was averted, but rioting continued spasmodically, and stones were thrown even at the royal palace. When Lola was asked whom she saw most frequently in her house, she replied, *"La canaille et le roi"* (The rabble and the king).

In retaliation, Ludwig had the remaining extreme Catholic professors removed from the university. This was a popular measure with students other than the Ultramontanes, as it ensured that some of the more restrictive rules of the university were relaxed. Ludwig was reported to have suggested ruefully that if his friend had been called Loyola (after Ignatius Loyola, founder of the Jesuit Order), instead of Lola, there would never have been a problem.

Despite the riots by the students against the dancer in Munich, there was almost nationwide approval of the new, more liberal ministry. Lola's popularity soared with the Bavarians in general, and shopkeepers did excellent business in trinkets, tiepins, cigarette cases and tobacco boxes bearing her portrait.

A young American, Charles Godfrey Leland ("Hans Breitmann"), was a student in Munich at this time, and described an evening of discussion in Lola's house: "When defending the existence of the soul against an atheist, [she would] tumble over a great trunk of books of the most varied kind, till she came to an old vellum-bound copy of Apuleius, and proceed to establish her views according to subtle neo-Platonism. But she romanced and embroidered so much in conversation that she did not get credit for what she really knew." And on another occasion: "There were few, indeed, if any there were, who really knew the depths of that wild Irish soul."

Rejuvenated by the surge of approval from the people for his new policies, the king decided to fulfill his promise and reward Lola with Bavarian nationality and a title. George Henry Francis observed at the time:

> One thing in her praise is, that although she really wields so much power, she never uses it either for the promotion of unworthy persons or, as other favourites have done, for corrupt purposes. Her creation as Countess of Landsfeld, which has alienated from her some of her most honest Liberal supporters, who wish her still to continue in rank, as well as in purposes, one of the people, while it has exasperated against her the powerless, because impoverished, nobility, was the unsolicited act of the king, legally effected with the consent of the Crown Prince. Without encroaching too far upon a delicate subject, it may be added that she is not regarded with contempt or detestation by either the male or the female members of the Royal family. She is regarded by them rather as a political personage than as the King's favourite.

The king chose to ignore any opposition to his decision. On August 14, 1847, he announced: "We have resolved to raise María Porris y Montez, of noble Spanish descent, to the dignity of Countess of Landsfeld of this our kingdom." The new countess also had the Order of St. Theresa bestowed on her with the agreement of the queen, the order's titular head. As well as her peerage, the king gave his "Lolita" a large estate, including feudal rights over "two thousand souls," and an income of 20,000 florins annually. All this enraged the largely Catholic aristocracy beyond endurance.

UNFORTUNATELY, THE COUNTESS of Landsfeld was not content with her rise in rank and wealth. As the slanders against her increased, ladies of society drew aside their children and their skirts as she passed; places would empty wherever she sat. Lola had never learned self-control; she had become intoxicated with power, and her rages and tantrums when thwarted increased. Furious at being snubbed by the conservative and rigidly Catholic aristocracy, Lola plagued the king to force society's doors open for her. Ludwig did his best to protect his beloved muse, even having the chief of police dismissed for daring to criticize her, but her megalomania had so distorted her reason that some considered her a danger to the state.

Lola's behavior became more irrational in the face of the persistent attacks against her in the newspapers. As the new ministry would not enforce censorship of the press—a most unliberal suggestion—Lola encouraged Ludwig to change his cabinet once again and appoint only those totally in agreement with the king and the favorite. An ally of Lola's, Councillor von Berks, became minister of the interior, and the anti-clerical Prince Wallerstein, the former Bavarian representative in Paris, was appointed foreign minister. Once again Lola was credited with the reforms. She was recognized as an able politician and hailed by Europe's liberals as Bavaria's savior. The country adopted the Code Napoléon, and Luther's bust was admitted to join the ranks of the immortals in Ludwig's Valhalla. Even *The Times* in London praised the new government, which was totally controlled by the dancer and inevitably called "The Lola Ministry."

To disenchant the population with the king's favorite, Count Arco-Vallée, leader of the opposition, offered to distribute 5,000 gulden to the people of Munich on the day Lola was deposed. Vile stories were circulated that she used the Alemannia as her harem and conducted wild orgies in a cottage at the bottom of her garden. It is surprising that, despite her youth, her beauty and her exciting new policies, Lola failed to win over Bavaria's youth (other than the Alemannia). Unrest increased at the university as students took sides for or against the dancer, and incidents involving Lola Montez became regular occurrences. Several times when she was recognized in the street, she was surrounded by groups of menacing Ultramontane students. On one occasion Lola was seen facing the mob with her small band from the Alemannia. Although they were outnumbered and forced to seek refuge in a church, even her enemies remarked on her courage and on how magnificent she looked in her defiance.

When the king heard of these latest demonstrations against his beloved, he was outraged, and on February 8, 1848, he closed the university. All foreign students were expelled and ordered to leave Munich within twenty-four hours.

This order had dire consequences. There were then at least a thousand foreign students in Munich, who brought much-needed revenue to the local tradesmen. A petition was signed by two thousand burghers and presented to the king two days later, urging him to change his mind. Impressed by their number and the seriousness of the economic repercussions for the city, Ludwig reconsidered, and promised to reopen the university after the summer.

The king's capitulation to pressure from the burghers was seized upon by Lola's enemies as a great victory, and a significant step toward ridding the country of the foreign strumpet. The next day, armed crowds gathered outside the palace and in the main squares, demanding Lola's expulsion from the city. The ministers informed the king that they could not rely on the police or the army to keep order. Nor could they assure him the Countess of Landsfeld would be spared if serious rioting broke out. Under tremendous pressure from his family, his ministers and the howling mobs outside the palace, Ludwig understood that the monarchy itself was in danger. He realized that the only way to save his crown, and the life of his Lolita, was to break all his promises to stand by her forever. On February 11, 1848, with great sadness and a shaky pen, King Ludwig signed an order for the banishment of Lola Montez from Bavaria.

After all his declarations of eternal loyalty, it was hard for Lola to believe that the king had finally deserted her; even harder to fully comprehend the feelings of the people who had been released from Jesuit bondage due to her efforts. The sentries posted outside her gates had been recalled, and the mob looked menacing. She hastily packed her jewels and, relying on her luck, hoped that the air of authority which gave her control over animals would have the same effect on the crowd. Silently they allowed her to depart unmolested, accompanied by three of her faithful Alemannia. She left by train, ostensibly travelling far from the capital. Once Lola was out of sight, the mob broke down her door and rushed into her house in a frenzy. Ludwig was informed, hurried to the Barerstrasse and appealed to the crowd to spare the house, as it belonged to him.

Reports differ dramatically about the events which followed. Some say Lola stole back into Munich the following night dressed as a boy. Other rumors circulated wildly that Lola returned several times to plead with the king to rescind her banishment. At midnight she was said to have visited Ludwig for an hour, urging him to stand firm and abdicate rather than destroy all the reforms he had achieved with her help. Lola's own memoirs naturally favor this version.

When the rumor spread that Lola had returned, the people demanded that the king withdraw her Bavarian citizenship and that she should be arrested or shot on sight.

Some years later, a number of letters came to light which were said to have been written by a German quack, Dr. Justinius Kerner. He claimed that, to his great annoyance, King Ludwig had sent Lola Montez to him to "drive the devil out of her." As Dr. Mesmer had only recently begun practicing his new techniques, hypnotists with only some vague knowledge sprang up everywhere. Kerner wrote to his daughter on the day Lola arrived:

> I am detaining her in my tower, where guard is being kept by three
> of the Alemannia. . . . As a preliminary to my magneto-magic treat-
> ment, I am beginning by subjecting her to a fasting cure. This
> means that every day all she is to have is a quarter of a wafer and
> thirteen drops of raspberry juice. . . . Don't tell anyone. Burn this
> letter.

In another letter Kerner admitted that the treatment was not working, the only result being a dramatic loss of weight in the patient.

It seems totally out of character that Lola should submit to such treatment unless the events of the preceding weeks had left her in a nervous depression, with a desire to placate Ludwig no matter what the personal cost. The exorcism cure did not last long. Lola escaped and made her way to Switzerland.

DURING THE FIRST three months of 1848, the Year of Revolutions, there were dramatic changes in the governments of Europe. In Munich, news of the revolution in France had inspired the people to press their demands on the king, and the dancer became a convenient tool for both parties, a scapegoat and focus for national ills. Revolution also broke out in Vienna, and by March 13 Lola's old enemy Metternich had resigned.

Reports that Lola was still in Bavaria, and had even been seen in Munich, caused further rioting. The king was informed by his ministers that if he did not accede to the people's demands he was courting revolution in his own capital. With deep regret, on March 17 Ludwig issued two decrees—the first withdrawing the rights of naturalization from the Countess of Landsfeld together with her title and privileges, the second ordering her arrest if she were discovered within his kingdom.

⟨⟨§§⟩⟩

RIOTS WERE REPORTED in Berlin on March 18, and there was similar news from Italy. With no support from Berlin or Vienna, and lacking the counsel of his beloved Lola, Ludwig felt he could no longer remain on the throne and rule without compromise as he had done for so long. On March 21, 1848, King Ludwig I of Bavaria abdicated in favor of his son, Crown Prince Maximilian.

⟨⟨§§⟩⟩

WE SHALL NEVER know if Lola Montez felt a sense of betrayal for the way her protector had abandoned her. She observed once: "It is said that there are some women who are foolish enough to love men and let themselves be ruled by them. I call that topsy-turvy *ménage*. For my part, I have never believed in such a path." In her lectures and her autobiography she always spoke of King Ludwig with the greatest respect: "No monarch of a whole century did so much for the cause of religion and human liberty as he."

With all hope lost of retrieving her position in Bavaria, Lola settled in Switzerland. According to her memoirs, the country welcomed her with gratitude, remembering that she had influenced Ludwig to "withhold his assent to a proposition from Austria which had for its object the destruction of that little republic."

In Berne, Robert Peel, son of the famous English statesman, gallantly escorted Lola. However, retirement in a sleepy Swiss town held little attraction for a young, energetic woman who had, in effect, ruled a country. In a letter to his friend von der Tann, Ludwig claimed that Lola had begged him to join her in Switzerland, but he chose to remain in Munich and continue embellishing his beloved city. He had been deeply hurt that his people had forced his abdication, and although his son, the new king, maintained many of the reforms of the Lola ministry, he disappointed Ludwig by making a number of petty changes to his financial and domestic arrangements.

⁂

LUDWIG WAS NOT immune to the copious abuse that the press hurled after Lola, presenting her as the cause of his downfall, the root of the country's problems and the greatest whore in Christendom. The former King of Bavaria was aware of the ridiculous figure he would cut in exile leaning on the arm of the scorned, though lovely Lola. Once she was out of his sight and unable to reassure him, he was tormented by daily accounts of her philanderings. Enough doubt crept into his sentimental heart for him to send her a poem expressing his disillusion and pain.

Ludwig I of Bavaria did not die of a broken heart. He even found another paramour, a charming, gentle young lady-in-waiting attached to his sister. Although his love was unrequited, the sensation of still being able to feel the familiar *frisson d'amour* kept a spring in his step and a twinkle in his eye.

⁂

FOR LOLA, THE years of wandering began. After six years on the Continent, she returned to London and made another attempt to revive her theatrical career. She starred as herself at Covent Garden in her own program, *Lola Montez: ou La Comtesse pour une heure*. Using her Bavarian money she bought a charming house in the West End with the intention of setting up a literary salon. Many visitors passing through London wanted to see the notorious Countess of Landsfeld, and her house in Half Moon Street became the meeting place for the daring among the fashionable, the literary, and international members of society.

Lola made one last bid for respectability when she married George Trafford Heald, a young officer in the Life Guards with a sizable inheritance. As the countess had chosen to forget that her divorce had never been finalized, she was denounced by her husband's scandalized maiden aunts, arrested, and charged with bigamy. Once again the fascinating adventures had shocked London, and tongues wagged over a delicious new scandal. Even Benjamin Disraeli wrote to his sister:

> The Lola Montez marriage makes a sensation. . . . She quite convinced him [Heald] previously she was not Mrs. James; and as for the King of Bavaria, who, by the by, allows her fifteen hundred pounds a year* and to whom she writes every day—that was only a *malheureuse* passion.

The ensuing brouhaha forced the couple to flee to the Continent, but marriage to a twenty-one-year-old did not hold much charm for a woman of Lola's experience, and they parted. Heald later drowned while swimming in the Tagus. The gossips claimed that Lola had two children with Heald which she abandoned, but this can be discounted. Lola had no reason to desert her children, especially as, initially, they would have been the most compelling reason for having her marriage to Heald recognized by the English courts.

IN THE NEXT ten years, Lola Montez crisscrossed the Atlantic. In New York she was greeted with fulsome accolades: "She is beautiful! She is irresistible! She is the embodiment of female grace!" Three years had passed since the events in Munich when she arrived in America, but her reputation guaranteed full houses, especially when her theatrical repertoire included *Lola and the King of Bavaria*. Although the box-office takings were good, she spent lavishly, and there were always problems with her troupe. When dancing became too much effort and the critics more severe, it became less lucrative.

---

* Ludwig continued to send Lola poems as well as money, and never demanded the return of the fabulous Wittelsbach jewels he had given her.

The celebrated Countess of Landsfeld took to holding receptions where she shook the hand of anyone willing to pay one dollar. Some of those who had availed themselves of that privilege announced that *they* found the countess charming and a great lady.

Lola travelled west and married again, this time a newspaper publisher called Pat Purdy Hull. With typical panache, the ceremony was conducted at dawn in the Mission Dolores in San Francisco. Hull was witty, attractive and a popular figure about town, the editor and part owner of the *San Francisco Whig*. Lola said she had married the Irishman because "he could tell a story better than anyone else I had ever met." Together they moved to the raw gold-mining town of Grass Valley (population four thousand) in California. Lola bought a small white house near the center of town with a "colonial door and an entrance too pretentious for the neat, square rooms inside." She loved gardening, and spent hours in old faded clothes, digging and weeding. Taking her pony into the surrounding hills, she collected an amazing variety of cacti. These she transplanted into her garden, creating one of the first cactus gardens in America.

A few months later she divorced Hull on the vague pretext that "his aroma had grown less attractive than my roses." The real reason seems to have been a German gold miner, Baron Adler, who was killed shortly afterward on a hunting expedition.

There was little in these wild surroundings to attract a sophisticated *mondaine* like Lola, but among the simple, rough mining community, with its adventurers and outcasts, she found a certain peace. She remained in her rustic cabin for the next two years, gathering what talent she could find into her little circle of admirers. Once a week the former countess, beloved of a king, held court in that cabin, and even occasionally agreed to give a small performance for her motley audience, showing them a glimpse of the legendary Spanish dancer.

She surrounded herself with animals: parrots, monkeys, wolf cubs, dogs, sheep, goats, hens, turkeys, pigs and her pony. Sometimes she would ride alone into the mountains, once bringing home a bear cub that she tamed. The cub grew into a huge bear, which she invited the strongest miners to wrestle. One day the bear bit Lola, and a newspaper editor wrote:

When Lola came to feed her bear,
With comfits sweet and sugar rare,
Bruin ran out in haste to meet her,
Seized her hand because 'twas sweeter.

A minister came to preach against the loose morals of the town, implicating Lola. True to character, when she heard this, she charged up to the church and danced before him in the aisle. With her haughty petulance, Lola always seemed to rub salt into any wound, no matter what the cost.

When a fire swept away the entire township, Lola moved on—this time to Australia and back to the stage.

After her tour of the principal towns, and many adventures (which included whipping an editor in Ballarat who dared to write a scathing review of her performance), Lola returned to America via Europe and, billed as the "Demosthenes in Dimity," she gave a successful series of lectures. These were gently autobiographical—with generous embellishments—and were published in 1858 as *The Art of Beauty and Gallantry,* with considerable success. There was one more visit to England. As always, her notoriety filled the halls in which she spoke, although no one who heard her could deny the charm of her stories or the good sense in the advice she offered her audience.

BY THE TIME she reached forty, her beauty faded, Lola Montez had turned her energy and intelligence toward religion. She had exhausted all that man could offer her; now it was God's turn. Lola kept a spiritual diary, and in it she appears totally sincere in her repentance. By 1860 she was back in New York, where she joined the Episcopal Church. Most of her days were spent in quiet retirement, reading and studying the Bible and visiting outcast women in the Magdalen Asylum. In December that year, Lola was stricken with paralysis down her left side, possibly a result of cerebral syphilis, which was widespread, and which she could have contracted years before. She spent the final weeks of her life in the Astoria Sanatorium in New York, a Bible by her side.

On January 17, 1861, Lola Montez died, aged forty-two. Her last words to the Episcopal minister attending her were: "Tell me more about my dear Saviour." She was buried in Green-Wood Cemetery, New York, as Mrs. Eliza Gilbert.

After she left Munich in 1848, King Ludwig of Bavaria never saw Lola Montez again. He outlived her by seven years, dying in 1868 at the age of eighty-two.

EPILOGUE

WITH FEW exceptions, Lola Montez has not been treated fairly or kindly by her biographers. Victorian historians had as hypocritical, jaundiced and intolerant a view of their own century's morality as they had of the morality of the preceding one. Most twentieth-century biographical efforts echo the double standards of the yellow press; beneath the censorious voice lurks the lip-smacking delight in "exposing" scandal. A free spirit and fiery temperament such as Lola's could expect no mercy or tolerance from her own press, and the media of other countries were inclined to be influenced by what was being said at home—after all, her own people should know . . .

Fame did not interest Lola. She lived for the present, not the future, using publicity to flatter her vanity and to secure theatrical engagements, not to leave lasting memorials to herself. "I have always been notorious, never famous," wrote the queen of scandal, without self-delusion.

Lola's incredible beauty belied, for a time, the life she lived; moving from country to country, from court to court, she remained always optimistic and energetic. She often believed her fabrications, especially those concerning herself; if in beauty there is truth, Lola's lies did nothing to distort that lovely face. A failure as a stage actress in the mannered tradition of her time, she was a consummate actress in her own terms, transforming herself, like a chameleon, into whatever role was expected by the audience she had chosen. She played, she *became,* in her mind, the aristocrat moving in European court circles, the intellectual *demi-mondaine* before Dujarier came into her life, the royal courtesan par excellence ruling king and country in Bavaria, the artiste back on the stage and, not surprisingly, the booted and spurred, cigar-smoking, horse-whipping señora in the Californian gold fields. Lola was, if nothing else, supremely adaptable.

The arrival of Mademoiselle Montez on the international scene followed the Romantic period, whose ideal was a woman of cultured, aesthetic sensitivity. Lola was this role model's antithesis; her wild, unpredictable presence was extremely exciting—and therefore it shocked the righteous. She was a gift to the gutter press, which savored every detail of the temperamental beauty's exploits, real or imaginary, and served them up to an audience ever ready to feed on the wickedness of others in order to feel virtuous. Readers from every class were able to take sides on the issue of Lola, and many would have agreed with Alexandre Dumas that she had the "evil eye."

It is easy to understand why Lola Montez has been called the "international bad girl of the mid-Victorians." Her name drew superlatives and exaggerations as a magnet draws pins: "She could raise instinctive passion, and was one whose seduction and whose glance was poison." "Lola's beauty, particularly the splendor of her breasts, made madmen everywhere."

Her circumstances and education made her a member of a society whose very existence depended on those who belonged to it keeping its rules. Lola broke them, and had to pay the price for flaunting convention and spitting in the eye of the establishment. In the hypocrisy of the Victorian era, which blessed couples who appeared faithful in public, yet led separate lives in private, a royal courtesan who flaunted her role and trod the boards could not be allowed access to society's drawing rooms. That such a woman should become an influential royal favorite, and was known as an avowed liberal and anti-clerical, made her eligible for condemnation from every direction. As an outcast from her own kind, she became the perfect scapegoat: beautiful, wicked, courageous, wild, mysterious and just a little vulnerable.

Her biggest mistake was to think she could return to the fold whenever it suited her—by acquiring a title in Munich, and by marrying a young gentleman when she returned to London. Her arrogance and inability to grasp the true nature of her image in the eyes of society were the product of her total belief in the infallibility of her own charm, beauty and intelligence. One glance from those magical eyes and the coldest heart would melt; the enchantress would conquer . . . it had happened so often since her earliest childhood, it would happen again. But once she was out of sight, Lola's personal magnetism faded; the vision that prevailed was of the wicked witch, not the good fairy. This was why Lola felt that if only she could *see* King Ludwig after her banishment, and talk with him, he would believe her and not her detractors. Whenever the king left her for a few days, as he did in the summer of 1847, Lola was frantic with worry that he might fall under another influence, one which might poison him against her. She bombarded him with letters and joined him as soon as she could. Once Lola was settled in Switzerland, her almost hypnotic hold on Ludwig faded without her daily presence.

In fact, Lola had the kind of energy and character which could have turned as easily toward either good or evil, and she held an enormous potential for both. If the James marriage had not sealed her fate at home, or Dujarier had lived and she had married him, Lola Montez might not have become "the most widely known and thoroughly discussed woman of the decade." As Dujarier's wife she would have continued to have access to the glittering beau monde and literary set of Paris, perhaps even had an influence within political circles, though she would never have tasted the narcotic power of ruling a country, nor been corrupted by the gratification of her every whim. But one should not discount the justified sense of satisfaction Lola felt when the reforms she instigated in Bavaria were acknowledged and acclaimed by the political world. It must never be forgotten that she was very good at being Bavaria's *éminence rose*.

The excitement and challenge of the nineteen months spent as the power behind the throne of Bavaria could never be matched afterward, and her subsequent choice of husbands and companions, from the very young Heald to the larger-than-life Irishman Hull, is evidence of her continued restlessness. Her travels can be seen as a search for a meaning to her life, as well as a relentless quest for adventure and novelty.

It is facile to suggest that her discovery of peace in religion took place merely because she felt her end was near. After all, Lola had tried everything else to calm that wild and troubled soul. Her religious notebooks show her to be entirely sincere; found by chance, they were not intended for posterity.

As a courtesan, Lola had few equals in her time. Born into the gentry, well educated, intelligent and beautiful, she had the spirit and the stomach for intrigues. By nature passionate, she took her pleasure from men of her choosing. As her confidence in her abilities grew, she inevitably made her choices from among richer and more powerful men. Like so many beautiful and intelligent women throughout history with access to men in positions of power, Lola was fascinated by politics, and she had the ideal qualifications for the role of a royal courtesan. The part she played in the destiny of Bavaria and its king was both a success and a failure. Her success lay in bringing life and laughter back into the heart of an older man, and inspiring him to carry out reforms long overdue and half-buried in his dreams and poetic memories. Her failure was that all too soon she and the king were compelled to awaken from their dreams into the harsh realities of 1848.

5

Lillie Langtry

1853–1929

MISTRESS OF EDWARD VII OF GREAT BRITAIN

"For the first and only time in my life I beheld perfect beauty."
The painter WALFORD GRAHAM ROBERTSON
upon seeing the young Lillie Langtry

Mrs. Langtry "arose from Jersey like Venus from the foam."
OSCAR WILDE

"A scandal was a romance until it was found out."
ANON.

"Let us not fuss, please."

LILLIE LANGTRY

*E*milie Charlotte Le Breton was born on October 13, 1853, in the Old Rectory, St. Saviour, Jersey. She was the only daughter of the handsome Dean of Jersey, William Corbet Le Breton, and his very pretty and worthy wife, Emilie Martin Le Breton; though after bearing him six sons in addition to Lillie (as their daughter was known), beauty deserted her mother* and only worthiness remained. Growing up surrounded by her brothers in the large Victorian deanery in the paradise that was Jersey was as near to perfect happiness as Lillie would ever know, and all her life she yearned to repossess it.

Her father, the Reverend William, a born Jerseyman, was educated at Winchester and Oxford. Six foot tall, blond, famous for his good looks, notably his astonishing blue eyes, he was also an idealist who as a young man energetically helped the poor in Southwark, a working-class parish of London.

The Jersey Le Bretons had history in their genes and a certain right to claim a distinguished ancestry. But their pretensions were somewhat excessive and did not justify their boycott of William's marriage to the lovely, though penniless, Emilie Martin of Chelsea. In 1859, once four sons were born, William was persuaded to leave the smog of London and take over the vacant position of Dean of Jersey. Now more accepting of William's marriage, the Le Bretons welcomed the young family back to the comfort and clean air of the island. Despite the advantages of space and fresh air, life on Jersey was inevitably provincial and constricted, particularly to a beautiful young woman brought up in the intellectually stimulating circles Mrs. Le Breton had known in London. When a girl, Mrs. Le Breton was described by her neighbor Charles Kingsley as "the most bewitchingly beautiful creature" he had ever seen. Emilie found herself restricted to good works in the parish and the society of a few island families. She withdrew into herself and poured her energies into cultivating her garden in the mild climate ensured by the Gulf Stream. While her plants conformed to her designs, her children grew wild, without much parental re-

---

* Nonetheless, in her old age, Lillie's mother was still described as quite lovely.

straint. The dean found his new parishioners less in need of his charitable efforts than the poor of Southwark, and time also hung heavy on his hands. The handsome William buried himself in his library.

With the birth of the fifth son in 1851, Mrs. Le Breton abandoned her efforts to maintain her looks. But if she no longer charmed her husband, he was not short of female attention in the community. The handsome dean found few of the island's flower sellers and serving girls could resist him. William was an incorrigible "ladies' man" and stories abounded of the numerous blue-eyed, blond children he fathered in the parish. In fact, in later years, Lillie would describe him as "a damned nuisance, he couldn't be trusted with any woman anywhere."* No wonder Mrs. Le Breton often took to her bed, as ladies did in Victorian times of stress. However, despite her legendary (and possibly phantom) illnesses, she long outlived her husband, to be described as "an exquisite little woman, plump and pink and white as a baby when she was seventy years old."† Never did a word against her "dear husband, the Dean" escape her lips.

William le Breton set the tone for his growing family, and that tone was unpretentious. He was an intellectual, but also unquestionably human, a kind man who saw good in most and who was liberal in attitude, treating everyone, high and low, the same—often to the disapproval of Jersey society.

His interference in the children's upbringing was minimal. They grew bold, energetic and daring, riding along the clifftops at breakneck speed, engaging in terrifyingly dangerous practical jokes which, although thoroughly good-natured, often went too far. There is a story that Lillie responded to a dare from her brothers and ran down a country lane stark naked at midnight. Yet the dean never admonished them except for their worst excesses and then only when he had no choice.

The family made their own rules and regulations and ignored the social mores of the island's society. Lillie's upbringing was totally unconventional, with little if any emphasis on typical Victorian virtues like embroidery, or watercolor painting or flower pressing. In fact, she

---

* Lillie Langtry, *The Days I Knew,* Lillie's memoirs. All future quotes are from this source.
† Laura Beatty, *Lillie Langtry: Manners, Masks and Morals.*

met few other girls and didn't care to. With six brothers to play with, her childhood was rough-and-tumble and devil-may-care.

Much later, Lillie would write her memoirs, *The Days I Knew,* extolling the freedom of her upbringing on Jersey, and the delight of the rambling old deanery covered with climbing roses. She described it as "a labyrinth of small, low rooms," presided over by a nurse whose son was said to be a smuggler—not an unusual profession on an island. Her mother features very little in the memoirs, and yet Lillie's life-long passion for flowers and creating her own gardens must have come from her. Alone of her siblings, and according to the custom of the time, Lillie never went to school. The boys attended Victoria College, while Lillie was educated at home by a French governess and then by several of her brothers' long-suffering tutors. She also sat in on her brothers' Latin, Greek and math tutoring in the evenings. Lillie was determined to keep up with her brothers in all their exploits, fully aware what a handicap it was to be a girl. She tried to excel in all they did—swim, fish and sail, and of course, to ride, another skill that would be most useful later. In the process, she learned the most important lesson for her life from her brothers—how to manage in a man's world, to handle men and even to dominate them.

Reggie, the youngest and just two years junior to Lillie, was her favorite brother. It was Reggie who shared her confidences and escapades. Each year there was a race meeting on the island and one year Reggie and Lillie hatched a plot to partake. Sharing the cost, they secretly bought a nag for 30 shillings whom they called "Flirt" and hid in one of their outhouses at home. Once they had nursed Flirt carefully back to health, Lillie, wearing boy's clothes, would ride her quietly about the lanes to allay suspicion and then Reggie took her out of sight and trained her along the cliffs. On the day of the race, with Reggie riding the unknown outsider, they won. Their father didn't even notice until he read about it in the local paper.

Inevitably, with so many brothers, Lillie grew up a tomboy, and as her mother's "health" kept her in bed, Lillie went with her father on his calls to the sick in the parish, which gave her a sense of adult importance. At the age of fourteen, she decided to join in the social life of the island, attending picnics and small dances. This transition was not easy; without the company of girlfriends to influence her during her youth; Lillie was not accustomed to cultivating friendships and alliances among other young women.

To add to her many social disadvantages, her headstrong outspokenness and general wildness, at fourteen Lillie was already seen as a beauty—not something that would endear her to the other young ladies on the island. However, it cannot only have been their envy which inspired the extraordinary stories about her at this time—that she would roll naked at dawn in the dew on the deanery lawns or use a facepack of raw mincemeat at night. Her long Titian hair always streamed behind her and her gray eyes laughed at the world. No wonder she received her first serious marriage proposal at the age of fifteen.

During the winter months, Jersey's ideal climate attracted some members of the aristocracy and London Society. In 1869, when Lillie was sixteen, Lord Suffield, who was a member of the Royal Household, declared that Lillie was so beautiful she ought to have a London season. Her mother took note as rumors of Lillie's attachment to a handsome young fisherboy reached her ears. Lillie refused to break with him until her adored father felt obliged to tell her the lad was his son. Not only was Lillie's heart broken over the boy, but it was also broken over her father, who until then could do no wrong.

Lord Suffield had a point about Lillie's future chances. A whole season was clearly beyond the family's resources; but fortified with a new dress and an invitation from Lord and Lady Suffield to a ball at his house in Gloucester Place, Lillie and her mother left for London.

Her launch into Society was a disaster. Her pretty new dress, made in Jersey, was completely outmoded, as was her hairstyle. She could ride like a goddess, swim like a mermaid, but waltz she could not, nor could she even walk like a lady. Her polite conversation was nil—in fact, Lillie had no social graces whatsoever and started at the serried ranks of cutlery by her plate in total confusion. Years later she wrote of that evening: "I felt like a clumsy peasant. My one 'party gown' which had been made for me in St. Helier, made me look like one of the serving maids."

She fled back to Jersey, aware for the first time that there was a world she had not known how to conquer. It did not take long for Lillie's self-confidence to rise again and to face the challenge: she

would conquer London—no matter how. The exposure of her ignorance hurt her deeply, and she was determined to learn how to be a
cultured lady. Immersing herself in books for the first time, with her
father's encouragement, she discovered a passion for knowledge.
Other young ladies might have cultivated manners, but few were well
read or had any real learning. She wrote in her memoirs: "Between
the ages of sixteen and twenty, I learned the magic of words, the
beauty and excitement of poetic imagery. I learned there was something in life other than horses, the sea, and the long Jersey tides."

Like her brothers, who all eventually found their escape from
provincial Jersey by joining the services, Lillie's goal was to find a suitable route to London where, she wrote, she was convinced her destiny lay. But for a young lady, short of marriage this was almost
impossible.

Lillie was twenty before an opportunity presented itself. Her
brother William returned to Jersey to marry the sister-in-law of Edward Langtry, a widower of twenty-six (although in her memoirs she
wrote that he was thirty). The Langtrys had made a fortune from
trading vessels, but by the time Edward came of age, the family resources were greatly reduced and their Irish tenants slow and often reluctant to pay their rents. However, Edward Langtry had several
boats, including a racing yawl, and gave all the impressions of landed
gentry who had no need for employment. For his sister-in-law's wedding (and more probably to impress Lillie) he held an elaborate reception, the sailors from his yacht lining the staircase and the hall in
their "whites." Lillie wrote that she wore a dress decorated with real
tea roses and was dazzled by the "Arabian Nights Entertainment."

Edward Langtry was not only dazzled by the ravishing Lillie, he
lost his head, cruising with her on his yacht, even to France, and always chaperoned by her father. All her life Lillie loved sailing and, as
she told a reporter years later, one day she saw a most beautiful yacht
come into the harbor. "I met the owner and fell in love with the
yacht. To become the mistress of the yacht, I married the owner."

At the time, Lillie clearly imagined herself in love with Edward
Langtry, because she ignored her parents' reservations. She did not
even demur when her father looked into Edward's finances and found
the results disturbing. We do not know precisely what her parents

thought of Ned (they most probably thought she could do better), but her adored brother Reggie was totally against the match. Lillie's inexperience was to be expected as she had not had the opportunity to "come out" in London; but as always, her strong will prevailed. Eventually she overcame everyone's objections, and on March 9, 1874, Lillie married Edward Langtry wearing her travelling dress because, as she claimed in her memoirs, she hated the idea of a big wedding in "the conventional bridal array."

The honeymoon was spent visiting the Langtry relations in Ireland. Lillie quickly made it clear she had no intention of living there. London was still her goal and to conquer Society her aim. Plump, dull Ned was the sort of man Lillie felt should bend to her ideas and not mind too much about her own ambitions. But Ned resisted a move to London and instead they moved to Southampton, where he could sail with his yachting friends. They rented a modest house called Cliffe Lodge overlooking Southampton Water and moved in with Dominique, Lillie's maid from Jersey.

The sailing made up in part for the lack of stimulating society, but soon Mr. and Mrs. Langtry had little to say to one another, and even less once the two yachts were sold for lack of money. Physically, Ned failed to inspire Lillie, but then that was often a wife's lot in Victorian times and expectations in that area were low. Lillie had gambled and lost. Her husband was an unattractive dullard with less money than she thought and no desire to enter London Society even if he could.

Perhaps from despair, Lillie fell ill. A delighted Ned was sure she was pregnant, but in fact it was typhoid and Lillie almost died. In her misery she did not even contact her parents, who had so disapproved of the marriage. Her recuperation was slow but somehow she persuaded her doctor to agree that London, despite its filth and soot, would be the ideal place for her lungs to recover. Having lost his first young wife to illness, Ned had no choice.

In January 1876, the Langtrys moved to modest rooms in Eaton Place. Lillie had achieved her goal. She was in London; but physically and emotionally weakened by her near-fatal illness, for the first time she accepted her vulnerability. London in January could not have been worse for a recuperating invalid and the smog from the chimneys at the time cannot have made it easier. Nor did the Langtrys have any friends to frequent, but London Society was much smaller than today and it was possible to meet acquaintances in Hyde Park. There fashionable people went to parade and admire one another on foot or riding splendid horses, and the greatest prize of all was to see members of the royal family on horseback or in their carriages on Rotten Row.*

For the next twelve months Ned accompanied Lillie on her sightseeing walks and tolerated her fantasies of running into one of the few fashionable London acquaintances she had met during their winters spent on Jersey. Knowing no one, they were always in each other's company, but Lillie does not mention in her memoirs any marital difficulties at this time. During the freezing winter of 1876, while the Langtrys shivered in their rooms and Lillie often remained in bed all day, she learned by telegram from Jersey that Reggie had taken a bad fall from his horse. By the time Lillie reached him three days later, her most beloved brother was dead. He had been found at the bottom of the cliff and had either slipped or been thrown from his horse. Dark whispers of incest and suicide circulated.

Edward rented a house on Jersey so Lillie could be near her grieving parents and away from the cold of London. Reggie's death would haunt her all her life. When she heard of his fall she had not hurried to be by his side and in her memoirs she denied even knowing of the accident before his death. The Langtrys remained on Jersey throughout the spring, when another tragic accident shook her. While Lillie was out sailing with two local boys in bad weather, their boat overturned, and although Lillie made it to shore, both boys drowned.

In April 1877, the Langtrys returned to London. On one of her solitary walks, Lillie saw the Prince of Wales out riding and noted in her journal that he was a fine horseman despite his bulk. She too had been noticed—by the painter Walford Graham Robertson, who described her, a young slender girl entering Hyde Park, as possibly being a milliner's assistant—until she looked up, and

The face was that of the lost Venus of Praxiteles, and of all the copies handed down to us, must have been incomparably the best.

* A corruption of rue du Roi or the King's Road.

. . . The small head . . . drooped slightly forward like a violet or a snowdrop, the perfect nose was made less perfect and a thousand times more beautiful by a slight tilt at the tip. The wonderful face was pale with the glow of absolute health behind the pallor, the eyes grey beneath dark lashes, the hair brown with glints of gold in it; the figure in its poise and motion conveyed an impression of something wild, eternally young, nymph-like. . . . *

As Lillie's most recent biographer Laura Beatty writes so aptly, this description gives the "thunderbolt" quality of her beauty. Soon all London would discover its impact.

Later that April, on a visit to the Aquarium at Westminster, the longed-for meeting with a member of Society happened. Lord Ranelagh, who had property on Jersey, was there with two of his daughters who knew Lillie, and he invited the Langtrys to spend a few days at his country property in Fulham. Lord Ranelagh had never married the mother of his seven children, and with his foppish appearance, tightly corseted waist and rakish top hat, he cut a somewhat unconventional figure in Society. Staying with him in the relaxed atmosphere of the countryside (that Fulham was at the time) gave Lillie the opportunity to ask him to help her meet some interesting people. And why not? Despite her poverty, Lillie was beautiful and acceptable, and jaded Society needed a bright new star.

IN THE 1870s, Society began to move away from Queen Victoria's stern code of behavior toward accepting a far more relaxed and sexually liberal way of life. This was due to Queen Victoria's heir, Edward, the Prince of Wales. Good-humored, well mannered, utterly charming, Edward liked the good life. When he was a young man, his father Prince Albert had become convinced that his son would amount to little and kept him away from all possible contamination with the adult world, notably university or the armed services. However, at nineteen, the prince was sent to a military camp for a few weeks. Until then, his con-

* Beatty, *Lillie Langtry*.

tact with young ladies had been minimal. One evening his fellow officers slipped a jolly, willing girl called Nellie Clifden into his bed, and the
prince's life-long devotion to lovemaking was the result.

Following Albert's death in 1861, which Queen Victoria always
blamed on Bertie's shocking behavior, she decided that the only way
to prevent Edward from philandering was to have him married. Victoria chose the pretty Princess Alexandra of Denmark, and at the age
of twenty-one, Bertie had his own household and independence.

As Queen Victoria refused to allow her heir to take part in politics
or to represent her in public, the Prince of Wales had nothing to do
but to indulge and enjoy himself. In fact, Bertie (as he was always
known) was not untalented. His charm was legendary and resulted in
useful diplomatic gifts; he had charisma and great vitality. But the
queen considered him irresponsible, and forbade her ministers to
show him any state papers. Bertie was kept in total ignorance of affairs
of state in case he might "meddle." Queen Victoria wanted him idle
and so he became, his goodwill and sense of responsibility eroded.
Following the death of Prince Albert, Victoria had become "invisible"
to her subjects, but she would not allow her son and heir to charm
them on behalf of the monarchy.

Edward Albert, Prince of Wales, had been seduced by France in
his teens. On his parents' state visit to Napoleon III and the lovely
Empress Eugénie,* Edward had been exposed to all that the French
court and Paris had to offer—the scented, seductive young ladies-in-
waiting swaying in their white crinolines around the empress, beautiful ladies who fussed and caressed, bending over the thirteen-year-old
boy and exposing their décolletés; elegant courtiers and a most fash-
ionably dressed emperor; and Paris, with its fine buildings and elegant
streets. Bertie fell in love with France and all that was French—from
culture to clothes to food, wine and entertainment. Throughout his
life he would spend time in France *en garçon* in Paris, Biarritz, the
South of France, and of course, Deauville for the racing. And Paris
had another attraction irresistible to Queen Victoria's heir: those ex-

* The tactful empress was so aware of the awful clothes the queen was sure to wear on her
state visit and worse, put on her young daughter Vicky, that the girl was sent a life-size doll
with her own measurements, and then a fashionable wardrobe for the doll that the girl might
also wear.

quisite *demi-mondaines* or courtesans, beautiful, witty, worldly women dedicated to pleasing a (rich) gentleman in every way. At home, he sought their equivalent among the married ladies of Society.

The Danish-born Princess of Wales was charming and quite beautiful, with a wonderful figure and natural elegance. She was good-natured and cheerful, slightly deaf and also, it was rumored, rather cool and not passionate. Even Queen Victoria, who loved her, admitted Alex was "not very clever" or witty. The prince, who was not a great intellectual either, enjoyed quick-witted women and those who held his attention throughout his life were that. Like many a spoilt prince before him, boredom was his greatest enemy and he needed constant distraction. Following the birth of their first child, Alexandra's deafness increased, which made her appear more stupid than she was, and she retreated further and further into her own world.

Neither his wife's deafness nor her lack of passion or wit could explain her husband's serial philandering. Unlike most young bloods of his class, the Prince of Wales had never had a chance to sow wild oats, so when he discovered their attraction, Bertie saw no reason to stop sowing just because he was married. To put it plainly, he loved women and making love to them, no matter what their class or background. Duchesses or prostitutes—it was all the same to him and he was never faithful to any of them.

Victorian society has the reputation of respectability, but this was confined to the middle classes. The aristocracy was an exclusive clan that kept to its own rules within a relatively small and closed group of people—roughly ten thousand from fifteen hundred families. These families were all titled and landed and owned approximately 90 percent of the country. A gentleman did not work and had an estate with a great house. Members of the upper classes intermarried and kept out anyone who was not of their own.

At the pinnacle of this pyramid was the royal family, who were respected and worshipped. To be in their company or entertain one of them was the height of a gentleman or lady's aspiration. It was not just snobbery that caused Society's ladies to succumb to the Prince of Wales, it was his aura, his charm, his way of making everyone feel they were the most important person in his orbit at that moment. As one of his biographers put it, the Prince of Wales was London's most "accomplished, persuasive and charming philanderer"* and, of course, heir to the throne of the British Empire.

Did Alexandra know or mind? She was wise and tolerant, and like most Victorian ladies of the upper classes, she ignored and accepted her husband's infidelities. Divorce was almost unheard of in the 1870s and certainly not as the result of an infidelity. Alexandra would only really have suffered humiliation in the event of a public scandal. Queen Victoria wrote early in Alexandra's marriage that her "lot is no easy one, but she is very fond of Bertie, though not blind."† Bertie was always kind and genial, and the worst Alexandra seems to have called him was her "naughty little man." At least, until the age of thirty-five, he had never fallen in love with anyone.

Queen Victoria's Hanoverian uncles had set such a bad moral example that she and Albert had worked hard to set the moral standard for the majority of respectable families in England—the middle classes, not really the aristocracy. Young gentlemen could gain experience from serving girls or prostitutes—and London had around a quarter of a million of them—but a young lady would invariably be a virgin on her marriage, and quite ignorant of her marital duties. Nor did she expect to enjoy them. Her young husband would often take a mistress and even install her somewhere with his second family. Such an option was not available to the Prince of Wales, nor could he really be seen in the company of chorus girls, prostitutes or serving girls. He solved his particular problem by having affairs with married ladies from Society. In this way, the Prince of Wales effectively condoned adultery.

⁂

SOON AFTER THE Langtrys' stay in Fulham with Lord Ranelagh, an invitation arrived from his friends, the Sebrights, to spend an evening in company at their house in Lowndes Square. On this famous

---

* Theo Aronson, *The King in Love: Edward VII's Mistresses.*
† From a letter to her daughter Vicky in *Beloved Mama: Private Correspondence of Queen Victoria and the German Crown Princess, 1878–1885*, edited by Roger Fulford (London: Evans, 1981).

evening in May 1877, three years after her marriage, Lillie Langtry was "discovered," and from the first she showed an unerring instinct for success.

Sir John and Lady Sebright liked to surround themselves with the cultural elite and included among their guests that evening more of the fashionable members of bohemia than the upper classes. Olivia Sebright was herself a talented amateur actress and singer who liked to entertain the best of these arts. This mix of aristocrats and artists was beginning to become the fashion for London hostesses. They all had money—at least enough to appear to have more—and they all dressed elaborately, with sumptuous gowns and jewels, hair piled high and ornamented. Describing the evening in her memoirs, Lillie wrote that she felt "very un-smart and countrified." Seated modestly in a corner of the room in her Jersey-made, simple black dress, her long hair in its habitual twist at the nape of her neck and no jewels ("I had none"), Lillie became, to her surprise, the center of attraction. "After a few moments, I found that quite half the people in the room seemed bent on making my acquaintance." Lillie had a *succès fou*.

Among the guests were some of the most fashionable artists of the day: John Everett Millais, James Abbott McNeill Whistler and Frank Miles. There was Henry Irving and the critic Abraham Hayward. Millais was a Jerseyman, quite the handsomest man in the room, and the most famous painter in the country. He took over his shy young countrywoman, leading her to supper and easing her into his group while extracting a promise that she would sit for him. The budding young artist Frank Miles sketched her portrait in pencil that same evening and worked it up when he came home. Before the month was out, his drawing of Lillie was displayed on every corner postcard stand. He claimed later that his sketches of Lillie in her first season made him more money than he had made on the largest commissions for his most expensive paintings. Due to Frank Miles, within weeks, Lillie's was one of the best known faces in London.

The more serious painters would take time to display their paintings of homage to the new goddess in their midst. Frank Miles became Lillie's first friend in bohemia and they shared a love of flowers. The buzz went around the cultural elite: there was a new goddess in town, and all those jaded palates had something else to feast upon. Lillie's soft, gentle features were a new kind of beauty, and without stays, her body also set a new, softer outline.

The next day, when the Langtrys returned from their daily walk, their entrance hall was littered with dozens of invitations from unknown hosts. Lillie had become the rage. It was not lost on Edward that everyone wanted to see her—not her ineffectual, dull husband. She was wanted, he was not. For the sake of propriety, however, she needed accompanying, so he had to be tolerated—and many a hostess complained. Poor shy Edward, how jealous he must have been with all the gloating over Lillie and ignoring of him.

At their next Society dinner Lillie was once again swamped by painters and writers of bohemia. The dinner took place at the home of Lord Wharncliffe, a future close friend to Lillie and not a very distinguished man himself. However, he had money and liked to be considered the leading patron of the artists' circle, and so he invited Lillie for their sake. As Lillie's most recent biographer Beatty so rightly points out, Lillie was invited "as bait for the painters." Once again wearing her simple black dress, she did not disappoint. Sir Edward Poynter immediately asked her to sit for him, and his later portrait of her in the Pre-Raphaelite style beautifully captured the famous swanlike bend of her head as she held a rose to her breast. She loved the "gorgeous golden gown" she wore for the sitting, and this was the only original painting of herself that she possessed. The celebrated though aging painter Burne-Jones was quite revived by her beauty, saying, "I can't imagine a face more radiant or a look more serene—like day itself she is . . ."* Among the many other famous people she met that night was Lord Randolph Churchill, who wrote to Jennie his wife that he took into dinner "a Mrs. Langtry, a most beautiful creature, quite unknown, very poor, and they say has but one black dress."†

Lord Wharncliffe introduced Lillie to the many artists in attendance that night. But the Wharncliffes, like most of the guests that evening, as at the Sebrights', were considered to be on the fringes of real Society—rakish, and most probably more fun. To judge from

* Letter from Burne-Jones to Lord Wharncliffe, quoted in Beatty, *Lillie Langtry*.
† Lady Randolph Churchill, The Reminiscences of Lady Randolph Churchill, quoted in Beatty, *Lillie Langtry*.

Lillie's memoirs, her hostess, Lady Wharncliffe, made a considerable impression on her—in particular, her wit and sophistication, which Lillie noted to her own detriment. The late nineteenth century saw the rise of a "New Woman" in many guises—Florence Nightingale or George Eliot or the suffragettes or the gorgeous heroines of Ouida's* novels, who somehow made it acceptable for women to be "sexy" so long as this was elaborately disguised as "art." It was Ouida who commented unwisely and in public that the Prince of Wales was afraid to meet Lillie—presumably because he would not be responsible for the consequences.

Due to the attention of these artists, Lillie's life changed considerably as she rushed from one sitting to another. She was the embodiment of the Pre-Raphaelite beauties of Holman Hunt, Dante Gabriel Rosetti and Millais, and had appeared like a vision to justify their paintings. Indeed, the handsome Millais became another of her painter-friends, whose features she described in her memoirs as "strong rather than sensitive in character, and his swinging walk suggested the moors and the sportsman. Manly is the only word which would accurately describe the impression he made."

It was in their studios that Lillie began to meet members of Society and make friends. But still at this time, most of her evenings would be spent quietly with Ned at Eaton Place. It was in Frank Miles' studio that Lillie was observed by Lord Roslyn and his young daughter Daisy, future Countess of Warwick. Both were overwhelmed by Lillie's beauty, and an invitation to the Roslyns' promptly followed. Millais painted a scene from Sir Walter Scott's famous novel *The Heart of Midlothian,* which he exhibited in galleries in King Street, choosing Lillie as his model for Effie Deans; engravings of his sentimental, tearful portrait of Effie Deans were bought in their thousands.

Lilly was twenty-three and lionized. But it was not just her extraordinary beauty which dumbfounded people, it was her air of calm self-assured control mixed with her vivacity: "the vitality, the glow, the amazing charm, that made this fascinating woman the centre of any

* The non de plume of the noted novelist Marie Louise de la Ramée.

group that she entered,"* wrote Daisy, Countess of Warwick. Lillie confused people, which made her even more attractive. She was so in control, which was almost a manly trait, and yet with her remarkable gray eyes half-closed, she spelt seduction. Although she may not have had any experience as yet, Lillie appeared most sensual—the wide mouth, slightly parted lips and voluptuous figure accentuated by a tiny waist. Furthermore (most unusually for the time), she wore no stays and her movement was described as almost animal, "like a beautiful hound set upon its feet."†

Lillie's triumph at the Roslyns'—again in the modest black dress—resulted in a steady flow of invitations; and Ned—described now as "fat Mr. Langtry"—trotted unwillingly behind his ravishing wife.

"Acts of worship" multiplied; the society poet Joaquin Miller, "perhaps the most picturesque personality of the literary world," scattered rose petals before her out of his sombrero as he mounted a huge white marble staircase backward before her, saying, "Thus be your path in life"—and declaiming poetry in her honor.‡ The invitations became ever more numerous, sometimes three a night—to balls, dinners and receptions, and even to political gatherings at the Duke of Devonshire's house. There the duke's heir, the staid politician the Marquess of Hartington, having given Lillie a personal tour of the untold treasures of Devonshire House, responded to her admiration of some water lilies in a pond by plunging in up to his armpits and uprooting them. Mr. and Mrs. Langtry rode home that evening in their carriage surrounded by the dripping lilies.

OVERNIGHT AND NOW just twenty-four, with no particular accomplishment, her one dull black dress and no fortune, Lillie was an acknowledged sensation. The country and its upper class were rich and the staid times of Victoria and Albert had slipped during the queen's widowhood into the wild excesses of what became known even before

---

* Quoted in Beatty, *Lillie Langtry.*
† Quoted in Beatty, *Lillie Langtry.*
‡ Beatty, *Lillie Langtry.*

his reign as Edwardian England. Edward, Prince of Wales, had no occupation, and despite his most honorable intentions, he was not provided with one. His mother the queen saw him as an unredeemable rake and up to a point she was right. The prince not only spent his time with the aristocracy but accepted into Society for the first time some of the nouveaux riches—Jewish bankers, some manufacturers, rich Americans or South African mineowners, a few artists and of course some politicians. The nouveaux riches entertained in great style and married their daughters into aristocratic families who needed money. Brains, beauty and business were the criteria for the new members of the Prince of Wales' society. The once firm lines of social delineation were becoming blurred. But the outward show of propriety continued, with rigid rules of dress for all occasions, requiring constant changes of clothing and jewels. Entertainments were devised to prevent boredom, and distraction of any kind was sought.

Seeing Lillie at Society functions in the same black dress, with no jewels and no corsets to turn her natural slim figure into a rigid statue, coupled with her extraordinary beauty, must have stunned her contemporaries. Her lack of artifice or pretension, her genuine sweetness and no-nonsense attitude must have been so refreshing to the jaded members of Society. Still, royalty made the rules and accepted or excluded the members of what amounted to their own club. As Lillie wrote later in her memoirs:

> Actors and actresses were not then generally received, the Stage being regarded as an undesirable vocation. Rank was more highly considered, and the line more finely drawn between the social grades, the inner circle being, consequently, comparatively small and rigorously exclusive, and people were more hypocritical and narrow minded. Travel was less easy and much less luxurious, and very few Americans were to be found in London.

In fact, Society was still quite small, and that was one of the reasons Lillie caused such a sensation. She was, of course, a lady, and not one of the new *arrivistes*. The Dean of Jersey's social standing was the same as that of landed gentry. Edward Langtry was a gentleman of leisure and did nothing so vulgar as work for his living, and for all her apparent sensuality, Lillie conducted herself in public and private like a lady. Even sitting for portraits by bohemian artists was an acceptable activity for a Society lady. All she lacked was money. She was a phenomenon, someone completely unknown, an astonishing beauty with extraordinary magnetism.

A NEW ART that flourished at the time was photography, and in particular demand were pictures of great beauties. Society ladies were photographed in romantic or tragic poses. They were known as "professional beauties" or "P.B.'s," and their images were avidly collected by all classes. "The multitude was learning to lust after its social betters," was how one writer succinctly put it. Lillie quickly joined their ranks, and hostesses would even urge guests to attend their evenings as "the P.B.'s will be there." As well as Lillie, there was the Duchess of Leinster; Mrs. Luke Wheeler; and the enchanting daughter of the Marquis of Headfort, Mrs. Cornwallis-West, known by all as "Patsy." But Lillie's photographs were the most popular of all.

The season began in late April, when everyone came to London from their country estates to meet and enjoy themselves. Like a great swarm Society would attend race meetings, balls in London's fine private houses, and boating parties on the Thames. In between, they would admire one another in "the Park"—which only meant Hyde Park, of course. Then in early August everyone would disappear to the country again for the shooting, the fishing, and other set programs of entertainment.

Lillie's first season, 1876, consisted mainly of sitting for the artists during the day, and between 4 and 6 p.m. meeting and making friends at their studios. Reading her memoirs, it is clear Lillie was most at home in bohemia, where she felt appreciated and admired, though she did make many friends among the aristocracy who also frequented the artists' studios. Lillie was not choosing her friendships; she accepted those that were offered. She would write of the "simplicity about the people which one finds only in those born to greatness." Lillie had been charmed, and her account of her first season seems to burst with the pride of being the guest of so many people of title.

Meanwhile, Edward Langtry had nothing better to do than to dress in his white tie and tails and accompany his dazzlingly successful wife to all the entertainments. Lillie makes it clear in her journal that Ned hated the social life he was now forced to lead, but he had no choice—no married lady could go into Society alone without her husband.

The influential artists in Lillie's life were to be James A. McNeill Whistler, who became one of her closed and most trusted friends, and Oscar Wilde. It was Frank Miles who introduced Lillie to the young Irishman Oscar Fingal O'Flahertie Wills Wilde, who had recently graduated from Magdalen College, Oxford, and had won a prestigious poetry prize. He came up to London and rented a floor of Frank Miles' house. This he adorned with peacock feathers, old china, and an abundance of flowers, just as he had done in his rooms at Oxford. Oscar Wilde was a dandy. He wore a flowered waistcoat under his shabby black frock coat, and nonchalantly carried a pair of lavender gloves—a theatrical touch. Lillie noted his dirty fingernails, his freckled pallor, and his stained dirty teeth framed by thick lips. He was not a pleasing sight. But she immediately appreciated his sharp mind, his seductive voice, and was struck by his "great, eager eyes." Oscar was three years younger than Lillie, but he recognized in her a shooting star and he actively attached his to hers. This Irish eccentric saw Lillie as a prop to his own social advancement: he was seen almost marching to her house carrying a single white amaryllis before him. Lillie wrote: "The scribblers construed his act of homage as a pose, and thus I innocently conferred on him the title 'Apostle of the Lily.' "

Like the Pre-Raphaelites, Oscar had a true love of botany. Since Society lionized him as much as it did Lillie, hanging on his every witty utterance, he inspired hostesses as well as his young male following to fill their drawing rooms with "meaningful" flowers—orchids, sunflowers, and of course, the lily in honor of Mrs. Langtry. He wore a simply daisy in his buttonhole and his young acolytes did the same. His bon mots, "Give me the luxuries, and I can dispense with the neces-sities" . . . "Nothing succeeds like excess" . . . "If one had the money to go to America, one would not go," which sounded so natural and spontaneous, were in fact practiced for hours, but Society was captivated.

Then there was the older painter, George Frederick Watts,* for whom Lillie also sat, spending some of the happiest time of her first London season in his company. From Watts she learned about art. He would lecture her for hours during the sittings, his flowing white beard reminding her, as she told him charmingly, of Titian. Lillie wrote in her memoirs that "subsequently when I came to visit the famous galleries of Europe, I realized what a debt I owed to him." Charm came naturally to Lillie because she enjoyed pleasing. And all her life she would find father substitutes.

Whistler wrote to her as "Most Beautiful Lillie" and his signature butterfly on her letter was sting-less.† Whistler's American cuisine was famous: Lillie recounts that it was with the artist that she first delighted in "buck-wheat cakes, pop-overs, corn muffins, and other cereals that make breakfast such a tempting meal in the most hospitable country in the world."‡

BUT IF THE artists painted her features, as yet, no one had claimed Lillie's heart. Ned still followed along, but it was clear to everyone that it was only a question of time before the ravishing Mrs. Langtry acquired a lover. Adultery was acceptable in London Society, and once the legitimate heir "and a spare" had arrived, married ladies more or less did as they pleased while outwardly observing the proprieties.

If a gentleman called on a lady of his choice in town, it would be between the hours of five and seven—the infamous *cinq à sept*—and having left his hat, gloves and cane on a chair outside the drawing room to indicate his presence to the staff or even to the husband should he return, the visitor could rest assured that he would not be disturbed. Young men were encouraged to take a married mistress from their own class.

---

* George Frederick Watts was married to the teenage Ellen Terry, who was later to advise Lillie about going on the stage.

† One could gauge his affection for his correspondent by the length of the butterfly's sting. Lillie's had none.

‡ Lillie was writing her memoirs later in life when she had often visited America.

Lillie's first two admirers had just this intention. They were John Leslie and Morton Frewen, who were both to become brothers-in-law. Frewen* was good-looking, a famous gentleman rider, considered the best in the country. It is related that on meeting him Lillie stared with her large blue eyes and asked, "What are your spiritual beliefs?" Nonplussed, he was instantly in pursuit. But even the gift of a horse she adored—a splendid chestnut appropriately called Redskin—did not persuade Lillie to succumb to Frewen. She pretended she could not ride, accepted lessons and fell off charmingly. She teased and laughed at her two admirers and thoroughly enjoyed herself. The actress in Lillie was practicing the many roles she would play during her life.

⁂

IN THAT FIRST season of 1876–1877, in addition to acquiring admirers, Lillie was making women friends. Among them was the beautiful giantess Lady Gladys Herbert, sister of the Earl of Pembroke, and her friend Lady Augusta Fane, daughter of the Earl of Westmorland. These two pillars of the establishment were drifting into the loucher elements of London's bohemia. In Augusta, Lillie met a soul mate who loved practical jokes as much as she did. The most socially experienced of them all, however, was that enchanting and daring Irishwoman, Patsy Cornwallis-West, who had so impressed Lillie during her first brilliant season. Patsy had married at seventeen and tired early of her husband. Lillie recounts in her journal that she arrived at dinner at the Cornwallis-Wests' house to find her host missing from the table. No mention was made of him; only when the wine ran out did Patsy declare they could not have more as she had locked her husband in the cellar following an argument and had no intention of letting him out.

Lillie was still being entertained by the great and the good in her one black dress, not only on account of her poverty, but also because she had the excuse of being in mourning for Reggie. Her dress became so famous that one evening Patsy borrowed it—it came back in

* Frewen left for America soon afterward and married one of the Jerome sisters, which made him Lord Randolph's brother-in-law and Winston Churchill's uncle.

rags and needed serious mending. Famous designers had been offering to dress Lillie on credit or even for free, but it was only when
Lady Dudley begged her not to wear black to her ball as it upset her
husband that Lillie gave up her famous dress. Instead, she now wore
white velvet embroidered in pearls, low cut and very fitted, the skirt
draped back into a bustle outlining Lillie's slender long legs. Lillie's
figure was always described as voluptuous or hourglass, a perfect example of the fashionable type of the time. She wrote: "As I entered
the ballroom the dancers stopped and crowded round me, and as I
pursued my way to greet my hostess, they opened out to allow me to
pass."

Lillie had arrived—and been noticed—by none other than the
most important person in Society: the Prince of Wales, who was its
leader, its arbiter of taste and judge of acceptability.

Lillie's first meeting with the Prince of Wales was not by chance.
Sir Allen Young, known as "Alleno" to his friends, was a dashing
bachelor, an explorer who had twice sailed his own yacht in hazardous
and futile attempts to find the Northwest Passage, the arctic route
joining the Atlantic and Pacific oceans. In May 1877, most probably
without Lillie's knowledge, he arranged a supper party for ten guests
following the theater. As the guests were in the drawing room awaiting dinner, the Prince of Wales suddenly arrived from another play,
full of apologies that he was a little late and uttering the hope that Sir
Allen's famous lobster curry was on the menu. Lillie noted that
though tall enough, he was shorter than she had expected, and that
he beamed good health, with an "outdoor" complexion. "Alleno"
may have told his royal friend about Lillie or perhaps he had expressed
a desire to meet her himself. Once she had stifled her initial desire to
climb up the chimney—she was standing by the fireplace when he entered—Lillie managed to contain herself. Whatever the explanation,
his genial presence ensured slightly less panic in Lillie than she had anticipated.

It must have flashed through her mind that he was the reason for
her invitation, and she knew what might be expected of her. The
ladies curtsied, the gentlemen bowed. Lillie noted her husband's embarrassment and his stuttered greeting to the prince and felt no pity
for him. As the prince appraised Lillie with his heavy-lidded blue eyes,

she touched his hand and curtsied—then was placed next to him at dinner. Prince Edward had just returned from his annual holiday in the South of France and Princess Alexandra was in Greece visiting her brother George of Denmark, who had been appointed King of the Hellenes. The timing was perfect.

The prince was his relaxed and charming self, glittering with medals and the Order of the Garter on its blue ribbon across his chest. Edward, Prince of Wales, was an accomplished *grand coureur*— a most skilled seducer. He was naturally affable and at the same time very conscious of his position. Wisely, Lillie did not try to impress and said little, allowing him to expound and charm. She wrote in her memoirs that he showed all the qualities she had expected: "dignity, good humour, consideration for his host, even compliments for the cook." Although she said little, and her husband even less, Lillie observed the prince and "I decided it would be a very brave man who, even at this little *intime* supper party, attempted a familiarity with him." Lillie does not recount their conversation, but it seems certain that he would have followed the usual pattern of seduction—a request to pay an afternoon call. There can have been no doubt in Lillie's mind how she would be expected to entertain her august visitor.

The Prince of Wales adored women—not just for their horizontal delights, but simply for their femininity. He loved to discuss their topics—clothes, domestic matters—and most of all, he loved to gossip. The company of a witty, pretty, well-dressed society lady was his ideal entertainment. Despite his affection for cigars and port, Bertie would always choose the company of ladies over that of his peers.

Until Lillie met the Prince of Wales, she had flirted with many but remained faithful to Ned and was known to be quick to cut any man who took liberties with her. The surprising thing is that Bertie and Lillie did not meet sooner. There were occasions in that first season when they were invited to the same event but somehow one or the other would be unable to attend. It was shortly after the meeting between Bertie and Lillie that C. J. Freake, a self-made manufacturer, entered the Langtrys' circle. He was a multimillionaire who had climbed the social ladder to become a friend of the Prince of Wales. It can be assumed that Bertie asked his friend to help the Langtrys and advise Ned on some investments.

That the Prince of Wales should call on Mrs. Langtry at her home for tea was seen as perfectly acceptable in the eyes of Society. Like all husbands, Mr. Langtry would be expected to spend the afternoon at his club (or taking tea with another married lady). Ladies entertaining a lover at home would wear a "tea-gown" or "teagie," a glamorous, delicious floating confection devoid of uncomfortable stays that required a maid if they were to be undone and replaced again. Ladies so enjoyed the comfort of these robes that they became essential to the wardrobe of a lady with or without a lover. Tea in the drawing room would center on the chaise longue where various degrees of courtship could be entertained, from the most chaste to the most flagrant.

Soon the Prince of Wales was calling openly on Mrs. Langtry at Eaton Place for tea. It was the first time that Bertie did not hide his relationship with a woman other than his wife. Hostesses began to realize that if they wanted the Prince of Wales to stay at their country houses, Mrs. Langtry would have to be included in the party, and with her own room not far from his. Lists of the guests at various social functions were often published, and Mr. and Mrs. Langtry would be listed after the Prince of Wales. Bertie was clearly smitten. He took to riding with Lillie in the Park in full view of everyone.* As Lillie explains in her memoirs, the fashionable hours for riding in Rotten Row during the London season were either dawn or dusk—at seven in the morning "when what was termed 'the Liver Brigade' made its appearance," or, preferably, at seven in the evening. This resulted in late dinners. Once, when Lillie was delayed by the prince—one could not leave the presence of royalty without being dismissed—a furious Ned was waiting to take her to a dinner. Happily for Lillie, on arrival at their hosts,' she was told that dinner had been delayed for her once the hostess heard Lillie was still riding in the Park with the prince.

Lillie had become a fashionable celebrity, and as such, being seen with her was more important even than becoming her lover. She was now a public figure. One biographer argues that this was how the Prince of Wales, who had always been most discreet in his *amours,* was able to be seen publicly escorting Lillie on her daily rides without

---

* 'The Park' always meant Hyde Park, never one of London's other great parks. The fashionable stretch was from Albert to Grosvenor gates, and included Rotten Row.

drawing outraged public criticism. Of course her other swains melted away. Toward the end of the century, his daily appearance in the Park was almost a ritual of Society. After breakfast and between tea and dinner, the world would come and gawp at the splendid shining carriages and horses, liveried footmen in attendance, gleaming and jingling harnesses, ladies in veils and tight riding habits (often sewn onto them) and other ladies in exquisite dresses and hats seated in carriages. The Princess of Wales would arrive in the afternoon in her royal-burgundy barouche, exquisitely dressed as always in ethereal muslins and silks, bowing graciously at the curtsying and hat-doffing public on foot. Sometimes the prince would ride in the carriage with her; more often he would be on horseback, surrounded by his friends and equerries.

Lillie would appear in the prince's group, in her veiled top hat and showing off her tiny waist in her tight riding habit, sitting prettily sidesaddle on Redskin, showing his paces. Sometimes when Lillie came home late from a ball, she would slip into her riding habit and set out for the Park without going to bed at all. But Edward Langtry always accompanied his wife to her social engagements, so that the prince and Lillie were never seen alone together. Scandal was averted—for the time being.

For the first time, Bertie was faithful. Lillie became his first *maîtresse en titre*, his official mistress. He was in love and wanted the world to acknowledge his favorite.

Eaton Place was too small for regular meetings, so the Langtrys, with the help of Freake's business advice, moved to a larger house at 17 Norfolk Street just off Park Lane; they hired more staff and acquired a carriage and pair. What Edward Langtry thought of these new arrangements, we do not know. Most husbands in London Society at the time would have been strangely flattered. All we do know is that his drinking bouts increased, and there were occasions when he was too drunk to accompany Lillie, who was then obliged to send last-minute regrets to her hostess. There was even a rumor that Freake advised Ned about his role in the ménage à trois. On at least two occasions, the Freakes were entertained at small dinner parties at Norfolk Street, and there was talk that Lillie and the Prince of Wales would meet for tea at the Freakes' well-appointed house. Neither the

Freaks, Lillie nor Bertie mentioned these meetings, but the stories persisted.

If the Prince of Wales paid for the rent—and we are not sure that he did—he was not about to give Lillie a palace in the traditional manner of the French kings whose generosity to their mistresses was legendary. His munificence to date had been limited to beautiful pieces of jewelry,* but then, the Society ladies whom he had chosen as his mistresses in the past all came from wealthy backgrounds and marriages and did not have Lillie's needs. Nonetheless, even if he did not lose his head and buy Lillie a mansion, no one doubted that Bertie was in love. Lillie fascinated him. It was not only her beauty—that perfect face and figure—but also her manner—her delicious sense of fun and of the absurd, of ridicule and mockery; in short, she was a delectable, natural, captivating woman.

Lillie's free and easy upbringing, roughhousing with her many brothers, had taught her to be tough and to understand men. This was, in part, the reason for her incredible success with them, and the Prince of Wales was, in this regard, no different than any other man. It seems that the Prince found Lillie's lack of obsequiousness or toadying refreshing, and distinct from many who surround royalty. Unlike some members of the royal family, who only allowed near them those who were of their own opinions, Edward, Prince of Wales, welcomed this free spirit. Just as he had accepted a new breed of self-made and confident achievers into his circle, in Lillie he recognized a similar will and intelligence. According to George Bernard Shaw, Lillie had no right to be intelligent, daring and lovely, and he declared it a frightening combination of attributes. She was practical and straightforward and the prince could discuss matters with her as a friend. The combination of all these qualities made Lillie Langtry irresistible to the heir to the throne. Interestingly, no one seems to have disapproved of either the Prince of Wales or Lillie Langtry for their adultery, despite the popularity of the Princess of Wales.

In fact, Alexandra was kindness itself to Lillie and welcomed her to both Marlborough House and Sandringham. Lillie would even ap-

---

* The Prince of Wales was a very wealthy man and loved to give jewelry to his mistresses. He gave Lillie a great many pieces—hers became known as one of the world's largest private collections of the time.

pear at official functions which the Princess of Wales also attended. Alexandra had entertained all her husband's mistresses, but she seemed to have a real affection for Lillie and her acceptance of Lillie was clear to everyone. The princess, who was renowned for her goodness of heart, despised jealousy and most probably instinctively liked Lillie's unaffected and open nature. Or perhaps she simply did not care; she was totally absorbed in her own life and in that of her children—and Bertie was sincerely grateful for her open acceptance of Lillie. Alexandra spent more time in Copenhagen with her own family and they came to visit her more often than before. Whatever she felt inside, Alexandra set the tone, and her acceptance of Lillie prompted Society to do the same.

That does not mean that Society's ladies unanimously accepted Lillie. She was breaking all the accepted rules in flaunting her relationship with the Prince of Wales. Officially, she had to be included in all invitations offered to the prince, but Lillie was in no doubt that apart from a handful, Society's ladies would not share Princess Alexandra's gracious generosity.

Was Lillie in love? She was certainly flattered, and by being accepted in Society, she had achieved more than her wildest ambitions. Established by the side of the Prince of Wales, no door was closed to her. In her memoirs, she writes of her amazement at the adulation she attracted once the public became aware of her new status. Until now, her image had circulated widely through photographers' postcards, but from the time of her association with the Prince of Wales, Lillie inspired the kind of public hysteria generated by pop stars today.

Whatever she wore, it was imitated; cheap versions of her hats appeared immediately in stores throughout London. The simple twist of velvet around her head with a feather attached became the "Langtry hat" and copies appeared in all the milliners' shops. Other accessories followed: the "Langtry shoe," the "Langtry knot" (of hair), and something called the "Langtry dress-improver." Lillie was venerated and imitated. The Prince of Wales placed her in his carriage for the royal parade down the grass racetrack at Ascot in front of the stands. They were escorted by outriders in scarlet livery and his equerries on horseback in shiny black top hats and frock coats. The particular shade of pink she wore that day became the color of the season, just as her muffs, shoes, cloaks and parasols resulted in sweatshop imitation. Lillie became the ideal every woman aspired to, beautiful, adored by the heir to the throne, and liberated. They copied her hairstyles as well as her clothes—anything to have a little of her life. The simple black dress that was a part of her initial appeal had given way to a fabulous wardrobe from the fashionable couturiers Worth and Ducret. She wore picture hats and elaborate dresses trimmed with pearls or tea-gowns edged with silver fox. When she walked in the Park, "people ran after me in droves, staring me out of countenance and even lifting my sunshade to satisfy their curiosity." It was customary for a lady's lover to pay the dressmaker's accounts and no doubt the Prince of Wales did the same. In fact, Lillie is often credited with the simplification of the elaborate fashions of the time. She wrote that man could dress as he liked; so woman should be entitled to "break the chains of fashion's tyranny and strike out on her own."

The London home of the Prince and Princess of Wales was Marlbrough House, which was often the setting for Lillie to shine in Bertie's circle. It was the most glamorous destination in London, a large house on the Mall, its huge ballroom used regularly for the entertainments of the royal couple. Strict protocol was observed, liveried servants attended, and yet the evenings spent there were always convivial. Only when all the guests had arrived would the Prince and Princess of Wales make their entrance and everyone would curtsy and bow. Alexandra stunned with her beauty and Bertie with his energy and good humor. Dancing was energetic, wine and champagne flowed and the food was delicious. On his many visits to France, Bertie had learned to live well.

SINCE HER CHILDHOOD, when she and her brother Reggie smuggled Flirt into a race in their first effort at training and riding a racer, Lillie had been enthralled by the world of the turf. The year he met Lillie was also the year the Prince of Wales first ran his own stable of horses; his racing colors of purple, gold braid and scarlet sleeves* were

---

* These are still the royal colors used by Queen Elizabeth II. Another exclusive royal distinction is a gold tassel on the jockey's black velvet cap.

first seen at Newmarket in July 1877. Among the prince's friends who joined in with his racing calendar were the Beresford brothers, the Lords Marcus, Charles and William, all superb horsemen and connoisseurs of thoroughbreds. Lillie adored their company, describing them as "handsome as paint and as merry as the traditional Irishman or sandboys . . . full of native wit, charm and bonhomie." June and July were spent at the numerous smart race meetings—Ascot, Goodwood, Newmarket—and Lillie loved everything about them.

She wrote: "As far as I am concerned the pleasures of the turf do not merely consist in owning horses and seeing them win. I like the routine of racing. The fresh air, the picnic lunch, the rural surroundings, all tend to make a race meeting a delightful outing."* Much later she would be a successful owner herself.† It seems Lillie met Prime Minister Disraeli one year just before Ascot. He was in his second term and felt confident enough to ask the Prince of Wales's mistress quizzically, " 'What can I do for you, my dear?' Without hesitation, Lillie replied, 'Four new gowns for Ascot.' 'You are a very sensible young woman,' commented the prime minister. 'Many a young woman would have asked to have been made a duchess in her own right.' "‡

Due to the spread of her pictures, Lillie was recognized everywhere and even chased down the street. Shopkeepers had to usher her out their back doors and even duchesses stood on chairs at balls to get a better look at her. A look-alike was mobbed in the Park until she fainted and had to be taken to the hospital. Lillie was a sensation; but she never lost her head, since she fully realized that this popularity depended on her association with the heir to the throne.

She wrote of being overwhelmed by all the attention she was receiving—"the murmur as I entered a room; to see my portrait roped around for protection at the Royal Academy" made her think London must have gone mad. In this famous portrait, *A Jersey Lily,* by Millais, Lillie is wearing her signature black dress, with just a lace collar and cuffs, and she appears in three-quarter profile holding a species of amaryllis that grows on Guernsey. Millais mistakenly called it a "Jersey Lily." So it remained, and the name clung to Lillie from then on. To

* Langtry, *The Days I Knew.*
† Lillie Langtry's horses would twice win the Cesarewitch.
‡ Langtry, *The Days I Knew.*

Millais, she was not only beautiful but, he claimed, for ten minutes out of every hour, she looked "amazing." Poynter painted her in seductive apricot yellow silk; Frederick Watts put her back in her black dress as *The Dean's Daughter,* and Edward Burne-Jones used her as a model for two of the faces in his painting *The Golden Stair.*

There is another interesting portrait of Lillie by Burne-Jones depicting her as "Dame Fortune" turning a wheel on which "kings, princes, statesmen, millionaires and others rise, reach the top, and then fall," as Lillie wrote in retrospect in her memoirs. The famous critic George Smalley saw her posing for Whistler in his studio and described her coloring as "brilliant and at the same time delicate; the attitude all grace. There was a harmony and a contrast all in one: the harmony such as Whistler loved; the contrast such as it pleased her Maker to arrange; between softness and strength; the lines of the woman's full body flowing gently into each other, but the whole impression was one of vital force." When Smalley came with other critics to view Whistler's portrait of another famous beauty, Miss Connie Gilchrist, he wrote describing Lillie's strong personality and opinions: "Mrs. Langtry, who even in those days passed Acts of Parliament for her private use, took command of the situation," and declared the portrait lovely.* No matter what the other guests, critics or even Whistler himself thought, the Act had been passed.

THE FACT OF her association with the Prince of Wales would have resulted in extensive credit everywhere, but Edward Langtry's Irish rents were unreliable, and as it was not the prince's habit to "keep" his mistresses, Lillie would have had to find an income elsewhere. It is highly likely that she received a percentage from the "professional beauty" photographs of her sold extensively as postcards. Throughout her life, Lillie proved she was a tough businesswoman, and she was not alone in taking such percentages. Other "P.B.'s" far richer than Lillie were doing the same. Lillie made an arrangement with one pop-

* Quoted in Beatty, *Lillie Langtry.*

ular photographer to receive a commission in exchange for his taking exclusive pictures of her and she studied the proofs very carefully.

The Prince of Wales was never followed on his assignations or hounded by reporters. Nonetheless, visiting Lillie in the afternoons in her rather modest house presented difficulties. Lillie gave small dinners there in décor enlivened by her friend Whistler, who painted the sky on her ceiling and gilded palm-leaf fans to decorate the purple walls of the drawing room. Oscar Wilde's touch was water lilies floating in glass bowls. Lillie mentions in her memoirs Bertie's consideration for the staff and that "he really worked hard to make one's dinners and parties successful—an easy task with his magnetic personality."

In that first year of their relationship, the prince decided to solve the problem of private encounters by building Lillie a house in the fashionable seaside resort of Bournemouth. Known as "the Red House" because of its red brick lower story, it was in the Tudor style and not untypical of the home of any other successful professional man. The foundation stone simply states the date, 1877, and the initials E.L.L.—presumably for Emilie Le Breton Langtry. This royal love nest was officially leased to one Emily Charlotte Langton and therefore had no connection with the Prince of Wales. Lillie was not mercenary, but she must have realized that to hold the interest of one of London's greatest womanizers was virtually impossible for long, and that she must think about the future.

Lillie wrote of her time spent at the Red House with the prince: "My only purpose in life was to look nice and make myself agreeable." This she did in what was an eminently sensible middle-class domestic environment, with a scenic view that must have given her great pleasure. The house stood on the top of sandstone cliffs and its large south-facing windows gave onto the beach below and the wide sea's horizon. The Prince of Wales was thirty-six and Lillie twenty-three.

Neither Prince Edward nor Lillie was sentimental. "Let us not fuss, please," became her answer to difficult situations. They were both practical and businesslike. In the society in which Lillie moved, she was remarkable in that she never gossiped, complained or explained, and although Edward loved to sit and chat with the ladies, he was never known to discuss anyone's personal affairs. In their domestic habits they were oddly alike, rising early, dressing quickly, eating simply breakfasts—he had coffee, she had China tea, both had toast and the morning papers. Unlike Princess Alexandra, Lillie could pin up her hair in minutes and be ready punctually. Carved onto one wall of the dining room at the Red House was the inscription: *"They say—What they say? Let them say."* It expressed their feelings. Later, Lillie wrote: "I have always been willing to take the blame for things I have done."

Many in the Marlborough House set could not fathom the attraction. After all, Society was full of beautiful, delightful young ladies fresh out of the schoolroom. But Bertie and Lillie suited one another. Lillie was clearly a sensual woman, who had not received physical satisfaction from her husband. She was ambitious and had not yet succumbed to any of the adoring gallants she had met. Perhaps she was always waiting to catch the biggest fish of all? Like so many princes throughout history, Edward was easily bored, and Lillie's disdain of most men, as well as her ambition, appealed to him.

Taught to be fearless by her many brothers if she wanted to keep up with them, although she could play the wilting flower, Lillie was something of an Amazon. She was never physically afraid, another trait she shared with the prince. Once, a carriage door was accidentally shut on his hand, but he brushed it off as nothing although it must have hurt a great deal. Despite the constant threat of nihilist assassins, the prince refused to be protected. Of course he was, surreptitiously. On his frequent visits to Paris he was unaware that the closest of the crowds around him were plain-clothed police officers. When a fifteen-year-old Belgian student fired a gun at him from just four feet away, Bertie's only comment was what a poor shot the boy must have been.

On the last Friday in July every year, the Prince and Princess of Wales gave a ball at Marlborough House that marked the end of the London season. Three days later, everyone left for Goodwood and the racing. In 1877 the Langtrys joined the Prince of Wales, who was staying with Baron Ferdinand de Rothschild (whom Lillie disliked), and then went on to Cowes on the Isle of Wight, where not only Society but even foreign royalty and European grandees arrived with their boats. Everyone who was anyone would be a member of the Royal Yacht Squadron, situated overlooking the harbor. The week spent racing their yachts thrilled those taking part and those watching from the deck of some great and elegant ship. Sailing was as much to Bertie's taste as horse racing and Mr. and Mrs. Langtry were made welcome. Ned no longer had a yacht—he had been obliged to sell his last two—but they were invited by Sir Allen Young, the friend who had brought Lillie into the prince's life. Lillie and Ned stayed on Alleno's yacht *Helen,* moored next to the royal yacht, the *Osborne.* Born and brought up on Jersey, sea and wind enthralled the tomboy in Lillie. Even Ned came out of himself when around boats and became friendly with the Danish royal family. According to Lillie's memoirs, the King and Queen of Denmark much enjoyed being rowed about by Ned in the *Helen*'s little dinghy. Each evening, the Prince of Wales gave dinners aboard the *Osborne*—sometimes they danced on the deck—and among the foreign royalty and the Austrian and German princes would be the exiled and widowed Empress Eugénie of France, said to be the most elegant of all the ladies in Europe. The Langtrys were always included. Years later, Lillie remembered how Sir Allen entertained "the Royal Party on the *Helen* for tea and a sail."

Lillie met the Danish royal family at Cowes and, being a fan of all royalty, exchanged photographs of herself for theirs. The prince introduced his beloved to everyone, including the Empress Eugénie. Since the fall of the Second Empire in 1870, she had been living in England and took a house each August at Cowes with her only child, her son the Prince Imperial. Louis-Napoleon was in his early twenties and a great favorite with Bertie. On one occasion, at a friend's seaside villa, Lillie encouraged some table-turning. Spiritualism was all the rage and Lillie seems to have believed in the power of the spirits to influence her destiny. The lights went out and the furniture flew. It did not take long to discover that the Prince Imperial was the "spirit." He was banished from the room and the group settled down to try again. This time, a ghostly figure was seen outside the window. Of course, it was the irrepressible Louis-Napoleon, completely covered in white flour. (Lillie was convinced her house in Norfolk Street was haunted and the staff swore to it as it stood near the site of Tyburn, where criminals used to hang.) The Prince of Wales loaned the Langtrys his yacht the *Hildegarde,* manned by sailors from the Royal Navy, on which Ned and Lillie sailed to Jersey. We do not know what the Reverend and Mrs. Le Breton thought about the relationship of their daughter with the Prince of Wales. Tourists came to stand outside the rectory, but the neighbors pretended nothing had changed in Lillie's circumstances.

With Cowes over, the round of country house parties began. While Lillie was staying with Lord Malmesbury, who prided himself on his chef's skill, he announced a splendid dish, gratin à la Grammont, and said Lillie should be the first to try it. She did, but it was so hot she burned her tongue so that her eyes watered. When her host demanded a comment, Lillie said it would be excellent if it were not cold. Astonished at his chef's lapse, Lord Malmesbury took a generous mouthful and almost choked on the boiling food, emptying all his glasses to put out the inner fire. On another occasion (it was raining) Lillie took a large silver tea tray from the sideboard and used it to toboggan down the staircase. The Prince of Wales was enchanted with her high spirits, so like his own, and roared with laughter at her tomfooleries. (Less so the host, who rescued his silver and locked it away.)

Weekends were known as "Saturday–to–Monday"—implying that gentlemen did not need to be in town to go to work for their living on a Monday morning. By the summer of 1877, all the Prince of Wales' hostesses realized that if they were to enjoy the company of the heir to the throne, they must invite the Langtrys. On the "Glorious 12th" (of August) the grouse shooting began, then pheasant shoots and foxhunting, all built around a huge house party, with dances and entertainments in the evenings after the sport. To entertain the Prince of Wales could be a ruinous honor, with between twenty and forty guests and their personal staff staying. But to own a photograph of Bertie sitting in the middle of such a large group, proving he had stayed at their house, was the ambition of anyone rich enough to entertain the heir to the throne—the highest social accolade of the Edwardian era.

Society was relatively small and everyone knew one another. Although the Princess of Wales was always invited with her husband, it had been her custom for some years to refuse and allow her husband to "go his own social way." These great houses were extremely comfortable and in a strange way, even cozy. Four-poster beds were hung with luxurious curtains and piled with deep soft pillows, the mattresses covered in exquisite linen, heavy with monograms and crowns. Rooms provided everything a guest would need—even a metal tub behind a screen. Of course, there would be no connecting bathroom. Enormous amounts of food were served and consumed—huge buffets for breakfasts and a minimum of ten courses for dinner, each with a different wine. As the men needed to change at least three times a day and the ladies at least four times, it would seem the most exercise was taken in dressing and undressing. While the men were out shooting, the ladies usually sat about waiting and gossiping until they changed into fancy tea-gowns for afternoon tea when the men returned. For dinner, the company would be in full evening dress.

Despite the opportunity for practical jokes, Lillie was not enchanted with these elaborate house parties and she disapproved of foxhunting and shooting. She never really enjoyed the company of women as much as men—she had not had the chance to make girl-friends as a child—and she did not know many Society ladies well. But she did enjoy learning about antiques and art, and some hosts, like Lord Malmesbury, would lead her around their remarkable collections. She wrote: "It was in these rooms that I learnt to distinguish the different periods of French furniture, china, etc. . . . It was, moreover, a pleasure to the owner to explain the most minute characteristics of each chair, cabinet, vase or table." There is a story that when Baron Alfred de Rothschild drew her aside from the dancing in his house and murmured, "What shall I give you, beautiful lady?" Lillie picked up an exquisite Louis XVI bejeweled gold box and said that would do very well. Gasping for air, the baron offered her something less precious instead.

House parties did give Lillie the opportunity to enjoy her genius at practical jokes. None of the prince's friends escaped without toothpaste in the toes of their slippers, apple-pie beds, pockets containing sticky candy, and so on. In her memoirs she described one occasion when a donkey was hoisted into a bedroom on the second floor, dressed in a nightgown and placed in the bed of a notorious young womanizer.

These great house parties were also renowned for the "corridor creeping" that took place at night. Married couples arrived together and often changed partners at night. After a brief exchange of signals, a whispered word here, a gentle touch there, a walk in the garden, an assignation for the night would be made. With up to forty guests in a house, it was not always easy to find one another's rooms, but outside on the door to each bedroom a brass slot contained a card giving the name of the occupant. Married couples invariably had separate rooms far apart. As all the guests came from the same society, there was little danger of scandal reaching the outside world, and discretion was paramount. After all, a gentleman's country house was a far more discreet venue than any hotel or restaurant.

At six in the morning, a gong rang to warn everyone back into their respective rooms ahead of the maids bringing up hot water or breakfast before the men left for the shoot. Should husbands and lovers meet while creeping along corridors to their respective bases, they would studiously ignore one another. Of course, amorous swains occasionally ended up in the wrong beds, with Feydeau-esque consequences. Serving maids were fair game, but no gentleman would be forgiven for seducing an unmarried lady. Nor could the staff behave as they saw their masters do. Should a member of staff be caught in flagrante with another servant, they were dismissed without references. The Edwardian era was one of double standards.

BY THE START of Lillie's second season, the summer of 1878, it seems all of the country suspected, and accepted, that Lillie Langtry was the mistress of the Prince of Wales. But if Alexandra appeared not to mind the affair, the same could not be said for Edward Langtry. According to Lillie, although they had ceased to have marital relations by the time they moved to Norfolk Street, Ned was not the complaisant husband of a royal favorite. He suffered from a mixture of jealousy and pride and had a violent temper.

There is a story that from Lord Malmesbury's house Lillie wrote a note to the prince to thank him for the gift of a small brooch. Edward Langtry saw writing on the blotter in Lillie's room, and, holding it up to a mirror, read it. There was a tremendous scene, with Lillie in tears and a furious host blaming the servants for not burning the blotting paper every day as instructed. Lillie informed the prince of her husband's anger. He immediately sent off a pair of monogrammed gold cufflinks, a typical royal gift, and arranged to have Edward Langtry presented at court. It seems Edward was mollified, though his drinking increased. As the prince said: "Society grows; it is not made." Lillie had certainly made her own place in Society, and judging from her memoirs, she may have enjoyed sex more than most women of her class. A rumor spread that Lillie was considered unsuitable to be presented to Queen Victoria. Lillie was afraid she might meet the queen by chance in public and be rebuffed, so Bertie immediately arranged for her to be presented to Her Majesty.

Whether the idea was Lillie's or Bertie's we do not know. Neither wrote or told anyone. Did Lillie need the public acknowledgment or did the prince want her to have it? Until Bertie came to the throne and abolished the custom of afternoon presentation, which he found irksome, it was essential for anyone who wished to be recognized as a genuine member of Society to be formally presented to the queen. Would this make Lillie somehow more acceptable? Under normal circumstances, ladies were presented during their first season. This was Lillie's second and also she was married, so a special exception was made for her by the Prince of Wales.

But first, in March 1878, Bertie personally presented Lillie's husband to his mother at a "levée." For confidence, Ned wore the gold cufflinks given him by the prince. It seems Queen Victoria spoke to him for all of five minutes, a rare occurrence. Lillie's presentation was to be some months later, in May,* at one of the queen's "Drawing Rooms," held at three in the afternoon. Mrs. Le Breton† came from Jersey to help her prepare. Months of practice preceded this important event in a young lady's progress into the world. But it was not only debutantes straight out of the schoolroom who went through the ritual. Foreigners, those who lived in the colonies, the foreign wives of Englishmen, or those who had achieved a senior position in

---

* May was also the month her portrait by Poynter was exhibited at the Royal Academy to such aplomb.

† Mrs. Le Breton had reached the end of her endurance with her shameless husband. Lillie decided to build her mother a house next to hers in Bournemouth, which would help with appearances.

public life—all could be presented provided they had a suitable sponsor. Bertie made sure that Lillie did, appointing a lady of the queen's household to accompany her.

Lillie was determined to make her presentation a success so that the prince could see her receive Society's acknowledgment of her position. She had chosen an ivory brocade dress, low cut, with a long train from the shoulders in the style made popular by the Empress Josephine. Her nine-foot-long train was lined in yellow. The queen had complained that the obligatory headdresses fixed to a tulle veil that the "presentees" were obliged to wear in their hair were becoming far too small and insignificant, and must be "at least visible to the naked eye." Lillie, daring as ever, chose three very tall white ostrich plumes, carefully arranged in the coil of hair at the nape of her neck: to stand up in exact imitation of the Prince of Wales' signature crest. The German motto of the Prince of Wales, then as now, is *"Ich dien"*—"I serve." Lillie noted that later that evening, the Prince of Wales "chaffed me good-humouredly on my conscientious observance of the Lord Chamberlain's order."

Lillie had hoped that by remaining at the end of the line her turn would come so late that the queen would have left and handed over the task to the prince and princess, as was her custom. But Lillie had not reckoned on the queen's curiosity. Victoria had certainly heard of Lillie Langtry's beauty and her association with her son and heir. Out of curiosity, the queen remained until the very end when Lillie came forward second from the last. The prince had sent her a wonderful bouquet of pale yellow Maréchal Neil roses to match the silk ones on her dress. Before she gave her card to the Lord Chamberlain, she heard him inform the queen that "Mrs. Langtry comes next, Your Majesty." Lillie trembled.

According to Lillie's memoirs, Queen Victoria looked annoyed when Lillie curtseyed to her, quite possibly for having been kept waiting for so long. Lillie was very nervous and rather afraid of the queen, but also of failing to execute the complicated ritual of stepping backward after her curtsy and catching her train, expertly tossed to her by a page. Despite her black mourning attire, Queen Victoria glittered with diamonds and orders, and tiny as she was, exuded great authority. She held out her hand and seemed to look through Lillie: "Queen

Victoria looked straight in front of her, and I thought, extended her hand in a rather perfunctory manner. There was not even the flicker of a smile on her face, and she looked grave and tired." Lillie's final word on the experience was that all the fuss for a few moments in the presence of the queen "made it seem a great deal of labour lost." It seems the Prince of Wales did not like to see the same dress twice. The fact that he saw so much of Lillie implies that she was able to surprise him and keep him guessing. In this she succeeded brilliantly at her presentation—her total ensemble was deemed a triumph.

The torment over, that evening there was a ball given at Marlborough House: Lillie had arrived. The prince seemed delighted with her performance and with her recklessness. Now she could be invited to balls at Buckingham Palace—occasions that were not exactly pleasurable due to their formality, but still the most important of the season. "These balls at Buckingham Palace completely realized my girlish dreams of fairyland," wrote Lillie. It is understandable that she was impressed by the ladies dazzling in their wonderful family jewels, the colorful liveries of the footmen, the gentlemen blazing decorations and sashes, and the Prince and Princess of Wales in their midst, the most impressive of them all. While sedate dances were the norm at the palace—"a preponderance of stately square measures"—at Marlborough House, "waltzes, gallops and the polka, with an occasional 'Highland schottische' after supper," were the norm.

There was only one other occasion when Lillie could have met the queen, and that was later the same year when she was included in a party of friends staying in Scotland for some shoots. The group decided to pay their respects to the sovereign by signing the visitor's book at Balmoral. This was the polite custom carried out without any intention of actually meeting with the queen. Only after the party had left did the queen realize Lillie had been there and send a rider after them. He was too late and missed them.

By now Lillie had met many of Bertie's relations: his in-laws the King and Queen of Denmark, Christian IX and Queen Louise—"remarkable for their simple manners and their affability to everyone" *; King Oscar II of Sweden; the future Emperor and Empress Frederick

* Langtry, *The Days I Knew.*

of Prussia (she was Bertie's sister Vicky); and of course, Bertie's two eldest sons, Prince Albert Victor (known as Eddy) and Prince George. In September 1879, Lillie gave a small charm bought at Cowes' jeweler's shop to Eddy, a dull boy, and another to his fourteen-year-old brother as they left for a seven-month cruise to the West Indies. Eddy was only really liked by his mother, so Lillie's kind gesture must have meant a lot. He told her he attached his gift to his watch chain. "I had to take off my grandmother's locket to make room for it."*

◦ʃʃ~

IT WAS AT the end of Lillie's second season that she became close to Oscar Wilde, who made it his mission to educate her. When he took her to a lecture on Greek art at King's College, London, not only did the cheering students mob them, but Lillie was asked to sit facing the audience as a living exponent of Attic beauty. Wilde urged her to study Latin as well and admonished her when Society's demands had her fall behind with her homework. Lillie was not taken in by Oscar's attentions and saw them for what they were—full of self-interest—but she was entertained by him and she was learning. They were foils for one another and both benefitted. Oscar wrote mock-petulantly to a friend: "The lily is so tiresome. She won't do what I tell her . . . I assure her that she owes it to herself and to us to drive daily through the Park dressed entirely in black, in a black Victoria drawn by black horses, and with 'Venus Annodomini' emblazoned on her black bonnet in dull sapphires, but she won't do it." The irreverent Oscar Wilde added to her praise by declaring that Lillie's beauty was as nothing compared with "Her charm, her wit and her mind—what a mind—[these] are far more formidable weapons."† Lillie had valid opinions and always spoke her mind; and by now she was extremely well read.

Despite her reservations, Lillie did lend Oscar the Poynter *Jersey Lily* portrait so that he could display it on an easel in the center of his white-paneled drawing room. There illustrious guests like Henry Irving and Ellen Terry were encouraged to sign their names on the

---

* Langtry, *The Days I Knew.*
† Walford Graham Robertson, *Time Was.*

panels. Oscar's next act of homage was to alter one of his poems in her honor. The first line, which originally read, "a fair slim boy, not made for this world's pain," became

A lily-girl, not made for this world's pain
With brown, soft hair close braided by her ears
And longing eyes half veiled by slumberous tears
Like blue water seen through mists of rain . . . *

Wilde then wrote a lengthy panygyric entitled "The New Helen" for her, had it bound in white vellum and dedicated it on the flyleaf: "to Helen, formerly of Troy, now of London." It was wearisome stuff and Lillie was not overwhelmed.

A year before his death, Oscar said there were three women in his life he really admired: Queen Victoria, Sarah Bernhardt and Lillie Langtry. "I would have married any one of them with pleasure." But it was more Lillie's notoriety that attracted him. This effete dandy let it be known he was in love with her. Lillie was never deceived but she enjoyed learning from him—even Italian. She did not present Oscar to the Prince of Wales, who only met him years later in Germany. Wilde was a successful playwright by that time and involved with the young Lord Alfred Douglas. Lillie's final word on Wilde was a quote from Sir Herbert Tree: " 'Oscar turned his words into gems and flung them at the moon.' "

IT SEEMS CERTAIN that for the first two or three years of the relationship, the prince was faithful to Lillie. His concern for her welfare, his touching correspondence when away gave every impression of a man devoted. When Lillie was not by his side he even boasted to her that he found himself, to his own surprise, not flirting. His solicitous letters always began "My fair Lily" and ended with his initials, A.E., for Albert Edward.

But that did not stop Lillie from receiving the unwanted atten-

* "Madonna Mia."

tions of other suitors. One who was most unwelcome was that legendary lecher King Leopold II of the Belgians, who enjoyed making incognito visits to London. When he presented himself uninvited and unexpected at Norfolk Street at nine one morning, Lillie hastened to dress and receive him. Stiff, polite conversation followed. The next day when he called again at 9 a.m., Lillie threw protocol to the winds and declined to descend.

Another unrequited but persistent suitor was the twenty-year-old Crown Prince Rudolf of Austria-Hungary. He arrived in London late in 1879, and Baron Ferdinand de Rothschild was to give a ball in his honor. In order to attract the most beautiful of Society's ladies, he offered all the "professional beauties" a new ball gown from Ducret— the best and most extravagant couturier of the time. Naturally, they accepted. Lillie's dress was pale pink crêpe-de-chine, and ravishing.

The young Rudolf could not have been unaware of Lillie's relationship with the Prince of Wales, who was also present. Perhaps he felt as a crown prince he too had a right to her favors. He was instantly captivated by Lillie and insisted on almost every dance. When supper came and Lillie was not included in the separate "royal" supper room, a message came that Austria's crown prince "insisted" she be placed next to him. After dinner, again Lillie was claimed by Prince Rudolf, who danced with her so energetically that he was marking her dress with his sweaty hands. Gently, Lillie asked if he would wear his gloves, whereupon the prince insisted, ungallantly, that it was *she* who perspired, not him.

Although she may have been flattered for a while, and the Prince of Wales seems to have been bemused, Lillie would never have risked endangering her relationship with Bertie at this time. Whenever Rudolf called, Lillie insisted her husband be present. One day, when Ned was away fishing, Rudolf presented her with a beautiful emerald ring (with bedroom strings clearly attached). Lillie reacted furiously and pretended to throw the ring into the fire. The young prince's frantic scrabbling for the jewel among the hot coals so disgusted her that she apparently told Somerset Maugham, "I could never have loved him after that." Of course she kept the ring.*

---

* Some years later, Lillie visited Austria and was graciously entertained by Prince Rudolf.

The foreign gutter press reacted as one might expect. One newspaper noted: "Lovely Lillie Langtry has added another royal scalp to her fast-growing collection." It was not true, but when was the truth allowed to spoil a good story? However Lillie tried, Rudolf would not be discouraged until his worried father, the Emperor Franz Joseph, cancelled the rest of his heir's Grand Tour and summoned him home.

It was all to much for Morton Frewen, the donor of Redskin, who wrote: "Quite impossible to compete with Prince Rudolf, much less the Prince of Wales." He sailed for America, to be confronted by a reporter in New York asking if he too had had an affair with Lillie. Frewen replied, "Alas, no," but added that he found her a bit dull, as she was always surrounded by people. "A lily," he added, "to bloom as it should, must be planted in its bed." It would take Lillie years to forgive him. She only did so when she herself came to America.

Had Lillie succumbed to Prince Rudolf, it would certainly never have remained a secret. However, a suitcase of love letters has been found, written by Lillie around this time over a period of some four years to a childhood friend from Jersey, called Arthur Jones.* The tone of these sixty-five passionate letters makes it clear Lillie was really in love with Arthur Jones and not the Prince of Wales. However, it was in both their interests to keep this relationship secret, and they did. Lillie may have loved Arthur but her future lay with the Prince of Wales. More and more often Lillie would appear in public as a woman driven only by ambition and without a heart; but her letters to Arthur Jones totally disprove this impression. "Please, please hurry back," she writes while with the Prince of Wales. "I want you so much."

IN 1879, THE Prince of Wales was still so infatuated with Lillie that he cancelled his annual "bachelor trip" to Hamburg. His contentment with Lillie resulted in his being much kinder to his wife, and instead, he took her to visit her family in Copenhagen. Ever the realist, Lillie knew that her time at Society's pinnacle and on the arm of the Prince of Wales was limited.

---

* Jones was one of the many illegitimate children of Lord Ranelagh.

In an effort to keep the attention and affection of the prince, Lillie's evening dresses became more extravagant. She describes one she wore to a Marlborough House ball as being of yellow tulle, "draped with a wide-meshed gold fish-net, in which preserved butter-flies of every hue and size were held in glittering captivity. . . . It could hardly have been considered a very serviceable garment, for the Prince of Wales told me that, the morning after, he picked up many of the insects, which were lying about the ballroom floor." But the bills were accumulating—Lillie referred to them as "our pigmy ocean of debt"—as Ned's income from his Irish rents dwindled and their lifestyle continued way beyond their means.

◈

BY LILLIE'S THIRD season, the spring of 1880, the ground rules be-tween her and her royal lover had shifted even further. On the pretext of visiting her family on Jersey, Lillie arrived but stayed only two days, moving on to meet with the Prince of Wales in Paris. She had her own suite at the Hôtel Bristol, as did the prince, naturally incognito and on a strictly private visit. Of course the French press knew exactly who they were and followed them—on carriage rides in the Bois de Boulogne, in fashionable restaurants, to Maxim's, where Bertie was said to have kissed Lillie on the dance floor, to pavement cafés where they sat and sipped coffee or liqueurs. Fascinated by ladies' attire, Bertie took Lillie to the grand house of Worth, the Empress Eu-génie's couturier, and bought her a complete new wardrobe. Accord-ing to the press, the prince also bought her two magnificent diamond bracelets, a large diamond and emerald ring, and a very large ruby and diamond brooch. These superb pieces were worn by Lillie all her life.

To be totally incognito was impossible for the Prince of Wales and he was naturally shadowed by officials who hid behind shrubs or lampposts whenever the lovers came near. The couple met the sev-enty-eight-year-old famous lothario and playwright Victor Hugo, saw his play starring Sarah Bernhardt and dined at his house. He offered Lillie the now famous toast: "Madame, I can celebrate your beauty in only one way, by wishing I were three years younger."

They visited Monte Carlo and there Lillie met for the first time

Bertie's young cousin-by-marriage, Prince Louis of Battenberg. He was to have a dramatic impact on her life. At the French coast, Lillie and the Prince of Wales parted ways, she heading for another brief stay on Jersey, the prince to England. During her absence, Edward Langtry had visited his father in Ulster in the hope that he might pay his debts. To his shock, his father insisted that Edward divorce Lillie on account of her adultery with the Prince of Wales or he would cut his son off without a penny. For reasons of his own, Ned absolutely and unequivocally refused to hear a word about divorce.

Despite Ned's financial troubles, Lillie was at her peak of fame and adulation. The famous lyricist W. S. Gilbert and his partner the composer Sir Arthur Sullivan wrote and scored these lives about her:

> Oh, never, never, never
> since I joined the human race
> Saw I so exquisitely fair a face.*

Lillie was the most admired woman in England. But it seems that the Prince of Wales, notoriously fickle, had surreptitiously drifted away into the arms of others now and then and was sometimes seen with another professional beauty, Mrs.—(and for decency's sake) Mr.— Luke Wheeler. And then the "divine" Sarah Bernhardt came to town with the Comédie Française. She had arrived the previous season to enormous acclaim, both for the skill of her acting on the stage and her extraordinary behavior off it. With Oscar Wilde as her "official" escort—thereby once again adding to his own fame—she was seen everywhere. Lillie came to know Bernhardt through Oscar Wilde and they became life-long friends. Not conventionally pretty, Sarah did everything she could to make herself appear astonishing, and succeeded. Her kohl-rimmed eyes stared out of a white-powdered face above the scarlet lips, and her slim, angular body was draped in sinuous fabrics, opening in the front. She admitted she even rouged her earlobes as "I went to extremes in everything." It would seem the divine Sarah had nothing to lose. Born the illegitimate daughter of a Jewish actress, she had an illegitimate son of her own. Lillie summed

* From *Trial by Jury*, quoted in Beatty, *Lillie Langtry*.

up her amazing talent: "Her superb diction, her lovely silken voice, her natural acting, her passionate temperament, her fire—in a word, transcendent genius—caused amazement."

Perhaps inevitably, with his great interest in the theater, the Prince of Wales was also fascinated by Sarah Bernhardt. He had met her years earlier in Paris and always called on her when there, the last time together with Lillie. When the actress arrived in London the previous season, the prince sponsored her acceptance into Society and invitations followed.

At twenty-seven, the "Jersey Lily" had reached such a pinnacle that she may not even have felt any little pangs of jealousy over Sarah's success with the prince. Lillie was mobbed wherever she went, painted by the best artists, and photographers lived up to take her picture. One photograph was even buried in the foundations of Cleopatra's Needle, an ancient Egyptian obelisk, when, in 1878, it was re-erected on the embankment beside the Thames in London. All this was due to her beauty—and her association with the Prince of Wales.

And Lillie had not been faithful, either. Not only was she still conducting an affair with Arthur Jones and writing him passionate love letters; there were others. According to Daisy, Countess of Warwick's, memoirs, it seems Lillie was sharing her charms with Lord Londsdale and Sir George Chetwynd.* Then there was her fledgling affair with the nineteen-year-old Lord Shrewsbury, encouraged by his mother for the boy's experience. Unfortunately, Lillie was with Shrewsbury one afternoon when the prince arrived at her house. He was not at all pleased.

Then as now, members of the royal family were considered legitimate targets by the popular press, but it took almost three years for the Prince of Wales' open liaison with Lillie Langtry to make the tabloids. The magazine that publicly exposed their relationship was called *Town Talk* and was edited by Adolphus Rosenberg. The article alleged that Ned had cited the Prince of Wales and two other gentlemen as co-respondents in a divorce suit. Publication of these allegations caused a sensation, but as the Langtrys did not issue a denial, Rosenberg continued writing. The next article mentioned that Lillie's

* Lord Londsdale was alleged to have been cited by Ned in a divorce petition, and a case of love letters written by Lillie to Sir George Chetwynd was auctioned in London in 2004.

picture could be seen on display in shops beside such lowlife as "well-known harlots. The question arises " 'Who is Mrs. Langtry?' " The journalist answered by saying enigmatically that "there was something not very pleasing to the loyal mind to see, in a dozen shop windows, Mrs. Langtry side by side or else beneath the Prince of Wales. . . ."

The Langtrys remained mute. The tirade from Rosenberg continued in the time-honored mock outrage of the gutter press. The two other co-respondents were named as Lord Lonsdale and Lord Londesborough. Still no response from the Langtrys.

Suddenly, and without reason, *Town Talk* claimed that Edward Langtry had withdrawn his petition for divorce and that he would shortly be posted to a diplomatic mission abroad. Lillie's plans, it added, were not known. But it was Lillie's friend, the lovely Patsy Cornwallis-West, who finally silenced Rosenberg. In the same issue of *Town Talk* in which Edward Langtry was allegedly removing his petition for divorce, the editor unwisely accused Patsy of making a fortune out of selling photographs for which she had posed in a number of studios and darkrooms set up in her home. George Cornwallis-West sued for libelling both his family and the Langtrys. On the stand, Ned denied having filed for divorce, and claimed he and Lillie were a happily married couple. His counsel added that the Langtrys frequented high society and that the Prince and Princess of Wales were frequent callers. He blamed the accusations on the editor's greed to make a profit on Lillie's fame, which was solely due to her beauty. Nor had Edward Langtry been offered a diplomatic posting. Rosenberg was imprisoned for eighteen months and the wags noted that "there was nothing between the Prince of Wales and Lillie Langtry; not even a sheet."

DURING THE SEASON of 1880, due to the trial, for the first time the whiff of scandal attached itself to Lillie Langtry. Her position in Society became harder to maintain. Lillie wrote that their "waning income had reached almost vanishing point" and bailiffs were knocking on the door. Ned had tried and failed to raise the money at home in Ireland to meet their debts. When the bailiffs called, Ned "frequently found it convenient to go fishing, leaving me to deal with the unwelcome intruders as best I could." He had sold his yachts already, and also Cliffe Lodge. His carriage and horses now went, as well as the staff—a butler, the cook, a coachman, and Lillie's maid. Dominique would fill her pockets and those of the guests with Lillie's jewels to save them from the bailiffs and her friends also helped remove precious items. Even the Prince of Wales left the house on Norfolk Street with a gold hand mirror in his jacket. "With money troubles as constant companions, there can be no compensation for the intolerable worry and anxiety," Lillie noted.

More anxious now than ever to hold on to the prince's interest, Lillie became less and less discreet. At a charity fête, gentlemen were asked to pay a guinea for the thrill of being given a cup of tea by Lillie Langtry once she had taken the first sip. When the Prince and Princess of Wales came to her stall with their children, Lillie poured the prince a cup and took the first sip without his asking; gently, the prince requested a "clean cup."

Then there was the famous "ice-down-the-back" incident. The Prince and Princess of Wales attended Lord Randolph Churchill's costume ball, the prince dressed as Pierrot but Alexandra in quite another outfit. Unsurprisingly, Lillie came as Pierrette. Accounts differ as to the exact details of the incident, but some guests claimed that Lillie, who rarely drank alcohol, had too much champagne. Eyewitnesses claimed that the banter between the prince and Lillie was becoming indelicate, that they argued, and Lillie was said to have popped an ice cube down the back of Bertie's costume. Instantly, the atmosphere changed. Lillie had gone too far. Eyewitnesses said the Prince of Wales fixed her with a cold stare, turned and left, his wife following hurriedly behind. All her life Lillie denied this act of lèse majesté, but the story stuck. Bertie was not the first nor the last Prince of Wales whose friends had to walk a fine line between friendliness and familiarity. Of course the prince forgave her and they remained close.

IN 1851, THE third son of the Grand Duke of Hesse had shocked his family by marrying a commoner, Countess Julie Hauke, daughter of a Russian general of Polish and Flemish descent and a French mother. Their four sons, designated princes of Battenberg, were each in their way outstanding and extremely good-looking. However, they were excluded from the Hesse inheritance and only "Serene Highnesses," not "Royal." This seems so unimportant today; but at the time it mattered a great deal, and the four Battenberg princes—Louis, Alexander, Henry and Franz Josef—would strive all their lives to excel.

Louis was tall, dark and extremely handsome. Having become a naturalized British subject, he joined the Royal Navy in 1863 at the age of fourteen. Louis worked seriously and conscientiously, gaining the respect of his peers, and was destined to go far. Although he worked hard, he also played hard and was known as an irresistible lothario. Related by marriage,* Bertie thoroughly enjoyed entertaining his high-spirited young cousin and may well have thought him the ideal person to inherit his position in Lillie's life. The Prince of Wales' passion for Lillie was on the wane. Although their "romance" would continue only spasmodically for many years, throughout his life Bertie's friendship and support never wavered.

As a senior sublieutenant aboard HMS *Serapis,* Louis had accompanied Bertie to India and formed a solid friendship with the heir to the British throne. After two years serving on HMS *Sultan,* Prince Louis arrived back in England in August 1878. No doubt due to Bertie's intervention, the Admiralty did not seem in a hurry to reemploy young Louis, and he spent much of his time with his older royal cousin while officially serving on HMS *Agincourt* and also on the royal yacht *Osborne* in commission at Cowes. With his striking blue eyes, dark short beard and the nonchalance of most naval officers, Prince Louis seemed irresistible to women. In fact, Lillie and Louis had met several times with Bertie the previous season, but it was only when Lillie realized that Bertie was encouraging them both that she felt free to explore this new possibility.

Lillie understood that the Prince of Wales would always be entertained by her and that she would retain his affection and remain his friend, but she took advantage of her situation in his circle to look about

---

* The Prince of Wales' sister, Alice, had married the Grand Duke of Hesse.

for her next protector. When Prince Louis was brought into her close circle, possibly with the connivance of the Prince of Wales, this dashing young naval officer and Lillie fell passionately in love. They had much in common. Beautiful and young, they shared a love of the absurd, of daredevil pranks, and of the artistic world of bohemia. With Ned away on arranged fishing trips—no doubt with the assistance of the Prince of Wales' friends—Lillie could be alone with Louis in Norfolk Street or at country house parties. As no gentleman could marry a divorcée, the couple never had that option. Prince Louis would have been cashiered from the navy. Having lived with the taint of his parents' morganatic marriage, he would never have done the same.

While at Cowes, Louis and Lillie danced often on the royal yacht and it seems Princess Alexandra was not unaware of the attraction between the young couple. One evening in 1880, Lillie became ill at one of the princess' small dinner parties. Alexandra urged her to go home and immediately sent her own doctor in attendance. The next day, when Lillie was lying on her sofa in her little sitting room, "the butler suddenly announced Her Royal Highness. The honour of the unexpected visit brought me at once to my feet, ill though I felt, but the Princess insisted on my lying down again, while she made herself tea, chatting kindly and graciously. She always used a specially manufactured violet scent and I recall exclaiming on the delicious perfume, and her solicitous answer that she feared possibly it was too strong for me." In fact, Lillie was pregnant.*

Lillie told Louis she was pregnant, and Louis told his parents. The pregnancy had to be kept secret. This presented the three involved parties, the Prince of Wales, Prince Louis and Lillie, with a dilemma. To resolve the first problem, Ned was sent to Ireland to try to recoup some of his income, though Lillie knew he would spend more time fishing—a sport he loved and that was cheap. Louis' parents arranged a financial settlement for Lillie and set about getting a naval posting for their son.

Possibly the most attractive quality of the Prince of Wales was his loyalty to his friends. Bertie was very fond of his young cousin Louis,

---

* Lillie seems not to have been sure herself who the father was. At this time she wrote to Arthur Jones asking him for medicine from the chemist to ascertain if she really was pregnant. Her note implied that he was the father.

and knew that should the truth of Lillie's pregnancy become known, and the likelihood of Louis' being the father, the young prince's naval career would be ruined by the scandal. He was regarded as a promising naval officer. Her husband's bankruptcy gave Lillie the excuse to "retire" to Jersey and there hide her spreading waistline. *The New York Times* reported that "Mr. and Mrs. Langtry have given up their London residence, and for the present Mrs. Langtry remains in Jersey. Is beauty deposed or has beauty abdicated?"

In fact, few in Society were aware of Lillie's relationship with the younger prince, and if there was innuendo, Bertie took the responsibility for Lillie's condition upon himself. This was both generous and typical of him, and frankly, the association with Lillie did more to enhance his reputation than harm it. Times were changing.

As all births in England and Wales had to be registered at Somerset House in London, it was easier for Lillie to give birth abroad. Bertie sent her to Paris with her mother and her faithful maid from Jersey, Dominique. There they stayed until a daughter, Jeanne-Marie, was born on or about March 8, 1881. Strangely, there is no official record of the girl's birth until her marriage certificate in 1902, which gave her age as twenty-one. Of course, Society gossiped and innuendos flew around Europe and even America; but the Prince of Wales' reputation as a ladies' man could not have suffered, although he did not assume the position of the child's father either.

Actually, it is not clear that Jeanne-Marie was the child of either prince. After all, Lillie was still seeing Arthur Jones and exchanging passionate letters with him, so he must be considered a contender. Lillie used to tell the story that one day some years later at her house in Newmarket, Bertie, Louis and Lillie were discussing Jeanne-Marie and which of them might be her father. The princes decided to toss a coin, a gold sovereign, and Louis won. The forfeit was paid by Bertie in the shape of a solid gold statue of Lillie that he commissioned, standing superbly naked. Whether the forfeit was true or not, Lillie's golden perfection always stood in the middle of her dining table.

Not until 1940, some sixty years later, was Lillie's relationship with Prince Louis of Battenberg made public by a journalist and politician named T. P. O'Connor, who wrote that "an aristocrat of great wealth was ready to abandon the old world, position and everything else if only Lillie Langtry would become his companion in exile."* It seems extraordinary that the hardheaded and ambitious prince was willing to give up everything he had fought so hard for, but this was the effect Lillie had on him. That year a play called *The Jersey Lily*, written by Sir Basil Bartlett, was put on in London, in which the Prince of Wales advises Louis and Lillie not to run away together as they planned. To be poor in exile was no life.

Not surprisingly, Prince Louis was hastily found an important role in the navy and he sailed off on his ship, the aptly named HMS *Inconstant*. He would be gone for two years, stopping at Montevideo, the Antipodes and various parts in the Far East. Once again Lillie would succeed in holding a lover's friendship, but not more.†

DURING HER PREGNANCY and since the birth of her daughter, Lillie had been taking stock. One month after Jeanne-Marie's birth, in April 1881, Lillie returned to London from France and was met by the Prince of Wales' solicitor, who had been taking care of her finances. Ned was on his way home from Ireland. She took lodgings in Ely Place, wrote a letter to Ned that she was leaving him, and sent her mother and daughter to Bournemouth, to the Red House.

In the same month, at the Duchess of Westminster's ball, according to Lillie's memoirs, she became conscious of the need to change her life. Stopping in front of a portrait of the celebrated actress Mrs. Sarah Siddons, Lille noticed that the artist had signed his name along the hem of her dress and "had declared himself satisfied to go down in posterity that way." Lillie saw that perhaps there could be a different path for her. With her possessions sold at auction, her reputation in shreds from the whispers of the birth abroad, and the Prince of Wales' attentions elsewhere, the time had come to reinvent herself.

---

* *The Telegraph*, February 1929.

† In accordance with King George V's wishes, all his German relations living in Britain anglicized their names. On May 17, 1914, Lillie, who was then in America, heard that Prince Louis's family name of Battenberg had become Mountbatten and his title was now Marquess of Milford Haven.

⌘

IT WAS NOT surprising that Lillie's Society friends drifted away; only Patsy Cornwallis-West remained close to her. Lillie's money had almost disappeared, and she was not prepared to ask Bertie for more. Her friends from bohemia were still there and so she asked for their advice as to what she should do to rebuild her life. Wearing black mourning for her brother Maurice (who had been killed by a tiger in India), Lillie had little need for an expensive wardrobe, and she now had her mother and daughter to provide for. (The child was officially described as the daughter of her dead brother. Jeanne-Marie was fourteen before she realized that Lillie was not her aunt but her mother.)* Whistler suggested Lillie try painting; but Oscar Wilde understood "the Lily" and recommended she go on the stage.

With the help of Mrs. Henrietta Labouchère, the wife of a member of Parliament, Lillie received an invitation to perform in an amateur theatrical for charity. She took lessons and the result was a success. The formidable Mrs. Labouchère persuaded Lillie—who, on the advice of Ellen Terry, first feigned reluctance—to accept a part in another, larger charity performance at the Haymarket Theatre. After all, Lillie was a celebrity and would draw crowds, and perhaps even the Prince and Princess of Wales would attend. Of course they came, and even the critics were generous in their praise. Princess Alexandra came with a group to see Lillie in her dressing room and impulsively kissed her cheek. At the age of twenty-eight, Lillie Langtry was launched on a new career. She was invited to join the company of the Haymarket Theatre and accepted. Lillie needed the money. Although she clearly still enjoyed the friendship of the Prince of Wales, once Lillie Langtry became an actress, Society's doors were thereafter closed to her. An actress was not regarded as a lady. But Lillie simply did not care.

In addition to the Prince and Princess of Wales, Lillie could always count on the support of her parents, and her father never missed her

---

* Prince Louis of Battenberg was the father of Earl Mountbatten of Burma and uncle of Prince Philip, Duke of Edinburgh. Lillie's daughter with the prince made her Lord Mountbatten's half sister and great-aunt to the present Prince of Wales.

opening nights. The Reverend Le Breton had lost his parish on Jersey on account of his philandering and was now living in London, working for the poor of his new parish.

As Lillie was no longer officially the mistress of the Prince of Wales, she needed another high-profile establishment figure in her life. This is where the genius of Lillie Langtry came into play. Who better than William Ewart Gladstone, once again prime minister? She had once briefly met "the great statesman" in Millais' studio, but only after she joined the theater in January 1882 did they become friends. It is very possible that Bertie asked Gladstone to prevent Lillie from being totally ostracized by Society. And yet, it seems extraordinary that Gladstone was willing to befriend the Prince of Wales' mistress, and correspond with her privately—he gave Lillie his secret code so that his secretaries would not open her letters. For Lillie, the prime minister's friendship must have flattered her, and she needed him. One can only imagine what that friendship gave the prime minister— was he, too, a little in love with Lillie? The friendship did, in fact, do the prime minister some harm, as all the old stories of his relationships with prostitutes resurfaced, although it is generally acknowledged that his intentions were always honorable. He brought Lillie improving literature and advised her: "In your new profession you will receive attacks, personal and critical, just and unjust. Bear them, never reply and above all, never rush into print to explain yourself."*

Lillie had actually asked the influential critic and society raconteur Abraham Hayward to bring them together. Hayward wrote to Gladstone and suggested he call on Lillie. And he did. Lillie would have been aware of Gladstone's reputation; he was known for his bizarre behavior in meeting with and admonishing prostitutes. His friendship with her predecessor with the Prince of Wales and also on the stage may have inspired Lillie to approach him. The prime minister's secretary wrote that "despite all the efforts of HRH, no one would receive [Lillie] in their house." To his colleagues, Gladstone was being used by Lillie, although it is doubtful that they had a physical relationship. That she did with Arthur Jones at this time is not in any doubt, and there were also the love letters to Sir George Chetwynd, which make

* Langtry, *The Days I Knew.*

Lillie's relationship with him perfectly clear. Considering that Chetwynd was a friend of the Prince of Wales, and was also being credited with the parenthood of Jeanne-Marie, Lillie was indeed spreading her favors in many directions.

Yet Bertie remained loyal. He loved the theater and could be counted on to come to her performances. The Prince of Wales' relationship with Lillie Langtry lasted five years. During that time she had evolved from a tomboyish, though ravishing, unschooled girl into one of the most beautiful and seductive women of her time. Her stage career would take her to the heights just as her social career had done.

Bertie encouraged her, coming up to town from Sandringham especially to attend her new play, and was often to be found chatting to her maid in her dressing room. Then there were the after-theater supper parties, or race meetings which she continued to enjoy with "His Nibs," as Lillie called him. Her professional career as an actress made her rich and even more famous, and the connection with the Prince of Wales was guaranteed to help her success in America. As for Ned, he was kept on an allowance from Lillie until he drank himself to death.

When his *affaire* with Lillie ended, the Prince of Wales was forty and still in his prime. He would go on to make other conquests, two of them as "official" as Lillie Langtry. At the Prince of Wales' coronation as Edward VII in 1901, his three great mistresses* sat together in specially reserved seats, referred to by the wags as "the King's loose box."

In 1910, Edward VII died and Lillie was summoned by Alexandra to Buckingham Palace. There the queen gave her Bertie's bequest, his terrier, whose collar read: *I am Caesar the King's dog*. He did not live long after his master.

EPILOGUE

AFTER A most successful career on the stage in America, in 1885 Lillie Langtry returned to settle in England. It was not long before she took up her old relationship with the Prince of Wales, although this

---

* Lillie Langtry; Daisy, Countess of Warwick; and the Hon. Mrs. Keppel.

time it was Lillie who fitted *him* into her schedule when her busy stage career permitted. They exchanged letters and he always came to her first nights, often with the princess, and visited her in her dressing rooms. He commissioned Lafayette to photograph her and begged to attend dress rehearsals of her play. Her reply was not always positive. In short, he was once again devoted to Lillie—but not exclusively.

Lillie was always fond of her father; his adoration made her happy, and his death in 1888 deeply disturbed her. Her memoirs are devoid of her feelings about personal matters like family feelings, especially her love for Jeanne-Marie. These were private and not for the public to devour. Lillie had become a goddess indeed and somehow more remote to her public than ever.

Her erstwhile friend Oscar Wilde wrote a play for and about her, *Lady Windermere's Fan,* the story of a woman with a grown illegitimate daughter. Actually, the play was a genuine tribute to Lillie, but she refused to read it and subsequently broke off her friendship with Oscar Wilde, one of the first to champion her cause when she arrived in London Society. And that Society began to regard her more negatively. The play was Oscar Wilde's attempt to reverse Lillie's "black" reputation. It was a tragedy that she rejected the gift, as it would have shown her in a more compassionate light. Unfortunately, Wilde had just met Lord Alfred Douglas and was on the edge of his own ruin.

Throughout the scandals that plagued Lillie, the Prince of Wales remained steadfastly her friend. Lillie had developed a passion for horse racing and this she could enjoy with him. The Jockey Club excluded women, so Lillie was obliged to register and run her horses in the name of "Mr. Jersey." When her Australian horse Merman won a brilliant race, the Prince of Wales delighted in escorting its owner, "Mr. Jersey," inside the Jockey Club to be toasted in champagne. Lillie approached her racing life with the same determination and professionalism that she applied to her stage career and her success was quite phenomenal. It is interesting that her racing photographs bear a choice of two captions, either "Mr. Jersey" or "the Goddess of Goodwood"—the one so masculine and the other a triumph of femininity. Lillie Langtry knew how to separate business and pleasure.

She adored her daughter but was insensitive to her needs. Dragged around the world on her mother's endless stage tours,

Jeanne-Marie could not form relationships with other young people. She grew to resent Lillie, and later in her life would have little to say to her own children about her beautiful, famous mother. Lillie's stage manager, Edward Michael, described her as having a man's brain while "possessing in a marked degree every feminine charm—wiles, fascination, and moods—she was at the same time possessed of an iron will power, immense courage, and a gift of instant decision . . ."* Lillie had to be in control of everything.

ON THE SAME night in 1897 that Lillie celebrated her horse's win in a great race, the Cesarewitch—an incredible feat and the first for a woman owner—she heard that Ned had died in a lunatic asylum. The news of his death and of her great win were reported in the press simultaneously the next day, and to Lillie's disadvantage. Once Ned had died she felt able to tell Jeanne-Marie that she was her mother and not her aunt, and she maintained that Ned was her father. Lillie then asked the Prince of Wales if Jeanne-Marie could be presented at court. He agreed with pleasure.

At the end of the century, 1899, aged forty-seven, Lillie married the twenty-seven-year-old Lord de Bathe. The marriage was a sham and no one really understood the reason for it. Even if she was fond of him, Hugo de Bathe clearly used her for her money and played around. Oscar Wilde is said to have commented that as her husband was a fool, no doubt Lillie may have thought he would be kind, "when of course, kindliness requires both intellect and imagination."†

In 1902, Jeanne-Marie made a good match, marrying the Hon. Ian Malcolm. It was at the wedding reception that a chance remark by a guest, the waspish Margot Asquith, disclosed the fact that Jeanne-Marie's father was Prince Louis of Battenberg. The girl was in shock and the shame of her illegitimacy far outweighed the knowledge of her royal birth. She never forgave her mother, and distanced herself completely for a number of years. Her husband, on the other hand, like most men, could not resist Lillie's warmth and charm.

* Beatty, *Lillie Langtry: Manners, Masks, and Morals.*
† Noel B. Gerson, *Because I Loved Him.*

When Edward VII died in 1910, Lillie mourned a true friend. Adding his loss to the loss of her daughter's love, Lillie felt there was nothing left for her in England. She sold her houses and her horses, bought a villa for Hugo in the South of France and another for herself in Monaco. Her old lover, Arthur Jones, himself over sixty, was Master of the Monaco Hunt. Arthur may well have been the passion of her life, but as he had no money and no place in Society, Lillie's pragmatic side would never have allowed her to marry him. What they shared were familiar things. From childhood Lillie was a survivor, and she made herself tough in order not only to survive, but to win.

In 1925, Lillie published her memoirs, *The Days I Knew*. But they were not considered sufficiently sensational to be a huge success. As Lady de Bathe, Lillie continued to visit friends in England and finally achieved some sort of reconciliation with Jeanne-Marie, who allowed her to see her grandchildren. Despite the attentions of her dear friend and companion of sixteen years, Mathilde Marie Peat, Lillie was lonely.

In February 1929, she returned to Monaco after spending Christmas in England. She had been suffering from bronchitis for some time, caught a vicious influenza, and quietly died. Once again the press gloried in her story, with every brilliant and sorry detail. Lillie Langtry could still sell papers. Of course she had lost her famous beauty in old age, but never her allure. She was noticed wherever she went, her life discussed, her fame dissected. But whatever her critics said about her, Lillie had a heart which she gave as freely as she exercised her indomitable spirit. It was her tragedy that Jeanne-Marie never understood her mother's wish to spare her the taint of illegitimacy. It was her love for her daughter that had been the reason for her silence.

Lillie was a giver, who learned the hard lesson of survival in a man's world. She was also a shrewd judge of men, and in Edward, Prince of Wales, she found one so very like herself: warm, generous and utterly charming. Her beauty attracted him, but it was her courage and character that kept her by his side until the end.

Bibliography

1: NELL GWYN

Ascoli, D. *A Village in Chelsea: An Informal Account of the Royal Hospital,* 1974.

Ashley, M. *Charles II: Man and Statesman,* 1971.

Aubrey, John. *Brief Lives,* ed. Anthony Powell, 1959.

Baker, Sir Richard. *A Chronicle of the Kings of England,* 1665.

Baschet, A. *Transcripts of the Despatches of the French Ambassadors in London* (Public Record Office).

Bax, C. *Pretty Witty Nelly,* 1932.

Beer, E.S. de. *The Diary of John Evelyn,* 1955.

Bell, W.G. *The Great Fire of London,* 1957.

Bevan, B. *Nell Gwyn,* 1969.

Boswell, E. *The Restoration Court Stage,* 1932.

Brett, A.C.A. *Charles II and His Court,* 1910.

Bryant, Arthur. *King Charles II,* 1933.

———. *Samuel Pepys,* Vol. I, 1935; Vol. II, 1947.

Buckingham, John, Duke of. *A Short Character of King Charles II,* 1725.

Burghclere, W. *Buckingham,* 1903.

Burnet, Gilbert. *History of His Own Time,* 1723.

———. *Life of Rochester,* 1681.

Cartwright, Julia. *Madame,* 1900.

Chapman, Hester W. *Great Villiers: A Study of George Villiers, 2nd Duke of Buckingham, 1628–1687,* 1949.

Chesterton, C. *The Story of Nell Gwyn,* 1911.

Clark, Sir George. *The Later Stuarts, 1660–1714,* 1955.

The Complete Peerage. Vol. 6, Appendix F, 1926.

Crawfurd, R. *The Last Days of Charles II,* 1909.

Cunningham, P. *Story of Nell Gwyn,* 1852, 1892, 1908.

Dasent, A.I. *Nell Gwynne,* 1924.

———. *Private Lives of Charles II,* 1927.

Drinkwater, J. *Mr. Charles, King of England*, 1926.

Etherege, Sir George. *The Dramatic Works,* ed. H.F.B. Brett-Smith, 1927.

———. *Letter Book,* 1928.

Evelyn, John. *Memoirs,* 1959.

Fairburn, J. *Life, Amours and Exploits of Nell Gwin,* 1820.

Forneron, J. *Louise de Keroualle,* 1887.

Fraser, Antonia. *King Charles II,* 1979.

Granger, J. *A Biographical History of England,* 1775.

Greene, Graham. *Lord Rochester's Monkey,* 1974.

Halifax, Marquis of. *Character of Charles II,* 1688.

Hamilton, A. *Memoir of the Comte de Grammont,* ed. N.J. Hartmann, 1930.

Hartmann, C.H. *A Vagabond Duchess,* 1927.

———. *Charles II and Madame,* 1934.

Hill, B. *Notes to Dr. Johnson's Lives of the Poets,* 1887.

Home, G. *Epsom,* 1901.

Hore, J.P. *History of Newmarket,* 1886.

Hutton, R. *Charles II,* 1989.

Imbert-Terry, H.M. *A Misjudged Monarch,* 1917.

Jameson, A. *Memoirs of the Beauties of the Court of Charles II,* 1851.

Jusserand, J.J.A. *French Ambassador at the Court of Charles II,* 1892.

Loch, D. *Royal Charles, Ruler and Rake,* 1931.

MacGregor-Hastie, Roy. *Nell Gwyn,* 1987.

———. *Charles II and the Theatre.*

MacQueen-Pope, W.J. *Theatre Royal, Drury Lane,* 1946.

Melville, L. *Nell Gwyn,* 1923.

Morah, P. *The Year of the Restoration,* 1960.

Ogg, David. *The Rochester-Saville Letters,* 1940.

Otway, Thomas. *Collected Works,* ed. M. Summers, 1926.

Pearson, H. *Charles II,* 1960.

Pepys, Samuel. *Diary,* 1962.

Pinto, V. de S. *Sir Charles Sedley,* 1927.

Prinz, Johannes. *John Wilmot, Earl of Rochester,* 1927.

Rochester, John Wilmot, Earl of. *Collected Works,* ed. J. Hayward, 1926.

Scott, Lord George. *Lucy Walters,* 1947.

Scott, Sir Walter. *Life of Dryden,* ed. George Saintsbury, 1882.

Sheffield, John Mulgrave, Earl of. *Works,* 1726.

Smith, A. *The Lives of the Court Beauties,* 1715.

———. *The Court of Venus,* 1716.

Soulig, J. *Nell Gwyn,* 1955.

Trowbridge, W.R.H. *Court Beauties of Old Whitehall,* 1906.

Warburton, E. *Prince Rupert,* 1849.

Watson, J.N.P. *Captain-General and Rebel Chief,* 1979.

Wheatley, D. *Old Rowley,* 1962.

Wheatley, H.B. *Samuel Pepys,* 1880.

Williams, H. *Rival Sultanas,* 1915.

Wilson, J.H. *Nell Gwyn, Royal Mistress,* 1952.

———. *The Court Wits of the Restoration*, 1948.

Wyndham, V. *The Protestant Duke*, 1976.

2: LA MARQUISE DE POMPADOUR

Aretz, Gertrude. *The Elegant Woman*, London, 1932.

Arneth, A. von. *Maria Theresa*, Vol. IV, 1863–79.

Asse, E., ed. *Mémoires de la duchesse de Brancas*, 1890.

Bernis, Cardinal de. *Mémoires et lettres, 1715–58*, 1878.

Broglie, Duc de. *Le Fils de Louis XV*, 1877.

———. *L'Alliance autrichienne*, 1895.

———. *Le Secret du roi*, 1878.

Butterfield, Herbert. *The Reconstruction of an Historical Episode*, 1955.

Buvat, Jean. *Journal de la régence*, 1865.

Calmette, Pierre. *Choiseul et Voltaire*, 1902.

Campan, Madame. *Mémoires*, 1979.

Campardon, Emile. *Madame de Pompadour et la cour de Louis XV*, 1867.

Caraman, Duc de. *La Famille de la marquise de Pompadour. Etude généalogique*, 1901.

Carre, Henri. *La France sous Louis XV*, 1891.

Cheverny, Dufort de (Comte et Duc). *Mémoires*, 1908.

Choiseul, Duc de. *Mémoires* (1737), ed. M. de Lescure, 1868.

Correspondance de Louis XV et du maréchal de Noailles ed. M. de Lescure, 1873.

Correspondance de Mme de Pompadour, 1875.

Coxe, William. *Memoirs of Horatio, Lord Walpole*, 1803.

Cröy, Duc de. *Journal inédit*, 1906.

Cushion, John. *Pottery and Porcelain*, 1972.

d'Argenson, Marquis. *Journal & Mémoires*, 1859–1867.

———. *Autour d'un ministre de Louis XV*, 1923.

———. *Lettres intimes*.

d'Estrée, Paul. *Richelieu*, 1917.

d'Haussonville, Count de. *La Duchesse de Bourgogne*, 1898–1908.

Duclos, C.P. *Mémoires secrets sur le règne de Louis XIV, la régence et le règne de Louis XV*, 1891.

Eriksen, Svend. *Early Neo-Classicism in France*, 1974.

Fromageot, P. *La Jeunesse de Madame de Pompadour*, 1902.

———. *La Mort et les obsèques de Madame de Pompadour*.

Gallet, Danielle. *Madame de Pompadour*, 1985.

Gauthiers-Villars, *Le Marriage de Louis XV*.

Goncourt, Edmond, and Jules de. *La Duchesse de Châteauroux et ses soeurs*, 1879.

———. *Madame de Pompadour*, 1894.

———. *La Peinture au dix-huitième siècle*.

———. *The Mistresses of Louis XV*, 1907.

Gooch, G.P. *Louis XV: The Monarchy in Decline*, 1956.

Hausset, Mme du. *Mémoires*, 1824.

Hénault, Président. *Mémoires,* 1911.

Inventaire des biens de Madame de Pompadour, 1939.

Lavisse, E., ed. *L'Histoire de France,* Vols. VII, VIII (Part 2), 1911–1922.

Lecky, W. E. *History of England in the Eighteenth Century,* 1878–1920.

Leroi, P.-A. *Relevé des dépenses de Madame de Pompadour depuis la première année de sa faveur jusqu'à sa mort,* 1853.

Leroy, Alfred. *Madame de Pompadour et son temps,* 1936.

Lescure, M. F. A. *Les Maîtresses du régent,* 1861.

Levron, J. *Secrète Madame de Pompadour,* 1961.

L'hermier, P. *Le Mystérieux Comte de Saint-Germain,* 1943.

Louis XIV. *Mémoires pour l'instruction du dauphin,* 1860.

Louis XV. *Lettres inédites de Louis XV à son petit-fils l'Infant Ferdinand de Parme,* 1938.

Luynes, Duc de. *Journal (1735–58),* 1861.

MacInnes, Ian. *Painter, King and Pompadour,* 1965.

Marais, Mathieu. *Journal et mémoires du M. M. sur la Régence et la règne de Louis XV, 1715–37,* 1863–1868.

Marquiset, A. *Le Marquis de Marigny,* 1918.

Masson, Frédéric. *Le Cardinal Bernis depuis son ministère, 1758–1794,* 1884.

———. *Napoleon and His Coronation,* 1911.

———. *Napoleon and the Fair Sex,* 1894.

Maugras, Gaston. *Le Duc et la Duchèsse de Choiseul,* 1902.

———. *Correspondence de Mme du Deffand,* 1885.

Mitford, Nancy. *Madame de Pompadour,* 1953.

———. *Frederick the Great,* 1970.

Nolhac, P. *Le Château de Versailles sous Louis XV,* 1898.

———. *Louis XV et Marie Leczynska,* 1900.

———. *La Marquise de Pompadour,* 1903.

———. *Louis XV et Madame de Pompadour,* 1928.

———. *Madame de Pompadour et la politique,* 1930.

Perkins, James Breek. *France Under Louis XV,* 1897.

Piepape, Général de, ed. *Lettres de Madame de Pompadour au comte de Stainville,* 1917.

Poulet-Malassis, P.E.A., ed. *Correspondence de Madame de Pompadour,* 1878.

Rosval, T.D. *The Mazarine Legacy,* 1969.

Sainte-Beuve. *Lundis,* 1869.

Saint-Simon. *Mémoires, 1714–1716.*

Terrasson, J. *Madame de Pompadour et la création de la "Porcelaine de France,"* 1969.

Thierry, A. *La Marquise de Pompadour,* 1959.

Tinayre, M. *A Study in Temperament: Madame de Pompadour,* 1937.

Tocqueville, Alexis de. *L'Ancien Régime et la révolution,* 1856.

Toth, C. *Woman and Rococo in France Seen Through the Life of Duclos,* 1931.

Trouncer, Margaret. *The Pompadour,* 1936.

Valfons, Marquis de. *Souvenirs.*

Vandal, A. *Louis XV et Elisabeth de Russie,* 1882.

Villars, Marshal. *Mémoires*, 1795.

Voltaire. *Le Siècle de Louis XIV*, 1751.

———. *Le Siècle de Louis XV*, 1739.

———. *Histoire du parlement de Paris*, 1769.

Vrignault, H. *Les Enfants de Louis XV: Descendance illégitime*, 1954.

Wyndham Lewis, D.B. *Fair Favourites*, 1948.

3: MARIE WALEWSKA

Aretz, Gertrude. *Napoleon and His Women Friends*, 1927.

Aronson, T. *Napoleon and Josephine*, 1990.

Bernard, J.F. *Talleyrand*, 1973.

Bernardy, Françoise. *Alexandre Walewski*, 1974.

Bertrand, Maréchal Xavier. *Les Cahiers de Sainte-Hélène*, 1828.

Binet-Valmer. *La Vie amoureuse de Marie Walewska*, 1928.

Bonaparte, Caroline Murat. *Mémoires*, 1840.

Bonaparte, Lucien. *Mémoires secrets*, 1818.

Broglie, Duc de. *Souvenirs*, 1886.

Brookes, Dame M. *St. Helena Story*, 1960.

Caulaincourt, A.A.L. de. *Mémoires (1812–14)*, ed. J. Hanoteau, 1955.

Cooper, A. Duff. *Talleyrand*, 1932.

Coxe, William. *Travels into Poland, Russia, Sweden and Denmark*, 1792.

Cronin, Vincent. *Napoleon: An Intimate Biography*, 1971.

Dixon, Sir Pierson. *Pauline: Napoleon's Favourite Sister*, 1964.

d'Ornano, Philippe. *La Vie passionnante du comte Walewski*, 1953.

———. *Marie Walewska, "l'épouse polonaise" de Napoléon*, 1947.

Greer, Walter. *Napoleon and His Family*, 1928.

Herold, J. Christopher. *Mistress to an Age: A Life of Madame de Staël*, 1959.

Iwaszkievicz, J. *Vie de Chopin*, 1949.

Kemble, J. *Napoléon Immortal*, 1959.

Kielmansegge, Comtesse de. *Mémoires*, 1849.

Las Cas, Comte de. *Mémorial de Sainte-Hélène*, 1823.

Macdonell, A.G. *Napoleon and His Marshals*, 1934.

Masson, Frédéric. *Napoléon et les femmes*, 1897.

———. *Napoléon et sa famille*, 1895.

Ménéval, Baron de. *Mémoires*, 1894.

Montesquiou, Anatole de. *Mémoires*, 1846.

Montholon, C.J. *Mémoires*, 1857.

Musulin, Stella. *Vienna in the Age of Metternich*, 1975.

Oman, C. *Napoleon's Viceroy*, 1966.

Orieux, Jean. *Talleyrand: The Art of Survival*, 1974.

Palmer, Alan. *Alexander I: Tsar at War and Peace*, 1974.

Petre, F. Loraine. *Napoleon's Campaign in Poland 1806–7*, 1901.

Potocka, Countess Anna. *Mémoires, 1794–1820*, 1897.

Pradt, abbé. *Histoire de l'ambassade à Varsovie*, 1819.

Savant, Jean. *L'Affaire de Marie Walewska*, 1963.

———. *Napoléon raconté par lui-même*, 1954.

Ségur, Comte de. *Mémoires: La campagne de Russie*, 1901.

Sutherland, Christine. *Marie Walewska, Napoleon's Great Love*, 1979.

Tour, Jean de la. *Duroc, duc de Friul*, 1897.

Tulard, Jean. *Napoléon*, 1978.

Wairy, Constant Louis. *Mémoires de Constant, premier valet de l'empereur*, 1830–31.

Wilson, Robert M. *Napoleon's Love Story*, 1933.

4: LOLA MONTEZ

Aretz, G. *The Elegant Woman*, 1932.

Banville, Théodore de. *Souvenirs*, 1832.

Beauvallet, L. *Rachel and the New World*, 1967.

Bernstórff, J. H. *Papers*, 1884.

Burr, C.C. *Lectures of Lola Montez*, 1858.

———. *Autobiography of Lola Montez*, 1858.

Carter, T. *History of the 44th Regiment*, 1864.

Channon, Henry. *The Ludwigs of Bavaria*, 1933.

Claudin, Gustave. *Mes Souvenirs*, 1884.

Corti, Count E.C. *Ludwig I of Bavaria*, 1938.

d'Auvergne, E.B. *Lola Montez*, 1909.

Dictionary of National Biography, Vol. 21, 2004.

Eden, Emily. *Letters from Upcountry*, 1866.

Englbrecht, J. *Drei Rosen für Bayern*, 1985.

Erdmann. *Lola Montez und die Jesuiten*, 1847.

Falk, B. *The Naked Lady*, 1934.

Fuchs, Eduard. *Ein Vormärzliches Tanzidyll*, 1904.

Gautier, Théophile. *Histoire de l'art dramatique en France*, 1859.

Gollwitzer, H. *Ludwig I von Bayern*, 1986.

Hawks, F. L. *Story of a Penitent*, 1867.

Heigel, Carl. *Ludwig I*, 1872.

Henningsen, Charles Frederick. *Revelations of Russia*, 1844.

Holdredge, H. *The Woman in Black: Lola Montez*, 1955.

Holland, N. *Lola Montez*, 1988.

Ireland, Joseph N. *Records of the New York Stage, 1750–1860*, 1866–1867.

Kelen, B. *The Mistresses*, 1966.

Kobell, L. von. *Unter den Vier Ersten Königen Bayerns*, 1894.

Leverson-Gower, Edward Frederick. *Bygone Years*, 1905.

Lewis, O. *Lola Montez: The Mid-Victorian Bad Girl in California*, 1938.

Metternich, Prinz von. *Memoirs*, 1880–1882.

Mirecourt, E. de. *Les Contemporains*, 1870.

Montemar, Julie de. *Folly's Queens*, 1882.

Montez, Lola. *The Arts of Beauty*, 1858.

Perenyi, E. *Liszt*, 1975.

Phelps, H.H. *Players of a Century*, 1880.

Ramann. *Franz Liszt als Mensch und Künstler*, 1880–1894.

Richardson, J. *The Courtesans*, 1967.

Ringhoffer, C. *The Bernstoff Papers*, 1908.

Sala, George A. *Life and Adventures*, 1895.

Sepp. *Ludwig Augustus*, 1869.

Vandam, A. D. *An Englishman in Paris*, 1892.

Victoria, Queen of Great Britain. *Journal*, 1847.

Walker, A. *Franz Liszt*, 1983.

Wyndham, H. *The Magnificent Montez*, 1935.

5: LILLIE LANGTRY

Aronson, Theo. *The King in Love: Edward VII's Mistresses*, 1988.

Asquith, Emma Alice Margaret, Countess of Oxford and Asquith. *The Autobiography of Margot Asquith*, ed. Mark Bonham Carter, 1920, 1962.

———. *More Memories*, 1933.

Beatty, Laura. *Lillie Langtry: Manners, Masks and Morals*. 1999.

Bernhardt, Sarah. *My Double Life*, 1907.

Brough, James. *The Prince and the Lily*, 1975.

Churchill, Lady Randolph Spencer. *Reminiscences of Lady Randolph Churchill*, 1908.

Dudley, Ernest [Vivian Ernest Coltman-Allen]. *The Gilded Lily*, 1958.

Ellemann, Richard. *Oscar Wilde*, 1987.

Fane, Lady Augusta Fanny. *Chit Chat*, 1926.

Gerson, Noel B. *Because I Loved Him: Lillie Langtry, a Biography*, 1971.

Hart-Davis, Rupert, ed. *The Letters of Oscar Wilde*. 1962.

Hough, Richard Alexander. *Edward and Alexandra: Their Private and Public Lives*, 1992.

James, Robert Rhodes. *The Prince Consort*, 1983.

Knutsford, Viscount Sydney Holland. *In Black and White*, 1920.

Langtry, Lillie (Lady de Bathe). *The Days I Knew*, 1925.

Lee, Sir Sidney. *King Edward VII: A Biography*, 1925.

Leslie, Anita. *Edwardians in Love*, 1972.

Magnus, Sir Philip Montefiore. *King Edward VII*, 1964.

Middlemass, Keith. *The Life and Times of Edward VII*, 1972.

Nowell-Smith, Simon. *Edwardian England*, 1964.

Pearson, John. *Edward the Rake*, 1975.

Ponsonby, Sir Frederick Edward Grey. *Recollections of Three Reigns*, 1957.

Ricketts, Charles. *Oscar Wilde Recollections*, 1932.

Robertson, Walford Graham. *Time Was: The Reminiscences of W. Graham Robertson*, 1931.

Sackville-West, Hon. Victoria Mary. *The Edwardians*, 1935.

Sebright, Arthur Edward Saunders. *A Glance into the Past,* 1922.

Victoria, Queen of Great Britain. *Darling Child: Private Correspondence of Queen Victoria and the Crown Princess of Prussia, 1871–1878,* ed. Roger Fulford, 1976.

————. *Beloved and Darling Child: Last Letters Between Queen Victoria and Her Eldest Daughter, 1886–1901,* ed. Agatha Ramm, 1902.

Warwick, Frances Evelyn Maynard Greville, Countess of. *Life's Ebb and Flow,* 1929.

Young, George Malcolm. *Victorian England: Portrait of an Age,* 1936, 1972.

Manuscript:

Town Talk, October 4, 1879. http://www.bl.uk/catalogues/newspapers/record .ASP?IngMTitle= 13285.

Index

Illustration Credits

Page 1

Portrait of Nell Gwyn, by Sir Peter Lely (1618–1680), The Art Archive/Army and Navy Club/Eileen Tweedy

Photo of Nell Gywn's reputed birthplace, photograph taken in 1858, photographer unknown, Hereford Museum, Herefordshire Heritage Services, Herefordshire Council

Page 2

City of London viewed from the Southwark, by W. Hollar, 1650, Museum of London

The Restoration, Charles II rides into London; unnamed engraver, circa 1750, Mary Evans Picture Library

Page 3

The Palace of Whitehall, by Hendrick Danckerts; from © Queen's Printer and Controller of HMSO, 2005, UK Government Art Collection

Londoners fleeing the plague, 1665, Mansell/Time Life Pictures/ Getty Images

Charles II, by an artist in the studio of John Michael Wright (1617–1694), National Portrait Gallery, London

Catherine of Braganza, by or after Dirk Stoop, circa 1610–circa 1685, National Portrait Gallery, London

Page 4

A woman sells oranges and lemons from baskets on her arm and balanced on her head, Cries of London—unidentified series, Mary Evans Picture Library

Louise de Kéroualle, Duchess of Portsmouth, by Pierre Mignard (1612–1695), Picture Library, National Portrait Gallery, London

Barbara Palmer (née Villiers), Duchess of Cleveland, unknown artist after Sir Peter Lely (1618–1680), National Portrait Gallery, London

Page 5

Madame de Pompadour (1721–1764), by François Boucher (1703–1770) in the Louvre, Paris, France; Bridgeman Art Library

Louis XV (1710–1774), King of France and Navarre, after 1730, by Maurice Quentin de la Tour (1704–1788), Musée Antoine Lecuyer, Saint-Quentin, France; Bridgeman Art Library

Page 6

Portrait of Marie Leczinska, Queen of France and wife of Louis XIV, by Jean-Marc Nattier 1748, Roger-Viollet/Rex Features

The Three Graces (The Nesle Sisters), by Van Loo, Château de Chenonceau

Page 7

Reclining Nude (Miss Murphy), by François Boucher (1703–1770), Wallraf Richartz Museum, Cologne, Germany; Bridgeman Art Library

Madame de Pompadour (1721–1764), by François-Hubert Drouais (1727–1775), National Gallery, London, UK; Bridgeman Art Library

Page 8

Marie Walewska, by Jacques-Louis David, Collection d'Ornano

Portrait of Napoleon Bonaparte (1769–1821), 1st Consul, 1803, by Baron François Pascal Simon Gérard (1770–1837), Musée Condé, Chantilly, France; Bridgeman Art Library

Page 9

Empress Josephine (1763–1814) at Malmaison, circa 1801, by Baron François Pascal Simon Gérard (1770–1837), Musée Nat. du Château de Malmaison, Rueil-Malmaison, France, Giraudon; Bridgeman Art Library

Marie and Napoleon, Patrick Rougereau

Page 10

Portrait of Marie Laczinska (1786–1817) Countess Walewska, 1812, by Baron François Pascal Simon Gérard (1770–1837), Château de Versaillles, France

The Divorce of Napoleon I (1769–1821) and Josephine Tascher de la Pagerie (1763–1814), 30th November 1809, by Charles Abraham Chasselat (1782–1843), Bibliothéque Nationale, Paris, France; Bridgeman Art Library

Page 11

Portrait of Marie-Louise de Hapsburg-Lorraine (1791–1847), by Pierre-Paul Prud'hon (1758–1823), Musée de Beaux-Arts, Chartres, France; Lauros/Giraudon/Bridgeman Art Library

Marie Walewska on a Polish postage stamp

Page 12

Lola Montez, dancer, lover of King Ludwig I of Bavaria, by Joseph Karl Stieler (1781–1858); 1847; AKG Images; Berlin, London, and Paris

Page 13

Ludwig I, King of Bavaria, by Gemalde; 1845; AKG Images; Berlin, London, and Paris

Queen Thérèse of Bavaria, by Gemalde; 1827; AKG Images; Berlin, London, and Paris

Page 14

"Lola Coming! Europe Farewell! America I Come!," by Marie Dolores Gilbert; AKG Images; Berlin, London, and Paris

"Lola has come! Enthusiastic Reception of Lola by an American Audience," by Marie Dolores Gilbert; AKG Images; Berlin, London, and Paris

Page 15

Mrs. Langtry, by Sir Edward John Poynter (1836–1919), © Jersey Heritage Trust, UK; Bridgeman Art Library

Edward VII, by W. & D. Downey, 1868, National Portrait Gallery, London

Page 16

Portrait of Oscar Wilde (1854–1900) wearing an overcoat with a fur collar bought for his trip to America, by unknown photographer, Private Collection, Bridgeman Art Library

A Jersey Lily, by Sir John Everett Millais (1829–1896), © Jersey Heritage Trust, UK; Bridgeman Art Library

About the Author

HER ROYAL HIGHNESS PRINCESS MICHAEL OF KENT is the author of *The Serpent and the Moon: Two Rivals for the Love of a Renaissance King* and *Crowned in a Far Country: Portraits of Eight Royal Brides.* For more than ten years, the Princess has pursued a successful career lecturing on historical topics. She lives with her husband, Prince Michael of Kent, in Kensington Palace in London and in their seventeenth-century manor house in Gloucestershire, England.